The Antebellum Kanawha
SALT BUSINESS
and Western Markets

T0307682

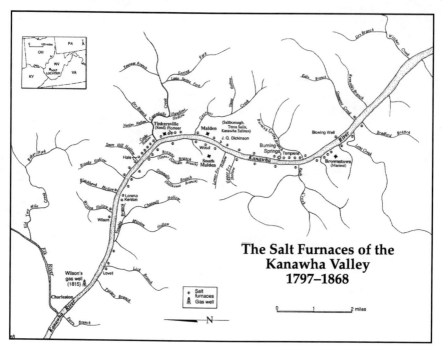

The Salt Furnaces of the
Kanawha Valley
1797–1868

*Adapted from a map produced by Chlor Alkali Division,
Food Machinery and Chemical Corporation, South Charleston, West Virginia.*

Illustration on title page: "Gt. Kanawha River, Va. Salt Works," a
previously unpublished watercolor by August Köllner that accurately
reflects the salt furnace vicinity, ca. 1840. Courtesy of
Mary Price Ratrie, Malden, West Virginia.

The Antebellum Kanawha
SALT BUSINESS
and Western Markets

By John E. Stealey III

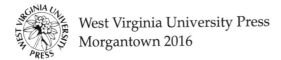

West Virginia University Press
Morgantown 2016

West Virginia and Appalachia

A Series Edited by Ronald L. Lewis, Ken Fones-Wolf, and Kevin Barksdale

Titles in the Series

*The Last Great Senator: Robert C. Byrd's Encounters with
Eleven U.S. Presidents*
David A. Corbin

*Life, Work, and Rebellion in the Coal Fields:
The Southern West Virginia Miners, 1880–1922*
David A. Corbin

*Memorializing Motherhood:
Anna Jarvis and the Struggle For Control of Mother's Day*
Katharine Lane Antolini

Working Class Radicals: The Socialist Party in West Virginia, 1898–1920
Frederick A. Barkey

"They'll Cut Off Your Project": A Mingo County Chronicle
Huey Perry

*An Appalachian Reawakening:
West Virginia and the Perils of the New Machine Age, 1945–1972*
Jerry Bruce Thomas

*An Appalachian New Deal:
West Virginia in the Great Depression*
Jerry Bruce Thomas

Culture, Class, and Politics in Modern Appalachia
Edited by Jennifer Egolf, Ken Fones-Wolf, and Louis C. Martin

Governor William E. Glasscock and Progressive Politics in West Virginia
Gary Jackson Tucker

Matewan Before the Massacre
Rebecca J. Bailey

Sectionalism in Virginia from 1776 to 1881
Charles Ambler; introduction by Barbara Rasmussen

Monongah: The Tragic Story of the 1907 Monongalia Mine Disaster
Davitt McAteer

Bringing Down the Mountains
Shirley Stewart Burns

Afflicting the Comfortable
Thomas F. Stafford

Clash of Loyalties
John Shaffer

The Blackwater Chronicle
Philip Pendleton Kennedy; edited by Timothy Sweet

Transnational West Virginia
Edited by Ken Fones-Wolf and Ronald L. Lewis

To Patty

ISBN:

PB: 978-1-943665-29-7
EPUB: 978-1-943665-30-3
PDF: 978-1-943665-31-0

Library of Congress Cataloging-in-Publication Data is available from the Library
of Congress

Cover design by Than Saffel. Cover images, clockwise from bottom: *Brooks Salt
Furnace*, used with permission of the West Virginia and Regional History Center,
West Virginia University Libraries; Engraving, "View of the Salt-Works on the
Kanawha," Henry Howe, *Historical Collections of Virginia* (1845): 345; *Colton's new
topographical map of the states of Virginia, Maryland and Delaware, showing also eastern
Tennessee & parts of other adjoining states, all the fortifications, military stations, rail
roads, common roads and other internal improvements*, used with permission of the
Library of Congress.

Contents

List of Illustrations, Tables, Chart   viii

Introduction to the New Edition   ix

Acknowledgments   xxi

1. Kanawha Salt's Savor   1

2. Early Development and Expansion   8

3. Growth, Chaos, and Combination, 1811–1824   17

4. Kanawha Salt's Use and Its Pre-1850 Markets   41

5. The Manufacturing Process and Technological Progress   48

6. Manufacturers and State Intervention   57

7. Merchant Capitalists, Independent Manufacturers, and Local Economic Developments, 1825-1835   76

8. Hewitt, Ruffner & Company and Depression, 1836-1846   89

9. The Kanawha Producers and the Salt Tariff   103

10. White Labor, Subsidiary Industries, and Furnace Managers   119

11. Slavery in the Kanawha Salt Industry   133

12. The Kanawha Salt Association and Ruffner, Donnally & Company, 1847-1855   158

13. Ruffner, Donnally & Company and the External Economy   170

14. Kanawha Salt Loses Its Economic Savor   184

15. Perspectives   191

Notes   199

Works Cited   239

Index   253

Illustrations, Tables, & Chart

Illustrations

"Gt. Kanawha River, Va. Salt Works"   iii
Kanawha County Courthouse   32
Oldest Dickinson brine well, Malden   50
Brine cistern at J.Q. Dickinson & Company, Malden   52
"View of the Salt-Works on the Kanawha"   96
J.Q. Dickinson & Company Salt Factory   100

Tables

1. Slaves Owned or Leased by Salt Firms in Kanawha County in 1850   138–139
2. Slave Inhabitants of Kanawha County in 1850 and 1860   154
3. Comparative Costs of Hired Common Slave Labor and Free White Labor, Kanawha Salt Industry, 1850–1854   155

Chart

1. Relationship of Average Annual Hire Rates for Common Slave Labor in the Kanawha Salt Industry to the Annual Purchasing Power of Kanawha Salt in the Cincinnati Market, 1844–1854   152

Introduction to the New Edition

Fortuitous selection of a fruitful topic for a PhD dissertation in history and the subsequent research and writing can open new historical venues and offer opportunities for subsequent publication of some articles and a university press monograph, thus enabling one's scholarship to enter the historiographical mainstream. If the resulting publications are especially prescient of future historical scholarship, they can maintain enduring intellectual relevance and value. In time, all of these hoped for outcomes arose from this investigation of the antebellum Great Kanawha River western Virginia salt industry. This project has exposed historical topics substantially broader and more consequential than the title might suggest.[1]

From the time of European settlement until the 1830s, salt was a scarce commodity in the United States. This critical deficiency inhibited agricultural and economic development because the element is a necessity for life, for processing of many products, and for preservation. No large-scale domestic commercial salt producers existed before the Great Kanawha's emergence in 1810. Since the colonial period, coastal salt ponds and scattered evaporators at interior brine springs, using crude vessels to boil and shallow wells to extract water, furnished very limited quantities of domestic salt. Americans depended on foreign salt, mainly from Great Britain and Turk's Island, for the necessary mineral. Initial development of the western Virginia salt industry between 1810 and 1815 radically changed the situation in the Ohio River basin. Kanawha Salines output made extensive and prosperous agricultural settlement and enterprise possible throughout the Ohio riverine system. Despite the Kanawha development and the later emergence of the salt field in Onondaga, New York, domestic producers could not satiate national demand during the antebellum period. Because of the mineral's weight, distance from sources and inadequate transportation created continual scarcity in many localities. Frequent mercantile speculation and forestalling in a commodity of need prevailed in many markets.

For these obvious reasons and for many more that emerged, study of such a vital and indispensible industry became compelling. Informed previous historians vaguely knew that the Kanawha salt manufacturers were important to regional economic development, used slave labor to some extent, and crafted seemingly modern-like legal arrangements to govern their industry. Yet no one ever launched a thorough research project to determine and expose the enterprise's important aspects and meaning. Studies of United States commodification of resources have become plentiful, but those explaining how things are made or produced are scarce.

Two early exposures to the shadowy Kanawha salt makers and their slave workers also greatly influenced the choice of topic. In a stimulating undergraduate course in state history at West Virginia University (WVU), Dr. Festus Paul Summers observed that the importance of the Kanawha salt industry should attract a curious researcher. Later, in a graduate history seminar on The Old South at the same institution, Dr. Edward M. Steel Jr. mentioned that the Kanawha County court records at what is now the West Virginia and Regional History Center, WVU Library, might hold extensive material about slavery. A cursory search revealed that the county records held voluminous information about the salt manufacturers and their slaves.

The trajectory of the extensively revised dissertation "The Salt Industry of the Great Kanawha Valley of Virginia: A Study in Ante-Bellum Internal Commerce" (1970) to publication differed from the academic norm. The demands of professional promotion and achievement of tenure usually compel rapid revision of the manuscript and submission to university press consideration for publication. For various reasons, this work appeared as a university press book more than two decades later. This beneficial hiatus allowed extensive contemplation, marinating of material, the appearance of new manuscript and printed sources, the weighing of the burgeoning historiography relating to the subject, and advantageous revision of writing.

In the interim, three important primary sources emerged to cause elaboration and refinement of conclusions. The deposit of the bound records of the Dickinson & Shrewsbury partnership in the Morrow Library, Marshall University, permitted the unique view of one salt company over time in all phases of its extensive mining, manufacturing, merchandising, and agricultural activities. The West Virginia Department of Archives and History acquisition of two cholera death registers for 1849 and 1850 allowed analysis of the scourge's relative effects on the Kanawha Salines white and African American populations and on manufacturing operations. The serendipitous discovery of a fugitive printed report of an obscure Virginia court case in the Law Library, Library of Congress, revealed the complete text of the only previously unknown associative arrangement between 1817 and 1851. Since 1993, no known major manuscript collections or additional primary sources affecting the narrative have surfaced.

Over time, the completed study and book anticipated several emerging modern fields of United States historical interpretation: slavery's profitability and adaptability, the rise of the market economy, the transatlantic connection of salt and cotton commerce, and the new capitalism before it enjoyed the designating label. The narrative of the Kanawha capitalists' often-blended activities to achieve profit indicates that investigations of capitalistic behavior might not be so new. The work exposed the interconnection between adaptable slave labor and manufacturing in the context of the larger regional and international economy.[2]

The Appalachian hills did not restrict the salt makers' worldview. The regional importance and the connections of the Kanawha business with its major markets in the Ohio River basin are obvious. Not as apparent is the salt makers' awareness of and participation in inter-regional and international markets. From the beginning, they informed themselves about very small, competing local salt works in the Ohio River basin. As canals connected Lake Erie and the Ohio River, the New York or Onondaga producers at times became competitive factors. The interior salt trade was an adjunct of the Anglo-American cotton trade that linked the inland Kanawha manufacturers' markets with the vagaries of the transatlantic and global economy. Salt constituted an important international exchange commodity for shippers in the Atlantic cotton trade. Ships, mostly British, arriving in New Orleans to transport cotton often were not fully loaded to capacity with trade goods and carried Liverpool, Turk's Island, and other foreign salts as ballast. Steamboats on the Mississippi and Ohio, bearing more downriver cargo than they could find to transport upriver, also used foreign salt as filler in their holds by attracting it with cheap freight rates. After 1820, when all physical barriers on the Ohio were removed, imported salt penetrated the Kanawha vendors' primary markets where it competed in price and quality. As cotton exports grew in the 1840s and 1850s, the competitive problem of foreign salt became more exacerbated. Very familiar with the dynamics of the effects of transatlantic trade, Kanawha salt agents frequently bought up what imported salt they could to control the market and prices.[3]

On the national front, Kanawha manufacturers worked to secure higher protective tariffs on salt by entering a complex political alliance with New England cod fishermen and coastal salt works to secure their objective. Senator Thomas Hart Benton of Missouri devoted his political career to representing western consumers against these combined interests. Since ancient times, governments throughout the world depended on taxing the commodity of necessity for revenue, and the United States government was no different. Although western Virginia people never thought the salt tariff was high enough, they did prevail in maintaining the levy until other factors arose to depress their enterprise.

Throughout the antebellum era, barreled pork from Cincinnati and river towns, besides supplying a preserved food to consumers in the regional and Lower South economy, was a major western export that fed British and other nations' sailors and people through the port of New Orleans. Using immense quantities of salt for preservation, the meat packing trade connected the Kanawha producers and their slaves to the regional and, in another way, the global economy. The Ohio River basin pork packers shipped great amounts of Kanawha salt overseas. The annual level of Midwestern hog production dictated the quantity of salt required by packers.[4]

As the initial version of the study was completed, a debate during the 1960s and early 1970s about the profitability of slavery raged among traditional historians, cliometricians, and econometricians. The "new economic history," according to proponents, promised to answer the question of slavery's economic effects. Stimulated by the debate and several historians' work, notably that of Robert S. Starobin and Charles B. Dew who were also concentrating on industrial slavery, the author cast into the fray an article about the extensive industrial use of slaves in all phases of Kanawha salt manufacturing that asserted that Kanawha usage was profitable and imminently adaptable to non-agricultural employment.[5]

New historiographical issues about slavery such as family structure and additional sources required revision of the article for the book chapter. Unfortunately, historians writing after 1993 often refer to the original article rather than the later version. John C. Inscoe's useful collection of essays about Southern Appalachian Mountain slavery includes an adaptation of the monographic chapter. Whichever version is employed, two reprints and numerous citations testify to the article's entrance into the historiographical mainstream.[6]

Simultaneously with the final production and publication of the present volume, a long-running controversy erupted about whether domestic colonial, early national, and antebellum economies were ever in a subsistence stage, and if they were, when they transformed into market mode. This debate might be regarded as foundational in launching the later "new capitalism" interpretations. Of the many articles and books that addressed the issue, the appearance of Charles Sellers's important volume, *The Market Revolution, Jacksonian America, 1815–1846*, in 1991 reflected the seminal flowering of this historiographical controversy that begat more publications. The Kanawha experience coincidentally furnished a timely case study of what actually occurred in a commodity enterprise in an inland river valley. If the area economy ever existed in a subsistence stage, it lasted at most two decades after initial settlement. Because of the sudden emergence of salt extraction, the salines quickly attracted merchant capitalists and integrated into the regional market economy. As the book's title indicates, market forces influenced the Kanawha salt makers in every aspect of their business.[7]

In the year of this book's publication, close analysis of Dickinson & Shrewsbury records resulted in an article that showed the power of genealogy in business, the intrastate migration of Virginians to seek potential economic opportunity, and a significant enterprise creating the foundations of family wealth in the Great Kanawha Valley that endured into the twenty-first century. This case study demonstrated the evolution of capitalistic business partners over decades, their management approaches, their employment of white and slave labor, their response to dynamic market conditions, and their attitudes toward associative attempts by other salt manufacturers to confront market forces. Dickinson & Shrewsbury, a militantly independent partnership existing from 1809 to 1856, engaged in extensive mercantile, mining, agricultural, and salt manufacturing and vending operations. Over time, the partnership amassed 130 slaves (and leased almost as many more) and seventy-seven parcels of land, including some of the best bottomland in the Kanawha Valley; in several other Virginia counties; in Nashville, Tennessee; and in Kentucky. A rare view of day-to-day operations of all facets of the salt-making enterprise occurs. Also, the exploration shows that historians who ignore genealogical relationships in commerce do so at their peril.[8]

Because slaves were the primary labor for the antebellum Great Kanawha salt industry, it is not surprising that this aspect of the work has attracted the most scholarly attention. The human condition, including bondage and treatment of people, has more appeal than other important aspects of the story. Contemporary historians as part of the new capitalism interpretive school are exposing the vital link between the rise of American capitalism and the slave institution. The story of Kanawha slavery is among the early studies that implicitly demonstrated that slavery was a major part of the regional capitalistic economy. In that historiographical era, explicit interpretation of this reality did not manifest itself. Contemporary narrative certainly would emphasize the significance of this economic connection.

Some historians of the new capitalism contend that most past writers have not properly linked slavery with capitalism and have viewed the institution as quasi-feudal and distinct while de-emphasizing its productivity and profitability. Slavery was somehow out of the mainstream of American economic development. Whether the contention is completely accurate or not, these new capitalism historians are taking the old capitalism interpretations a giant step forward by highlighting slavery's centrality in the national and international economy. Several works emphasize slavery and capitalism's connection and more are certain to come. Among the most notable are those by Seth Rockman, Calvin Schermerhorn, James D. Rothman, and Sven Beckert. Edward E. Baptist's *The Half Has Never Been Told: Slavery and the Making of American Capitalism* is the most strident and provocative volume. To oversimplify Baptist's interpretation, slavery was a fundamental, efficient, dynamic system of capitalism that drove antebellum economic growth. Southern slavery was integral to constructing American capitalism and fostering northern prosperity. The growth of slavery showed no sign of slowing down at the Civil War's outbreak. Able critical reviews place Baptist's arguments in context rather than rejecting them.[9]

The bibliography of slavery's essential role in the growth of the nineteenth-century American economy is burgeoning. Almost contemporaneously with Baptist's work, Calvin Schermerhorn published *The Business of Slavery and the Rise of American Capitalism, 1815–1860* (2015). A student of Sven Beckert at Harvard University, Kathryn Boodry, wrote an important dissertation, "The Common Thread: Slavery, Cotton and Atlantic Finance from the Louisiana Purchase to Reconstruction" (2014). An essay collection demonstrating the fashionable eruption of the important slavery/capitalism pursuit is Sven Beckert and Seth Rothman, eds., *Slavery's Capitalism* (2016).[10]

Kanawha slavery, like the institution elsewhere in the South, was an integral part of the local and regional economy. Midwestern and Kentucky agricultural enterprise, mostly livestock-raising and meat packing, and processing industries such as tanning relied upon Kanawha slaves' output. To meet their industrial needs, the salt makers depended on what labor was available and the cheapest, and they did not hesitate to rely on slaves. They knew that slaves furnished a stable, manageable, and profitable workforce that adapted to all requirements of a twenty-four-hour manufacturing process, including extraction of furnace fuel initially by wood-cutting and later by coal mining. Kanawha entrepreneurs secured most of their slaves by purchase or lease from Piedmont, Virginia. This process of labor transfer was a small alternative part of the maritime and overland slave trade from the Upper South to the Lower. To cope with capital scarcity to purchase slaves and to maintain flexibility in the labor force to respond to market demand for salt, Kanawha producers leased over one-half the slaves employed in any given year in their industry. Salt prices governed hire rates. To minimize risk to owned slaves who often possessed specialized skills, managers normally placed hired slaves in the most dangerous occupations. The hire system had other adverse implications in regard to treatment of slaves. Owners and overseers had a full arsenal of incentives and punishments to maintain control of the work force. Some absentee owners enjoined lessors to keep their slaves away from the river because of the possibility of drowning and escape. Despite surveillance of steamboats departing downstream, slaves did flee in this way or by simply following overland the river's course to Ohio. Leasing even eliminated this risk.[11]

Surprisingly few scholars have plumbed in depth antebellum southern Appalachian natural resource industries that often have connections to the regional and national economy. Notable exceptions include, among others, Charles B. Dew on iron, Katherine A. Harvey on coal, Ronald L. Lewis on coal and iron, and Kenneth W. Noe on Virginia's southwestern railroad that opened the area. Randal L. Hall, showing the great potential of such studies, recently examined the myriad extractive industries in southwestern Virginia from colonial times to the modern day.[12]

The most virginal area of historical inquiry of the southern Appalachian region is the borderland between law and the economy. Law, being a profession that attracts the economically motivated and often the most intellectually gifted people of the Appalachian region, is an unexploited frontier for historians and legal scholars. Appalachian legal history studies are scarce as law schools in the region eschew emphasizing the pursuit because such study does not seem to unappreciative individuals to contribute to winning cases. The practice of natural resource and commercial law is an activity where in-migration of practitioners to Appalachia actually transpires. Some of the most creative intellectual accomplishments in Appalachia and West Virginia have been achieved in the law affecting land tenure and natural resources. Much about the legal area begs historical discovery. Research is difficult as such creativity being proprietary and intellectual remains veiled as it is the innovative and artful legal practitioners' stock-in-trade. Careful review of recorded and unrecorded legal instruments—especially deeds, leases, agreements, and depositions; the filings and reports of court cases on all judicial levels; and attention to the process of legislative draftsmanship and statutory results—can expose the crucial creative elements affecting

the fundamental historical and economic development of specific resource activities in the region.[13]

The present volume addresses the impact of legal activities on natural resource development, production, and marketing in an Appalachian industry. It highlights the originality and empirical progress of
creative Kanawha legal minds that drafted several agreements of concert, combination, and association that anticipated by decades national
corporate legal developments of the post–Civil War era. It demonstrates
that not all innovative legal contributions occurred in New York, Massachusetts, or the Middle Atlantic states as many studies contend. So far,
no earlier examples of output pools or proposals for a trust arrangement
than those on the Great Kanawha have surfaced in the legal literature.
The Kanawha salt producers also refined the organization and operation of contemporary joint-stock companies and sales agencies.

Many factors dictated the legal and business organization and
operation of the several dozen salt firms as they responded over time
to the commercial and industrial environment. Established companies
that owned their land, furnaces, and other facilities tended to be the
larger manufacturers and could take a long-term view of their operations. Others, holding short-term leases of their factories, had different economic objectives. Some were single proprietorships or partnerships in manufacturing; others were complex partnerships or joint
associations that vertically integrated by melding mining, mercantile,
agricultural, multi-furnace, and sales operations. Some firms resulted
from various combinations of manufacturers who attempted to attain
economies of scale and to control market forces.

The legal evolution of the antebellum Great Kanawha salt industry's business organization was unique and distinctive. It is quite important to understanding American legal history as it altered what was
previously known about the application of nineteenth-century American associative and contract law. Upon discovery of a missing sales
agency agreement, it became possible to supplement this present volume by publishing all the Kanawha salt makers' agreements of concert
and combination during the antebellum period. The innovative legal
instruments, including original lease/re-lease agreements, placed into
the salt manufacturers' contemporary economic and legal environment,
were explained in the context of current associative and contract law
in the United States and Great Britain. The resulting publication was
*Kanawhan Prelude to Nineteenth-Century Monopoly in the United States: The
Virginia Salt Combinations* (Richmond: Virginia Historical Society, 2000).[14]

Verifying the adage that a person who selects a dissertation topic
better choose one he or she likes, as one will be living with it for a

long time, in 2003, the author summarized six decades of the salt industry's history in a very brief overview for a Kanawha Valley chemical heritage symposium. This essay, taking advantage of a railroad surveyor's 1850–1851 maps, also demonstrated the transitory physical characteristics of an Appalachian extractive enterprise. These maps show the salt makers' extensive industrial footprint: fifty-two active and six abandoned salt furnaces, ninety-six brine well rigs (thirty feet tall), and thirty-two coal railroads from the adjacent hills to the furnaces. Today, hardly a sign, except for structures in Malden, of this past industrial presence of the enterprise remains.[15]

Republication of a monograph after many years represents a reaffirmation of its timely intellectual value to current scholars in an era of new, exciting interpretations and to other curious readers. It is also an intellectual investment in the state and regional citizens' knowledge about themselves in the realm of economic, commercial, and legal accomplishment. West Virginians can view this volume as a positive appraisal of their forbearers' entrepreneurial acumen, technological innovation, and worldview. The study emphasizes that what initially seems very local actually has very important, far-reaching meaning. The antebellum Great Kanawha salt makers, their leased and owned slaves, and their activities in manufacturing and in confronting the harsh market have established their place in the tapestry of narratives about Appalachian extractive industries that show their importance to the regional, national, and international economy. The manufacturers' industriousness, entrepreneurial nature, technological progress, and their legal activity demonstrate how original and premodern their thinking was in areas often ignored. Perhaps this work will stimulate additional probing on the legal frontier and about other important Appalachian industries such as early modern chemical production. Adapting to new economic realities, the few post–Civil War Kanawha salt manufacturers and others began producing by-product chemicals.

Because of an extractive industry's nature in Appalachia and everywhere, its history necessarily has a funereal denouement. The lessons of the sudden rise and extended decline of the Kanawha salt industry (beginning in the 1850s) and other like enterprises remain constant and clear. When they develop, they herald great prosperity and change for all, but after periods of boom and depression, the industry will pass, leaving in its wake acquired wealth for a few, outmigration, economically stranded people, and an altered landscape. Hope for revival of a transitory extractive enterprise, especially when the resource is depleted or national and global markets permanently change, to its former prosperous status is futile.

NOTES

1. For the best scholarly, global view of the importance of salt and it sources, see Robert P. Multhauf, *Neptune's Gift: A History of Common Salt* (Baltimore: Johns Hopkins Univ. Press, 1978). For a popular account that reached the *New York Times* bestseller list, see Mark Kurlansky, *Salt: A World History* (New York: Penguin Books, 2002), 250–54 for the Great Kanawha Industry.

2. No definitive definition of what historians mean by the term *new capitalism* exists. For a learned, wide-ranging discussion by practitioners that reveals a great breadth of thought about the concept, see "Interchange: The History of Capitalism," *Journal of American History* 101, no. 2 (September 2014): 503–36. For a general history, see Joyce Oldham Appleby, *The Relentless Revolution: A History of Capitalism* (New York: W. W. Norton & Co., 2010). For an avocation, see Seth Rockman, "What Makes the History of Capitalism Newsworthy?" *Journal of the Early Republic* 34, no. 3 (Fall 2014): 439–66.

3. For the opportunities for transatlantic research that has implications extending beyond the span of title dates, see John J. McCusker and Russell R. Menard, *The Economy of British America, 1607–1789: Needs and Opportunities for Study* (Chapel Hill: Univ. of North Carolina Press, 1985). Also, see Cathy Matson, ed., *The Economy of Early America: Historical Perspectives and New Directions* (University Park, PA: Pennsylvania State Univ. Press, 2006). For New Orleans as an *entrepôt* from 1837 to the 1880s, see Scott P. Marler, *The Merchants' Capital: New Orleans and the Political Economy of the Nineteenth-Century South* (New York: Cambridge Univ. Press, 2013). For the global cotton trade in the new capitalism school, see Sven Beckert, *Empire of Cotton: A Global History* (New York: Alfred A. Knopf, 2014).

4. Margaret Walsh, *The Rise of the Midwestern Meat Packing Industry* (Lexington: Univ. Press of Kentucky, 1982). Using Immanuel Wallerstein's world-systems pattern, sociologist Wilma A. Dunaway employed the author's dissertation, not the monograph, to demonstrate the interconnectedness of the Kanawha salt producers and other Appalachian industries with the international economy. She contends that southern Appalachia, being on the periphery of the commodity chain, was a frontier of the capitalistic system from the beginning with the commoditization of everything of worth to the world. *The First American Frontier: Transition to Capitalism in Southern Appalachia, 1700–1860* (Chapel Hill: Univ. of North Carolina Press, 1996). For a critical review, see John E. Stealey III, *North Carolina Historical Review* LXXV, no. 1 (January 1998): 108–9.

5. For the original article, see John Edmund Stealey III, "Slavery and the Western Virginia Salt Industry," *Journal of Negro History* LIX, no. 2 (April 1974): 105–31. Charles B. Dew, *Ironmaker to the Confederacy: Joseph R. Anderson and the Tredegar Iron Works* (New Haven: Yale Univ. Press, 1966). Robert S. Starobin, "Disciplining Industrial Slaves in the Old South," *Journal of Negro History* LIII, no. 2 (April 1963): 111–28; "The Economics of Industrial Slavery in the Old South," *Business History Review* 44, no. 2 (Summer 1970): 131–74; *Industrial Slavery in the Old South* (New York: Oxford Univ. Press, 1970). Numerous scholars espoused the "new economic history" in many works; however, Robert W. Fogel and Stanley L. Engerman wrote the primary controversial study: *Time on the Cross: The Economics of American Negro Slavery*

(2 vols.; Boston: Little, Brown & Co., 1974). The main rebuttal of many by historians is Herbert G. Gutman, *Slavery and the Numbers Game: A Critique of* Time on the Cross (Urbana: Univ. of Illinois Press, 1975). Fogel later wrote a toned-down version of the joint work, *Without Consent or Contract: The Rise and Fall of American Slavery* (New York and London: W. W. Norton & Co., 1989). A thorough review is Peter Kolchin, "More *Time on the Cross*? An Evaluation of Robert William Fogel's *Without Consent or Contract*," *Journal of Southern History* 58, no. 3 (August 1992): 491–502.

6. An early reprint of the piece appeared in James E. Newton and Ronald L. Lewis, eds., *The Other Slaves: Mechanics, Artisans, and Craftsmen* (Boston: G. K. Hall & Co., 1978), 109–33. For the recent reprint, see John C. Inscoe, ed., *Appalachians and Race: The Mountain South from Slavery to Segregation* (Lexington: Univ. Press of Kentucky, 2001), 50–73. For entrance into the mainstream, see John B. Boles and Evelyn Thomas Nolen, eds., *Interpreting Southern History: Historiographical Essays in Honor of Sanford W. Higginbotham* (Baton Rouge: Louisiana State Univ. Press, 1987), 87, 152, and Gavin Wright, *Slavery and American Economic Development* (Baton Rouge: Louisiana State Univ. Press, 2006), 149.

7. The historiography of market capitalism is quite extensive. Some of the important works, beside that of Sellers (New York: Oxford Univ. Press, 1991) are: Allan Kulikoff, "The Transition to Capitalism in Rural America," *William & Mary Quarterly* 46, no. 1 (January 1989): 120–44; Allan Kulikoff, *The Agrarian Origins of American Capitalism* (Charlottesville: Univ. Press of Virginia, 1992); and Steven Hahn and Jonathan Prude, *The Countryside in the Age of Capitalist Transformation: Essays in Social History of Rural America* (Chapel Hill: Univ. of North Carolina Press, 1989). An appraisal of Kulikoff's work is Harold D. Woodman, "Review: Independence, Dependency, and Economic Change," *Reviews in American History* 23, no. 3 (September 1995): 464–71. A bibliographical summary is Michael Merrill, "Putting Capitalism in Its Place: A Review of Recent Literature," *William & Mary Quarterly* 52, no. 2 (April 1995): 315–26. The *Journal of the Early Republic* 16, no. 2 (Summer 1996): 159–308, devoted an entire number to the subject of capitalism, entitled "Special Issue of Capitalism in the Early Republic," containing articles by Joyce O. Appleby and Gordon S. Wood, among others. See especially Paul A. Gilje, "The Rise of Capitalism in the Early Republic" (159–81) and Cathy Matson, "Capitalizing Hope: Economic Thought and the Early National Economy" (273–91) for excellent reviews.

8. "Virginia's Mercantile-Manufacturing Frontier: Dickinson & Shrewsbury and Great Kanawha Salt Industry," *Virginia Magazine of History and Biography* 101, no. 4 (October 1993): 509–534. For wealth formation from the salt enterprise, see Bill Drennen, *One Kanawha Valley Bank: A History* (n. p., 2002): 5–106.

9. Baptist (New York: Basic Books, 2014). Important review essays in response are: Matthew Pratt Guterl, "Slavery and Capitalism: A Review Essay," *Journal of Southern History* 81, no. 2 (May 2015): 405–20, and Scott Nelson Reynolds, "Who Put Their Capitalism in My Slavery?," *Journal of the Civil War Era* 5, no. 2 (June 2015): 289–310. Baptist published a precursor article that showed the interconnection between slavery, cotton, and national financial speculation that led to the Panic of 1837: "Toxic Debt, Liar Loans, and Securitized Human Beings: The Panic of 1837 and the Fate of Slavery," *Common-Place* 10, no. 3 (April 2010), http://www.common-place.org. Books are Rockman, *Scraping By: Wage Labor, Slavery, and Survival in Early Baltimore* (Baltimore: Johns Hopkins Univ. Press, 2008); Schermerhorn, *Money over Mastery, Family over Freedom: Slavery in the Antebellum Upper South* (Baltimore: Johns Hopkins Univ. Press, 2011); Rothman, *Flush Times and Fever Dreams: A Story of Capitalism and Slavery in the Age of Jackson* (Athens: Univ. of Georgia Press, 2012); and, Beckert, *Empire of Cotton.*

10. Schermerhorn (New Haven: Yale Univ. Press); Boodry (Unpublished diss., Harvard University); and Beckert and Rothman (Philadelphia: Univ. of Pennsylvania Press).

11. Works about slavery are voluminous. A few recent parallel ones most related to the Kanawha situation are: (borders and regions) Adam Rothman, *Slave Country: American Expansion and the Origins of the Deep South* (Cambridge, MA: Harvard Univ. Press, 2007), Walter Johnson, *River of Dark Dreams: Slavery and Empire in the Cotton Kingdom* (Cambridge, MA: Harvard Univ. Press, 2013), and Matthew Salafia, *Slavery's Borderland: Freedom and Bondage Along the Ohio River* (Philadelphia: Univ. of Pennsylvania Press, 2013); (slave trade) Steven Deyle, *Carry Me Back: The Domestic Slave Trade in American Life* (New York: Oxford Univ. Press, 2005); and (slave hiring) Jonathan D. Martin, *Divided Mastery: Slave Hiring in the American South* (Cambridge, MA: Harvard Univ. Press, 2004). For the legal implications of hiring on control, and treatment of slaves, see John E. Stealey III, "The Responsibilities and Liabilities of the Bailee of Slave Labor in Virginia," *American Journal of Legal History* XII, no. 4 (October 1968): 336–53.

12. Charles B. Dew, *Bond of Iron: Master and Slave at Buffalo Forge* (New York: W. W. Norton & Co., 1994); Katherine A. Harvey, *The Best-Dressed Miners: Life and Labor in the Maryland Coal Region, 1835–1910* (Ithaca, NY: Cornell University Press, 1969); Ronald L. Lewis, *Coal, Iron, and Slaves: Industrial Slavery in Maryland and Virginia, 1715–1865* (Westport, CT: Greenwood Press, 1979); Kenneth W. Noe, *Southwestern Virginia's Railroad: Modernization and the Sectional Crisis* (Urbana: Univ. of Illinois Press, 1994). Especially relevant is Randal L. Hall, *Mountains on the Market: Industry, the Environment, and the South* (Lexington: Univ. Press of Kentucky, 2012). A useful bibliographical essay about writings in Southern Appalachian history is Kenneth W. Noe, "Appalachia before Mr. Peabody: Some Recent Literature on the Southern Mountain Region," *The Virginia Magazine of History and Biography* 110, no. 1 (2002): 5–34.

13. For the blending of public policy and the law with an extractive industry, see Ronald L. Lewis, *Transforming the Appalachian Countryside: Railroads, Deforestation, and Social Change in West Virginia, 1880–1920* (Chapel Hill: Univ. of North Carolina Press, 1998).

14. An able economist has conducted important research that connected the antebellum Kanawha associative activities with those in Michigan where the salt producers eventually produced bromine, a chemical by-product of salt manufacturing. Her research led to explorations of the Dow Chemical Company and its early confrontation with international cartels. Margaret C. Levenstein, "Vertical Restraints in the Bromine Cartel: The Role of Distributors in Facilitating Collusion," National Bureau of Economic Research Historical Paper No. 49, Cambridge, MA, July 1993; "Price Wars and the Stability of Collusion: A Study of Pre-World War I Bromine Industry," National Bureau of Economic Research Historical Paper No. 50, Cambridge, MA, September 1993; "Mass Production Conquers the Pool: Firm Organization and the Nature of Competition in the Nineteenth Century," *The Journal of Economic History* 55, no. 3 (September 1995): 575–611; "Price Wars and the Stability of Collusion: A Study of the Pre-World War I Bromine Industry," *The Journal of Industrial Economics* XLV, no. 2 (June 1997): 117–37; and *Accounting for Growth: Information Systems and the Creation of the Large Corporation* (Stanford, CA: Stanford University Press, 1998).

15. John E. Stealey III, "An Overview of the Antebellum Great Kanawha Salt Industry," in Lee R. Maddox, compl., *Great Kanawha Valley Chemical Heritage Symposium Proceedings*, Institute for the History of Technology and Industrial Archaeology Monograph Series, Vol. 6 (Morgantown, WV, May 3, 2003), 1–13, for map interpretation, 2.

Acknowledgments

The genesis of this investigation of the antebellum western Virginia salt industry and the economy of the western United States occurred about thirty years ago when Hubert H. Humphrey's and John Fitzgerald Kennedy's presidential campaigns, the latter's New Frontier domestic program, and contemporary writings by journalists and scholars focused national attention on Appalachia and its condition. At that time my youthful academic goal of becoming a lawyer in Appalachia, presumably to profit from West Virginia's extractive industries, switched in an intellectually exciting undergraduate environment to vaguely philanthropic objectives of investigating the origins of influential regional enterprises, of earning a doctorate in history, and of attempting to teach the crucial importance of history. Whether the change reveals imprudence or wisdom is irrelevant here, but this detailed study of the Great Kanawha salt makers and their responses to market forces is a long-term result of my intellectual quest. In a crowded undergraduate history lecture hall at West Virginia University, the late Festus Paul Summers broached the topic that sparked my original interest. His later simultaneous warnings about the academic tolls of research in antebellum western Virginia enterprise and warm encouragement launched a fledgling project that reached far beyond the Allegheny Mountains to Liverpool, England, to Turks Island, British West Indies, to Onondaga County, New York, and to New England.

Historical investigation of nineteenth-century United States business enterprises and economic development incurs special difficulties and high costs. The investigator usually confronts the problem of scarce materials and the requirement of a separate inquiry for each industry, which prohibits the transfer of most acquired expertise to other studies. The discrete research required to qualify the historian to present a narrative is similar to accruing excavation or productive costs in the mining of low-grade ore and in the evaporation of low-density brine in extractive endeavors. When this high investment combines with the cost of refining and distilling local legal records, the price becomes even more prohibitive and the indebtedness greater.

Many people, more than can be specifically mentioned or repaid, have eased my research of the Kanawha Salines. While inspiring me and fellow students about the joys and exactions of Clio, William Derrick Barns, my graduate school adviser, patiently oversaw the first tentative writing efforts. Edward M. Steel, Jr., aided production with his many stimulating insights and a critical review. A valued colleague at Shepherd College, Jerry Bruce Thomas, was a helpful critic who was always ready to review various versions with discernment. Otis K. Rice of the West Virginia Institute of Technology warmly encouraged this work from the beginning. Anders Henriksson, chairman of the history department at Shepherd, wholeheartedly supported the effort and secured institutional funds for some typing.

Numerous librarians and curators at many collections and institutions cited in the bibliography have greatly aided the research process, and their unfailingly gracious help is gratefully acknowledged. Several persons have devoted more attention to my extensive requests than even professional courtesy required. Foremost are the late J. William Hess, George Parkinson, John A. Cuthbert, A.D. Mastrogiuseppe, Jr., Pauline Kissler, and Harold M. Forbes at the West Virginia and Regional History Collection of the West Virginia University Library and Floyd W. Miller, George R. Gaumond, Joseph W. Barnes, and all their numerous past and present assistants at the Ruth Scarborough Library at Shepherd College. Timely assistance with technical and research problems has come from Dr. David M. Gillespie, now of Frostburg State University; Dr. James C. Klotter of the Kentucky State Historical Society; Cora P. Teel, Special Collections Department, James E. Morrow Library, Marshall University; Frederick H. Armstrong, West Virginia Department of Archives and History; and Connie Hunt of Scott Depot.

Colleagues in the academy often deplore the vanishing of gentlemen editors, but they have not encountered William Jerome Crouch. His quiet yet firm prodding over a decade brought this work to fruition when he had no reason to think that it would ever appear. His two anonymous reviewers made constructive criticisms that have strengthened the presentation. For permission to use the previously unpublished watercolor by August Köllner, I thank Mary Price Ratrie, a direct descendant of prominent salt makers. The Association for the Study of Afro-American Life and History has kindly authorized the use of the copyrighted portions of the chapter on slavery that previously appeared in the *Journal of Negro History.*

Many dedicated secretaries have typed parts and versions of the manuscript at various stages, thereby earning my gratitude. They are Betty L. Crampton, Janice S. Sheaff, Kathy G. Jamison, Patsy C. Wilt, and Brenda M. Feltner. Jeanne Norris's secretarial support was especially crucial, comprehensive, and exemplary.

Finally, to my wife, Patty, I owe the greatest debt, not only initially for her secretarial skills but also for her enduring companionship through three decades of involvement with me and the Kanawha salt makers. To her I dedicate this volume, as she is definitely seated above the salt in all aspects of my life.

1

Kanawha Salt's Savor

Salt, essential for life, processing, and preservation, is a substance that animals and humans not only need but often crave. This aspect of the commodity's nature emphasizes the importance of the enterprise that developed in the first years of the nineteenth century on a ten-mile stretch of a major Ohio River tributary, the Great Kanawha, at Kanawha Salines (Terra Salis or Malden), two or three miles above Charleston, Virginia (now West Virginia). It accounts to some extent for the unique, perhaps unparalleled, premodern business and legal activities of some remarkable manufacturers who confronted a vagarious market. Although other sources of salt existed, none rivaled the Kanawha brine in ensuring the emergence of large-scale agricultural development in the Ohio River basin. Thomas Childs Cochran explained in his classic survey of the frontiers of economic change that rapid expansion in early United States industry resulted from culture, geography, and resources, and the same convergence was true on the regional level in the Great Kanawha salt business.[1] Agricultural prosperity in the West and the growth of the pork-packing industry at Cincinnati, Louisville, and other river towns could not have occurred without it.

Operating in a state and local economy that was for the most part laissez faire, Kanawha salt makers dominated their locality in capital access, labor supply, and government programs. The market was the only factor that they could not master, but they did attempt to control market forces. Temporary successes resulted, but Kanawha producers achieved more in other areas. They blended the plantation slavery system into a factory environment. They adapted the common law and the Virginia legal system to meet their economic needs. And they dominated state and local government, shaping the policies and programs that touched their industry. The Commonwealth of Virginia, however, though it seldom interfered, did little of positive value for the industry. The state did not legally intrude in the industry's formulation of agreements that could have been construed as contrary to public welfare. Its attempts to make internal improvements on the river and to provide banking facilities were feeble. The Kanawha manufacturers obstructed and eventually reversed the commonwealth's taxation of salt during the War of 1812, and later, by controlling county government and its administrative processes, they harnessed the operation of the state inspection statutes.

This microcosmic investigation of the Kanawha salt industry relies almost totally upon local legal records. These records have the potential to support fruitful research into antebellum United States business enterprises, as they were primarily local and regional. For the Kanawha industry, the absence of sources other than those that originated in court, however, also inhibits interpretation. No business records of a single salt company over an extended period exist. Therefore, the conclusions that can be formulated from tracing the growth of one manufacturing proprietorship, firm, or group cannot be made. The result is a series of horizontal views through time of the industry and its milieu. It is a legal record internally generated by the salt makers themselves.

Because of the documentary limitations, a kind of self-oblivion created by the nature of salt makers' lives and by the effects of transitory extractive industries, this analysis concentrates on the evolution of the industry, how the business functioned, the Kanawha manufacturers' market responses to their internal and external circumstances, the producers' forging of legal remedies to better their economic standing, and their reaction to public policy as it affected them. Many Kanawha salt makers were short-term operators, running their businesses for less than a decade. Some long-term individual and family firms existed, but only a few extended beyond the 1850s. When one considers this lack of permanence, combined with the continual flooding of the Great Kanawha bottomland, where furnaces, stores, and homes were located, and the ravages along a primary Civil War military route, it is understandable why few records survive. As a group, Kanawha salt makers were men of action, not writers, who acted unobserved at the furnace, at the company store, at the distant river port, or in the field. Their laborers, free and slave, were unable or too busy to create a documentary record except in indirect ways. Few contemporaries, reporters, or travelers were extensively interested in the workers or gained insights into their thinking. A relatively comprehensive view of owners and laborers in society like that of Alan Dawley's shoemakers in Lynn, Massachusetts, or Anthony F.C. Wallace's Rockdale textile enterprise and anthracite coal miners is impossible. Although clues about lives and thoughts of the furnace owners, managers, and workers flicker from the record, generalization about their self-proclaimed motives and impact on society must be slight.[2]

The Kanawha salt business dramatically demonstrates the truism that economic development in the United States cannot be separated from legal history. Legal and economic historians consciously work within what Harry N. Scheiber aptly calls the borderland of law and economic history.[3] This study attempts to marry the approaches within the context of a deterministic market. With few exceptions, studies involving legal and economic history have focused on business or industry that faces an externally generated legal environment emanating from the state through public policies determined by the executive and legislature or by judicial interpretation of statutes and equity questions. Most of these investigations of the external legal climate center on the state's effect on transportation enterprise. While not denying the importance of the interplay of antebellum transportation and the state, one might appropriately focus on producing and manufacturing enterprises and their legal situations. The inside-out, rather than the outside-in, approach to legal development might alter surveys of American legal evolution. The legal responses of Kanawha producers, for example, generally were internally generated rather than externally imposed through public policy or public instrumentalities.[4]

The Kanawha salt makers' creation and adaptation of legal forms and arrangements to achieve their end of profit were advanced to an extent previously undiscovered by historians of American combination and monopoly. The legal devices, both adopted and proposed, and the economic environment that caused their formulation forged a new chapter in American legal history. Salt manufacturers demonstrated Adam Smith's observation that those who employ their stocks to supply markets to raise their price above the natural price are careful to conceal the attempt, but such secrets can rarely be concealed. Contemporaries and later historians generally knew of the salt makers' monopolies, although only a few of the formal combination arrangements had surfaced. Over twenty years of concerted effort has been expended in a systematic pursuit of these contracts.

The combinations of Kanawha producers raised a major Jacksonian Era theme of popular reaction against privilege and vested economic interests. Although the Kanawha salt makers' solutions to their economic dilemmas varied in nature and effectiveness, they ran counter to deeply engrained notions of fair, if not free, trade. The salt makers' activities attracted the national legislative attention of Senator Thomas Hart Benton, who, knowing a good issue, guided and expressed the views of many western salt consumers. Benton considered his exposés of the Kanawha "monopoly" and his advocacy of free salt importation as important as his stand on the expunging resolution. His intermittent attacks constituted the only contemporary questioning on public policy grounds of the legal and business methods of Kanawha manufacturers. The issue of Kanawha combinations and their exposure to foreign importations as beneficial to western consumers became part of the fabric of Jacksonian Era debates.[5] One of the mysteries to previous scholars who had become slightly familiar with the attempts of Kanawha producers to combine to raise salt prices was why little public outcry and no legal objections resulted. Thomas Senior Berry explained the slight response by noting the constant, drastic reduction of antebellum salt prices. An additional explanation is that from the western consumers' viewpoint, what the Kanawha salt makers tried to do was the same as what they routinely experienced with their local merchant when any commodity became scarce.[6]

Most studies of antebellum legal history and evolution, technological innovation, managerial structure and accomplishment, and general pre–Civil War economic history focus upon developments in the textile industry of New England and the Philadelphia–Delaware Valley area, early iron manufacture, and railroads and center progress in New England and the Middle Atlantic states. The importance, primary nature, and scale of these industries, the availability of sources, and the location of leading centers for the study of business and economic history, rather than geographic bias, probably explain this tendency. Investigations of midwestern and southern industries are so scarce that one cannot gain a full comprehension of the legal and economic evolution of American business. Among local and regional economic activities in the Midwest and South that need exploration are lumbering and sawmills (millwork and containers), gristmills and flour production, distilling, glassmaking, tanning (saddle and harness making, hatmaking, and belting), textiles, conveyances (wagons, carriages, and coaches), brick making and quarrying, machinery construction (gins, engines, and implements), pottery, and building construction. The salt industry's story, one of a basic commodity, might suggest that economic and legal activity in the South and West contributed more than historians have recognized.[7]

Their vision unobstructed by the hills of the Allegheny Plateau, the Kanawha salt manufacturers had a national and international view of their enterprise. They thoroughly understood the domestic salt trade, agricultural commodity markets, the impact of the transportation revolution, and the ramifications of the international cotton trade for salt manufacturing. They were more than parochial capitalists who reacted to market circumstances to attain their prosperity. They confronted a full-time manufacturing process that had a widely dispersed labor force engaged in many simultaneous functions; an enterprise that might include more than one furnace, a coal mine, and a company store; and a geographic reach that stretched from western Virginia to the Mississippi. The Kanawha salt makers coped with the organization and structure of managerial functions and fashioned premodern solutions as early as did the railroad men described by Alfred Dupont Chandler, Jr., separating what Chandler identified as the entrepreneurial from the operational functions. The move toward organizational rationalization occurred both within the individual production unit and in the producing brine field as a whole. This early confrontation with the dynamics of extensive enterprise explains to a great degree the quest for legal combination. The agreements of consolidation, particularly the later ones, specify the organization of the enterprise beyond the individual producing unit.[8] By eliminating intermediaries and controlling the distribution of their commodity, the producers anticipated what later nineteenth-century manufacturers would encounter when they tried to control the price and distribution of their products. What limited their control of their economic destiny was not their comprehension but their time in history, the nature of salt as a widely deposited mineral, and the external economy.

From their industrial beginnings, the Kanawha manufacturers extensively employed slave labor in all phases of the extractive enterprise. A sufficient free labor supply never existed. The examination of the adaptation of the peculiar institution to these circumstances supplements many recent studies that generalize about industrial use and the hire system. The extensive Kanawha lease-hire system freed capital that might have been invested in slaves for other purposes. A plantation mentality did not inhibit the economic awareness or the resourcefulness of salt makers in responding to market imperatives or in exploring technological innovation. Control and manipulation of the legal system proved crucial to the adjustment of slavery to an industrial situation.

Students of modern extractive industries in general and of those in southern Appalachia in particular will readily see the linkage between the Great Kanawha Valley salt industry and post–Civil War regional economic development in mineral and forest industries. In regard to labor supply, the social organization of the labor force, the characteristics of capital investment and marketing, and the boom-and-bust business cycle, the similarities are striking. The bituminous coal industry recruited labor from domestic sources, just as the Kanawha furnace operators went to Piedmont Virginia. Coal operators went to the same geographic source but extended their net into the Carolinas and northern Alabama.[9] Appalachian whites, alienated from the land, and immigrants supplied post–Civil War operators but were not available to early nineteenth-century salt makers. The class system, the company house and store, and the subtle means of social and economic control were not new in the Gilded Age. Post–Civil War extractive industries in mining and lumber were decentralized in ownership of production and faced vicious national business cycles, alterations in transportation policies and facilities, and vigorous competition, like the earlier Kanawha enterprise. The domination by salt makers of local government was as thorough if not as authoritarian as was any later coal operator's. Subject to an external market for its prosperity, the Kanawha industry foreshadowed the evolution of the local and regional economy characteristic of coal, lumber, and natural resource commodities.[10]

Based on historiographic interpretations of evolving economic development in the Western world (having modern worldwide ramifications in all developing economies), modern differences about development have emerged. A pioneering 1972 article by Franklin F. Mendels about preindustrial industry, or what he called proto-industrialization—which described the transition from feudalism to capitalism and from household to factory manufacture, as well as the passage from local to international markets for goods—ignited the European phase of research.[11] The discussion in the United States focuses upon early industrial beginnings in the transition of capitalism in rural America, emphasizing the farmer. To oversimplify the sometimes complex interpretations, one group explains rural capitalism by examining market development and sees farmers as active capitalists, and the other views farmers as not completely market-oriented, but primarily concerned about their subsistence, independence, and household integrity.[12] The stimulating differences practically compel one to place, if only briefly and superficially, the western Virginia salt makers in an evolutionary context.

The Kanawha salt producers fit somewhere between the age of the merchant capitalist and the "strategy and structure" of modern enterprise. By the War of 1812 the western Virginia industry had expanded beyond the household and local market and met increasing regional demands. The Kanawha boom attracted capitalist adventurers who sought a fortune in manufacturing or vending a commodity of necessity. They moved into an agriculturally undeveloped river valley. A few subsistence settlements and farmsteads existed before 1808, fourteen years after the Indian danger. Revolutionary era land speculators held most of the prime river bottom, and their economic objectives had retarded agricultural settlement.[13] The early salt discoveries rapidly thrust the area's economy into an extensive and expanding market oriented to the demands of the entire Ohio River basin.

Because substantial agricultural development did not precede but was simultaneous with or followed the construction of numerous salt factories, subsequent growth in farming and other endeavors supplemented industrial requirements in a subsidiary fashion. To separate the Kanawha factories completely from the rural and agricultural environment would oversimplify the capitalist context. Evolution, like most aspects of economic development, is characterized by erosion and gradualism rather than stark contrast or suddenness. Salt makers blended endeavors, as some firms farmed while others did not. Always, however, they primarily reacted to the local and regional market. If salt makers grew and produced food for themselves, it was to lessen their economic dependence on the uncertain marketplace.

When they confronted Adam Smith's invisible market forces, the Kanawha salt makers were ahead of their time and premodern in their commercial and legal attempts to control their factories and their industry. In the legal and economic dimension, the Kanawha businessmen demonstrate the transitory aspect of historical development while they exhibit the characteristics of British and colonial endeavors and the crass methods of postbellum "robber barons." Condemnation of their rational economic and legal behavior does not result in enhanced comprehension of the dynamic economy that Kanawha salt makers confronted. By following their adaptations to the realities of the marketplace of the western United States, one may gain a broader perspective on the complexities of nineteenth-century commodity industries and their role in the legal and economic development of the United States.

2

Early Development and Expansion

The Allegheny Mountains and the heavily forested areas that stretched westward to the Mississippi contained numerous licks, where salt brine seeped from underground sources to the porous surface to satisfy a basic natural requirement for man and beast. Because ruminants such as buffalo and deer congregated at salt licks, Indians and later white hunters focused their fur-gathering efforts at these locations. The connecting traces carved between Allegheny and Ohio River basin salines by migrating animals became the paths of the *coureurs de bois* and Anglo-American settlement.

Strangely, until the American Revolution, the early frontiersmen, with the exception of the French at Misere near Sainte Genevieve, Missouri, ignored the salt-making potential of the licks and relied upon importations from the eastern seacoast. Salt shortages, induced by the conflict with the British, and the increasing requirements of growing western settlement in the trans-Allegheny stimulated salt production at various Kentucky licks in the 1780s. Manufacturing at many other Ohio River basin salines, following the Bluegrass State's lead, attempted to meet the enormous salt requirements necessary for development of a prosperous agricultural enterprise and a commercial economy in the American West.[1]

For centuries, a great salt lick existed on the northern side of the Great Kanawha River, six miles above the mouth of the Elk River, in western Virginia. This particular seepage, known as the Great Buffalo Lick, attracted ruminants in great numbers. Opposite the lick in a low passage named Thoroughfare Gap, the buffalo and deer had cut deep trails, which remained visible throughout the nineteenth century. The first white explorers discovered an absence of foliage near the ground in the immediate vicinity.[2]

The existence of the salt spring and plentiful wildlife on a primary buffalo trail leading over the Allegheny Mountains from the Valley of Virginia to the Ohio Valley lured Indians, white explorers, and land speculators to the Great Kanawha Valley. Indians had utilized this salt lick frequently: the first white settlers found the remains of pottery and primitive wells. In 1755 the Indians had carried Mary Ingles, her new-born baby, and others as captives from the Draper's Meadows settlement of New River to this spot on the Kanawha to obtain a salt supply.[3] In the autumn of 1774 the farmer-soldiers of the army of Colonel Andrew Lewis had viewed this alluring site on their way to Point Pleasant in Lord Dunmore's campaign against the Ohio Indians. In the year following Dunmore's campaign, Colonel John Dickinson of Bath County, Virginia, patented 502 acres at the mouth of Campbell's Creek on the Great Kanawha River that included the Great Buffalo Lick and some surrounding bottomland.[4]

For several years the salt spring at Thoroughfare Gap owned by Dickinson remained unexploited. In 1795 Joseph Ruffner, Sr., of Page County, Virginia, purchased the Campbell's Creek property, including the salt lick, without ever seeing it.[5] Ruffner, a prosperous farmer, had inherited improved property on Hawksbill Creek from his Swiss-German parents, who had migrated from Lancaster County, Pennsylvania, like many other residents of the Valley of Virginia. Severe losses by fire on his farm in the Shenandoah Valley moved Ruffner to consummate the speculative purchase and to explore the Great Kanawha Valley.[6] While on the Kanawha River, he purchased an additional tract of approximately five hundred acres from Jemima and George Clendinen. The great fertility of the bottomlands of the Kanawha and the potential value of the salt lick induced Ruffner to move westward with his entire family in September 1795.[7]

The original purchase agreements between Dickinson and Ruffner and a fraternal quarrel between the heirs of Joseph Ruffner, Sr., upon his death prevented the development of the salt spring on Campbell's Creek for a decade. In addition to paying £500 for the property, Ruffner had signed three conditional bonds upon purchase. Each of these bonds obligated Ruffner and his heirs for £2,000 to exert "all pains and Industry" to produce salt from the spring. Ruffner had to pay Dickinson, his heirs, executors, or administrators £1,000 worth of salt (at the current selling price) on each of the three bonds for each ten-bushel amount (up to thirty) boiled in a twenty-four-hour period.[8] If more than ten bushels were produced, Dickinson agreed not to require the payment of more than one bond annually, and interest would not accrue on outstanding bonds.[9] If successful development had occurred, Ruffner could have owed the grantor up to £3,000 value in salt.

For very good reason, Ruffner never made any salt at the spring during his lifetime. In 1797 he leased the lick to Elisha Brooks. Brooks sank three hollowed sycamore tree trunks ten feet into the ground as wells and erected a small, primitive furnace of twenty-four kettles to evaporate the brine bailed from the wells. Using four or five cords of wood as fuel, he could manufacture 150 pounds (three bushels) of impure salt daily.[10]

In his will of 1803, Joseph Ruffner, Sr., enjoined his sons to explore for saltwater on the former Dickinson property within one year of his death. If the "water proves good and lasting," the profits arising from salt making would be divided into six equal parts to be distributed to his five sons: one part each to Joseph, Tobias, David, and Daniel and two parts to Abraham. If the experiment did not prove fruitful, the Dickinson property was to be conveyed to Abraham. If Abraham did not want the land and the lick, the executors were to dispose of the tract and give £750 to Abraham from the proceeds.[11] Joseph's sons David and Joseph, the executors, attempted to obtain brine, but their efforts were probably superficial because of the Dickinson bonds and agreements. They announced that the salt lick "was of little or no value."[12] Despite their claims, the executors would not convey or sell the property as provided by the will and pay their brother Abraham £750.

In 1805 several interested parties began contesting the legal position maintained by Joseph Ruffner, Sr., during his life and later by his executors. After the deaths of the principals, the executors of John Dickinson's estate sued Joseph Ruffner's executors on October 28, 1805, on the ground that the elder Ruffner had never attempted to manufacture salt at Campbell's Creek as provided by the bonds and agreements of the original sale. The defendants contended that their father had expended all possible effort during his lifetime to produce the greatest amount of salt, but the spring could not yield the requisite brine. In the course of the trial, the plaintiffs obtained the vital deposition of William Dupuy, who had worked for Elisha Brooks at Ruffner's salt spring in 1798–99. He deposed that Brooks made seven to nine bushels every twenty-four hours and that twenty bushels could have been manufactured on a larger furnace. Furthermore, Dupuy said that Joseph Ruffner, while obstructing the manufacturing process in minor ways, stated that the progress Brooks was making "would ruin him."[13]

In March 1806 the prodigal Abraham thwarted the executors' plan of awaiting the passage of time to avoid the intent of the Dickinson agreements. He sold his portion of his father's estate—the Dickinson tract including "the Salt lick on Kanawha river," one lot in Charleston, and a set of sawmill irons—to Andrew Donnally, Jr., for £750 Virginia money.[14]

Fortunately for his heirs, Joseph Ruffner, Sr., had purchased from George Alderson a 266-acre tract of land that adjoined the Dickinson salt spring. With their decade-old fraud collapsing in the summer of 1806, David and Joseph Ruffner began serious experiments to obtain saltwater on the Alderson tract. Dr. Henry Ruffner, son of David, writing about his family's quest for brine after his retirement from the presidency of Washington College in 1851, ascribed the motivation and eventual success to Divine Providence. Relating his activities after 1807 to a boyhood friend, however, Henry Ruffner conveyed a less romantic version. He recalled that he and his family worked "at sinking hollow sycamore trees into the mud, until we were all sick of it, but my father was deeply in debt and it was sink or nothing."[15]

At a low-water mark on the north bank of the Great Kanawha River, a short distance below the Dickinson salt spring, Joseph and David Ruffner began their experiment to obtain a plentiful source of brine. They cut a straight sycamore tree, three and a half to four feet in diameter, for the outer casing of the well (called a gum). The gum had an outer living shell, three to four inches thick, and was squared off at eighteen feet in length. The gum, with a beveled outer edge, entered a hole, large end first. To keep the casing upright and perfectly perpendicular to the ground, two sets of parallel beams were crisscrossed horizontally on its rim. Men worked on a platform built upon this superstructure. As the excavation progressed, the weight of the workmen and of the material placed on the platform forced the gum into the ground. A fifty-foot sweep was balanced on a high forked post as an axis. This sweep reached into the casing with a slender pole suspending a large bucket (half of a whiskey barrel). The men on the platform helped to lower, raise, and empty the bucket.[16]

The first twenty-six feet of excavation proceeded very smoothly. One man worked in the well with a shovel, pick, and crowbar. At a depth of ten feet, water began pouring into the casing. The drillers removed a half bucket of sand for each six buckets of water bailed. At thirteen feet, they struck a six-inch-thick cemented gravel bed, which they broke with a crowbar. Three feet below the gravel bed, they encountered solid rock. The water rushing into the well between the gravel and the rock was not any more saline than that found at the spring.[17]

This result caused the Ruffners to believe that the saltwater emanated from the hill to the north of the valley. They temporarily abandoned the well at the river and began a new excavation in the bottom between the river and the mountain. Here they dug a well that was five-foot square, lined with hewn timbers. The men soon reached the same level as the top of the abandoned casing. With a three-inch borer, they fashioned a twenty-foot-long white oak tube. A rod that could be withdrawn was fitted into the tube. A heavy block of wood hoisted by a windlass drove the tapered tube into the ground. At seventeen feet, the drillers, encountering the same solid rock as in the abandoned well, could not drive the tube further.[18]

The Ruffners had reached the point of no return in their exploration for saltwater, as about ten men had labored nine months without any significant discovery. In November 1806 the brothers had obtained a deed of trust on the Alderson property to secure a seven-hundred-dollar debt. In the summer of 1807 they returned to the well at the river's edge. To solve the water problem, they constructed an eighteen-gallon bucket with a valve in the bottom to bail water without the aid of the well digger. Five men could bail 150 gallons per minute. The digger could then work for a maximum of two hours under the splashing and dripping of the bucket in thigh-deep water. In this way, the persistent workmen penetrated fifteen feet with the gum onto another rock. Wedges driven around the base of the gum prevented the influx of fresh water, and Joseph Ruffner, finding the water issuing from the rock itself very salty, concluded that the rock contained veins of saltwater.[19]

The Ruffners had to muster their inventive genius to devise a way to penetrate the rock. In the early nineteenth century, techniques of drilling wells into rock had not been developed to any degree. Rock blasters with chisels could drill two- to three-foot holes in rock by hand. The Ruffners adapted a drilling method using spring poles that were commonly used to work the pestels of honing mortars. They attached a long-shanked stone chisel with a two-and-a-half-inch bit to a spring pole. They fastened the spring pole on the ground by the thick butt-end, supported it in the middle with a post, and worked the drilling tool by the vertical movement of the small flexible end. The chisel, frequently lengthened and sharpened, pecked very slowly into the rock of the well. The hole guided the auger while the water worked loose borings out of the drill hole.[20]

The spring pole method penetrated the rock to the brine fissures. On November 1, 1807, at a depth of thirty-two feet, the chisel sank into a rock fissure that emitted saltwater of good quality. So confident were the Ruffners of ultimate success that they began erecting a furnace. They decided to continue experimenting with the drilling until the furnace was completed. They struck a second, stronger vein of brine at forty-three feet and a third and superior vein at fifty-five feet.[21]

While preparing the well and constructing a furnace for salt manufacture, Joseph and David Ruffner confronted their legal difficulties. A shaky case and their discovery of brine compelled them to settle with Dickinson's executors. By the consent of both parties, the court appointed two men to arbitrate the action of debt. In September 1809 the arbitrators concluded that the Ruffner executors should pay the Dickinson executors a total of £3,000 in good merchantable salt in three equal installments. Interest on the three payments, based on the current selling price of salt on the delivery dates of September 28, 1810,

September 20, 1811, and September 20, 1812, would accrue from the time of decision.[22]

After discovering the saltwater and settling with the Dickinson executors, Joseph and David Ruffner refused to surrender the Dickinson property to Andrew Donnally, Jr., who had purchased the tract from Abraham Ruffner. The court recognized the halfhearted efforts of David and Joseph as meeting the requirements of their father's will. Thus the land was Abraham's to convey to Donnally.[23] The Ruffner brothers contested the suit outside the courtroom. While the case was pending, David stabbed Donnally in the left hip with a Dutch anvil and assaulted a laborer in Donnally's service. David was lodged in jail and indicted for assault and battery; Joseph was indicted for aiding, abetting, and concealing the act. Eventually, both brothers paid twenty-dollar fines and presented five-hundred-dollar bonds to guarantee good conduct for a year.[24]

Upon reaching the third vein of saltwater, the drillers stopped the process and concentrated on preparing the well for production. Simultaneously, the salt furnace was constructed. The Ruffners built a fitted plank floor in the bottom of the gum to exclude fresh water. Then they drove a short tube, the same size as the auger hole, from the floor into the well hole. After suitable caulking and pinning, the drillers ran wooden tubing down to the third vein. Salt production began on February 11, 1808, a date that was recorded in the Ruffner family Bible. A few days later, Henry Ruffner joyously reported, after "Digging gumsinking and boring We have at length got good Salt Water at the Alderson place at the Rivers edge." He noted that the brine was three times better than that at Scioto Salt Works in Ohio.[25]

Financial embarrassment prevented the Ruffners from rapidly expanding their salt manufacturing capacity. By the summer of 1808 they had sixty-four evaporation kettles in operation under temporary housing. Initially, two hundred gallons of brine from the shallow well were required to obtain one bushel of salt. The Ruffners manufactured twenty-five to thirty bushels of salt daily, which they sold at two dollars per fifty-pound weighed bushel. A young lawyer of Alexandria, Virginia, estimated the expense of making one bushel at one shilling and sixpence. Noting the manufacturer's need for capital, he thought that salt could be purchased for one dollar per bushel cash money if the buyer agreed to resell at two dollars.[26]

Over a year passed after the Ruffner discovery before a drilling boom and widespread furnace construction occurred on the Kanawha. No one knew if saltwater could be obtained in other locations, and most people lacked the mechanical inventiveness necessary to undertake explorations. The year 1809 witnessed other successful exploratory efforts,

continued experimentation and refinement of drilling tools and procedures, and the arousal of national interest. By the end of the year six
successful brine wells and four manufacturing furnaces existed. On
New Year's Day, 1810, Henry Ruffner reported: "I expect you have heard
of the great success of the people in Kanawha in obtaining Salt Water."
Without mentioning members of his family, he wrote that he believed
that "A. Donnally, C. Brown, S. Reynolds, S. Shrewsbury, Cle Jarred,
and R. Lewis" had capitalized on the new growth. Four furnaces owned
by Colonel Robert Johnson, Charles Brown, Daniel and Joseph Ruffner,
and Andrew Donnally were operating. Donnally, he tersely noted, "obtained water at the Old Lick which is considerably better than any of
the rest."[27]

The year 1809 saw several refinements in drilling techniques and the
attraction of inventive men in the quest for possible wealth to the bud-
ding industry. In drilling an additional well, Tobias, the ingenious me-
chanic of the Ruffner family, devised an effective method of excluding
fresh water from well holes. As a blacksmith, he supplied drilling bits
and other tools to individuals who were boring exploratory wells. Robert Johnson, father of a future vice president, migrated from a Kentucky
saltworks and leased a well from David and Joseph Ruffner. He brought
experience gained in another brine field and an auger with screw joints
and poles, with which he deepened the original well. By the end of 1809
Johnson was manufacturing salt.[28]

William Whitteker, a native of Princeton, Massachusetts, possessed
a mechanical ability that was very much in demand by Kanawha River
landowners who desired to explore their potentially valuable property.
Whitteker, who had been a farmer, carpenter, and sailor, moved inland
to become a fur trader in Canada, Detroit, Chillicothe, and Kentucky in
the early 1800s before he settled in 1806 in the Kanawha Valley.[29] In the
year after the Ruffner furnace began production, Whitteker exchanged
his inventive ability and energies with two landowners, who conveyed
to him control over wells and furnaces that resulted from his successful experiments.

Immediately upon the Ruffner success, Charles Brown, who owned
land on the south side of the river opposite the Alderson tract, per-
suaded Whitteker to bore for saltwater on his property. Whitteker, with
characteristic enthusiasm, concluded that "if the water was got by boring in the Rock it was likely to be on both sides of the River." In June
1809 Whitteker struck saltwater at fifty-seven feet, and by the first of
September a new fifty-kettle furnace manufactured fifty to sixty bushels
of salt per twenty-four-hour period on the Brown farm. In two legal
agreements, one signed before exploration and the other afterward,
Whitteker gained complete possession of the factory and premises for a

ten-year term in exchange for assumption of all exploratory and manufacturing expenses and a monthly delivery of two hundred bushels of
salt to Brown after January 1810.[30] In September 1809 Isaac Noyes, a
New Yorker who had been a successful fur trader, secured William
Whitteker and his brother, Levi, to search for brine on his river property. After drilling a successful well, the parties jointly erected a sixty-
kettle furnace, shared expenses, and split profits for a ten-year term. The
Whittekers drilled one dry hole to a depth of 150 feet and then a producing one. The furnace began production in 1810.[31] Whitteker, capitalizing upon his technical abilities, obtained potentially favorable business
opportunities and factory ownership without owning any real estate.

In 1810 the embryonic Kanawha salt industry achieved a remarkable
expansion. In the period from January to August, seven furnaces began
production. From August to December, five more became operational,
bringing the total number of manufacturing facilities to sixteen by the
end of the year. In 1810 each furnace had a productive capacity of 35 to
50 bushels daily or a total annual production between 204,400 and
292,000 bushels.[32]

Before the development of the Kanawha Salines, only two great
sources of salt existed in the interior United States: the Wabash Salines
and salines in Onondaga, New York. Although numerous small licks in
the West produced limited quantities of salt for local use from weak
brines, the expense of evaporation and the difficulties of transportation
inhibited distribution. After deeper drilling, between 90 and 130 gallons
of Kanawha brine yielded one bushel of salt. The closest competitor in
brine strength was the United States Saline in Illinois, where one bushel
of salt required the evaporation of 180 gallons. The Scioto Salt Works
required 500 gallons, and the various Kentucky saltworks extracted one
bushel from each 1,000 gallons of brine.[33] It was difficult to carry sufficient quantities long distances against the current of western rivers or
overland from New York State by packhorses, which could each bear a
maximum of two hundred pounds.[34]

Salt was thus a very expensive necessity—when it could be obtained—because of scarcity and transit costs. In the last decade of the
eighteenth century, salt prices ranged between six and sixteen dollars
per bushel in central Ohio. The price fluctuated between three and a
half and five dollars in the early 1800s. Kanawha output had the immediate effect of lowering western salt prices, a trend that persisted
throughout the antebellum period. The Ruffners initially sold their salt
at two dollars per bushel, but the expanding production at other furnaces reduced the current price in 1810 to approximately one dollar.[35]
A contemporary Pittsburgh chronicler suggested that large quantities
could be obtained at the works for seventy cents.[36]

Using Pittsburgh, 283 miles up the Ohio from the Kanawha, as an example, the effect of the Ruffner discovery on inland markets can be well illustrated. Before 1810 Onondaga salt was transported overland to Lake Erie, then overland and by the tributaries of the Allegheny River to Pittsburgh. Each year four to five thousand barrels of New York salt worth nine dollars per barrel reached the Pittsburgh market. In 1809–10 twelve to fourteen thousand barrels selling at eight dollars per barrel passed to this outlet. Kanawha manufacturers estimated that they could ship and retail their product in the same market for five or six dollars per barrel.[37]

In 1810 the salt factories on the Great Kanawha River constituted the nation's largest salt production area. Lewis Summers, who explored the area before moving from Alexandria, Virginia, prophetically recorded: "Their works being immediately on the margin of so nobile a river, the water so strong, and the extent to which salt may be made so great, that it must enhance the value of the whole country of the Kanawha and the adjoining rivers."[38] Manufacturing a scarce necessity in the Ohio River basin, the Kanawha County industry seemed assured of great growth and prosperity because of almost unlimited demand for its product.

3

Growth, Chaos, and Combination, 1811–1824

The War of 1812 and its effects provided the major impetus for the rapid overdevelopment of the Kanawha salt industry. Since large amounts of Onondaga salt could not be safely transported overland, the American West became totally dependent upon the Kanawha product and the few local sources for the necessity. American armies operating in the Northwest against the Indians and British obtained salt for their provisions from Kanawha furnaces. Kanawha producers never allowed congressional investigators or anyone else to forget about their role in the "second struggle for independence." During the war, imported salt from Liverpool was unavailable, and the British navy drove ships from the sea that might have carried salt from other foreign sources. The Atlantic seaboard and Gulf Coast lacked a sufficient salt supply throughout the conflict. Although high prices for scarce salt did stimulate the erection of seashore factories, in November 1814 the commodity sold for five to six dollars per bushel in many eastern cities. In the interior, the Kanawha manufacturers raised their weekly output to twelve thousand bushels to fulfill western demands. Prices ranged between sixty-two and a half cents and one dollar per bushel. In 1814 the Virginia industry produced approximately 640,000 bushels annually, double the output from any other state.[1]

The years from 1810 to 1815 were the boom era of the Kanawha salt industry. The number of furnaces grew from sixteen to fifty-two, and production capability roughly quadrupled to approximately one million bushels annually. According to David Ruffner, more furnaces were under construction. The existing fifty-two furnaces had forty to sixty thirty-six-gallon kettles capable of a daily output of 2,500 to 3,000 bushels of salt.[2] This period of rapid expansion delineated the Great Kanawha saline production field. The search for brine led to the drilling of wells outside the usual territory. In 1810 speculators drilled a brine well on Elk River. After the erection of a furnace in 1811, the high salt prices occasioned by the War of 1812 enabled the operation to profit even with its very weak brine. Within two years, to the relief of established producers, the more efficient Kanawha River wells forced the closing of this furnace, foreclosing the possibility of the expansion of the production area.[3]

The Kanawha salt industry would have expanded tremendously even if the war had never occurred, because of the almost insatiable western market. The army in the Northwest did create a temporary demand for salt, but the later emphasis on the importance of the role of the Kanawha manufacturers in the War of 1812 was intended mainly for national and congressional consumption. Before the Panic of 1819, the Kanawha salt economy was somewhat removed from international and national conditions and depended upon internal regional development in the Ohio River basin. British Liverpool salt, which flooded American shores after the Treaty of Ghent, did not intrude into the market area of the Kanawha product: the current of western rivers protected the inland salt market from competitive importations until the advent of the steamboat.[4]

Depression struck the Kanawha salt industry before the end of the War of 1812. Sometime in 1814, the collective productive capabilities of Kanawha furnaces extended to the optimum point to meet current demand. The producers informed the Virginia General Assembly that their salt output "was fully adequate to, and rather exceeding the quantity demanded for the supply of the tract of Country, then drawing its supplies from that source."[5] The rapid expansion of the industry simply enabled Kanawha salt makers to saturate the market that could be reached via the deficient, unimproved river distribution system.

By 1815 the Kanawha salt industry, decentralized in ownership, manufacturing capability, and the distribution and marketing of its product, was ill prepared to organize producers to attain a measure of control over production quantities, distribution, and marketing. Many salt makers knew they had to conclude arrangements among themselves to ensure their future prosperity. Widespread ownership and possession by lease practically foreclosed any possibility of combination. Of the approximately fifty-five furnaces in existence in 1815, nine individuals, partners, or firms possessed thirty-three. Only one firm controlled as many as four furnaces. Three different organizations operated three furnaces, while ten entities ran two furnaces. The remaining facilities consisted of single-furnace establishments.[6] Any analysis of ownership in determining total control of production quantities can be somewhat deceptive, because the manufacturing capacity of individual furnaces varied greatly.

After 1814 rumors of capitalists and speculators who might attempt to control the industry through purchase or lease of depressed salt properties abounded on the Kanawha Salines. One story had the partnership from Richmond of Samuel G. Adams, Harry Heth, and Beverley Randolph, after its purchase of three furnaces, buying twenty. Joel Shrewsbury thought "the day not far distant when the furnaces will be held by men of property and carracter."[7] The Steele brothers of Kentucky and Andrew Donnally, Jr., who operated as Donnally and Steele and Company, were the centralizing forces in the combination of the industry. Donnally, along with the Ruffners, was one of the industry's founders and one of the largest proprietors. Having been in the business from the beginning and during the boom, his extensive tracts of land inherited from his father, who had migrated from Greenbrier County, Virginia, had appreciated greatly and had produced wealth. The Steeles, arriving in 1812 in the Salines with extensive mercantile connections in the West, allied themselves with the resource-rich Donnally in speculative ventures.[8]

The Steele brothers—William, Richard, and Robert Makemie of Maysville and Louisville and Adam of Shelbyville—were four of six sons and five daughters born to pioneer Scotch-Irish Kentuckians Richard Steele and Martha Breckinridge Makemie, who migrated from Mercersburg, Pennsylvania. Adam was born first, in 1770; Richard, second, in 1775; William, eighth, in 1788; and Robert Makemie, ninth, in 1790. William primarily directed the Kanawha business and also represented John Steele of Mississippi Territory, probably a distant kinsman, eventually becoming his attorney in fact on the Kanawha. John Steele, a wounded veteran of the battle of Point Pleasant, was a colonel from Virginia in the Revolution and served on the Governor's Council before moving to Mississippi in 1798. He was secretary and acting governor of Mississippi Territory and served in other capacities before dying in 1817. His extensive landed interest on the Great Kanawha dated from the 1700s. Upon his death, the Steele brothers would acquire most of his salt estate. No record of an agreement between the Steeles and Andrew Donnally exists, but certainly the prominent Steele family's mercantile connections throughout the Ohio River basin and the established wealth of Donnally enhanced the combine's possibilities of obtaining adequate funds and markets to engage profitably in the salt trade.[9]

Donnally and Steele and Company was created in December 1812 and January 1813. Andrew Donnally had held valuable property for salt production since the Ruffner discovery. William Steele began acquiring interests in the industry in October 1812, with the acquisition of the salt interest of Robert Hening, who held a partnership in a salt factory with Charles Venable. Steele paid six thousand dollars, due in eighteen months, for Hening's undivided half interest. The purchase price included a new untested well, but if the brine was insufficient to supply a single furnace, Steele was to be allowed a thousand-dollar deduction from the total price.[10] In the same month, Charles Brown sold William Steele his contract with William Whitteker that called for the delivery by Whitteker of two hundred bushels of salt per month for seven years from February 22, 1811. In addition, Steele received the right to remove all specified timber from a certain tract of land. Steele assumed all of Brown's responsibilities and obligations to Whitteker and promised to return the property to Brown at the end of the seven-year term. For these privileges, Steele paid $6,250: $450 in hand, $1,050 before December 1, 1812, $1,500 in six months, and the remaining $3,250 in three equal installments.[11]

Donnally and Steele and Company immediately expanded by leasing other furnaces. In January 1813 the firm rented two furnaces for a one-year term from John, Samuel, and John D. Shrewsbury for a yearly rate of $2,000 per furnace. In June it leased a single furnace on the Leonard Morris plantation until November 16, 1816, at the same rate. In November the partnership obtained control of three furnaces owned by David Ruffner for four years for $3,500 per year and secured a factory owned by Leonard Morris and Sons for a four-year period for a total of $8,000. By the end of one year, Donnally and Steele and Company controlled by lease, in addition to the interests of Andrew Donnally and John and William Steele, two furnaces for one year, one for three years, and four for four years. In the same period, the partnership secured additional brine supplies and fuel sources. It paid $1,250 for a one-year lease of one-half of the water from a well that John Reynolds held with Silas Reynolds and acquired on a long-term basis extensive acres of woodland for a dependable and adequate supply of cord wood.[12]

In succeeding years the Steeles considerably extended their holdings in Kanawha River properties. In November 1814 William Steele, in partnership with Reuben Slaughter, acquired undeveloped land that adjoined the Burning Spring tract, owned by the Washington and Lewis families, from Joseph Fletcher of Gallia County, Ohio. In the next month John Steele obtained a brine well and three acres of adjoining land by trading part of a tract of woodland to John Warth.[13]

In 1815 John Steele employed his extensive forest lands to secure more salt. In January he conferred upon William Steele a power of attorney, authorizing Steele to transact all business and to dispose of land in Kentucky, Ohio, and Virginia. The attorney in fact allowed John, Samuel, and John D. Shrewsbury to remove wood for fueling their salt furnaces from Steele land on Simony and Witcher's creeks in return for 1,200 bushels of good salt on a yearly basis for each furnace that was fired. The Shrewsburys had to deliver the salt quarterly, and short-term use could be satisfied proportionally. In addition, Adam, Richard,

Robert M., and William Steele purchased three tracts of land for seventeen thousand dollars from Madelain Françoise Charlotte and John Peter Roman Bureau of Gallipolis, Ohio. One tract of 17 acres, 32 poles, contained several furnaces and outbuildings and was located across the Kanawha River from the Burning Spring tract; another consisted of 2,500 acres on Davis Creek; and the third contained 303 acres on Rush Creek.[14]

In 1816 John Steele acquired the three salt furnaces of David and Tobias Ruffner on a 19-acre section of the old George Alderson survey on George's Creek and a one-half interest in another part of the original Alderson survey. In exchange, Steele surrendered 1,500 acres of undeveloped property on Campbell's Creek to the Ruffner brothers.[15] In the same year John Steele conveyed to William Steele a one-third interest in several tracts of his Kanawha County property. William obtained his part in three tracts of 27,000 acres, 19,000 acres, and 63,500 acres. He also received a third of the Three Furnace property obtained from the Ruffners, a share of the John Warth furnace property on Burning Spring Creek, and the appropriate interest in John Steele's various salt agreements with Eli Jarret, John Reynolds, John Morris, James E. Harris, and John, Samuel, and John D. Shrewsbury.[16]

The specific operations of the Donnally and Steele partnership cannot be determined from the extant records, but there is no doubt that it was the largest single manufacturing concern on the Kanawha. Between 1813 and 1816 Donnally and Steele and Company probably controlled from 15 to 25 percent of total salt production with its delivery agreements, leases, and the output of partners' properties. The actual percentage of output control varied from a low in 1814 to the height of the company's domination in 1816. Not only did the partnership exercise control over the largest portion of production, but it also owned undeveloped properties with future productive capability that could limit the entry of new proprietors and that could be exploited for more production if needed. Along with these furnaces went control of brine wells and wood supplies.[17]

Although total dominance of the industry was impossible, advantages did accrue to the Donnally and Steele partnership. Because of its large productive capacity, it could manage sales in markets where salt supplies were usually inadequate. Merchants had to cooperate in order to secure reliable stocks for their customers. Donnally and Steele, for instance, dictated pricing policy for one Ohio mercantile firm. Woodbridge and Pierce, commission merchants of Zanesville, sold Donnally and Steele salt for a 5 percent commission. In November 1813 the salt company instructed Woodbridge and Pierce to sell its consigned salt in Zanesville for $2.50 per fifty pounds.[18]

Donnally and Steele and Company's possession of almost unlimited production facilities secured a commercial position with which most individuals, proprietorships, and partnerships in single- or double-furnace operations could not compete. The economies of scale permitted more efficient use of transportation and marketing systems in distant towns. Salt production in a multifurnace operation made possible the effective maintenance of facilities: a single furnace had to cease production completely for repairs. In addition, the approbation of Andrew Donnally and the Steele brothers would be necessary before the implementation of any future schemes for reviving the prosperity of the Kanawha salt industry.

Kanawha salt manufacturers did not formulate plans for combination suddenly and without precedent, as previous chroniclers indicate, but developed their legal forms gradually, as mercantile and legal talent merged in the Salines. Forged by contemporary economic conditions, the individual legal and pecuniary situation of salt makers and their empirical business experience governed the evolution of antebellum legal forms. Most accounts, particularly state and local, of the collective attempts of Kanawha salt producers to control production and sales assert that a trust, the first in the United States, was framed in November 1817 to achieve these ends.[19] Historically, the copartnership of November 1817, called the Kanawha Salt Company, had extensive legal and economic precedent, which present-mindedness has marred in an attempt to attribute the formation of the business trust to a group of entrepreneurs who had merely created an antecedent legal form. The firm of Steele, Donnally and Steeles, for which no written articles of copartnership exist, effectively operated during 1817 and preceded the Kanawha Salt Company. It guaranteed a set purchase price to manufacturers and operated as an exclusive sales agency to manage all vending of Kanawha salt.[20] The Kanawha Salt Company, when it did operate, functioned as a copartnership that manufactured on its own, controlled production of members, and acted as a central sales agency. Organized as an output pool, by strict legal definition it was not a trust. The first trust proposal for Kanawha manufacturers arose in 1829 and was never adopted; the idea, however, preceded the famous Standard Oil Trust by a half century.[21] National historians of combination and monopoly have done little better than local chroniclers. Traditional authorities usually date pools from the Civil War. They often cite the efforts of the cordage pool in 1860, the Michigan Salt Association in 1868, the first anthracite coal combination in 1871, and activities of Gilded Age railroads.[22] The Kanawha salt industry of western Virginia furnishes a much earlier example of advanced legal combination and suggests to legal and economic historians that post–Civil War monopolists had antebellum legal and business antecedents.

The continuation of overproduction and the resultant unprofitable and damaging competition forced many independent Kanawha salt manufacturers to consider centralization of all their production and marketing functions in order to achieve order and prosperity. Notwithstanding common problems shared with small proprietors, the dominant Steele and Donnally interests could not entertain any notion of surrendering any portion of their production for common goals until certain leases began expiring in 1816 and 1817. Many of these leases were formulated with rental payments based on projected productive capabilities of individual furnaces. The copartners, unwilling to risk the chance of financial loss in a violation of legal contracts, could not reduce production in the absence of any concrete plan or arrangement for increasing profit margins on sales of reduced quantities of salt.

As early as the winter of 1814–15 the Steeles and Andrew Donnally had the idea of purchasing all Kanawha River saltworks. One of the Steele brothers approached Harry Heth, a partner in Beverley Randolph and Company, proposing that Heth's firm join him and Donnally to control all manufacturers. Steele and Donnally projected that a total of two hundred to three hundred thousand dollars was needed to control the entire production field, but only one hundred thousand would be required immediately. The remainder could be discharged from cash-flow profits, as the total investment might be cleared within one year. The Steeles and Donnally impressed Heth as men of character, industry, and enterprise, but his unfamiliarity with the business caused him to decline participation. Steele approached other proprietors to determine possibilities. Continuing depressed economic conditions caused serious discussion of plans to revive the prosperity of the Kanawha enterprise to surface in 1816. Henry Ruffner reported that the salt makers were "loud and melancholy" and saw the folly of increasing production to compensate for shrinking profits. They talked of entering arrangements to stop half of their furnaces.[23]

In January 1817 the firm of Steele, Donnally and Steeles succeeded Donnally and Steele and Company. This new organization consisted of the joint and separate salt properties of William, Adam, Richard, and Robert M. Steele and Andrew Donnally. The combination included the partnership of William Steele and Company, in which William Steele held a one-third interest, Robert M. Steele, one-third, and Richard and Adam Steele, one-third jointly. Steele, Donnally and Steeles was controlled in the following proportions: Andrew Donnally controlled one-third of the whole, and the Steele family, two-thirds of the whole, with William Steele allotted one-third part of two-thirds, or two-ninths, Robert M. Steele, two-ninths, and Richard and Adam Steele, two-ninths jointly.[24]

In the late winter and spring of 1817 Steele, Donnally and Steeles became the sole purchaser and marketer of the approximately five hundred thousand bushels of salt produced by Kanawha furnaces until January 1818. William Steele and Company issued purchase notes, and Andrew Donnally personally secured the bonds. The firm paid seventy-five cents for each bushel delivered in barrels monthly between the first and sixth day at the river and one dollar and twelve and a half cents per bushel delivered at Cincinnati or Louisville. Payment was one-third cash on delivery, a 90-day note for one-third, and a 180-day note for the balance. No limitations existed on the amount a producer could deliver.

Steele, Donnally and Steeles, by centralizing the sale function, could dictate prices of the commodity in western towns by regulating supply. Also the contract guaranteed a measure of profit to manufacturers. Average production costs were sixty-two and a half cents per bushel, but the margin was so low that renters of furnaces could not survive. Because of payment in actual money and notes, credit to new-comers and renters was not available. The attraction for the firm was the high profit margin on its own substantial output rather than the slight profit made on its purchases from others. The defect for Steele, Donnally and Steeles was its inability to regulate production quantities. Salt output was very elastic, and with guaranteed prices, manufacturers had incentive to maximize deliveries. It is impossible to determine the profitability of the firm for 1817, but a profit resulted, especially from its own output. By raising sale prices and profit, it undoubtedly increased the capitalization of the Kanawha enterprise. Its short-term success demonstrated the potential for cooperation and aroused ideas for future legal arrangements in the Salines.[25]

The primary legal adviser to the firm of Steele, Donnally and Steeles and to all early combinations was Joseph Lovell, a young English nobleman who had migrated in 1815 to the Kanawha Valley from Richmond. He had come to Virginia at age five and had studied law in Richmond. He and his stepfather, James Bream, had a close business and family relationship. Upon his arrival in the Salines, Lovell immediately became active in local affairs as coroner, lawyer, and militiaman. By marriage in 1818 he established family connections with the Steeles. He and Robert Makemie Steele married sisters, grandnieces of President George Washington, from Mason County, Virginia. Lovell married Betty Washington, and Steele married Ellen Joel. Both were daughters of Howell Lewis, son of Colonel Fielding Lewis and Betty Washington.[26]

Lovell believed that the profit from any combination "might and ought to be concentrated in the hands of the manufacturers" and that "the same amount of profit might be made at less expence of capital by reducing the quantity manufactured and increasing the price."[27] Moreover, he proposed

as far as practicable to consolidate the works and reduce the quantity manufactured to 300,000 Bushels per annum which may be vended at 125 or 150 cents per bushel at the works, which would leave to the manufacturers a profit of $225,000 or $300,000 per annum which at 6 per cent would give the property a value of from 5 to 6 millions, if it is enquired why the reducing of the quantity would enable us to increase the price the answer is plain, we can vend 300,000 bushels without competition, when the quantity exceeds this we must go into the markets of other works, who could in their own marketts under sell us, but we have marketts without competitors, and there the monopoly will enable us to demand our own prices.[28]

Lovell, not solely interested in the legal welfare of his clients, reported the negotiations to his wealthy stepfather, James Bream. Bream, a former London merchant, had migrated in 1798 to Richmond, where he engaged in the mercantile business. Allured by the reports of his stepson, he moved to the Kanawha Valley, where he made extensive investments in real estate and salt factories.[29] Lovell forwarded a detailed plan whereby his stepfather might prudently speculate on the success of his legal advice to the salt manufacturers. He proposed that Bream purchase five specified salt properties for seventy-nine thousand dollars, with an advance payment of thirty thousand and deferred payments over three years from the proceeds of the property. After payment of an additional three thousand dollars from him and other partners in the association to silence the smaller concerns, Bream would possess one-fifth or one-sixth of the salt factories, worth, in Lovell's opinion, a million dollars. He added:

I am next to show you how the property is to be paid for. You would probably be limited to run five or six furnaces say 5 to 7 months of the year and manufacture each 10,000 bushels would be fifty thousand which if sold at one dollar would give a profit of $25,000 per annum and pay for the works, but you may rely on sales at $1.25 giving a much larger proffit, attached to the works I propose you should purchase you could have near 800 acres of cleared bottom land worth at least $5.00 per acre per annum is $4,000 the estimate low this land with out the works is nearly worth the price which they might now be had, and determined me in the choice I have made for you; View this speculation in every shape and you will approve it, first you cannot lose but may gain; beyond the probable annual income by the arrangement, the property is increased fourfold the day the purchases are completed, and here again, I must warn you the most profound silence on the subject is necessary.[30]

Following the legal counsel of Joseph Lovell and the dictation of economic necessity, most salt producers, including Steele, Donnally and Steeles, favored a new plan of combination whereby production could be reduced and profits increased. Steele, Donnally and Steeles was financially strained to purchase and vend all Kanawha salt produced in 1817 and was unwilling to assume full risk for Kanawha salt makers. Producers would have to share in the risks as well as in the potential profits. As early as October 1817 the larger firms had concluded that they would attempt to purchase the smaller furnaces and continue to raise prices. Some consolidation through purchase did occur, but the prospect of higher prices through centralization gave incentive to those who were not financially desperate to refuse to sell or to hold out for an inflated price or high production quotas. Joel Shrewsbury, of the vibrant firm of Dickinson & Shrewsbury, informed his partner: "I encourage them all I can tho not to join them, & inform them your & my articles of co-partnership prevents my becoming one of the contracting parties." Shrewsbury observed that one manufacturer whose property was worth ten thousand dollars refused to join and desired to sell his furnace for double its worth. The manufacturers had easily agreed on the total production quantity of four hundred thousand bushels and the selling price of at least a dollar per bushel. Steele, Donnally and Steeles had "bought out several small establishments under strong faith there would be a company and the purchases so made to belong to the company." Shrewsbury specified fifteen furnaces purchased from eight entities. While remaining independent and accepting a high production quota of thirty thousand bushels, Shrewsbury urged others "to get the people to come into arrangements believing it would be much to our Interest."[31]

On November 10, 1817, Daniel Ruffner, Tobias Ruffner, David Ruffner, Stephen Radcliff, Aaron Stockton, John Reynolds, John Shrewsbury, Samuel Shrewsbury, John D. Shrewsbury, Joel Shrewsbury, Leonard Morris, Charles Morris, Charles Brown, Isaac Noyes, Bradford Noyes, and John J. Cabell with William Steele, William Steele and Company, Joseph Lovell, and Andrew Donnally formed the Kanawha Salt Company "for the purpose of manufacturing and disposing of salt on a general and uniform plan and method." For the faithful performance of the covenants, the twenty individuals and firms each bound themselves for the penal sum of fifty thousand dollars. The company was to begin operation on January 1, 1818, and expire on December 31, 1822. The subscribers to the agreement promised to take "all legal and proper means" to reduce the quantity of salt manufactured at their own and other furnaces for the remainder of 1817, as "it is suggested that there is too great of quantity of salt manufactured for the demand of the present year."[32] The individual members of Steele, Donnally and Steeles pledged to sell their remaining salt at the end of the year in accordance with the price set by the president and directors of the Kanawha Salt Company.

The copartnership agreement specifically limited the amount of salt to be manufactured in 1818 by the signatory parties to a maximum of 450,000 bushels. The initial allotments reflect the size of individual manufacturing operations and their relative economic strength in the industry: William Steele and Company was allotted 53,000 bushels; Andrew Donnally and David Ruffner, each 40,000; Leonard and Charles Morris, 33,000; John, Samuel, and John D. Shrewsbury, 32,000; Isaac and Bradford Noyes, 30,000; Joel Shrewsbury, 30,000; Joseph Lovell, 25,000; John J. Cabell, Tobias Ruffner, William Steele, and Aaron Stockton, each 20,000; Charles Brown, 16,000; John Reynolds, 12,000; Stephen Radcliff, 10,000; and Daniel Ruffner, 9,000, for a total of 410,000 bushels. If a manufacturer believed that the quantity assigned to be produced was too small, he could appeal to his fellow subscribers who were disinterested in the involved property for a decision by majority vote. If a majority of copartners believed that the quantity prescribed to an individual was excessive, they could readjust and fix the amount to be manufactured. The decision of the subscribers was always binding.

The company purchased the property and salt interests of seven individuals and partnerships. The acquired interests were to be the joint property of all the copartners, held in the same proportions as the manufacturing allotments. The president and directors could lease the property at a fair and reasonable price if it was in the best interests of the association. The agreement provided for the company to lease or purchase five enumerated properties and all other salt properties that were not included in the copartnership.

The existence of long-term leases and other legal arrangements prevented the company from fully controlling the Kanawha industry. Subscribers were not responsible for the delivery of more salt than that which actually belonged to them or came into their possession as a result of a legal obligation. If the lease of a property owned by a subscriber expired, it reverted to his control and became subject to the production allotment of the copartnership. No signatory could transfer, lease, or sell any furnace while the company existed without posting a sufficient guarantee with the president and directors that all salt manufactured on the leased premises would be delivered to the Kanawha Salt Company.

Every six months the subscribers or a majority of them elected by ballot five directors out of their own number. The directors in turn had to select a president of the company from among themselves. The president and directors managed the affairs of the company for the following six months or until a new election. The directors could call a general meeting of the copartners whenever the interest of the company required one. At any time, two-thirds of the subscribers could meet and choose new directors, if two-thirds of the copartners agreed, and the new appointees could hold office until the regular election.

The agreement empowered the president and directors to receive all salt manufactured by the subscribers, to regulate and fix prices, to set the sale terms, to sell the salt, to arrange its transportation, to negotiate contracts, and to receive all payments. Management could employ clerks and agents, and it could compose all business correspondence. It could also borrow money from banks or individuals as necessary. After the deduction of expenses and losses, the president and directors had to declare monthly dividends on any selected day. The dividend payment was based on the apportioned salt interest of each copartner, but no one could receive a dividend proportionally larger than the quantity of salt actually delivered to the company. Dividend payments could be detained or suspended in order to meet financial obligations of the company. The copartners, by majority vote at any time, fixed the salaries and rate of compensation of the president and directors. The president and directors set the wages of the clerks, agents, and other employees, who were paid out of the company treasury.

The association established certain regulations for manufacturing and delivering salt. Each manufacturer had to deliver all salt on hand, packed in barrels, at least once a month under a shelter on the bank of the Great Kanawha River. The company's authorized agent had to weigh each barrel and mark on it the gross weight and the name of the manufacturer. The producer received a receipt from the agent for the salt delivered. The receipt was returned to the clerk of the company, who credited the amount on the books.

The agreement gave the management sufficient discretionary power to ensure the manufacture of a quality product. The president and directors could make appropriate deductions for poor-quality salt and weak barrels. They could penalize producers who used tallow to speed crystallization, to increase the salt's weight, and to enhance its appearance. (Tallow coagulated the salt and ruined its preservative qualities.)

The short-lived Kanawha Salt Company never incorporated all independent salt producers under its restrictive wings. At least five firms remained outside the arrangement. Small producers could flourish as a result of the production restrictions of the larger association, while not being subject to centralized control and limited output. They could enjoy the economic cake without making any sacrifice.

The attitudes of the members of the association and the independents created a strained situation on the Kanawha. The politically and economically powerful copartners began exerting various pressures on the independents to cooperate with the company and its policies. Andrew Donnally apparently accused one independent of theft, and Donnally's henchman Macker Cheek instituted a suit in the Circuit Superior Court for recovery of the value of the goods alleged to have been stolen.[33] John B. Jenatte, the independent, in turn sued Andrew Donnally for slander. Jenatte claimed that Donnally "wickedly and maliciously" intended to injure his "good name fame and credit" and "bring him into public scandel infamy and disgrace" among his neighbors and fellow citizens by accusing him of being a thief. Donnally allegedly threatened, "You took our salt and I can prove it by Macker Cheek, he will swear to it. I'll have you to the Penitentiary else it will cost you a dam'd sight of money." Jenatte, in consideration of the "great personal influence" of his antagonist, petitioned the Circuit Superior Court for a change of venue for the two pending cases. Extenuating circumstances arising from Donnally's attempt to monopolize the Kanawha salt trade prevented the possibility of a fair trial. Jenatte remained an independent producer, and he had heard others state that "he ought to be crushed as an enemy" and that the present suit was the means to do so. The Court, agreeing with Jenatte's contentions, moved the cases to Mason County.[34]

Both the copartners and the independents could employ coercion and sabotage to achieve their objective. Independent producers and a few association members petitioned the Virginia General Assembly for a statute making plugging a well a felony. A person could easily fill the small well hole to stop production of brine. "It has happened in the County of Kanawha that in secret and under the cover of the night wrongs of this sort have been committed." The injured party would have to sue for redress and damages, and then the offense could be punished only as a trespass. The petitioners desired a statute like the one in the Commonwealth of Kentucky, where such an offense was a felony and punishable by confinement.[35]

The first attempt by the majority of salt makers to combine for common ends lasted one year. Although the initiation of the Kanawha Salt Company temporarily inflated the value of salt properties, the effect was short-lived. Whether Kanawha salt makers could agree to act in their mutual interest for the full term of the company became a moot point when the national financial contraction began in 1818. As late as the spring of 1819 Joel Shrewsbury still hoped for an arrangement, but he thought it unlikely because "the great pressure for money & ruined State of the Banks will operate strong against a sale of salt." Steele, Donnally and Steeles offered eighty-five cents per bushel if all salt makers would sell to it, but three saltmakers, wanting ninety cents, absolutely refused. Shrewsbury worried that the price would decline to fifty cents: "If the markets of the West is not supplied cistamatically no Capitalist will vest money in the purchase of salt." He regretted the failure to agree, as "the Salt business will get out of that regular line of Trade it was last year & finally fall in a state of confusion & irregularity again." Salt prices fell rapidly to fifty to seventy-five cents per bushel. Alarmed, the producers met in March 1819 to make a gentleman's agreement to hold the price at one dollar per bushel and to limit production. Each swore upon a Bible. Even though manufacturers tried to maintain prices, cash sales dramatically declined by the summer of 1819. Joel Shrewsbury, noting that some salt had been sold on credit, related that Kanawha operators collectively had not received a thousand dollars in cash during the spring and summer. They could not pay their white laborers or meet other obligations in cash.[36] These depressed conditions effectively suspended the salt trade in 1819. Steele, Donnally and Steeles itself suspended active operations in early 1820.[37]

The Kanawha Salt Company and all proposed combinations were destined to fail because of contemporary financial conditions in the United States and in the West. At a time when the combination needed extensive credit and prompt payments from Cincinnati to raise the capital necessary to begin operations, a national financial contraction was occurring. The association required large amounts of capital initially in order to gain control of the production field and then later to regulate output. After achieving domination, the company had to vend its product in a decentralized market dependent on small merchants and farmers in order to liquidate its debts. To attain success, the producers had to obtain credit and sell their salt for specie or good notes or on very short-term credit. None of these requisite financial conditions existed in the West after 1818.

The financial crisis began in Cincinnati on July 20, 1818, when the local office of discount and deposit of the Second Bank of the United States was instructed by the main office in Philadelphia, headed by William Jones, to collect outstanding balances owed by various Ohio banks at a rate of 20 percent of the total every thirty days. The speculative, inflationary western economic bubble received a mortal deflation. After October 30 no credit was extended to city banks, and the local financial institutions could not redeem their notes because they needed specie or United States bank notes. In 1819 specie could be obtained at a 20-percent premium, and the paper of the four local institutions, the Bank of Cincinnati, Farmers' and Mechanics' Bank, the Miami Exporting Company, and John H. Piatt and Company, was redeemable at 30 to 40 percent below par in United States bank notes. The local land office agent would accept only specie and United States bank notes in payment for public lands. In May 1819 the Cincinnati branch of the Second Bank of the United States had a capitalization of $2,400,000, a sum greater than that of any branch except Boston. On October 1, 1820, the Cincinnati branch closed its doors, with local banks and individuals indebted for $2,289,414, secured mostly by local real estate. The only local currency then available was that of the Miami Exporting Company, which circulated at a 65-70 percent discount.[38]

The stagnant credit situation and depression prevented businesses from raising capital for operation and expansion. For industries primarily dependent on consumer sales, the panic also imposed insurmountable financial barriers to the redemption of debts and legal obligations. Western agriculture, in addition to suffering from deflationary land values and tight money, was readjusting to a smaller export market as a result of the restoration of normal European agricultural production at the end of the Napoleonic Wars. Farmers, merchants, and manufacturers resorted to the barter system in western towns for commercial survival.[39] This deflationary spiral ensured the disruption of the Kanawha salt industry, which had been plagued with economic problems since 1814.

Depressed economic conditions continued to harm the salt makers in the wake of the suspension of business by Steele, Donnally and Steeles. The number of manufacturers between 1817 and 1820 remained fairly stable, at twenty-three individuals and partnerships with an estimated invested capital of $686,500 in factories, excluding land, and an annual manufacturing capacity of about 478,000 bushels.[40] The reduction of the number of salt producers since the War of 1812 might have made agreement among proprietors likely.

Many meetings of salt makers held in the winter and spring of 1820 finally resulted in an ineffective arrangement in April. In initial discussions, most manufacturers favored a continuation of the 1819 gentleman's agreement. When they learned that Steele, Donnally and Steeles had contracted for downriver sales with the expectation that other vendors would adhere to the 1819 agreement, however, dissension resulted. Some wanted the right to ship immediately 20 percent of their annual production at market prices. Andrew Donnally met with the group, showed them the Steele, Donnally and Steeles correspondence and contracts, and offered the documents to them if they formed a combination. In February Joel Shrewsbury proposed that each manufacturer be permitted to ship 10 percent of his annual production for sale at one dollar per bushel, that a committee of four be appointed to review all sales, and that in case of a violation the committee "call a general meeting of the Salt makers, the person to be fairly tried & if found Guilty to be

The Kanawha County Courthouse, 1817–1888. Reflecting the early prosperity of the salt industry, this brick edifice replaced the first log courthouse and was the scene of the salt makers' extensive legal and public
business. This photograph was undoubtedly taken shortly before demo-
lition of the building. Courtesy of the West Virginia Division of Archives
and History.

disgraced." Agreement could not be reached on this proposal because several producers in financial distress sold some salt at fifty cents per bushel. Several manufacturers, to avoid loss, had resolved to make no salt. Finally, the producers agreed to ship one-fifth of their annual production at one dollar per bushel.[41] Because of the financial problems of most manufacturers, the great supply of salt, and the lack of coercion, adherence to production quotas and set prices did not result.

In November 1820 William Steele and Company offered to sell all Kanawha salt during 1821 if all manufacturers agreed to the idea and to production controls. The firm would earn only a reasonable commission on sales, estimated to be twenty to twenty-five thousand dollars, and would return all profits to the manufacturers. Seven producers agreed to the idea, but all others refused. A young merchant, who later became the president of the Charleston branch of the Bank of Virginia, observed that "many [a] jealous person" opposed the agency idea and that three or four salt makers would not agree to become jointly responsible for purchase of all output because they were unwilling to put up or borrow the twenty to thirty thousand dollars necessary to begin. The merchant erroneously predicted that, in the absence of capital, the salt makers would adopt the sales agency plan before 1822.[42]

Facing these circumstances, William and Robert M. Steele attempted in 1822 to obtain control of Kanawha salt production for a one-year period in an effort to recoup their severe financial losses in previous joint and individual ventures. Like the indebted gambler with all his chips on the table, the Steeles staked their future on this one speculation. Perhaps fiscal desperation rather than calculation inspired their bold move. The William and Robert M. Steele speculation became effective on March 1, 1822, and was projected to expire on March 1, 1823. The Steeles concluded purchase and production agreements with as many manufacturers as they could. Their contract with John J. Cabell and Walter Trimble was typical. On March 18, 1822, the Steeles agreed to purchase all the salt that would be manufactured at the furnaces owned by Cabell and Trimble or at furnaces that they would acquire, up to a maximum quantity of twenty thousand bushels, before January 1, 1823. The Steeles covenanted to pay fifty cents per bushel for the salt delivered on the bank of the Kanawha River "in good & sufficient barrels, well packed & nailed, each barrel having not less than ten hoops—the salt of good quality, white & dry, & which shall have lain at least six days after being packed, before being weighed." To prevent the disposal of Cabell and Trimble salt elsewhere and to secure the delivery of the exact quantity specified, the salt price was to be reduced to thirty-three and a third cents per bushel if a lesser quantity was delivered because

Cabell and Trimble had sold some to parties other than the Steeles. Moreover, the reduction penalty did not prohibit the Steeles from seeking legal damages that might be sustained by such a violation of the contract. Cabell and Trimble were not to be subject to any penalties or damages if they failed to deliver twenty thousand bushels, provided that they had delivered the entire quantity of salt manufactured at their furnaces or under their possession or control.[43]

Cabell and Trimble were to begin deliveries of salt on April 17 and to continue deliveries between the fifth and tenth day of each successive month before January 1823. Cabell and Trimble promised to vend salt already under their control on the date of the contract at least twenty miles below the Falls of the Ohio at Louisville. After January 1, 1823, or when the entire amount was manufactured or received, the producers were to cease furnace operations until March 1, 1823. Upon delivery, the Steeles were to pay sixteen cents cash per bushel, to execute a note payable in 120 days at the rate of seventeen cents per bushel, and to give a receipt stating the total quantity delivered. After 240 days, the delivery receipt entitled the bearer to a further sum of seventeen cents per bushel unless Cabell and Trimble had disposed of any salt manufactured at their furnace or in their possession to other parties, in which case the receipt and payment were forfeited. All payments had to be in specie or bank notes of the chartered banks of Virginia or their branches, the bank of Chillicothe, or the Bank of the United States or its branches, provided that the offices were making specie payments.

If any controversy arose over the quality of salt delivered or the condition of the barrels, the parties agreed to submit the dispute to Andrew Donnally, William Brigham, and Isaac Noyes or to any one of them for decision. The written decision of a reduction or penalty in price was to be binding on all parties. Also, Cabell and Trimble agreed not to sell or transfer their saltworks or furnaces during the term of the agreement without giving sufficient security guaranteeing that all covenants would be observed by the purchaser.

Legal obligations of independent salt producers complicated the task of the Steeles in extending their control of output. They obtained a twelve-thousand-bushel portion of the total production of the Stockton and Tompkins partnership from William Tompkins on terms similar to those in the Cabell and Trimble agreement. The only deviations were the elimination of the clause specifying the currency acceptable for payment and the identification of different arbitrators.[44] As a result of the existence of a previous legal obligation of Aaron Stockton, the Steeles had to alter their stipulations in order to gain a measure of control over Stockton's portion of the output. Stockton had contracted to deliver twenty-thousand bushels of salt at the mouth of the Cumberland River in order to discharge a debt to Joel Shrewsbury for previously borrowed salt. Stockton promised that he would not produce more than the twenty thousand bushels at any saltworks that he controlled, directly or indirectly, or in which he had an interest. In case he could not deliver the entire quantity of salt to the mouth of the Cumberland, Stockton agreed to "throw" the remaining portion into the Nashville market "at a price not less than that agreed upon . . . as the standing price for said Market." In return, the Steeles covenanted not to send to the Nashville area "an unusual quantity of salt." They would be "governed in the sale of the salt there by a price or prices, which may be for the mutual benefit of the parties hereto." If any controversy arose, Woods and Seay, commission merchants of Nashville, would decide the question concerning the Tennessee market, and Joel and John Shrewsbury would settle any other differences. All decisions or awards by the appointed judges were binding and conclusive.[45]

William and Robert M. Steele apportioned other market areas to producers. The Steeles had purchased the salt production of John D. Shrewsbury and John B. Crockett's furnace, but then they resold the fifteen thousand bushels to the original manufacturers for sixty cents per bushel and other stipulations. Besides making ten cents per bushel before the salt was produced, the Steeles confined the sales area to Sinking Creek, Kentucky (110 miles below Louisville on the Ohio River), "down as far as the Red banks and up Green River." Shrewsbury and Crockett had to pay the $1,500 to the Steeles in two installments, one-half on January 1, 1823, and the other half on April 1, 1823. The Steeles promised to send no other salt to the defined market area during 1822.[46]

Although it is impossible to determine the extent of the Steele partnership's success in controlling Kanawha salt production, it implemented new business ideas and procedures to ensure the monopolization of production and markets. These innovations would serve as legal precedent for future combination. Since the Steele agreements were based on the manufacturers' experience gained in the active operation of furnaces and marketing and in previous attempts to control production and sales, one can draw certain conclusions about the industry's problems and the preferences of centralizing forces. Contemporaries undoubtedly viewed overproduction as the primary problem confronting the producers. In the Steele agreements, manufacturers who did not deliver the stipulated amounts incurred no penalties. The delivery quota was probably set at an amount that ensured a profit to the producer while limiting collective overcapacity, so that the purchaser could vend smaller quantities more advantageously in starved markets. Sales agencies and purchasers of production must have experienced serious problems with unscrupulous manufacturers who took advantage of the commercial umbrella afforded by the combination and violated contracts to sell their product for more money than they would receive from the agency or purchaser while undercutting the set price in a distant market. Violators of this type ran the risk of the most severe financial penalties. By designating certain markets for producers, the Steeles demonstrated the preference of Kanawha manufacturers for the Ohio River sales area above Louisville, where steamboats did not, at that time, bring cheap, competitive foreign salt. Also, the shorter river haul to Cincinnati, the great emporium, reduced transportation expenses, eliminated some risk of a more distant water carriage, and made for efficiency in marketing. Evidence of an attempt to avoid costly litigation by contracting parties was apparent in the provision for binding resolutions of controversies by referees or arbitrators.

In addition to the harsh economic situation braved by the Steeles, climatic conditions caused great hardships for the industry. On December 1, 1822, a severe flood on the Great Kanawha, a thirty-five-foot rise, damaged the saltworks and surrounded the courthouse in Charleston. It inundated factories and salt supplies, ruined riverside wells, and devastated moored watercraft.[47]

In December 1822 William Steele conceded financial defeat by conveying a deed of trust to secure his many debts. The firms of William Steele and Company and Steele, Donnally and Steeles had not been dissolved. Their accounts were unsettled, so the amount of their indebtedness was undetermined. William Steele assumed that he, individually, was indebted to Steele, Donnally and Steeles and to William Steele and Company. William Steele and Company owed Steele, Donnally and Steeles and Andrew Donnally each an undetermined amount. Andrew Donnally himself provided security for the unknown indebtedness of William Steele.[48]

Wanting to discharge his debts to the several firms and to Andrew Donnally, William Steele conveyed his share of extensive real estate and other interests to the trustees to manage. An undivided third part of 2,379 acres, once owned by William Steele and Company, which bounded the southeast side of the Great Kanawha River, comprised separate tracts of 17 acres, 200 acres, 1,500 acres, 12 acres, and 600 acres, purchased at various times from several individuals. These tracts contained extensive saltworks and a steam mill. Steele held an unenumerated interest in "what is called the dead property at Kanawha by the Manufacturers of Salt." He owned a one-third interest with Adam, Richard, and Robert M. Steele in lot 3 with a brick house in the eighth square on Main Street in Zanesville, Ohio. Also in Zanesville, he held one undivided third part of two third parts of two tracts, one of eight acres bounded by the public barging ground and Marietta Street, and the other, lots 12 and 13 in the fifth square of the town plat. Another two-ninths interest included lots 9, 10, and 11 in the eighth square on Main Street. In the latter two groups of Ohio properties, Andrew Donnally owned a one-third interest, and Richard and Adam Steele held two-ninths. Additional Kanawha County real estate conveyed by William was one-third part of 63,500 acres on the Elk and Pocatalico rivers shared with Adam, Richard, and Robert M. Steele. Finally, he transferred his one-third share of two third parts held and owned by William Steele and Company of the personal and real assets of Steele, Donnally and Steeles.[49]

Extensive provisions about the disposal of William Steele's real estate and interests reveal the extent of his business indebtedness and the procedure and order of payment by which his liquidation was to proceed. The trustees or their survivors or any two of them could sell any portion of the properties or interests conveyed in trust upon any terms or for such sums of money as they might think to be in the best interests of William Steele. The trustees could make conveyances and were empowered to rent any portion of the real estate until it could be sold advantageously. The trust deed specified that William Steele's interest in the various Kanawha salt factories should be "occupied and carried on and worked" until a sale was consummated. The trustees or any two of them were to exercise control, and Andrew Donnally and Robert M. Steele or anyone selected by the trustees was to actively manage the furnaces.[50]

Andrew Donnally further extended his control over the defunct Steele interests in salt properties by purchasing on February 24, 1823, the one-third interest held by Robert M. Steele and his wife, Ellen, for five pounds. (The sum stated in the deed of conveyance does not necessarily indicate all considerations. For instance, Donnally could have released Robert M. Steele from various financial obligations in consideration of the transfer.) Donnally obtained a one-third interest in the 2,379 acres that bounded the southeast side of the Kanawha River. Also, he received a one-third share of the 63,500 acres on the Elk and Pocatalico rivers, originally patented by John Steele. William, Richard, and Adam Steele had shared both these parcels with Robert M. Steele, but William had previously granted his one-third to trustees to discharge his indebtedness. Only Richard and Adam retained a third. Robert M. and Ellen also transferred their interest in the "dead property" and other real estate purchased by the Kanawha Salt Company.[51]

On January 10, 1824, Adam, Richard, Robert M., and William Steele and Andrew Donnally met at Louisville for a final reconciliation and settlement of the accounts of the firm of Steele, Donnally and Steeles. They concluded that the copartnership owed Andrew Donnally $53,353.39.

At the same time, the Steeles agreed that William Steele and Company was obligated to various individuals for approximately $25,000. Of this total, Donnally had loaned $2,000 and had provided security for nearly $5,000.[52]

To satisfy their joint indebtedness to Andrew Donnally and others, Adam and Richard Steele conveyed a deed of trust in some real estate to Levi Welch, Andrew Parks, and Joseph Lovell on January 12, 1829. Adam and Richard held a one-third part of two third parts or two-ninths of the liabilities of Steele, Donnally and Steeles and a third part of the total obligations of William Steele and Company. The two Steeles conveyed their one-third share of the 2,379 acres on the Kanawha River and their share of the "dead property" purchased by the Kanawha Salt Company.

If their interest in the property could not be sold to pay the total amount of the debts of Richard and Adam Steele before January 1, 1829, the trustees were to surrender their share to Andrew Donnally at its valuation or at as much of its assessment as might be necessary to discharge their indebtedness to Donnally for money owed by Steele, Donnally and Steeles and William Steele and Company. Two respectable citizens of Kanawha County were to join the trustees in appraising the trust property. Meanwhile, before the date of the sale or January 1, 1829, the trustees were to appoint Andrew Donnally as agent to manage the one-third portion of the salt factories and steam mill. Donnally agreed to sell the trustees' salt along with his own on a yearly basis and to use the proceeds to satisfy the debts of William Steele and Company. All sums earned in excess of the company's obligations were to accrue to Donnally. Adam and Richard Steele retained the option to redeem their salt interests until January 1, 1829, if they could discharge all their financial liabilities.

Andrew Donnally thus became more dominant in the Kanawha salt industry than he had been previously. He survived the financial depression of 1818 and its aftermath and indeed emerged as the largest possessor of production capability and of strategically located factory sites for future development. Donnally and some others had owned extensive but relatively inexpensive property when the primitive furnaces converted the first discoveries into financial advantage. He and other original landowners benefited greatly from the early prosperity: their salt enjoyed an unlimited demand, and their lands had appreciated rapidly in value. They were able to start with a relatively small investment and accumulate capital.

After the initial discoveries, the purchase of brine-producing land along the Kanawha was the largest single fixed cost for future producers. The Steeles and other latecomers had to raise huge sums of money to purchase well sites, to construct furnaces, and to hire labor, or they had to grant high lease prices in kind or cash to obtain suitable property or salt. The original holders and their heirs had only to drill wells and construct furnaces to begin business. Later, when large amounts of capital were necessary to control production, Donnally was in a position to loan money and to secure potentially valuable real estate as collateral. Although the depression undoubtedly affected the cash assets of Donnally and other original landowners adversely, it also enabled them to extend their real estate holdings, whether voluntarily or not. They required only capital to make their property productive and potentially more valuable.

A source of outside funds to small salt companies for construction, development, and operations was the merchant capitalist or commission merchant. Cincinnati, the center of the wholesale trade, provided mercantile capital for the Great Kanawha Valley. Merchants often advanced cash sums to salt firms in order to guarantee future salt deliveries on promissory notes. Salt company stores often received upon consignment dry goods and other wares. Producers would sign notes promising the delivery of salt on certain terms at particular times and places in exchange for cash advances and merchandise.[53]

Although the independent salt maker could secure a dependable market and capital by exchanging his product with a wholesale merchant, he incurred several disadvantages under favorable economic circumstances. He was obligated to purchase only at the wholesale house concerned even if he did not have a contractual agreement specifying that, because the lack of capital that induced him to enter an initial arrangement with a store would prevent him from seeking and obtaining advantageous terms elsewhere. The merchant would gain the profit on the exchanged salt and on the merchandise. The producer lost the potential profit on delivered salt and conceded flexibility to enter other possible sales arrangements. The existence of previous agreements and obligations with merchants delayed and inhibited plans for reduction of output and control of sales to achieve prosperity within the Kanawha field.

Western steamboat activity and canal construction, which would foster competition, made the future prosperity of the Great Kanawha salt industry very uncertain. General depressed economic conditions did not rapidly change, and internal problems plagued the Kanawha manufacturers. Between 1819 and 1823 salt prices in Cincinnati dropped from $1.50 per bushel to a low of 30 cents. David Ruffner reported to his son in the fall of 1823 that "salt is selling at Market from 42 to 45 cents:

we sold some here at 30 cents and lately a small quantity at 28 cents."[54] Technological innovations in the production process could partially off-set this reduction in prices, but to regain profits and prosperity, the Kanawha manufacturers had to control their decentralized production capabilities and to manage all market sales of their commodity.

4

Kanawha Salt's Use and Its Pre-1850 Markets

Few commodities seem more necessary or more satisfying to human beings than salt. Scientific writers, however, differ greatly in their conclusions about the amount of salt that humans and animals need. The average worldwide consumption per capita is 4.5 kilograms or approximately 10 pounds per year. When authorities estimate culinary human consumption, along with salt usage for such activities as animal feeding, food preservation, and tanning, average per-capita individual consumption is 7.5 kilograms or approximately 16.5 pounds per year. Empirical evidence indicates that the per-capita consumption of salt in the United States may be higher. The increase in population in the Ohio River basin, the new West, clearly offered Kanawha salt producers a growing market after 1810.[1]

The primary single market for Kanawha salt came to be the meat-packing industry, especially pork packing. Although beef preservation was possible, pork became the main object of stock growers' and packers' attention in the West, because hogs were more efficient than cattle in transforming corn into consumable meat, in gaining weight, and in reproduction. Pork was more easily preserved than beef, and as a result, it enjoyed a sizable southern and export market. Chemically, Kanawha salt was perfectly suitable for preservation of pork when used with other salt. Valley salt was a "soft" salt that was extremely soluble because it contained small quantities of the chlorides of calcium and magnesium. With the absence of gypsum as a result of the presence of barium chloride, Kanawha salt penetrated meat very rapidly, a desirable characteristic in a warm climate.[2]

Salt was used in every stage of the process of preserving pork. For best results, packers in the interior mixed the soluble Kanawha product with "hard" salt from New York or coarse imported salt, both of which contained gypsum. English purchasers recommended that the animal carcass be placed in pickle with saltpeter for two days and then packed in barrels with pickle strong enough to float an egg. Kanawha salt was inserted between the layers of meat, with coarse "hard" salt packed on the ends to renew the pickle solution. If the pork was to be shipped in bulk, salt was applied in the ratio of fifty pounds for every two hundred pounds of meat.[3]

Before 1850 the chief avenue for the sale of the agricultural produce of the western states was the interior river system. The salt factories of the Great Kanawha Valley were optimally located to supply the needs of the domestic packing industry. Early pork packing was decentralized, so a central market for Kanawha salt never existed. Although pork packing became centralized somewhat in Cincinnati during the 1830s, individual farmers and interior towns collectively packed great quantities of hogs during the antebellum period. By the mid-1840s 123 listed towns, mostly in the Ohio River tributary system, consumed greater quantities of salt than their populations would suggest.[4]

The antebellum western pork-packing industry focused on Cincinnati. The Queen City emerged as the supreme packing center because of its proximity to the most important western livestock-raising regions and its location on the Ohio River, the main artery of commerce. It had access to plentiful supplies of domestic and foreign salt. The city also enjoyed superior banking facilities and financial connections with the East. Packinghouses operated before 1820, and during the succeeding decade, the number of establishments multiplied. In 1823 Cincinnati packed an estimated forty thousand hogs, and in the early 1830s the number reached one hundred thousand per year. In January 1834 a Cincinnati newspaper claimed that the city was "decidedly the first pork market in the world."[5] Pork packing was the Queen City's leading industry. In the late 1830s and early 1840s, Cincinnati packed around 30 percent of all hogs slaughtered each year in the West. In 1846 the city packed 68 percent of all hogs slaughtered in Ohio.[6]

Outside Cincinnati, the packing centers in Ohio were Chillicothe and Hamilton, but twenty-five other Buckeye towns packed a thousand or more hogs between 1843 and 1846. The Queen City drew considerable numbers of swine from both Indiana and Kentucky, although sizable packing establishments existed in both states. Louisville, the leading packing center in Kentucky in the late 1830s, attracted swine from both the Bluegrass area and southern Indiana. Between 1843 and 1846 Louisville increased its hog pack from 68,000 to 101,000 head. Also located on the Ohio River was Madison, Indiana, a vigorous competitor and the largest packing center in the Hoosier State. Other centers of the pork trade in Indiana were situated along the Wabash River at Lafayette and Terre Haute. Before the rise of Chicago, the Illinois packing centers were in the Ohio and Mississippi network. None of the Illinois centers, however, was as large as Terre Haute or Madison. The leading towns were Alton on the Mississippi and Beardstown on the Illinois. With the settlement of Illinois and Missouri, St. Louis developed as a packing center in the 1840s.[7]

Several variables always present from year to year in the antebellum pork-packing industry complicated any attempt of Kanawha salt manufacturers, individually or collectively, to adjust their production to market demands. Packing was an extremely seasonable enterprise. Dependent upon low temperatures, the packing season was relatively short, usually lasting from the middle of November to February. The Kanawha shipper could not predict the beginning of the packing season, and he could not ship salt during the peak demand period, because the same drop in temperatures froze the rivers. The manufacturer thus had to keep a large inventory in market for an extended time. The vendor of salt could not predict with certainty the numbers of swine that were to be packed in any given season, nor could he determine the location where they would be slaughtered.[8]

Hog growing depended upon the corn crop. Factors affecting the corn available to hogs included general growing conditions, flooding of corn-growing land along rivers, and the supply of old corn. These and other factors could cause feeder pigs to be driven from area to area. The hog pack in Kentucky depended upon the number of swine driven by drovers to the Carolinas. Also, drovers and other sellers had several packing towns from which to choose. Even if quantities were predicted, the heaviness of the hog crop affected the number of barrels packed and, hence, the amount of salt needed.[9]

Competition between Kanawha salt and other salt, foreign and domestic, became more intense as the transportation revolution gained momentum. Before 1820 the Falls of the Ohio at Louisville protected the upriver market of Kanawha salt makers from imported foreign salt such as Liverpool blown and Turk's Island, usually shipped to New Orleans as ballast in the cotton trade. The steamboat's passage around the falls opened the previously restricted market to competition. Salt from western Pennsylvania and Muskingum, Ohio, remained an important competitive element for Kanawha manufacturers to overcome on the upper Ohio at Wheeling, Marietta, and Parkersburg, and dominance between Parkersburg and Louisville became more difficult, as international factors increased in importance. The amount of foreign salt entering depended on the particular dynamics of the cotton trade, salt consumption levels of lower Mississippi markets, the availability of surplus cargo space on upriver steamers, and national tariff policy.[10]

Kanawha salt makers responded to the dynamics of transportation change. As early as 1820 salt makers Isaac Noyes and Andrew Donnally purchased for over thirteen thousand dollars a two-thirds interest in a steamboat constructed in Wheeling, but they had to dispose of the *Andrew Donnally* within a year because of financial conditions. Noyes and Donnally bought another Wheeling steamboat, called the *Eliza*, for thirty-five thousand dollars. This craft was the first steamboat to reach Charleston in 1823, but the salt makers again had to sell when the vessel failed to overcome the Ohio River current at Point Pleasant. In 1824 the *Fairy Queen*, owned by Andrew Donnally and A. M. Henderson, established the first regular packet service between Cincinnati and Charleston. The steamboat did not change the reliance of salt makers on flatboats for transporting the bulk of their commodity. They used the steamboat for small regular and strategic distribution.[11]

As the American West developed, domestic salt competition reduced the noncompetitive markets available to Kanawha producers. Locally produced salt could capture local markets and could sometimes intrude into the prime Ohio River markets, including Cincinnati. Before 1824 production in western Pennsylvania and New York could threaten the dominance of the Kanawha product. During the War of 1812, manufacturers constructed saltworks on the Conemaugh and Kiskiminetas rivers, tributaries of the Allegheny, north of Pittsburgh. Endowed with abundant supplies of Upper Freeport coal and brine of adequate saturation, the Conemaugh and Kiskiminetas salt makers reached competitively downriver to the Wheeling area and, at times, to Cincinnati.[12] The Onondaga works of New York had supplied western settlers in Ohio and Pennsylvania by packhorse before the War of 1812, but the gravity of the possible threat of this field to the Kanawha manufacturers became more apparent with the opening of each section of the New York canal system.

Local salt factories did not threaten the economic position of Kanawha salt as much as Conemaugh and Onondaga output, but the many western factories did restrict sales. In Ohio, the Scioto Salt Works, started in 1798 in Jackson County, were very important to early settlers, especially during the War of 1812, but with the revival of commerce and overexpansion, the Kanawha producers closed the weak brine field by capturing control of the Chillicothe market. More important were the Muskingum River salt factories, which were first developed on a large scale in the Zanesville area in 1817. By 1826 the estimated production of the Muskingum works was three hundred thousand bushels annually, but the entire quantity was consumed locally.[13] The primary Kentucky works were at Vanceburg on Salt Creek and the Ohio River. Even though Vanceburg was not far from Cincinnati, the weak brine and the lack of an economical fuel source forced the Salt Creek Works to cater to a local clientele. Another small Kentucky manufacturing operation was the Goose Creek Salt Works on the South Fork of the Kentucky River, near Manchester.[14] The salines near Shawneetown, Illinois, provided the major internal salt source for Illinois and Indiana. In 1827 the Gallatin County field manufactured a hundred thousand bushels of salt for area residents.[15]

Besides imported salt, a main rival in most western markets became New York salt originating in the vicinity of Syracuse. Before the early 1830s the expense of overland transportation confined Onondaga salt to the Great Lakes trade complex. The opening of the Erie Canal to Buffalo in 1825 greatly extended the market area of Empire State salt. Some consumers preferred New York salt over the Kanawha commodity because of its coarseness (made possible by solar evaporation). All things being equal, the Kanawha product held a slight economic advantage, because production costs were slightly lower as a result of the cheap fuel resource of bituminous coal.[16]

Encouraged by the phenomenal economic success of the Erie Canal, Ohio, Indiana, and Illinois began to project canal plans to connect the Great Lakes area with the Ohio River basin. Such projections posed a distinct threat to Kanawha salt producers, who already had to contend with imported salt and with local salt sources. The first trans-Ohio canal was begun in 1825 and was completed from Portsmouth on the Ohio River to Cleveland on Lake Erie, a total of 334 miles, in 1832. One branch of this canal extended through Zanesville to the Ohio River and eased the transportation of Muskingum River salt. Another Ohio project, begun in 1825, extended a canal 67 miles from Cincinnati to Dayton within three years. The Miami Canal reached 113 miles further to a point 8 miles west of Defiance on the Wabash and Erie Canal in 1845.[17] The Wabash and Erie Canal was an Indiana work built originally from Lafayette on the Wabash River through the Maumee Valley to Manhatten, four miles from Toledo, on Lake Erie. The Indiana canal eventually reached Evansville on the Ohio River. The Illinois canal plan, though less important to Kanawha producers, was designed to connect Lake Michigan and western rivers with the Illinois and Michigan Canal.[18]

Cross-state canals, started on the Ohio River but not reaching Lake Erie, temporarily expanded the market area for Kanawha salt. On the other hand, waterways built from Lake Erie enlarged the market for Onondaga salt. The penetration of central Ohio from Cleveland wrought a fundamental change in the interior's salt supply. In 1833 twenty-eight thousand barrels of New York salt cleared Cleveland for the interior; by 1839 the amount had risen to one hundred thousand barrels. When the Wabash and Erie improvement was completed, New York salt penetrated the Wabash Valley via Toledo.[19]

The completed canals brought New York salt to the very doorstep of the Virginians' markets. Onondaga salt flowed in four directions from its production site: to the Tidewater, northward to Oswego and Lake Ontario, through the Welland Canal to Upper and Lower Canada, and into Lake Erie to Pennsylvania and the Old Northwest. The Erie Canal directorate allowed a refund of tolls paid by state salt makers if the salt was shipped out of the state. New York salt was carried as ballast in the Great Lakes trade. In 1841 the *Buffalo Commercial Advertiser* estimated that three-quarters of the salt carried for Ohio consumption was transported free by shipmasters who preferred loading and unloading salt instead of sand.[20]

The completion of the trans-Ohio canal broke the total control of southern Ohio domestic markets by the Kanawha salt industry. Other than general merchandise, salt was the only commodity that passed north to south on the Ohio Canal.[21] Although great quantities of Onondaga salt were received by the canal at Cleveland, the growing agricultural population of the northern section of the state absorbed a major portion of the supply before it reached Portsmouth. Between 1833 and 1844 the total number of barrels of Empire State salt that started on the Ohio Canal at Cleveland and actually reached Portsmouth approached significant quantities in only three years. In 1835, the first year any salt passed the entire length of the waterway, only 18 percent of the total quantity begun at Cleveland reached the Ohio River. In 1839 and 1840, the percentages were 15 and 16 respectively.[22]

Manipulation of canal toll rates by the Ohio Board of Public Works in 1839 and 1840 to encourage through shipments of salt from Cleveland to Portsmouth accounted for the extraordinary deliveries of New York salt into the Ohio River basin in those years. The rebate of twenty cents per barrel on New York salt enhanced through traffic revenues yet protected Muskingum and Hocking Valley salt producers in their interior Ohio markets. After the Ohio salt producers had access to their own canals, in 1840 the canal board revoked the rebates and began levying discriminatory tolls on New York salt that passed beyond Roscoe, in north central Ohio. The board also enacted high tolls to exclude Kanawha salt on the Muskingum improvement. The state of New York, in response, allowed rebates on Erie Canal tolls on New York salt destined for Ohio markets. Virginia salt makers thus became victims of other states' public transportation policies.[23]

Levi Welch, a prominent Kanawha salt maker, manifested in 1844 a strategic understanding of the dynamics of the salt market when he informed his congressman that "no danger of monopoly" of the commodity could exist because of Ohio canals and the low freight rates from New Orleans. Low rates from New Orleans would continue, because three to four times the volume of freight descended the Mississippi than ascended. Returning steamboats would rather carry salt cheaply than be empty. Salt was brought to St. Louis and Nashville for eighteen to twenty-five cents per four-and-a-half-bushel sack.[24]

More ominous for the future of the Kanawha salt industry than canal improvements was the construction of railroads in the Old Northwest. In 1840 twenty-two miles of the Jefferson, Madison, and Indianapolis Railroad extended northward from the Ohio River. The Little Miami Railroad reached Springfield, Ohio, from Cincinnati in 1846 after nine years of construction. In the same year, the Mad River and Lake Erie Railroad connected the line with Sandusky.[25] The implementation of the plethora of railroad projects spanning the Old Northwest would not threaten the Kanawha enterprise because of domestic salt competition, however. More damaging would be the basic alteration of the agricultural economy of the western United States.

5

The Manufacturing Process and Technological Progress

A relatively simple simultaneous manufacturing process produced Kanawha salt. The heart of the factory was the furnace that evaporated salt from the brine pumped from nearby wells. An elevated storage cistern fed the brine by gravity through pipe logs to the evaporation pans. Wooden stopcocks on each pan controlled the flow of water. After boiling, the water was drawn into a brine trough, where the oxide of iron settled and the water became clear. After sedimentation was complete, conductors guided the clear water into the graining or crystallization kettles. After some boiling, the brine yielded impurities that were skimmed off the surface. As boiling progressed, salt crystals formed on the surface of the water until the weight of the accumulation forced them to sink. When the kettle or pan was boiled dry, the salt was lifted or shoveled onto a tilted platform or trough, where the bittern could drain. After drying, the salt was transported to the salt house, where it was stored or packed.[1]

Technological progress in the Kanawha salt manufacturing process was empirical and resulted from the modification of detail rather than from the development of new productive systems. No spectacular inventions revolutionized the industry, but innovation spurred evolution. The sudden fall of the rate of profit during the War of 1812 and the constant downward trend of the product price throughout the antebellum period provided incentives for the application of technology. Kanawha salt makers had to reduce their production costs to remain in business and to earn some profit. Overproduction of salt, whether it resulted from the proliferation of furnaces or from the application of inventions, stimulated further technological developments. The intense competition between enterpreneurs fostered the quest for more efficient factories and processes. Salt manufacturers could extend their influence in the industry and their market share of sales through innovation and the rapid adoption of new methods. Constant operation caused salt furnaces to deteriorate. Salt factories were not permanent and unalterable structures. The forced maintenance and renovation of furnaces allowed and indeed encouraged quick application of inventive modifications and new ideas.[2]

The Kanawha salt manufacturers, led by the Ruffner brothers, devised techniques and tools in drilling brine wells that formed the technological basis of all later developments in the subterranean search for brine, oil, and natural gas in the United States.[3] Constant experimentation led to the invention of new drilling tools and deeper boring. Wells progressed from the original depth of fifty-seven feet to the denser brine in the Lower Salt Sand in the Pottsville Series of the Pennsylvanian Period, one hundred to one thousand feet below the surface of the Kanawha River bottom.[4]

Initially, the motive power for drilling was furnished by a person who operated a spring pole. Kanawha drillers continued to use sycamore gums as casing.[5] The spring pole method was replaced by a horse or horses on an inclined tread wheel. When the horses walked on the wheel, a lever lifted and dropped regularly. Attached to the moving lever was the boring auger, which was connected by ash poles. A grass rope that held the connecting poles suspended from a high frame gave the cutting bit a slight rotary motion with every descending movement. The ash poles used as connecting rods were twenty-five feet in length and two inches in diameter. The rods could be joined together by sockets and screws to obtain any desired length.[6]

As drilling progressed, it was necessary to keep the auger sharp and the hole free of obstructions. If the diameter of the drilling bit became smaller, the danger of lodging the tool in the bottom of the well hole greatly increased. Drilling filled the hole with muddy borings, which could impede the motion of the auger. In 1810 William Whitteker fashioned a crude sand pump to remove obstructions. Later, a copper tube, five to six feet in length and three inches in diameter, became standard equipment for removing cuttings from the borehole by allowing material to pass through a valve in the bottom. Tubing was necessary in most Kanawha salt wells to prevent caving in and the entrance of fresh water from the surface. At first wooden tubing was employed, but William Whitteker substituted soldered tin. Screw joints later replaced the soldering, and copper gradually displaced corroding tin tubes. The Ruffners developed a packer that prevented surface water from entering the tubing and diluting the brine in the well. A leather sleevelike bag filled with flax seed and tragacanth was secured around the tube and inserted into the well hole to form a tight expansion seal.[7]

Perhaps the most important drilling tool invented in the Kanawha Valley—still in use throughout the world—was the slips or jars. In 1831 William ("Billy") Morris developed this device that made faster and

The oldest Dickinson brine well at Malden, West Virginia, in 1934. Originally drilled in the 1830s, this 1,700-foot well on the river bank, 200 feet from the furnace, produced brine from several sands. Courtesy of the West Virginia and Regional History Collection, West Virginia University Library.

deeper drilling possible. Thirty-inch-long, closely fitted double links of high-proof steel were dovetailed to slide up and down. With a pin and socket joint, they connected the drilling bit and the rod or rope running to the spring pole or tread wheel lever. This sliding mechanism made possible a delayed power motion that on the downward, drilling stroke allowed a quick and more powerful cut, unobstructed by the slack movement of the connecting rods or rope. On the upward stroke, the delayed power motion dislodged the bit from the base of the hole on the snapping of the sliding links.[8]

Facts of geography and the availability of natural resources spurred technological progress in the adaptation of a new fuel source to evaporate salt. Cord wood cut from the heavily forested hills bordering the Great Kanawha River provided the initial fuel source. Wood was a finite fuel, and as convenient stands were depleted, the expense of cutting, handling, and transporting wood increased. The presence of bituminous coal in the hills behind the salt furnaces was well known, but certain difficulties had to be overcome before coal could be used in salt furnaces. The primary problem was the removal of cinders, as the intense heat caused the cinders to melt into cakes of slag that were difficult to break and expel.[9] The heat gained from coal in comparison with wood provided a great incentive to salt manufacturers, who wished to obtain a cheaper and more efficient fuel source. In 1815 David Ruffner prophetically observed: "Fire wood, in the course of time, must become scarce or difficult to get—but stone coal may be used instead of it, and of this our stock is inexhaustible."[10]

Several early attempts to use coal as fuel in salt furnaces proved unsuccessful.[11] Eastern Virginia coal operators Harry Heth, Beverley Randolph, and Samuel G. Adams recognized the potential value of coal on the Kanawha and in 1815 conducted an extensive experiment. In March 1815 Beverley Randolph and Company signed a contract, sharing expenses and profits, with Nathaniel Bosworth, a New Englander, to construct a furnace fueled by coal to manufacture two hundred bushels of salt per day: "The water from the Reservoir shall pass through a conducting pipe into the highest of a range of Boilers, & thence gradually descend by its gravitating power to where it is finally concentrated & chrystalized & the whole process is to be performed by the use of Stone Coal without the aid of wood or Charcoal." Bosworth was "not to communicate or put in use his improvements" without the consent of the salt company.[12] Plagued by misunderstandings from the beginning, this experiment was a disaster. Bosworth, who had estimated a cost of $300.00 for the iron in Pittsburgh, ended up spending $3,810.22, which the salt company refused to pay despite legal proceedings. The firm escaped responsibility for the debt because it had not authorized the

A brine cistern at the J.Q. Dickinson & Company works at Malden, West Virginia. This twentieth-century photograph shows an antebellum style reservoir that collected brine from several wells for delivery to the furnace. Note the well in the right background. Courtesy of the West Virginia and Regional History Collection, West Virginia University Library.

purchase. Nevertheless, Randolph had hoped that somehow the effort would prove successful. In July he abandoned all hope: "I believe manufacturing with coal will not be introduced."[13]

Joel Shrewsbury and other manufacturers closely observed the construction of the experimental furnace to determine the effort's success. Noting that the experiment cost around five thousand dollars, he further described it: "[T]he apparatus was very costly the boilers made of Sheet Iron in the shape of a gum about 3 feet in diameter, thro which went a copper tube about 6 inches in diameter, the two boilers about 60 feet long, the steam that went thro those tubes in the boilers was to operate on two large copper pans for graining off the Salt, in shape and size like a Billiard Table the plan is thought wilnot answer."[14]

The Ruffners pioneered the use of coal. Henry Ruffner overcame the obstacle of slag removal by directing jets of steam under the bars of the grate. The contact of the steam with the fire fractured the slag into small-grained gravel that was easily removed. In 1817 David Ruffner was the first manufacturer who completely adapted his furnace and pans to use the new fuel. Within five years all salt manufacturers converted their furnaces to coal. In 1842 Lewis Ruffner noted: "Bituminous coal is the fuel exclusively used for twenty year past in salt making here."[15]

The use of bituminous coal made possible the refinement of the evaporation process and furnace construction. The first type of furnace usually contained from thirty to sixty kettles of thirty-five gallons each. Usually half of the kettles were used to boil brine, and the other portion crystallized the partially evaporated brine. If the brine was weak, a higher proportion of the kettles were employed for boiling. Successive improvements altered the shape and size of kettles. Kettles for boiling reached a capacity of 150 to 200 gallons, because it was more economical to fuel fewer large containers than several small ones. These giant vats weighed up to 1,900 pounds each, but only five or six were needed in each furnace. With the intense heat produced by coal, the furnace operators discovered that a much larger boiling surface could be fired, thereby producing a greater quantity of salt. Instead of employing kettles or vats, the producers substituted evaporation pans. Placed over the hot coal fire, the cast-iron pans were twenty-five feet long, six and one-half feet wide, and two to three inches deep. The pans were sectional and were connected with screws. The connecting joints were filled with molten cast-iron borings. Furnace capacity could be increased simply by enlarging the evaporating surface of the pan. Between 1817 and 1830 coal-fired furnace production jumped from 250-300 to 900-1,000 bushels of salt per unit per week.[16]

With their greatly increased output, the evaporation pans required four times the amount of brine than was formerly needed in a given operating period. Old methods of pumping brine from the well to the storage cistern impeded the productive capabilities of the new furnaces. Mechanical pumps worked by horses had replaced hand sweeps, but they were still inadequate. In 1828 one manufacturer installed a small steam engine to pump brine rapidly and continuously. Other producers employed more engines in the next year, and by the early 1830s steam engines pumped every well in the Salines. The scale of the adoption of these small two- or three-horsepower engines in the Kanawha salt industry was quite remarkable. By 1836 the sixty-two high-pressure stationary steam engines in the Salines constituted one-half of all stationary engines in Virginia. The western Virginia salt business employed more stationary devices than existed in fifteen other states.[17]

The availability of brine supplied from deeper wells drilled by improved tools permitted the development and construction of larger furnaces using more fuel-efficient evaporative processes. A coarse salt manufacturing method, originally patented by Calvin Guiteau of New York State, was introduced into the Kanawha Valley by George H. Patrick, who held exclusive rights to use of the design in Virginia. In February 1832 Patrick entered a complex agreement with Andrew Donnally and Isaac and Bradford Noyes for the experimental application of the new idea within a year. Through a complicated exchange of patent rights, furnaces, construction rights, reversionary real property, and potential profits that resulted in a copartnership if the process were successful, the parties would share the Virginia patent rights and factories.[18]

Instead of crystallizing the salt from the partially evaporated water by direct firing, the Guiteau method used the steam generated by the fire for the crystallization process. Whereas the old way required a fire under both the evaporation pan and crystallization kettles, the new mode employed direct heat only under the evaporation pan. The steam was captured in the sealed furnace and conveyed by a 16-inch-square wood and lead truck to a large plank vat that was 135 feet long and 16 feet wide. The raw well water first ran into the pan, where it was rapidly evaporated into highly saturated brine. The brine then settled impurities in a vat before passing into the large plank vat, where crystallization occurred. At the bottom of the crystallization vat was the leaden top of the 16-inch-square steam trunk, which contained the 150-degree steam heat. Besides employing fuel and heat more efficiently, the Guiteau process manufactured a desirable coarse salt product.[19]

The Guiteau innovation was a precursor to a production process that for a century was unique to the Kanawha region and to the Pomeroy, Ohio, area. Within a decade Kanawha salt manufacturers who had observed the efficiencies of the Patrick, Donnally, and Noyes furnaces improved their operations by refining the graining procedure. By altering the Guiteau method, they avoided the patent monopoly and achieved an evaporative factory ideally suited to their locality.

The Kanawha grainer process was unusual in salt production in the United States because it used low steam pressure and efficiently converted a low-density brine into salt with a small quantity of cheap fuel. Other brine areas could not use this grainer process, because only Kanawha water contained barium, which dissolved sulfate of lime. Lime sulfate would cake on the instruments of heat and water transfer, thus limiting efficient production in other areas.[20]

Ideally suited to the fuel-rich area's weak, dissolved-lime brines, the indigenous Kanawha grainer system of the 1840s made maximum use of fuel, heat, and brine. The entire continuous manufacturing process required about eighteen hours. Workers usually lifted or removed the salt every twenty-four hours. The only waste products were condensed water, ash, and bittern. (After the Civil War, the producers used bittern to create several chemical by-products.) The basic factory consisted of a masonry furnace with a grate, pans, and chimney and the attached settling and graining pans.[21]

The furnace actually formed a giant steam chest. In the front and bottom was a grate, where the sole coal-firing was done by banking in a twelve-by-nine foot floor area, eight feet in height, under the first of three heating pan sections located on the next level. Over one hundred feet to the rear of the furnace was a a chimney. Above the pans was a sealed chest, which captured the evaporating steam to be conveyed to the mud and draw settlers and to the grainers. The steam, under a low pressure of approximately four pounds, passed to and between the settlers and grainers by pine and poplar logs with a six-inch bore, in which it condensed only slightly. The steam was conveyed through the settlers and grainers by five-inch copper pipes with very thin walls that permitted maximum heat transfer.

The brine ran from a storage tank into the first of three sections of pans at the front of the furnace, where initial heating and evaporation occurred. Each of the three sections had ten cast-iron pans bolted together, forming a container thirty feet long, ten feet wide, and one foot deep, divided every three feet by eight-inch partitions. Melted iron filings or borings caulked the seams between the individual ten-by-three-foot cast-iron pans. After boiling from the front to the rear of the furnace across the partitions and through the three sections (thirty pans), the brine ran by gravity into two mud settlers over one hundred feet long and ten feet wide. Heated by the copper pipe containing steam from the chest, the brine circulated around a central partition in each settler to deposit the mud or sludge and iron oxide. The clean brine then ran by gravity into the first or second draw settler, where it remained until it was needed in the grainer. The five grainers were set on two levels slightly below the draw settlers. The first, second, and fifth settlers were on the same level; the third and fourth were paired lower. The concentrated brine ran initially into the first and fifth grainers, where the next grade of salt was formed, and into the third grainer, which produced an inferior salt. The last level and the lowest of the crystallization process was the peacemaker or small grainer, which recirculated the low-grade salt that it produced into the first mud settler and held the bittern for disposal. All the settlers and grainers except the smaller peacemaker were over one hundred feet long, ten feet wide, and two and a half feet deep. All vats were constructed of four-inch pine or poplar planking.

The economies of the Kanawha grainer system forced the salt makers to adopt the process and to rebuild their furnaces on the new plan in the 1840s. Steam evaporation doubled the output of the old-style furnace with the use of the same amount of brine. The innovation produced a greater quantity of a higher-quality product at a cheaper cost. In 1845 Lewis Ruffner observed: "Every body has first, or last, to adopt the changes particularly in regard to the Steam." William Tompkins concurred: no prudent manufacturer, he believed, could maintain his competitive position with an old-style furnace.[22]

The cost of labor is often a prime factor in stimulating technological discovery and adoption of more efficient manufacturing processes. The intense competition between decentralized entrepreneurs and the constantly reduced retail price of salt in free western markets forced the quick adoption of new methods. This change reduced labor costs per unit of manufactured product. The same labor force produced more bushels of salt.

Increased labor productivity resulting from improved furnace construction and manufacturing procedures did not cause technological unemployment. At certain stages, manufacturing improvements actually increased the demand for and the price of labor. Coal mining required more preparation for production (such as excavation, building of tramways, and removal of slate), demanded more skill, and represented more capital risk than woodcutting. Increased production of salt created the need for more coopers to fabricate containers for shipment. Also, since slaves were the basic labor in the factories, the available evidence does not suggest that the institution of slavery retarded technological innovation.

6

Manufacturers and State Intervention

Kanawha salt manufacturers consistently sought the active intervention of the state to maintain and augment the economic progress of their industry. For approximately thirty-five years, the entrepreneurs hoped that the Commonwealth of Virginia would adopt appropriate public policies, especially in banking and internal improvements, to aid their enterprise. By the 1840s they had abandoned all expectation of receiving more than the most remedial legislation from an eastern political establishment that discriminated politically against western Virginians and that possessed conservative agrarian attitudes toward state involvement in economic development. Virginia did establish a self-supporting, locally administered salt inspection system, but state activity in the creation of adequate banking facilities and internal improvements was far less than salt producers needed.

In 1814 the Virginia General Assembly took advantage of the supposed wartime prosperity of the state's salt manufacturers and levied a twelve-and-a-half-cent-per-bushel tax on the commodity along with excises on lead, cigars, and iron products. The assembly, believing the demand for the commodity far exceeded the supply, thought that the salt manufacturers could simply add the excise to the price and become the collectors, not the actual payers, of the tax.[1]

After February 10, 1815, each manufacturer had to obtain a license from the commissioner of revenue to produce salt, and a complete inventory of the stock on hand had to be forwarded to the revenue officer. Thereafter, salt makers had to submit monthly returns stating the total production and the amount of salt sold or otherwise disposed of. A producer also had to enumerate the "number of furnaces which he employs in his manufactory, the number of boilers or kettles, their contents in gallons, and the number of gallons of salt water requisite to furnish fifty pounds of merchantable salt." During the first ten days of February, May, August, and November, the commissioner of revenue had to file his quarterly returns with the sheriff, county clerk, and auditor of public accounts. The sheriff had to collect and pay the taxes into the state treasury in May and November. If a manufacturer failed to pay his taxes, the license permitting him to operate would be revoked. Revenue commissioners were required to visit all factories every quarter and were empowered to examine each manufacturer's record book and to question white employees over fourteen years of age. The revenue officer received compensation at the rate of 3.5 percent for all taxes collected in his district. Severe penalties were imposed for falsification, delinquency, and failure to comply with the statute.[2]

Despite the elaborate provisions drafted by the legislature, the state failed to collect the salt levy efficiently. The local political influence of manufacturers prevented quick and vigorous application of the statute. Upon learning of the tax, the Kanawha salt makers developed a strategy to defeat its collection. When they discovered that an unpaid tax would not constitute a lien on their real estate, they rented their furnaces to undercapitalized lessees. One observer noted, "If the Renter is only bound they will Rent to such hands as they can command, and the Law can not." Former governor Beverley Randolph recorded: "Almost all here will evade the tax by keeping between them and the law some worthless fellow under the pretext of renting." The commissioners of revenue were unable to secure cooperation from the manufacturers from the first quarter of 1815. Most producers secured the necessary license but did not file the monthly returns. The returns that were submitted seldom contained the proper information.[3]

Nonpayers of the salt tax now enjoyed a price advantage over law-abiding manufacturers in an already depressed salt market caused by the end of wartime demand and expanded output. Randolph lamented: "Now what do honor & honesty require of us: Must we be the only sufferers from an unjust regulation of the government? Those who will evade will be enabled to undersell us the amt of the tax."[4] After state noncollection for six months, he asked his partner to determine the present governor's attitude: "Has the Executive under the conviction that the Law laying the Salt tax is oppressive & unjust, suspended its execution till the meeting of the Legislature." His partner advised, "I can form no idea as to the temper of the Executive on the subject of the Salt tax—the least said on the subject the better—I never knew them over loaded by a feeling of Justice towards their fellow men."[5]

The salt tax fell especially hard on the manufacturers of the Kanawha Valley and the eastern seacoast, as well as on King's Salt Works in Washington County. The establishments in Accomack, York, Northumberland, and Princess Anne counties produced only 8,241 bushels, on which they paid an assessment of $1,030. King's Salt Works turned out 73,109 bushels, taxed at $9,146.12.[6] The total amount of the salt tax outstanding in Kanawha County after February 10, 1816, was $30,418.92.[7]

The manufacturers succeeded in obtaining a remission of six and a half cents of the tax on each bushel from the Virginia General Assembly, but they wanted the cancellation of the total amount. In their petition to the assembly, the operators, disputing the legislative assumption of undersupply of salt, noted they produced more salt than could be consumed in the West during the War of 1812. The restoration of peace reduced salt prices to such an extent that the amount of the tax exceeded their profits.[8]

The salt makers of Kanawha County forwarded a list of the persons and firms charged with the salt tax and their probable financial conditions. Thirty-five people, who owed $16,204.87, had left the state. Seventeen who remained were unable to pay $4,769.35. Four debtors of doubtful financial capability owed $788.85. The seventeen solvent firms, mostly partnerships, were assessed with $8,655.85 of the total tax load of $30,418.92. The financially able operators desired to be released from the onerous tax obligations imposed by the act of January 11, 1815. After the Committee on Claims reported that a bill achieving the goal was "Reasonable" on December 31, 1817, the legislature relieved the solvent salt producers of this financial burden.[9]

The boom in the salt business initially caused by the War of 1812 stimulated the influx of transient producers from outside the Kanawha basin. The newcomers employed questionable manufacturing methods that aroused resentment among established producers. The permanent operators accused some transient opportunists of manufacturing an impure, adulterated product that threatened the reputation of the commodity in western markets. The established operators, emphasizing that they were not only the pioneers in the industry but also the largest producers, petitioned the Virginia General Assembly for the creation of a salt inspection system to maintain the reputation of the Kanawha product. Asserting that their prosperity depended on the sale of wholesome salt, the manufacturers contended that "a few rapacious adventurers" who leased property for short terms, "possessing no permanent Interest in the property or even in the County, destitute of moral honesty," had made state intervention necessary.[10]

Within a month the Virginia General Assembly responded with a statute providing for a uniform salt inspection system to be effective on May 1, 1814, in Kanawha and Mason counties on the Kanawha River. The county courts of each jurisdiction were to appoint in May or June "a person of good repute and who is a skilful judge of the quality of salt" to be salt inspector on an annual basis. If the quantity of salt was too great for one man to inspect it with dispatch or if the inspector became ill, he was empowered to appoint any number of assistants, subject to the approval of the county court. The assistants had the same powers as the head inspector. No inspector or his assistant could be, directly or indirectly, concerned in the production of salt or its sale or purchase except as a consumer. Every inspector and assistant had to affirm that he would "without favor, malice, or partiality, carefully inspect all salt" and that he would not approve any containers without judging them to hold "clean and merchantable" salt. Provision was made in the case of the death of an inspector, and the county courts retained the power to remove inspectors "for neglect of duties, malfeasance, or corrupt practices."[11]

Standards were established for barrel construction and for identification of weights. All salt barrels had to be made of good seasoned wood and tightened with ten hoops, fixed with four nails in each chine hoop and three nails in each upper bilge hoop. Each salt manufacturer had to provide a distinguishable mark to brand each barrel. He also had to imprint the tare and net weight on each container. If barrels were moved from the place of construction without being branded and nailed as prescribed, the producer incurred the risk of a one-dollar fine for each one. Any person who falsified the amount of tare to the injury of the purchaser would be subject to forfeit ten dollars for each barrel wrongly labeled. The salt inspector or his assistant, "upon suspicion, or at the request of the purchasers," could require the producer to unpack any barrel to determine the tare. If an unpacked barrel was found to weigh more than declared, "making a reasonable allowance for the moisture of the cask," the manufacturer had to bear the penalty and the expenses of the investigation. Otherwise, the inspector or purchaser had to pay the packing charges.[12]

Each barrel of salt had to pass inspection before being loaded on a boat or other vessel for transportation. The inspector could examine the salt by drilling through the head of the cask. If the salt was satisfactory, the hole was plugged, and the inspector branded the name of the county with a public mark and noted the quality—first, second, or third—on the barrel. The manufacturer had to pay five cents to the inspector for each barrel examined. If the salt was inferior, the inspector condemned the salt and marked the barrel appropriately for the same fee. Any person who felt aggrieved by the decision of the salt inspector could apply for relief to a justice of the peace. The justice could issue a warrant to direct three impartial persons to examine the salt in question. If a majority declared the salt to be merchantable or of a quality superior to the decision of the inspector, the inspector had to erase the former brand, mark the new rating as directed, and repay the complainant his costs. If the judgment of the inspector was confirmed, the owner of the salt had to bear all the costs of the review and reward the inspector ten cents for each barrel.[13]

A person who reused a container without first erasing the earlier inspection marks would be subject to a ten-dollar fine for each offense. Attempts to alter or to imitate the public mark or to repack condemned salt in barrels previously branded incurred fines at the rate of ten dollars per barrel. The penalty for transporting uninspected salt was twenty dollars per barrel for the owner or navigator of the boat or other vessel and the same for the manufacturer.[14]

Salt transported in bulk or packed in containers other than barrels or casks was also inspected. Certificates for complete cargoes could be issued. Such a declaration had to state the quantity and quality of the salt, the name of the owner or owners, the name of the vessel, and the market for which it was destined. Both the manufacturer and the boat owner were responsible for obeying the statute.[15]

The county court had to procure the proper weights and scales for the salt inspector to use. The inspector had to examine all weights, steelyards, or patent balances used in the county. If the devices were accurate, he marked or stamped them. The inspector received $2.50 for each of the scales he tested. A person who persisted in employing inaccurate weights in a manufacturing establishment was legally liable, and the inspector could destroy the false scales.[16]

All penalties and forfeitures imposed by the statute were recoverable on behalf of the Commonwealth of Virginia in the superior court of law or county court, provided that the offending parties received ten days' previous notice of the motion. The inspectors had to return in June of each year to the county court an account of the quantity of each grade of salt inspected.[17]

In 1826, when the cost of production exceeded the selling price of salt, the manufacturers violated state statute and refused to have their salt inspected so that they could avoid the inspection fee. The justices of peace who sat as the Kanawha County Court simply refused to appoint the salt inspector as required by law.[18] The General Assembly of Virginia reacted immediately. Amending the general inspection act of January 8, 1814, for the first time, the General Assembly compelled the appointment of a salt inspector during every March term of the county court. The clerk of the county court had to issue a summons to the sheriff for all justices to appear to appoint an inspector or to fill vacancies in the office. After the summons was executed and returned by the sheriff, each of the justices who failed to make the necessary appointments had to pay a twenty-dollar fine for the benefit of the literary fund. The fine was recoverable in the superior court, with costs including a $2.50 reward for the commonwealth's attorney who prosecuted the case.[19]

Before a container of salt was placed in a wagon or boat for transportation, the inspector or his assistants had to test the contents for "its grain, dryness, colour and purity." On the head of each cask, the first-, second-, or third-quality mark had to be imprinted with the gross weight. A standard tare of twenty-eight pounds was set for each salt barrel, but if the inspector suspected that a container weighed more, he could empty the contents for a thorough examination. For doing this he would receive an extra one-cent-per-barrel fee. No salt could be weighed or inspected until it had drained at least twenty-four hours.[20]

The statute did temper the mandatory nature of the inspections, allowing for flexibility on the part of the county court in setting inspection fees. The inspector was to receive two cents for each barrel examined, but the county court had discretionary authority to raise or lower the fee by one cent. If an inspector or his assistants failed to perform their duties, they were liable to a fine of twenty dollars. Each manufacturer of salt had to furnish two workmen to aid in the inspection process.[21]

A person who loaded uninspected salt on any wagon or vessel was subject to a one-dollar penalty for each container. In all cases of violation, the manufacturer of the salt was liable for the fine, and if a renter, agent, or manager was unable to pay, the owner of the furnace or property involved was responsible. Penalties were also levied on the owner, master, or navigator of the vessel and on the owner, driver, or conductor of the wagon.[22]

A concession to local consumers permitted them to convey loose salt in bags by packhorses or canoes without inspection or payment of fees. Provision was made for bulk carriage of salt. The inspector received three mills for each bushel transported in this manner. Bags and boxes of salt could be sold, but the inspector had to declare the tare of each container. In each quarter, the salt inspector had to return to the county clerk an abstract of the amount of salt examined at each furnace. He also had to account for all salt that was carried by canoes and packhorses for local consumption.[23]

On February 19, 1830, the Virginia General Assembly enacted a statute that standardized barrel sizes for Kanawha salt. Salt had to be packed in barrels that did not exceed thirty inches in length and eighteen inches in diameter across the head within the chine. The inspector had to refuse to examine salt packed in barrels of larger dimensions. A factory had to brand the head of each barrel before it could be legally moved from the place where it was manufactured. The penalty levied by the enactment and previous statutes was recoverable by the commonwealth in the superior court of law or the county court provided that the offending party received ten days' previous notice of a motion.[24]

In 1831 the General Assembly provided for the compensation of the salt inspector. Before an inspector was appointed, the Kanawha County Court had to fix the rate of payment for the entire forthcoming year and enter the amount into the record. The sum could not be more than two cents or less than one cent for each barrel examined. A majority of justices had to concur in the decision, and if they failed to set the compensation for the inspector, they were liable to the same penalty as if they had failed to fill the office. If a vacancy occurred in the office for any reason, the successor was entitled to the same fixed fee. In all prosecutions against the inspector for neglect of duty, malfeasance, or corrupt practices and in all motions for removal from office, the superior court of law enjoyed concurrent jurisdiction with the county court.[25] The possible arbitrary power of the county court over inspection policy was reduced by the removal of its power to adjust fees within a term of office of an inspector and by the restriction of its exclusive jurisdiction.

Another amendment in March 1832 stipulated that all penalties, fines, and forfeitures imposed by the various salt inspection acts for benefit of the literary fund were recoverable before any justice of the peace if the amount involved did not exceed twenty dollars. If the final judgment exceeded five dollars, the decision could be appealed during the next term of the county court after the appellant entered into bond with sufficient security guaranteeing that he would prosecute his appeal and pay the amount of judgment with all costs if the decision was affirmed. If the amount involved exceeded twenty dollars, the case had to be heard by the county court with the defendant held to bail. All penalties had to be paid to the salt inspector, who had to render a fair and just account of the fines in the September term of the county court. The amount was certified by the county clerk, who transferred the copy to the auditor of public accounts, who in turn charged the inspector for the total. The inspector paid the amount due every January after deduction of a 6-percent commission. If an inspector failed to remit, the state could recover the amount, and the offending person would be ineligible for reappointment to the office.[26]

In 1832 the assembly empowered the Kanawha County Court to appoint two salt inspectors and to "divide and lay off the salt works . . . into two districts, as nearly equal as maybe as to quantity of salt manufactured, and assign one inspector to each." Each inspector had jurisdiction only in his respective district. A salt manufacturer could not appeal the decision of one inspector to another, as the judgment of each was final.[27]

An adjustment for the examination of output had to be made for the new manufacturing process for coarse salt. The amendment of February 9, 1833, asserted doubt about "whether the alum salt now manufactured . . . can be conveniently or properly inspected in the usual mode." The inspector had to view the product in bulk, and after it was packed in barrels or other containers, he had to brand or stamp KANAWHA ALUM SALT, the quality, and the actual weight on each container. The inspector was to receive two cents for every six bushels of alum salt examined. In all other respects, the general inspection laws applied. In 1837 the county court was empowered to fix the inspection fee on alum salt at one or two cents per barrel.[28]

Besides desiring to regulate the quality of Kanawha salt to maintain its reputation in western markets, the salt makers had other motivations in generally supporting the state-established inspection system. The Kanawha County Court, a body controlled by the dominant producers, administered the inspection process, which provided for uniformity and standardization in packaging and gradation among all manufacturers. It set the lick weight as the unit of sale to all consumers. Very important was the foreclosure of the necessity for inspection by municipal authorities in river towns who might have different ideas about quality and weighing procedures. After passage of the 1826 amendment to the inspection statute, the city of Cincinnati repealed its ordinance that required an examination of the Kanawha product. The editor of the *Western Virginian* called for authorities in Louisville to remove the "vexation" and expense of a second inspection so that consumers could enjoy cheaper prices.[29]

Before 1832 no local bank existed in the Kanawha Valley to serve the commercial requirements of the salt business. Manufacturers wanted the establishment of a bank so that capital might be available for expansion and for the normal operation of the enterprise. An office of discount and deposit would be convenient for routine financial transactions. In 1830 they petitioned the Virginia General Assembly for the establishment of a branch of either the Bank of Virginia or the Farmers' Bank of Virginia in the town of Charleston. They based their justification of the new proposed location on the needs of the salt factories and developing agriculture. The petitioners predicted that the potential exchange business would be sizable because of the salt industry's connections with other commercial centers. They estimated that two hundred thousand dollars' worth of merchandise, mostly from Philadelphia, Baltimore, and Pittsburgh, was sold annually on the Kanawha. The citizens asserted that a bank in Charleston would be profitable and would benefit the area and the state.[30] In response to the desires and needs of Kanawha Valley residents, the General Assembly provided for the establishment of an office of discount and deposit of the Bank of Virginia in Charleston after March 19, 1831. In May 1832 the branch began active operations.[31]

In the organization of the new financial institution, Lewis Summers, judge of the highest court in Kanawha County, constantly worried that the dominant salt manufacturers would become the controlling directors of the new bank. When attempts to form a producers' association materialized in December 1832, Summers, who had previously urged salt makers to subscribe generously to bank stock, feared that the producer-stockholders would use the bank as "a mere instrument of Monopoly in their hands." After the new salt company surfaced to eliminate the smaller, uncooperative producers, he cautioned: "If the associators and the Bank directors, turn out to be the same persons, all who stand in their way may quake and tremble."[32]

After acquiring a branch of the Bank of Virginia for Charleston, salt makers and residents were dissatisfied with the statutory limitation upon the total capitalization of $150,000, a sum considered inadequate for the institution to ease the transaction of business in the valley. They also resented the control exerted by the central bank in Richmond over the local office. Kanawha Countians believed that their banking needs could not be met while the bank was tied to Richmond-promulgated banking policy. The Panic of 1837 and its aftermath merely stimulated the expression of latent feelings of area residents.

Several Kanawha County citizens succeeded in obtaining a legislative act in March 1837 incorporating the Kanawha Savings Institution, to be located in Charleston. The statute vested commercial and corporate powers in the stockholders to elect officers and directors, to receive and invest deposits, and to discount and purchase notes, with certain restrictions. Members of the corporation enjoyed limited legal liability. By the end of 1841, the Kanawha Savings Institution had a paid capitalization of thirty thousand dollars.[33]

In December 1837 many salt manufacturers and other prominent citizens of the Kanawha Valley petitioned the Virginia General Assembly, advocating the incorporation of a state bank to be located in the county with a total capitalization of five hundred thousand dollars. Affirming their approval of the basic concept of a central Virginia bank with local branches throughout the state, the petitioners desired a "proper degree" of autonomy for the branches in determining policy. Not favoring a free banking policy that could lead to the operation of an "injurious and oppressive" monopoly, they wanted a central bank with "local and particular interests" handled by the branch officers. The petitioners condemned the policy that had resulted in the placement of only two state banks in western Virginia, at Wheeling and Charleston. Eastern

Virginia interests centered at Richmond controlled the Bank of Virginia. Current policy had placed the commercial and business interests of the entire commonwealth "at the mercy of the merchants of a single city, and all must yield in passive submission to that course of trade which the wisdom or the whim, the interests or the passion of the central directory may decree." The signatories could not "perceive the grounds of policy or necessity which should retain the resources, the commerce and the business of all Western Virginia in a state of interminable pupilage to a Richmond Directory, ignorant of our peculiar situation, our wants, and the character of our commercial operations." They desired another state banking organization with directors from each section of the state.[34]

The Kanawha salt manufacturers believed that inadequate banking capital inhibited the commercial operations of the marketing of salt to the detriment of the producers. They did not want new capital to invest in real estate and manufacturing facilities, but sufficient funds for a bank "to advance . . . that portion of the value of the salt manufactured, which consists of the annual expenditure devoted to its production." The amount of capital needed depended upon the total "of the floating, unfixed capital which is required for the vigorous and successful prosecution of the business." The average Kanawha salt producer lacked the commercial facilities and individual financial resources to arrange for the discharge of all production costs while he awaited an advantageous time to vend his product in a market. The manufacturer shipped his salt during slack demand seasons but had to sell immediately to discharge his expenses. As a result, the Virginia producer enriched speculators. A bank of adequate capital could reverse this situation by advancing the expected proceeds from the salt in market on bills of exchange.[35]

Amid the national financial recession of 1838, a large number of citizens met at the Kanawha County Courthouse "to take measure for laying before the Legislature the wants of this community in regard to Banking Capital." With David Ruffner as chairman and Robert A. Thompson as secretary, Lewis Ruffner explained the object of the meeting. A second petition was prepared and duly adopted for presentation to the Virginia legislature. The citizens appointed James Craik, Lewis Ruffner, Levi Welch, Robert A. Thompson, James C. McFarland, James M. Laidley, George H. Patrick, Joel Shrewsbury, Jr., and Levi Best as a committee to procure signatures for the petition and to correspond with residents of neighboring western counties "to urge their vigorous cooperation . . . in this effort to give a new impetus to the Agricultural, Commercial, and Manufacturing interests of Western Virginia." The petitioners, repeating verbatim most of the assertions of the December 1837 document, desired the location of a bank in the county with a capital of at least five hundred thousand dollars, "in which they can themselves have some interest and over which they may exercise some control." As western Virginians, they attested to their special competence to testify about the social and economic effects of the absence of a banking system when they competed with western merchants, especially those of Ohio, who enjoyed adequate commercial facilities.[36]

Responding to Kanawha County grievances, the General Assembly in 1839 incorporated the Bank of Kanawha, to be located at Charleston. The total capitalization of the new institution could not exceed three hundred thousand dollars. The statute designated Joel Shrewsbury, Sr., Luke Willcox, William Tompkins, Levi Welch, James Hewitt, John D. Lewis, William B. Clifton, Andrew Donnally, John Rogers, James Bream, Lewis Ruffner, Joel Shrewsbury, Jr., Dr. Goodrich Wilson, James Capehart—all associated with the salt business—and eight other men, or any five of them, as commissioners to open stock subscription books within two months at any selected place. In addition to being subject to the general regulations governing the incorporation of banks enacted on March 22, 1837, the Bank of Kanawha was restricted in other ways. Loans and discounts could not exceed twice the amount of capital stock actually paid in. No person or company could owe as a drawer, acceptor, or endorser an amount in excess of fifty thousand dollars. The bank was subject to all restrictions imposed by the General Assembly upon the Bank of Virginia, the Farmers' Bank of Virginia, and the Bank of the Valley of Virginia. The bonus to be paid to the state was not to be invested in additional bank stock. Also, the charter of the Bank of Kanawha was to expire on March 1, 1857.[37]

The House of Delegates had initially enacted the bill establishing the Bank of Kanawha with the provision that left the choice of location to the vote of the stockholders after the shares were subscribed, but a Senate amendment fixed the location at Charleston. As a result of this statutory specification, the salt manufacturers simply refused to subscribe for stock in the new institution. Only two shares were taken. In January 1840 the salt makers petitioned for an amendment that would leave the decision of ultimate location to stockholders. They reminded the legislature that the object of establishment was to afford adequate facilities to the salt industry at Kanawha Salines, not Charleston. The petitioners asserted that most prospective subscribers resided at the Salines and had no interest in an institution at Charleston. Besides, the county seat had a bank office, one supported by the business of the salt industry.[38]

Opposing the desires of the salt manufacturers, many counterpetitioners residing in Charleston and other parts of Kanawha County warned of the consequences of leaving the selection of the site of the new bank to subscribers of stock. They described Charleston as the "only fit and proper" location. The stock was not subscribed because of "the peculiarly embarressed condition" of the area and the noncooperation of salt makers, who wanted the bank to be located at Kanawha Salines. Since the active capital of the county was held by salt producers, any provision leaving the selection of location to subscribers of stock would be tantamount to placing the bank at Terra Salis. After reciting the manipulations by the joint stock organization of Hewitt, Ruffner and Company in reducing salt production and in controlling prices, the counterpetitioners cautioned the General Assembly about granting the salt interest the means to extend its power: "The inevitable result will be to Make the whole County tributary to schemes of aggrandizement which are dangerous to public safety, and adverse to the public weal." Laws should not extend the "influence of Capitalists and Monopolists," who would "bring under their subjection the industry and resources of a whole community." It was not good policy to permit a situation to arise whereby the directors of a bank might become the borrowers. The petitioners urged the General Assembly to maintain the statute without alteration, as the additional capital was necessary and the salt makers would have to cooperate, regardless of the controversy about location.[39]

The Bank of Kanawha did not become an immediate reality because of the rivalry over location and the severe financial contraction. Salt factory owners had to use their available funds to modernize their facilities in order to maintain their competitive position upon the expiration of Hewitt, Ruffner and Company. The rivalry over the location of the bank would tend to encourage politicians to pursue a policy of delay in forcing the issue. Vested interests in the existing branch of the Bank of Virginia would undoubtedly articulate a policy of postponement. Finally, in 1845 the salt manufacturers quietly achieved their object when the General Assembly empowered the president and directors of the Bank of Kanawha to locate the office at either Charleston or the Salines as the majority of stockholders should direct, provided that proper notice of their meeting had been published in a Charleston newspaper.[40] In 1842 the residents of the Salines successfully petitioned for the incorporation of a savings bank to be located in their community. The General Assembly limited the capitalization of the Kanawha Salines Savings Institution to a total of one hundred thousand dollars.[41]

The effects of the national depression tempered most petitions from Kanawha County concerning state banking and financial policy.[42] In 1841 valley residents complained about the statute that prohibited state banks from receiving or paying out notes of other banks in denominations less than ten dollars. Since Kanawha trade was with western states that issued bills of smaller denominations and that furnished most of the currency of the region, the prohibition operated very harshly upon the citizenry. They requested reduction of the limitation to five-dollar bills and notes.[43] At its spring term in March 1842, the Kanawha County Court under the chairmanship of David Ruffner drafted a petition that requested the enactment of stay laws (although the term was not used) to delay foreclosures by the branch Bank of Virginia at Charleston.[44]

By 1837 the Virginia General Assembly had contributed all that it was willing to offer to the banking facilities and capitalization in the Great Kanawha Valley. The entrepreneurs desired higher capitalization, more liberal and expansive lending policies, and more local control of the branch of the state bank. The creation of relatively small private banks under state charters did little to meet their commercial needs. The salt makers still depended on western mercantile centers such as Cincinnati for their banking requirements. State policy, formulated by eastern Virginians, would be as insufficient in this area as it would be in programs designed to overcome impediments to transportation.

Western Virginians and prominent residents of the Tidewater had long dreamed of surface connections between the East and the westward flowing rivers of the trans-Allegheny. Since the creation of the James River Company in 1785, the inhabitants and absentee landowners of western Virginia hoped and fought for state internal improvements so that the resulting prosperity in agricultural enterprise and the likelihood of increased settlement would cause land values to appreciate.[45] After the salt industry developed, the residents of the middle section of the Great Kanawha Valley looked with great interest upon all proposals designed to improve their river for transportation. At times they desired eastern connections with the Allegheny area and with Richmond, but Kanawhans generally looked westward. Spurred then by the favorable report of John Marshall and the other commissioners appointed by the state to survey transportation routes, who recommended a tortuous east-west internal improvement following Dunlap's Creek, Howard's Creek, the Greenbrier River, and the New River, Kanawha commercial interests worked for efficient market outlets.[46] The eyes of the salt makers were longingly viewing the West in 1815, when they petitioned the Virginia General Assembly to improve the navigation of the Great Kanawha River but warned that it was not necessary or advantageous to devote expenditures to improvements higher up than the Elk River. The producers wanted to avoid paying for nonbeneficial improvements through tolls on their commodity.[47]

After being greatly affected by the transportation revolution in downriver markets, the salt makers petitioned the Virginia General Assembly in 1817, requesting the incorporation of the James River Company to raise funds to improve east-west connections. They contended that they had delayed making any effort to improve the Kanawha River for navigation because they had hoped that the commonwealth would have engaged in construction of turnpikes connecting the James and Great Kanawha rivers. The petition, written by Joseph Lovell, constructively suggested a method of achieving the necessary financial resources for the huge project: "The creation of a commission to superintend the work under the controul of the Legislature with power to sell stock, bearing a fixed interest, would readily produce funds for the execution of the work."[48]

The salt manufacturers asserted that in four years they sustained losses owing to the unimproved river far greater than any improvement would ultimately cost. The Kanawha had to be rendered navigable for smaller steamboats, because the invention afforded the only method whereby transportation costs might be reduced. A safe navigation system "would enable them to meet and to encounter with success the competition, which is now growing up between their Salt, and the foreign Salt, brought by Steam Boats from New Orleans to the markets which they have been accustomed to supply." Moreover, "the enormous expence of transportation, together with the risque of loss, operates upon them like an export duty and is a bounty to their competitors, and unless counteracting measures are adopted, must result in consequences, extremely injurious."[49]

In 1817 several citizens of Kanawha County met at the courthouse and resolved that Andrew Donnally, Joel Shrewsbury, and Daniel Ruffner should be appointed as a committee to forward an estimate of the yearly imports and exports on the Great Kanawha River so that the General Assembly might have some basis on which to project tolls for proposed river construction. The committee, after noting that the sole export was nine hundred thousand bushels of salt, enumerated a lengthy list of imports, ranging from agricultural products to iron manufactures. Besides revealing the lack of self-sufficiency in both industry and agriculture, the estimates presented a taxable base for navigational improvement projects.[50]

The reorganization of the James River Company in the 1819–20 Virginia General Assembly expanded the scope of the enterprise to include the Great Kanawha River and necessary wagon roads in the trans-Allegheny area.[51] The new, revised statute provided for collection of tolls upon boats and various commodities "so soon as the improvements for the navigation of the Kanawha river shall be completed . . .

from Slaughter's Creek to the Ohio river." Salt was to be assessed a two-cent-per-bushel toll. In the subsequent session, the James River Company received discretionary authority to levy a toll on a bushel of salt not higher than two cents or lower than one cent until the projected improvements were completed.[52]

Relationships between the Kanawha salt manufacturers, residents of the area, and the James River Company were always strained. In November 1826, at a public meeting held at the county courthouse, the citizens with Andrew Parks as chairman and Joseph Lovell as secretary petitioned the state legislature for improvements on the Kanawha River. They contended that the construction had not been completed as provided by the enactments of 1821. Much of the work had been abandoned and left undone. The sluices intended to ease passage through the shoals were excessively steep, and the few jetties, wing dams, and side embankments were unmarked. The petitioners asked for the completion of the construction, the placement of buoys, and the improvement of sluices. After tracing the erosion of the price of salt between the time of the enactment and 1826, they suggested the revision of the toll levied on salt, since "a tax . . . to be rightful, must be at all times graduated by the value of the article taxed."[53]

In November 1827 another public meeting was held at the Kanawha County Courthouse concerning navigation of the Great Kanawha River. With Andrew Donnally as chairman and Lewis Summers as secretary, the assembly selected Joel Shrewsbury, Joseph Lovell, and George W. Summers as a committee to compose a protest of general river conditions. They emphasized that while the total expenditure for improvements was forty-five thousand dollars, between twenty and twenty-five thousand in tolls was collected annually. The petitioners desired the completion of the works or the suspension of tolls. Since legislative fiat provided for the improvement of the Kanawha River to a minimum three-foot depth in all seasons, David Ruffner and Andrew Parks tested the construction along the entire length of the river with a flat-bottomed thirty-by-sixteen-foot boat weighted to draw exactly two feet of water. The test boat, manned by four experienced watermen, contained the necessary gauges for depth measurement. In addition, the construction engineer of the Kanawha improvement accompanied the test run. The group recorded generally critical remarks about the sluice construction through the six shoals between Elk and Coal rivers. At the Coal River they reduced the draft of the vessel to twenty-two inches. From Coalsmouth to Point Pleasant, shallow water conditions in eight bars and shoals impeded the passage of the test boat. The group's report verified that the James River Company had not fulfilled statutory construction requirements.[54]

Reacting to the severe criticism, the Virginia General Assembly reduced the tolls levied and added other provisions rectifying injustices. It reduced the salt toll to one cent per bushel and exempted commodities on boats plying the river above Elk Shoals from tolls. A Charleston collection district was established within the boundaries of Slaughter's Creek and the north side of the mouth of the Elk River on the Great Kanawha.[55]

Strong resentment against the James River Company continued among the salt manufacturers and others. The grand jury in the spring term of 1828 of the Kanawha County Superior Court indicted the president and directors of the James River Company on several counts of negligence and noncompliance with statutory requirements. The company failed to attach large rings on bolts to rocks or other stable bodies along the sluices to allow ascending boats to use warps and cords to progress. Also, the company had refused to remove all impediments to navigation as required by law, as the depth of the river channels rarely exceeded two feet. Concluding the indictment with a unique judicial statement of grievances, the grand jury, with Andrew Parks as foreman, found that "the Kanawha river is in a worse state, and more difficult of navigation than when they commenced working upon it.—With the knowledge of those facts, we consider the act of Assembly passed last winter authorising the collection of Tolls upon the Kanawha river to be an unjustifiable oppression, and a total disregard of the rights, interests and priveleges of the citizens."[56]

Armstrongs, Grant and Company balked at paying certain tolls to the collector and defended its refusal upon the ground that the James River Company had violated statutory injunctions. The salt company also contended that the transportation company interfered with interstate commerce, since the Great Kanawha River had always been considered a navigable stream without obstructions. In July 1828 the citizens of the area again met at the courthouse to protest incomplete construction and excessive tolls on the river. They appointed Joel Shrewsbury, Joseph Lovell, George W. Summers, Andrew Donnally, and David Ruffner as a committee to open correspondence with William G. Giles, president ex officio of the Board of Public Works, for adjustment of complaints.[57]

In February 1829 the Virginia General Assembly revised the toll schedule that reduced the salt levy to one-half cent per bushel, while providing for the strict enforcement of collections and the appropriate legal remedies for handling evaders. The toll collector could prosecute for penalties in the name of the president and directors of the James River Company. Provision was made for the installation of buoys and beacons, sluice rings for the use of ascending vessels, and the removal of all obstructions. Total expenditures for improvements were limited to one thousand dollars. At the season of low water, the principal engineer was required to view the defects of the river improvement and to suggest remedies in a report to the Board of Public Works.[58]

Kanawha salt makers hoped that they might secure a railroad line for their valley that would make their exertions for river improvements moot. In 1827 Lewis Summers, Philip A. Thompson, Joseph Lovell, Joseph Fry, James C. McFarland, and Daniel Smith petitioned the president and directors of the Baltimore and Ohio Railroad for a route through the Great Kanawha Valley to the Ohio. They proposed that the railroad be constructed down the Valley of Virginia to Covington and then parallel to the proposed James River Company improvement to the Ohio River, a distance of 494 miles from Baltimore. The primary inducement for the railroad officials was the commerce of Kanawha Salines and the undeveloped natural resources of timber, coal, and iron ore.[59]

Although the Baltimore and Ohio officers viewed the proposed Kanawha location favorably, the idea of a Baltimore venture's tapping the valley and the West to the detriment of Richmond forced the aware but regressive easterners to reject this proposition in the charter grant. In 1827 the unreformed General Assembly restricted the western terminus to some point on the Ohio River north of the mouth of the Little Kanawha. The existence of considerable sentiment in eastern Virginia against the railroad's entrance into the Old Dominion made Kanawhans fearful about the possibilities for future railroad projects.[60]

In the Virginia General Assembly session of 1830–31, Kanawha County interests employed a legislative stalking horse in an attempt to achieve their objectives. This assembly incorporated several railroad companies, including the Staunton and Potomac. George W. Summers, delegate from Kanawha County, attempted to amend this incorporation bill to permit the railroad to extend its lines from Staunton to the Ohio River via the Great Kanawha. This amendment, which could have nullified the territorial restriction in the Baltimore and Ohio Railroad charter, aroused the opposition of the easterners, who feared the possible economic impact of the Baltimore enterprise. They defeated the proposal in a sectional vote, as they believed that the Baltimore and Ohio would eventually purchase the Staunton and Potomac.[61]

Both hope and hostility characterized the Kanawha salt makers' split view of the James River Company. The residents vigorously supported, financially and otherwise, the internal improvement project because they stood to profit immensely from the opening of east-west commerce. When they saw the opposition of other sections to the company, the high tolls, and the shoddy construction that actually restricted navigation, however, their wishful views altered. By December 1828 the

Kanawha salt makers had concluded that the enterprise was misconceived. The question was "whether the expense of it shall be cast on the Manufacturers of salt who had no agency in it, or bourn by the State generally, whose functionaries devised, adopted, & executed the project." Nevertheless, when the enterprise was reorganized as the James River and Kanawha Company in 1832, Kanawha County residents subscribed for $107,000 worth of the stock.[62]

Those engaged in commerce on the river believed that no tolls should be charged until they benefited from the improvements. As Judge Lewis Summers cautioned: "Better have no improvement than one so oppressive. . . . Nothing should be done here, until the other work was so advanced, as merely to leave time to make the improvements designed on this river in time for the whole line to go into operation together—never put it in the power of the company to distress us with tolls until the advantages of the full trade of the line are enjoyed."[63] Summers and the salt makers were not surprised when the company levied tolls before completion of the project.

Salt makers constantly pushed for more durable construction improvements on the Kanawha, but their efforts met with failure. In the depth of the financial contraction of the 1840s, they abandoned all hope for any real internal improvements in the valley through a state-supported agency. In 1843 Andrew Parks, a member of the House of Delegates, reported great opposition to the James River and Kanawha Company in all legislative quarters, identifying "a settled purpose it seems to me if possible to break it down entirely."[64]

In the financial crisis, Kanawha manufacturers resisted the payment of tolls on salt to the James River and Kanawha Company. In January 1842 the canal company had to sue Hewitt, Ruffner and Company for $22,678, the amount of unpaid tolls on 4,383,803 bushels of salt shipped from Kanawha Salines downriver through the Charleston Collection District. Hewitt, Ruffner and Company unsuccessfully pleaded nonassumpsit to the charge and based its defense on five grounds. Since the river was not improved to the specifications provided by the statute, the plaintiffs could not legally collect tolls or compensation. During periods of high water, the salt company did not employ the meager improvements of the canal company in downstream passage. The canal company could not collect tolls on goods that employed the natural condition of the river: "Every citizen of the United States, had a right to pass and repass thereupon, free from charge on hindrance." Much of the salt shipped on the so-called improvements was sunk because the canal company improperly constructed the sluices and refused to remove obstructions. Since the salt was transported beyond the limits and jurisdiction of Virginia, it was part of the commerce of the

United States. Thus, collection of tolls or duties by the state corporation was an unconstitutional impediment to interstate commerce.[65]

Juries in Kanawha County courts reflected the bitter feeling of residents against the James River and Kanawha Company. In 1844 a salt maker, William A. McMullin, had to pay the company a judgment of approximately $50.00 for nonpayment of tolls. Angered by the result, McMullin successfully sued the canal company for $937.82 for damages incurred in the sinking of his salt boat in a negligently repaired sluice.[66]

Salt manufacturers finally concluded that no improvement on the Great Kanawha could meet their transportation and distribution needs. As a result, they came to oppose all efforts of the James River and Kanawha Company and the imposition of tolls upon commodities. The canal company could never control water levels in the river. Therefore, traffic on the watercourse would always remain seasonable. The desirable goal of matching shipments with market demand could not be attained. Since salt shipments had to be dispatched during periods of adequate or high water, benefits from channel improvement in shoals and bars would be minimal and never worth the toll payment.[67] The producers found themselves nearly as dependent upon the whim of nature in transportation as they were in the early years of their industry, and neither the state nor the steamboat could free them from this natural restraint.

7

Merchant Capitalists, Independent Manufacturers, and Local Economic Developments, 1825–1835

The darkest period of the economic crisis enshrouded the Kanawha salt industry in 1826. From 1820, except for the brief rally stimulated by the faltering efforts of William and Robert M. Steele, salt prices constantly plunged downward from a high of thirty-seven cents per bushel. In 1826 the sale price per bushel fell as low as twelve cents—after the product was packed in barrels. So desperate were the salt manufacturers that those who sat on the Kanawha County Court refused to appoint a salt inspector in order to avoid payment of the inspection fee. An autumn traveler in the Great Kanawha Valley noted: "It is estimated that it costs the manufacture[r] at least 25 cents per bushel—but the rivalry, competition & mismanagement is such, that the salt is sold for 18 3/4 & sometimes 12 1/2 cents—thus ensuring a loss to the owner of the property."[1]

Production costs per bushel of salt far exceeded the sale price. Depending upon the density of the brine, the distance of fuel from the furnace, and the thickness and burning qualities of the coal seam employed, Kanawha producers estimated the manufacturing cost at sixteen to twenty-five cents per bushel. The average production cost was nineteen cents, but this figure was based on optimum operating conditions without breakdowns or accidents. The estimate did not include interest on capital invested, depreciation of machinery, and depletion of the fuel supply.[2] Only the fixed costs involved and hope forced the factories to produce in order to minimize their losses.

The only encouraging event for Kanawha manufacturers was the extension of their market eastward over an improved road to Covington. In the fall of 1826 wagons carried fifteen thousand bushels to Greenbrier, Monroe, Giles, Allegheny, and surrounding counties, where salt prices dropped by 75 percent.[3] Other road-building programs in Virginia could accomplish the same result, because the primary expense of salt to the consumer was the transportation cost.

Economic conditions were auspicious for the successful organization of an arrangement to control production of Kanawha furnaces. In December 1826 seven individuals from Maysville, Kentucky, and Cincinnati formed a joint stock company for the purpose of controlling both production and sales of Kanawha salt. William Armstrong, Johnston Armstrong, James S. Armstrong, Peter Grant, Gilbert Adams, James Hewitt, and William B. Philips associated with John D. Lewis and Andrew Donnally of the Kanawha to create Armstrongs, Grant and Company with a total capitalization of eighty thousand dollars. Each of the seven out-of-state partners held a share, while the actual manufacturers in the firm, Lewis and Donnally, split one share of ten thousand dollars' paid value. Negotiations lasted the entire month of December 1826. With the relatively small capitalization, Armstrongs, Grant and Company cleverly obtained almost complete control of an industry that in 1828 had an estimated total invested capital of $548,000.[4] Through the use of lease and re-lease agreements and delayed payment clauses, this joint stock company, which lasted from January 1, 1827, to December 1830, effectively restricted the output of the desperate producers and managed sales in distant markets.

The lease and re-lease arrangement enabled Armstrongs, Grant and Company to exercise maximum control with a minimum investment of capital. Under this type of contract, the manufacturer retained possession and management of his factory, but he could not control sales or the amount of production. For example, Walter Trimble leased for a three-year period, commencing on January 1, 1827, all his interest in his property and appurtenances necessary for the manufacture of salt. After obtaining control, Armstrongs, Grant and Company re-leased the property to Trimble for the same period. In the lease-back agreement, Trimble promised to manufacture ten thousand bushels of salt per year at "his sole and entire expence" and to deliver the production every thirty days after March 1, 1827, at his salt yard. He was to have the salt packed in good barrels of prescribed specifications and to have it inspected by the "properly appointed Legal Inspector." Relying on the inspector's weights and gradations, Armstrongs, Grant and Company would pay Trimble twenty cents per bushel for first-quality salt, eighteen cents for second-quality, and thirteen cents for third-quality, one-half of the amount on delivery and the remainder in six months. To discharge its original rental payment of five hundred dollars, the company would pay two and one-half cents on delivery and execute six-month notes for an additional two and one-half cents per bushel. If an accident delayed or prevented manufacturing operations, the rental payments would cease until production resumed. Trimble would not incur any penalty except the expense of repairs. To secure compliance with the contract and to ensure absolute control, Armstrongs, Grant and Company reserved the right to reenter and to take possession of Trimble's property if he manufactured a larger quantity than that specified or if he sold his salt to others. The company allotted Trimble an additional quota of ten thousand bushels to manufacture each year on the same terms, except the five-cent-per-bushel rental payment was not to apply.[5]

Armstrongs, Grant and Company appears to have formulated the same type of contract with other Kanawha producers that it had with Walter Trimble, but it did maintain contractual flexibility to achieve organizational goals. The firm had leased the saltworks of Littleberry Leftwich and Joel Leftwich for the customary rent and had re-leased it to them for ten thousand bushels of salt per year. Meanwhile, for five cents per bushel, the company purchased from Leonard Morris, with whom Armstrongs, Grant and Company had an identical contract, the allotted privilege of manufacturing ten thousand bushels yearly. The firm then sold the Leftwichs seven thousand bushels of the Morris three-year manufacturing privilege for $350 per year. The Leftwichs agreed to resell the entire seventeen-thousand-bushel annual allotment, after it was produced, to Armstrongs, Grant and Company for twenty-five cents per bushel, one-half on delivery and the remainder in six months. Then the company resold to the Leftwichs fifteen thousand of the seventeen thousand bushels for seventeen and a half cents per bushel the first year and thirty cents per bushel the second and third years. In the first year of delivery, ten thousand bushels were due before May 1, 1827, and the balance on June 1. In the second and third years, the entire fifteen thousand bushels were to be delivered before May 1. The Leftwichs agreed to dispose of the entire quantity only on the Tennessee River. The company promised not to vend salt to anyone who might enter the Tennessee River market for the three-year term. The Leftwichs could produce only the seventeen thousand bushels annually. Armstrongs, Grant and Company reserved the right to reenter the property if the Leftwichs disposed of salt to unauthorized parties. If the Leftwichs sold their salt interest, they had to place their salt furnace with the company to assure compliance with the various contracts by other persons.[6]

Besides engaging in repurchasing of manufacturing privileges and apportionment of markets, Armstrongs, Grant and Company leased outright for a three-year period the four salt furnaces owned by Aaron Stockton and his brother-in-law William Tompkins. The company obtained control of the property with wells and coal rights for a bargain price of two thousand dollars per year. Perhaps the firm secured these advantageous terms because Tompkins had first married Jane M. Grant and after her death had married Rachel Marie Grant, half-sister of Peter Grant, aunt of Mrs. James Hewitt, and aunt of a future general in the Union army and president of the United States.[7]

Armstrongs, Grant and Company, in its attempts to restore prices and to limit supply, restricted each furnace under its control to the production of ten thousand bushels of salt annually. Since the partnership tried to ensure the operation of every furnace to a limited extent, fifty-six of the sixty-five furnaces were producing at the end of 1827. After one year's trial, the company found its policy of restricting production on all furnaces to be uneconomical. An average salt furnace could evaporate ten thousand bushels in six months. Producers usually contracted for slave labor by the year and incurred other fixed costs that made the lack of income very unsatisfactory. Idleness caused furnaces and supporting fixtures to deteriorate. To solve this problem, the partnership decided that fewer furnaces operating at full capacity could produce more efficiently the necessary supply to meet all the demands than all furnaces could with limited production. The company compensated multifurnace operators to allow some designated furnaces to lie idle. It permitted single-furnace owners to continue production on an increased level. Armstrongs, Grant and Company could more than compensate for the lost rental payment on "dead furnaces" that would have accrued to the company and for the lost profit potential on the amount between the price that would have been paid for delivered first-quality salt and the basic production prices actually paid to owners of idle furnaces. At the end of 1829, twenty-four of the seventy-three furnaces were "dead."[8]

Except for at least two firms, the company exercised complete control over the industry. Armstrongs, Grant and Company neglected to obtain control of a furnace leased by Charles Venable to Frederick Brooks, a son of the first president of the Baltimore and Ohio Railroad. Protected by the restrictions imposed on all other salt factories, Brooks realized full economic advantage from his independent position. During part of the first year of the existence of the company, he ran a single furnace on his rented "independent property." He used his profits to erect a second furnace. With the capital accumulated during the second year, Brooks prepared three furnaces in 1829. Brooks later deposed that "the two first years I made but little money, and that was expended in improvements." During 1829 Brooks's three furnaces manufactured one hundred thousand bushels of salt, on which he was able to clear eighteen thousand dollars. He attributed his success to factors beyond his control: "I think the existence of that company was the cause of my making the profit."[9]

Dickinson & Shrewsbury continued its usual policy of not entering combinations or agreements that would limit its production. Joel Shrewsbury crowed about the situation: "Times in this Country is much better since the great part of the Salt is bought up by a Company . . . those like ourselves who has nothing to do with the Company, we can calculate upon now with certainty making our Salt nette us 50 Cents p Bus." On two furnaces, Dickinson & Shrewsbury annually projected manufacturing thirty-five thousand bushels.[10]

Armstrongs, Grant and Company successfully raised the price of Kanawha salt in primary markets. It held prices around thirty-five cents a bushel at the works and from forty to sixty-two and a half cents in Ohio River markets. By districting sales areas to large wholesale dealers, the combination achieved equal distribution without surpluses or scarcities in markets. The wholesale dealers who enjoyed exclusive districts generally were located in remote, decentralized river markets where the company could not exercise effective control. Armstrongs, Grant and Company devoted its energies to management of all markets in and around Louisville, Cincinnati, and Maysville.[11]

The most convincing testimony on the economic success of Armstrongs, Grant and Company was that after three years of operation, it realized a net profit in excess of fifty thousand dollars on each of eight shares of capital stock. A contemporary traveler observed that Armstrongs, Grant and Company, the lessees, "had made a large fortune; the manufacturers, jealous of their success would not renew it, and again fell back to their old condition."[12]

All Kanawha manufacturers did not share equally in the prosperity and profit generated by Armstrongs, Grant and Company. The average producer received twenty-five cents per bushel for his limited output, while the combination reaped the full benefit of its control by acquiring the difference between the manufacturer's price, transportation costs, and other incidental expenses and the sale price. The company realized ten to forty cents per bushel sold, but the manufacturer made only six cents per bushel (if his average manufacturing costs were nineteen cents). This margin for producers was far in excess of their pre-1827 profits, and it was guaranteed. Only Frederick Brooks with his "independent property" and Dickinson & Shrewsbury realized economic advantage without sacrifice. Andrew Donnally, Peter Grant's estate, and James Hewitt benefited as stockholders in the company and as manufacturers. Donnally owned four furnaces completely and shared eleven with other parties. Hewitt held eight furnaces, and Peter Grant (and later his heirs) controlled one manufacturing facility.[13]

Western reaction to the formation of Armstrongs, Grant and Company was almost immediate. Large public meetings in Kentucky's Ohio

River counties of Lewis, Mason, and Bracken convened to express indignation through resolutions, to plan boycotts of the Kanawha product, and to seek alternative salt sources. In a furious letter to the editor of the *Maysville Eagle* in February 1827, a consumer warned of the dire consequences of centralized control of Kanawha salt sales. He wrote that the avaricious engrossers, by fixing prices and raising them in times of scarcity, sought exorbitant profits. To prevent the Virginians from becoming demigods and from acquiring princely estates, he urged the Kentucky legislature to enact the appropriate legislation to prohibit engrossing, forestalling, and regrating. He also implored Kentuckians to petition Congress to remove the duty on imported salt as a method to break the monopoly. It was ironic that the financial desires of fellow westerners from Maysville, who accumulated the greatest portion of profit, excited such resentment among their neighbors.[14]

Before the expiration of the three-year Armstrongs, Grant and Company contracts on January 1, 1830, Kanawha Valley salt makers viewed their future fiscal welfare with great anxiety. In February 1829 an anonymous penman using the name Salt Lick advocated a plan of future combination whereby actual salt manufacturers might retain the profits arising from any arrangement and the resentful feelings of westerners might be assuaged. In order to quash misconceptions about the history of the salt trade, Salt Lick acquainted his readers with business realities. He observed that supply and demand basically governed the market price of salt and that the success of commodity dealers and speculators rested upon their knowledge of these changing aspects. The writer charged Kanawha Countians with the lack of perception to recognize the modifications of these basic economic elements as they related to the salt trade. For example, many residents believed that salt's reaching the hands of small traders caused the low prices of 1826, when the converse was true. If the article had been scarce and, therefore, more valuable, small dealers could not have bought or handled it. Everyone knew that a surplus existed, and as a result, speculations would not touch salt. "When the supply is short, there is always competition among the purchasers: when too large among the vendors." The complete control of a commodity by a few sellers who have concluded an agreement on restricting competition has the same effect on the price as a short supply of the article. Restricted competition can keep the price above its fair market value and can arouse the cry of monopoly from consumers.[15]

To guard against overproduction and bankruptcy of salt producers, the writer proposed a five-point program:

1. Let all the salt property be valued by three or more disinterested commissioners of ability and the quantity of salt be apportioned by the estimate.

2. Let all the property be conveyed to certain individuals, in trust, for a term of years for a specified purpose.

3. Let a quantity of salt equal to our present means of producing be distributed among the manufacturers for the first year—subject to diminution or enlargement in subsequent years.

4. Let agents, or commission merchants, some three, five, or more men of good character, of capital and commercial experience be engaged, either for a percentage or liberal salary, giving bond and security to receive the salt from the hands of the inspector, ship, sell, and account for the proceeds.

5. It should be the care as it would be the interest of all parties that a highly qualified inspector should be appointed; and the salt sold in market at his weights after having lain at furnaces not less than a week.[16]

Salt Lick justified each proposed stipulation. He identified the allotment of production quantities as the chief obstacle to agreement. Without some provision for production quotas, no durable system of cooperation could be established. All salt makers would have to agree to abide by the decisions of the commissioners. The estimate of the total production of a property should be based upon its permanent value as well as on its current production capability. The commissioners should have access to all information. Salt Lick advocated the revolutionary use of the trust conveyance of furnaces to ensure full compliance with agreements. A manufacturer predisposed to comply with his obligations would not hesitate to furnish a guaranty to others. Allowance for subsequent regulation of production quotas would assure necessary flexibility to meet demand and would prevent the possible financial loss occasioned by surplus supply. Accurate and competent inspection of the commodity would furnish a check upon the merchants' weights and would enhance the reputation of Kanawha salt with consumers.

The major barrier to the implementation of Salt Lick's scheme was the idea that "agents" or "commission merchants" would supply the capital and assume all risk while assuring the dominance of Kanawha producers in the arrangement. He demanded that the commission merchants possess unlimited funds and be experienced and of unimpeachable character. The merchants should engage the transportation and advance funds upon the delivery of salt. Losses in shipment should fall upon the shippers through the required use of insurance or upon the whole body of manufacturers. Merchants should bear all losses in sales. The Kanawha producers needed the commission merchants with capital more desperately than Salt Lick surmised. Merchant capitalists had alternative investments available and did not have to subordinate themselves to Kanawha salt makers. The independent Kanawha producers, having limited means, had the alternative of overproduction and ruinous competition.

The stockholders of Armstrongs, Grant and Company were anxious to renew the expiring contracts in January 1830, but many salt makers were not satisfied to receive a minimal return on their production while the joint stock company reaped tremendous profits. One nonresident salt producer favored continuation of Armstrongs, Grant and Company because he would have to expend scarce capital to recondition his furnaces for active production. To avoid this expense, he would have been satisfied to accept a dead rent payment or compensation for limited output over a long term.[17]

The merchant capitalists and Kanawha manufacturers compromised. They established a sales agency or factorage called Dickinson, Armstrongs and Company. Producers could share in the excess profits above the set delivery prices.[18] Dickinson, Armstrongs and Company had a total capitalization of sixty thousand dollars, with six shares of ten thousand each. Isaac and Bradford Noyes jointly, the extensive manufacturing firm of Dickinson & Shrewsbury, James C. McFarland, James Hewitt, Johnston Armstrong, and James S. Armstrong possessed one share apiece. Isaac and Bradford Noyes were permitted to discharge the cost of their share with salt deliveries.[19] Perhaps the other manufacturing members of the firm were allowed to do likewise.

Dickinson, Armstrongs and Company paid an advance price of twenty-five cents for each bushel of salt delivered to it, one-half immediately and the balance in six months. After sale of the commodity, the agency paid the balance of the sale price, if any, to the manufacturers on a pro rata basis, after the deduction of the original advance, transportation expenses, and a commission of three cents per bushel for the company.[20]

In the absence of adequate documentation, one cannot determine the degree of success of the sales agency arrangement. In the two-year period of the existence of the agency, Kanawha salt prices fell 15 to 20 percent. Upon its expiration, one manufacturer estimated that at least fifty thousand dollars' worth of surplus salt remained in downriver markets. As late as 1845 a full settlement of the accounts of Dickinson, Armstrongs and Company had not occurred. Isaac and Bradford Noyes willingly sold their ten-thousand-dollar share of stock to James Hewitt for three thousand dollars and the understanding that if the company sustained a loss, their portion of the burden would not exceed three thousand dollars.[21]

As early as July 1831 it was generally known that Dickinson, Armstrongs and Company would expire as a sales agency for manufacturers in January 1832. The company allowed the two-year contracts to terminate because it discovered that the salt makers had the more advantageous position. Unlike Armstrongs, Grant and Company, the sales agency gained only the three-cents-per-bushel commission. In December 1831 James C. McFarland was attempting to close the business of the company.[22]

In the last half of 1831 the manufacturers tried to formulate an arrangement to achieve control of their production and sales for mutual benefit. Most of the producers were as dismayed as John J. Cabell: "The consequences will be that there will be too much made for the supply of the markets & a reduction of prices will of course follow. I am much perplexed & some what at a loss how to stear my course to suit the changes to take place." In November, Cabell reported that all the manufacturers had agreed that one million bushels was the proper production quantity for the Kanawha field, but they could never establish a quota satisfactory to each producer. At the beginning of 1832, Cabell feared that any understanding was unlikely after a proposed agreement barely failed in December 1831. Cabell, blaming three individual salt makers for the problem, marveled: "It is very astonishing, the very men that are obstinate & will not come in will loose" as much as anybody.[23]

The dominant Kanawha manufacturers, annoyed by the same small producers, embarked upon an ominous tactic to purge the salt industry of uncooperative elements and to prepare the way for a beneficial combination. The local superintendent of the James River and Kanawha Company reported to Judge Lewis Summers that the strategy of large companies was to reduce salt prices for an extended period to ruin those who had refused to cooperate in any arrangement.[24] The major producers organized three separate, autonomous trading companies to manufacture and market salt and to secure through various means the eventual economic control of the smaller, independent furnace operators. Andrew Donnally, John D. Lewis, Joel Shrewsbury, William Dickinson, Isaac Noyes, Bradford Noyes, James Hewitt, James Bream, James C. McFarland, Henry H. Wood, Levi Welch, and Johnston Armstrong formed Donnally, Bream and Company; William Dickinson and Joel Shrewsbury as Dickinson & Shrewsbury, Lewis Ruffner, John D. Lewis, William D. Shrewsbury, Joseph D. Stratton, and Moses M. Fuqua created Dickinson, Ruffner and Company; and Henry H. Wood and Levi Welch established Welch, Wood and Company.[25]

The three dominant companies attempted to gain control of the small furnaces by extending credit through their respective company stores. An antagonist in a later legal controversy charged that the "big three" furnished the small operations with "large supplies at high profit on credit and taking their bonds therefor, secured by deeds of trust on their Salt Property with which the Records of Kanawha bound." The respondent in the same suit answered that he knew of no "sinister purpose" directed against the independents and charged that such suspicions were "the mere fancies of a diseased imagination."[26] As the major sources of local mercantile credit, the large trading firms did exert a certain measure of control over some independents. By supplying goods through their stores, the copartnerships exacted economic concessions from the financially pressed. It was the custom of company stores located at Terra Salis to average a 33-percent profit upon the first cost and carriage charges of dry goods sold.[27]

Small operators could readily obtain working capital from the larger companies while they dispensed with marketing problems by guaranteeing their salt output for payment. For example, in the autumn of 1833 Reuben Roy promised to deliver to Donnally, Bream and Company sixty thousand bushels of salt in barrels within a specified time in return for a set price of twenty-two cents per bushel, ten cents on delivery and the remainder in merchandise from the company store. If Roy took less than four thousand dollars' worth of merchandise, the bushel rate of payment would be reduced to twenty cents, and payment for the balance due would be rendered in a four-month note at the end of the delivery term.[28]

As the dominant producers intended, the Kanawha salt industry entered a severe recession. Between 1831 and 1835, in the absence of controls, salt production more than doubled, from 956,814 to 1,960,583 bushels. The relative buying power of Kanawha salt in the Cincinnati market fell sharply, as Kanawha salt prices slid from the fifty-to-sixty-cent range to approximately thirty-two cents per bushel. Later, when asked about the prosperity of the industry in this period, Lewis Ruffner emphatically denied the existence of profits for manufacturers. Upon visiting the Salines during the Christmas holidays of 1834, Judge Lewis Summers reported that the salt makers expected to produce more than two million bushels in 1835. Such a record output would leave five hundred thousand as a year-end surplus unless the manufacturers decided to endure financial sacrifices to vend the excess quantity. Anticipating the onslaught of profitable times for country lawyers and an increase in his court docket, Summers predicted a "considerable derangement in the business of the salt works."[29]

To measure the purge's effect on small manufacturers, the salt producers caucused daily in the last part of December 1834 and the first half of January 1835 to conclude an agreement for the regulation of production and price. James Hewitt and John Rogers proposed various plans for combination, but their efforts failed. During their deliberations, the manufacturers considered asking the Virginia General Assembly for an act of incorporation. Some consulted Judge Lewis Summers about the feasibility of incorporation and urged him to prepare a bill implementing their desires. Summers refused to encourage the project on the ground that insufficient time remained in the current legislative session to arrange the legal details. Ignoring Judge Summers's counsel, the producers sent to Richmond a hastily prepared petition requesting an act of incorporation.[30]

In the instrument written by Charleston attorney James Craik, the twenty-seven petitioners asserted the economic importance of the Kanawha salt industry to the surrounding territory, the Commonwealth of Virginia, and the West generally. They foresaw that individual effort and diligence would not avert economic ruin and that no hope for future prosperity existed. Believing the purpose of government to be the protection and preservation of the individual citizen's property and the adoption of every "just expedient" to increase the national wealth, they requested a simple act of incorporation, so that their "united capital and united will" might overcome all obstacles to prosperity. The petitioners emphasized that the grant of liberal incorporation charters was not an extraordinary legislative enactment.[31]

The petitioners enumerated the major obstacles to their achievement of prosperity under two headings: the increasing costs of production and severe competition from abroad and from production areas in other states. Deeper brine wells, higher fuel costs, a scarce labor supply, and Kanawha River tolls caused increased production costs. Receding brine levels made deeper boring necessary. Fuel costs rose because of increased transportation expenses resulting from longer distances between the furnaces and the mine entrances. Slave labor was relatively expensive because of the occupational hazards in the industry and the proximity of the Salines to Ohio. River tolls raised the commodity's sale price to consumers and limited possibilities for competitive pricing. Conversely, tolls on manufactured goods and agricultural products brought upriver for consumption at the saltworks increased production costs. Reduced import duties on foreign salt stimulated domestic competition. The opening of the Ohio Canal to Portsmouth brought New York salt in direct conflict with the Kanawha product, while Pennsylvania, Illinois, and Muskingum River production fields closed local market outlets. Anticipating opposition, the petitioning salt producers claimed that opponents of corporations possessed "distempered imagination, filled with chimaeras." They pointed to the contemporary successes of beneficial state-chartered commercial endeavors and urged the General Assembly to incorporate the Kanawha Salt Company.[32]

Opposing the incorporation proposal, thirty-eight counterpetitioners vigorously attacked the plan for centralization. They declared the scheme to be "inexpedient, and fraught with much mischief" to many manufacturers and to the citizenry of the Great Kanawha Valley. It would "tend, ultimately, to the complete ruin of a larger number of manufacturers, and to the creation of an unjust and odious monopoly." Advising the General Assembly that previous centralized control had aroused fierce western public opinion and had caused a ruinous reduction of the salt tariff, the petitioners asserted that "a free trade in an article of such prime necessity, and of such universal consumption, would best comport with the general welfare of the country, and of the great body of Salt makers themselves."[33]

The opponents attributed the proposal to the five or six larger manufacturers. If these dominant producers obtained a corporate charter, they could easily monopolize all available bank capital. They could use their aggregate wealth to undersell small manufacturers for two or three years to break them, and thus they would consolidate their properties "for a trifle." Dangers were also inherent even if the small producers did subscribe to the capital stock of the proposed corporation, because the richest manufacturers, the largest stockholders, would formulate company policy. The large holders could operate the corporation at a loss without dividends to force small shareholders to sell their equity interest at any price. The petitioners averred that "this intent is not disguised, but it is openly avowed that some five or six persons will ultimately own all the Salt property in Kanawha Salines."[34] The independent producers, who anticipated much criticism of corporate practices in future, cautioned that the proposed corporation could greatly affect many people engaged in subsidiary industries who depended upon the salt industry for their livelihoods. If the corporation destroyed independent operators, it could regulate the prices of products it consumed. As a result, people would lose their jobs and leave the area. The corporation's power, the opposition said, would last as long as its charter.

The controversy placed George W. Summers, Kanawha County's delegate to the General Assembly, in a potentially dangerous political situation. Any position that he might take could be politically fatal. His brother, Lewis, advised him that the question had excited local feeling. Since incorporation would likely become an issue in the next election, his position should be "as unexpectionable to both sides as practicable." Judge Summers observed that the incorporation of the salt company was "an important experiment on the vital interests of the county, and ought not to be left to the mere repealing power of the next Legislature." The elder brother suggested that delaying tactics be adopted if the measure seemed likely to be enacted: an amending clause could be inserted, suspending the organization of the corporation until a valuation was submitted to an ensuing legislative session. In this way, George W. Summers could, without arousing any suspicions, better assess the political ramifications of the situation while preventing the corporation from sliding into existence by inattention.[35]

Both Lewis and George W. Summers feared the creation of an economic monopoly on the Kanawha. Judge Summers was wary about the result of incorporation: "I think as a corporate body the salt interests might be managed much more to the advantage of the owners, than by the unavoidable competitions among themselves, both in making & selling the salt but the effects of such a consolidation upon the general interests of the county, are a good deal to be feared." He rhetorically asked his brother, "Will not the corporate body gradually become the merchants—the Bankers—the purchasers—and the vendors, of all that will be wanted in making & sending the salt to market?" Summers answered his own question in the affirmative by forecasting "that this state of things would be brought about, as soon as capital can be provided by admitting New Share holders, or by reserving annually a part of the profits to be devoted to this end."[36]

Caused by the issue's discussion near the end of the legislative session, the vehement opposition of small manufacturers, and the subtle reluctance of the Kanawha County delegate to support incorporation wholeheartedly, the failure to secure legislative sanction forced all salt makers to renew internal attempts to seek some arrangement for mutual accommodation. Decentralization had created the economic atmosphere for renewed attempts at centralization. The desperate industry had not shared in the general economic prosperity of the time. In the absence of production and marketing controls, all manufacturers, regardless of size and relative financial strength, would suffer continued losses and eventual ruin.

8

Hewitt, Ruffner & Company and Depression, 1836–1846

In the late autumn or early winter of 1835 all Kanawha salt manufacturers met to initiate negotiations for an arrangement to control their industry so that they could avert financial disaster. William Tompkins later recalled, "I do not think any one could be called a leader in forming the company—at least I did not hear of any who were not." At the first meeting, with James C. McFarland presiding, the salt makers appointed a committee composed of Charles G. Reynolds, John D. Lewis, and others to lay before the manufacturers propositions for the formation of a salt company that all interests might accept.[1]

Exhaustive negotiations occurred at many meetings throughout the early winter months, as the producers considered various plans and proposals. In January 1836 James Hewitt, hoping to revive the scheme of Armstrongs, Grant and Company, proposed that he become the sole purchaser and marketing agent for Kanawha salt. The manufacturers quickly rejected the idea. In the first few days of February, Hewitt suggested the organization of a joint stock company. Lewis Ruffner remembered, "Little or no hope or expectation was entertained . . . of the formation of a company upon any other plan." No certainty existed that an arrangement for the control of salt production and sales would emerge until February 16, 1836, when the producers consummated various agreements. Upon the suggestion of Andrew Donnally, the salt makers named their new joint stock company Hewitt, Ruffner and Company.[2]

The salt makers created the copartnership for a five-year term, beginning January 1, 1836. A majority vote based on the number of shares could dissolve the joint stock company on January 1, 1839, or in any succeeding January thereafter. The copartners were Richard E. Putney, William Shrewsbury, Charles L. Shrewsbury, Joel Shrewsbury, Jr., and John Rogers, Jr., trading as William Shrewsbury and Company; John Lewis, William R. Cox, Frederick Brooks, Andrew Donnally, John D. Lewis, Moses M. Fuqua, Henry Fitzhugh, James Hewitt, and Luke

Willcox, associated as Hewitt & Willcox; James C. McFarland, Samuel Shrewsbury, Jr., Henry H. Wood, Levi Welch, William Tompkins, Daniel Ruffner, Lewis Ruffner, John D. Lewis, and William D. Shrewsbury, partners in Lewis & Shrewsbury; Bradford Noyes, Jr., Benjamin H. Smith, and William I. Rand, dealing as Noyes, Rand & Smith; Isaac Ruffner, Samuel Q. Anderson, Robert Anderson, and Robert N. Anderson, trading as Samuel Q. Anderson and Company; and Crockett Ingles, Nathaniel Hatch, John Warth, George H. Warth, and Job English, manufacturing as Warth & English.[3]

According to the articles of agreement, the manufacturers formed the company for the purposes "of buying a portion of the Salt made & to be made on the Great Kanawha River . . . for the term and during which this agreement is to exist," of "buying and leasing certain Salt & Coal interests," of "purchasing all articles & provisions necessary to be had and used in carrying on the purposes for which this agreement is entered into," and of "vending . . . Salt, in such markets as may be deemed expedient for the like period."[4] The cashier of the Bank of Virginia described with extreme candor the specific purposes of Hewitt, Ruffner and Company and of centralized salt companies in general: "Advancing the price of Salt to the manufacturer & increasing the value & rents of the property holders who might prefer taking a rent to making Salt." Under centralized management, he continued, a salt company can secure credit easily and operate without vending the produce immediately so that the price can be raised and stabilized. This result made country dealers more willing to handle the commodity without fearing sudden loss. Centralized transportation and marketing reduced the expenses of sale.[5]

The copartners allotted the fifty-four thousand-dollar shares to the respective parties to the agreement, and signatories could subscribe for as many shares as they desired. To raise the capital, the subscribers had to pay into the company 20 percent of the value of their stock before March 15. Two 15-percent installments were due on April 15 and May 15. The remaining half of the value of the subscribed stock fell due in 10-percent increments on the fifteenth day of each of the succeeding five months. If any subscriber failed to pay at the specified times or within twenty days thereafter, the principal agents of the company could sell the defaulted shares. If the shares sold at par value or more, the amount paid in would be refunded to the shareholder or his legal representatives, but if any loss accrued upon the sale, the defaulting shareholder had to compensate the company accordingly.[6]

Under certain conditions, transfer of company shares was possible with the registration of a certificate of transfer. The stock transferred could not be voted if the grantor was indebted to the company unless the prospective grantee paid the debt. The grantee could only vote if he was already a member of the firm or an owner of salt interests in Kanawha County. In addition, the death of any shareholder of subscriber would not dissolve the organization. The dividends accruing to the capital stock of the deceased would be paid to his legal successors, to whom the shares would be transferred.[7]

By written proxy, any shareholder could authorize another person to vote in his place at any meeting or election. Unless otherwise provided, "the majority of voices" would decide every matter. Three shareholders could call stockholders' meetings, but only a meeting with a majority of shareholders present could transact business. Unless otherwise stipulated, a majority of all shareholders, not a majority of shareholders who might be present, decided all propositions submitted for consideration.[8]

Shareholders had to select three principal agents from among themselves to conduct the business of the association. In the election of the agents, each shareholder had one vote regardless of the number of shares held. The duties of the agents mainly concerned the diligent attendance "to the best interests of the company in all the business and transactions thereof." No other member of the company had any direct control over business transactions. The three principal agents enjoyed absolute authority in policy formulation and implementation. They could receive, ship, and market salt, make necessary contracts, execute monetary transactions, and select subordinates to carry out instructions. They had to maintain records of all the firm's business transactions. All books and papers of the company were open to the inspection and examination of the shareholders at all times. Any one of the principal agents could appoint another shareholder to act in his place temporarily if he could not attend to his duties. Removal and replacement were possible in cases of ill health or mental incapacity or if the agent failed to conduct business in an honest and discreet manner.[9]

In their first meeting after the company was organized, the stockholders selected Levi Welch, William Tompkins, and Lewis Ruffner as the principal agents of Hewitt, Ruffner and Company. All three held their offices throughout the existence of the firm. The company also appointed three bookkeepers: James Norton and Levi Welch to keep the salt books and Henry Tompkins to maintain the store books.[10]

No member of the association could use the name Hewitt, Ruffner and Company in any agreement or transaction, in drawing, endorsing, or accepting any note, bill of exchange, draft, check, receipt, or other paper, or in any binding manner unless it was for the sole purpose of achieving the objectives of the company. Any shareholder who improperly used the name of the firm was liable for all losses arising from the misuse.[11]

The principal agents could lease or purchase coal and salt properties in Kanawha County by pledging or binding the funds of the firm for payment. Any such purchase or lease, however, had to be "deemed expedient" by the vote of the majority of shares of the capital stock. The agents also declared dividends, which were paid on the basis of the number of shares outstanding to the stockholders or their legal representatives.[12]

The benefits of any contract made by any subscriber for the purchase and delivery of salt in Kanawha County during the existence of the association were to accrue to Hewitt, Ruffner and Company. If the agents deemed the contract expedient, the company would meet all contractual obligations of the subscriber and assume all benefits. The parties to the agreement and the firm retained the mutual right to sue for breach of any contract or for recovery of debt.[13]

The salt makers who voluntarily desired to purchase the shares of stock were the copartners in Hewitt, Ruffner and Company. No stock was automatically apportioned to specific properties or manufacturers.[14] It was in the interest of the company to spread stock ownership as widely as possible among the producers so that economic interests would be allied directly with the enterprise. The delayed payment feature allowed small and less solvent operators to subscribe for shares. Subscribers also used the Charleston branch of the Bank of Virginia to finance stock purchases through the use of delayed notes payable. Levi Welch, a member of the bank's board of directors, an active organizer of Hewitt, Ruffner and Company, and later one of the firm's three principal agents, declared in public upon formation of the new association that the bank would extend thirty to fifty thousand dollars' credit to those manufacturers who desired to finance stock purchases. Welch said that "the Bank would take this course because it saw that the formation of the company would be a benefit to the County generally."[15]

The original subscribers in Hewitt, Ruffner and Company were Andrew Donnally, James Hewitt, and William Shrewsbury and Company (five shares each); Lewis & Shrewsbury and Lewis Ruffner (three shares each); Frederick Brooks, William R. Cox, Hewitt & Willcox, John Lewis, James C. McFarland, Noyes, Rand and Smith, Richard E. Putney, Daniel Ruffner, and William Tompkins (two shares each); and Samuel Q. Anderson and Company, Henry Fitzhugh, Moses M. Fuqua, Nathaniel Hatch, Crockett Ingles, John D. Lewis, Isaac Ruffner, Samuel Shrewsbury, Warth & English, Levi Welch, and Henry H. Wood (one share each). As each of the fifty shares had a par value of four thousand dollars, the total capitalization of the new association was two hundred thousand dollars.[16]

Andrew Donnally, James Hewitt, and Lewis Ruffner dominated Hewitt, Ruffner and Company. In addition to direct holdings, Lewis Ruffner held an undetermined interest in the three shares belonging to Lewis & Shrewsbury, and Andrew Donnally and James Hewitt owned portions of the two shares subscribed by Hewitt & Willcox. The copartnership agreement did not reveal the full involvement of Hewitt, who had purchased four shares in the names of Richard E. Putney, Isaac Ruffner, and Henry H. Wood for the purpose of concealing the extent of his interest. Immediately after the subscribers affixed their signatures to the agreement, the parties reconveyed the four shares to Hewitt. Full knowledge by small producers of Hewitt's ownership might have jeopardized the creation of the company. Thus Donnally, Hewitt, and Ruffner controlled, directly and indirectly, 44 percent of the company's shares.[17]

Although several large producers did not become shareholders, Hewitt, Ruffner and Company controlled the entire Kanawha production field from 1836 through 1840, with the exception of one firm for a three-year term. Using purchase agreements, lease and re-lease contracts, and dead rents, the association ensnared production facilities and managed market functions for optimal return.[18] The familiar lease and re-lease agreement seemed to be the primary legal instrument employed. The producer would lease his facilities to the company, which would re-lease them to him with specific stipulations concerning purchase prices and reentry rights of the association in case of contract violations. It appears that production controls or limits were not imposed on most manufacturers who signed lease contracts. Most lessors and lessees sold their entire output to the company for a guaranteed price of twenty-three cents per bushel for first-quality salt and twenty cents for second-quality. The company paid half the amount in cash on delivery and the remainder with six-month notes. Goods and merchandise charged by operators at the company store were deductible from the second portion. Manufacturers were liable to a fifty-cent-per-bushel penalty if they sold to any purchaser other than the association. Bonuses were paid on the delivery of high-quality salt.[19]

The absence of some major producers from the joint stock company subscription list did not adversely affect the association, since the company gained control of output by outright purchase. James Bream, Brayton Allen, Silas Reynolds, Isaac Noyes, and Charles G. Reynolds refused to purchase stock. Isaac & Franklin, a single-furnace operation, remained outside, and the major firm of Dickinson & Shrewsbury did not acquire a direct interest in the company.[20] The larger manufacturers who were not stockholders, especially James Bream and Dickinson & Shrewsbury, sold their output to the company for twenty-five cents per bushel. They received a two-cent-per-bushel bonus because they agreed to certain production controls.[21]

The only firm not controlled completely during the existence of Hewitt, Ruffner and Company was Donnally, Noyes and Patrick, a partnership that manufactured and marketed steam salt independently during 1836, 1837, and 1838. Finally, the association was able to purchase the firm's total output in 1839 and 1840 for the premium price of thirty-seven and a half cents per bushel. Levi Welch justified this high price by surmising that coarse salt was "much more valuable than other salt." But at the same time, Frederick Brooks received only twenty-six cents per bushel for the coarse salt produced at his new steam furnace in 1839 and 1840. Brooks's production was already obligated to the company.[22]

Hewitt, Ruffner and Company leased some salt furnaces for the sole purpose of removing them from production. In 1836 the company estimated the number of factories that it should dead rent so that it could market the salt manufactured by active furnaces at a higher margin of profit. Initially, rent payments for keeping a furnace idle ranged from $1,200 to $1,500 annually.[23] In the absence of output restrictions, the active proprietors increased their production by adapting the more efficient Guiteau manufacturing process in rebuilding enlarged furnaces. As a result, the company had underestimated the total Kanawha salt output in the first year and faced a serious marketing problem. Levi Welch later observed that "the Salt was accumulating on the hands of the company to an extent somewhat alarming. . . . and they were compelled to throw idle some of the active furnaces on the best terms they could procure from the proprietors." James Hewitt and other persons interested in the association informed the cashier of the branch bank of Charleston that "there was more Salt made than could be profitable sold & that it would be to the interest of the company to expend 40 or 50 thousand dollars in throwing furnaces idle." In April 1837 Hewitt, Ruffner and Company committed itself to expend around forty thousand dollars annually to dead rent approximately fifteen additional furnaces to reduce production. The company leased the furnaces for a twenty-one-month term and secured the option to retain them an additional two years. It held these dead furnaces until the end of 1840.[24] Because of the company's need to close the factories, proprietors received a much higher rent of $3,000–3,500 per year for each furnace.[25]

Extensive interlocking connections between the stockholders and officers of Hewitt, Ruffner and Company and the directors of the Charleston branch of the Bank of Virginia placed the bank at the dis-

posal of the salt company. Hewitt, Ruffner and Company could effort-
lessly secure from the branch bank necessary capital for business operations. Shortly after commencement of the venture, the bank refused to
lend any money to individual merchants who wished to purchased store
goods in the East, but it readily accommodated the salt company. In
1835 Andrew Donnally, Joel Shrewsbury, and Levi Welch served as
bank directors. James C. McFarland was president of the Charleston
branch from its organization until the Civil War. In 1841 the bank stockholders selected Joel Shrewsbury, Lewis Ruffner, and William R. Cox as
directors.[26]

Hewitt, Ruffner and Company created its own currency, which was
accepted by the Charleston branch of the Bank of Virginia. The notes
issued by the company in payment for manufacturers' salt deliveries re-
sembled bank notes and circulated in the Kanawha Valley as money. A
contemporary later recalled that "the Salt Company's note[s] in those
days were regarded as good as any Bks note & much desired by Debtors
to pay the debts."[27]

The most sordid case of collusion between the bank and the salt
company was the affair of the Tennessee money. It confirmed the worst
suspicions of Judge Lewis Summers. People in Charleston business cir-
cles knew that Hewitt, Ruffner and Company had brought a sizable
quantity of Tennessee currency to Charleston. The currency was circu-
lating below par elsewhere when the Bank of Virginia credited the company's account with the face or par value of the money. After the
company discharged several debts with the Tennessee currency, the
Bank of Virginia refused to accept it.[28]

Hewitt, Ruffner and Company succeeded in its attempt to control
and limit Kanawha salt production. Output had reached a record
1,960,583 bushels in 1835, a 90-percent increase from the 1832 production of 1,029,207 bushels. The salt company stabilized and slightly reduced production in the years of its existence: 1,762,410 bushels in 1836,
1,880,415 in 1837, 1,811,076 in 1838, 1,593,217 in 1839, and 1,419,205 in
1840.[29] Since the company did not have to sell the commodity immediately at a sacrifice in order to raise capital, it regulated shipments in proportion to downriver demand. Quantities of salt actually shipped down
the Kanawha to markets varied considerably with the inspector's returns of the amount manufactured: 1,692,290 bushels in 1836–37,
1,874,879 in 1837–38, 1,810,090 in 1838–39, 1,840,490 in 1839–40, and
1,548,858 in 1840–41.[30] The variation in quantities is owing to the difference between the calendar year employed by salt inspectors and the
adjusted year used by the James River and Kanawha Company officials
in compiling statistics. Also, an estimated eighty thousand bushels of
Kanawha salt per year were consumed locally.[31]

"View of the Salt-Works on the Kanawha," a wood engraving in Henry Howe, *Historical Collections of Virginia* (Charleston, S.C.: Babcock & Co., 1845), 345.

The partners in the firm of Donnally, Noyes and Patrick concluded that it was more profitable to accept a lesser but guaranteed price from Hewitt, Ruffner and Company than to assume marketing risks and collection problems. In 1837 these independent producers had sold their output wholesale to agents for forty-seven cents per bushel, but in the face of risk and intense competition from imported salt, they chose to sell their entire production to the company for thirty-seven and a half cents per bushel. The firm's relatively small output could not support permanent sales agents in western towns, and controlling commission merchants proved virtually impossible. Donnally, Noyes and Patrick restricted one independent agent to sell below the Falls of the Ohio, but he violated his agreement and unloaded a large quantity of salt in Madison, Indiana. The manufacturers lost sales in a very profitable market, and their Madison agent was burdened for nine months with a surplus supply.[32]

In order to avail itself of a guaranteed transportation system for the carriage of imports and salt to and from the Salines, Hewitt, Ruffner and Company acquired interests in four steamboats: the *Hugh L. White*, the *Tide Shylock*, the *Harry Tompkins*, and the *Lynchburg*.[33] The salt company could carry its own supplies on more regular schedules, and it could deliver larger quantities of salt more safely on downriver voyages. Extra income arose from incidental freight and passenger business.

Since the demise of Armstrongs, Grant and Company, Kanawha salt manufacturers had not shared in the general economic prosperity of the 1830s. The formation of Hewitt, Ruffner and Company reversed the trends of the declining price and the lower relative purchasing power of Kanawha salt even in the face of the economic dislocations of 1837 and 1839. After gaining control of production, the company immediately increased local prices from seventeen to twenty cents per bushel to thirty-five to forty cents.[34] Prices in Cincinnati generally remained at a profitable level during the firm's existence. There the mean monthly price even jumped for a short period in excess of seventy-five cents per bushel. Hewitt, Ruffner and Company thus enabled Kanawha salt to buck the downward trend of other basic commodities in the Cincinnati market.[35] Hewitt, Ruffner and Company and Kanawha manufacturers did not, however, emerge unscathed from the national economic crisis of 1839. In the last two years of its existence, the company began experiencing difficulties in collecting payments for salt deliveries. The squeeze seriously affected producers who sought capital to expand or to remodel their plants.

The first phase of the economic disorder in the United States fell in 1837 on financial institutions, but the second phase in 1839 seriously impaired the prosperity of agricultural interests. The fiscal demands of the Specie Circular, the dwindling specie reserves of British creditors' banks, American security sales in foreign markets, and the distribution of surplus national revenue from urban eastern depositories through rural banks to the states fomented a specie crisis. National excesses in speculation in both public and urban land and the precipitously planned internal improvement programs halted. The inability of British firms to rediscount the bills drawn on the southern cotton crop of 1836 caused commercial houses in New Orleans to fail and drag under their New York correspondents. By 1837 New York, Boston, and Philadelphia banks had suspended specie payments. During the next two years commercial revival appeared imminent, when Nicholas Biddle attempted to restore support to the British market for American cotton and other agricultural staples. American bond sales hit an all-time high, and some banks resumed specie payments. In October 1839 the Bank of the United States, Biddle's institution, suspended specie payments, and other domestic banks followed suit. The severe national depression of 1839–43 had begun.[36]

The Panic of 1837 and its aftermath cut Hewitt, Ruffner and Company's profits greatly by creating a large reservoir of unpaid debts. The cashier of the Bank of Virginia in Charleston later observed that there was "a large surplus of bad or doubtful debts due the Company." In 1844 William Tompkins estimated that the bad and doubtful debts due the firm were not less than fifty thousand dollars or more than three hundred thousand. The agents, in a notice dated one year after the dissolution of the firm, warned that indebted individuals and partnerships would incur lawsuits if they did not pay by February 1, 1842. Also, they notified the public of authorized collection agents located outside Kanawha County. In 1846 Hewitt, Ruffner and Company began to sell its bad and doubtful debts at tremendous discounts to individuals who were willing to attempt to collect them.[37]

The organizers of Hewitt, Ruffner and Company expected to clear a million dollars during the five-year operation on an invested capital of two hundred thousand. A later purchaser of stock in the enterprise voiced his high hopes: "From my Knowledge of the business and from information I had received at the time I purchased Stock, I thought they would make a profit of four or five hundred percent."[38] The financial results of Hewitt, Ruffner and Company disappointed the organizers and stockholders. The per-share profit in 1845 was approximately $6,000; additional payouts from 1845 to 1849 raised the profit to approximately $7,550 per share.[39] As William Tompkins later testified, this figure included "the profits on all business done by Hewitt, Ruffner & Co including steamboats, merchandise, groceries, salt and every thing else, except the bad and doubtful debts." In 1844 Bradford Noyes transferred one share of stock of $4,000 par value (which he had purchased for $6,000 from Frederick Brooks) in barter for an estimated value of $9,500 on the assumption that company profits would not exceed $6,000 per share. With the same expectations, Joseph Friend paid $9,000 to William R. Cox for a share but ended up receiving $11,550 by 1849.[40] On a total capitalization of $200,000, Hewitt, Ruffner and Company made in excess of $337,000 by 1849. On each share of stock of $4,000 par value, such a profit annually amounted to 34 percent in simple interest during the term of the company. Contemporaries were disappointed, but most antebellum investors in extractive and manufacturing enterprises would have been satisfied.

After the financial contraction, the producers who rented property or sold their salt under contract to Hewitt, Ruffner and Company enjoyed an economic advantage over the firm's stockholders. Regardless of the difficulties of collecting payments upon sales, the joint stock company had to pay for the furnace property and salt upon delivery or immediately on due dates specified by the lease and delivery contracts. All losses on sales through bad debts and financial failures fell upon the stockholders, not on the producers or lessors. Lewis Ruffner recalled: "I may say with sincerity that the original object was to divide the advantages between the manufacturers renters and Stockholders—But that in a conclusion of the whole matter, the renters & manufacturers had the best of it."[41]

In December 1840 the recession made successful negotiations for an arrangement to succeed Hewitt, Ruffner and Company highly unlikely. As early as 1838 Judge Lewis Summers forecasted a state of industrial collapse because of the excessive capital requirements needed to reactivate properties decayed by the dead rent system. The salt makers had formulated another combination to manage production and marketing, but they could not surmount the contemporary economic situation. Summers predicted the result despite the apparent optimism of the negotiators: "The difficulty of paying dead rents to restrain the quantity . . . combined with the almost impracticability of raising funds to go on with till furnished by sales, will present insuperable bars to their present schemes."[42]

The dissolution of Hewitt, Ruffner and Company and the failure to negotiate another agreement forced all Kanawha salt makers to experience economic adversity. In the absence of production controls and sales management, salt prices plummeted to eighteen to twenty-five cents per bushel on the Kanawha in 1841. Prices struck a disastrous low in the Cincinnati market in 1842 and 1843: sales, if they could be made, were at fifteen cents per bushel. In 1844 prices improved somewhat, to twenty-two to twenty-six cents, but by 1846 salt sold for fifteen to eighteen cents in the Cincinnati market. Annual production increased from 1,419,205 bushels in 1840 to 2,197,887 in 1843 and 3,224,786 in 1846.[43]

Scarcity of capital greatly affected the producers, because they needed funds to refurbish decayed properties and to adapt their furnaces to technological advances. The dead rent system employed by the company left proprietors with deteriorated factories. A salt manufacturer, noting that furnace inactivity was "a very great injury," described the economic result: "A furnace which has been run one year, will go to decay entirely if left idle for three years—it puts a property in such a condition that it cant well be rented out, it costs so much to improve it."[44] In 1841 prudent manufacturers concluded that to remain competitive they had to shift their production process to the steam evaporation method pioneered by Donnally, Patrick and Noyes. The conversion would require between three and four thousand dollars per furnace.[45]

Even when individual producers did invest the necessary capital to remodel their plants, they met with loss. In the summer and winter of 1841 Brayton Allen rebuilt a furnace for active production, but in two years of operation he could not clear enough profit to repay the expenses incurred in restoration. Samuel Hannah and William R. Cox experienced the same difficulty and gladly leased their reconditioned

J.Q. Dickinson & Company Salt Factory, ca. 1930, Malden, West Virginia. Except for housing an area to manufacture chemical by-products such as bromine and calcium chloride, the modern factory had changed little from the antebellum period. Notice brine wells at right and left and the abandoned, brush-covered steps to the river at right for rolling barrels to boats. Courtesy of the West Virginia and Regional History Collection, West Virginia University Library.

property for $1,200 annually in 1842. Richard C.M. Lovell and his brother personally supervised the production of seventy-five thousand bushels of salt on a new steam furnace and lost $5,000 in one year.[46]

Some owners of salt properties devised a way to shift the burden of modernization to adventurous lessees. They would lease a decayed furnace for a five-to-ten-year term on the condition that the tenant improve the property at his own expense. Usually, after improving the furnace, the lessee would default on rental payments. The lessor would reoccupy the new plant and enjoy the fruits of the lessee's sacrifices.[47]

In 1842 the salt manufacturers' outlook descended to even greater depths. In January, Judge Lewis Summers reported that the producers had attempted but failed to form a cooperative production and marketing arrangement. In March, the judge related that the salt makers, who were "depressed and disponding," could not sell salt or collect for that already delivered. One partnership made a general assignment of its assets to forestall creditors from obstructing its business and to induce them to compromise on favorable terms. After presiding at the May term of the Circuit Superior Court of Law and Chancery in Charleston, Summers itemized the wretched financial condition of individual salt makers and appraised the depressing prospects for profitable sales and for reliable collection of receipts. The debts of one partnership exceeded $110,000. In 1841–42 Andrew Donnally had sold $12,000 worth of salt in one area, but his agent could collect only $3,000 of the amount.[48]

By midsummer conditions were slightly better for Kanawha salt makers. Summers observed: "The dark gloom which seemed to overshadow the most indebted salt makers as I am inform^d becoming the means of their relief." The difficult times compelled creditors to accept depreciated salt in payment for loans and debts. Rather than incurring the risk of a lengthy lawsuit that might terminate unsuccessfully or in a trust sale of a deteriorated furnace at a price that could not satisfy the judgment, creditors settled for salt, a commodity of some value, to salvage a portion of the debt. Producers were pleased to discharge debts in this fashion, since salt was plentiful.[49]

Beginning in March 1842 Kanawha salt producers began extensive negotiations to formulate a production and sales plan that all manufacturers would accept. The major obstacles in these attempts to relieve mutual economic distress were the necessity for unanimity and the requirement of adequate capital to initiate an enterprise. Most producers possessed no investment capital, and the few who had the means would not gamble during the depression on the success of a combination. Control of sales would be difficult, because sizable quantities of salt had passed through creditors into many hands. Some manufacturers required immediate cash advances to save themselves from creditors, but sales of salt on this basis were impossible to consummate. Negotiations continued throughout the remainder of 1842 and in January 1843, but such efforts failed. Judge Summers noted "that many of the old furnaces are to be put in operation, and that the prices in the upper markets are receding, as the stock on hand exceeds the demand. . . . salt like everything else continued on the downward march."[50]

Responding to inquiries from Kanawha's congressman, who was preparing for a tariff debate, Levi Welch candidly summarized the salt business for 1842 and 1843 with a price history and bottom-line appraisal. "I am certain a majority of the salt manufacturers have lost during the last two years, a few having ample means of holding up their Salt until wanted in the Markets and economizing in every possible way made a little, while others (and a majority) have been obliged to force sales when the article was not wanted, have lost." He assured his representative that his conclusion could "be sustained by thousands of witnesses."[51]

For a two-year period the salt makers abandoned all hope for the formation of an arrangement for control of production and sales. Half-hearted negotiations between manufacturers resumed in January 1845, but the problems of oversupply and inadequate capital could not be surmounted. Lewis Ruffner reported: "All hope of agreeing upon some general system of management is not abandoned but I confess I have small expectation of a favorable result." Painting a dreary picture of future economic prospects, he related: "The increased pressure on the business of salt making has so upset all calculation of results, that we are now only carrying on a warfare of defences against loss." Ruffner himself abandoned the salt enterprise to engage in a general commission business on Strader's Row in Louisville.[52]

In the winter of 1845–46 the Kanawha salt manufacturers, heeding economic necessity, again attempted to conclude an arrangement. On March 17, 1846, John D. Lewis reported to his agent: "We are still making efforts for a company, but with very doubtful success." Four days later he observed: "The prospects for a salt company has now assumed a very unfavorable appearance."[53] Lewis's assessment of the situation was accurate, as all attempts to agree on common economic goals failed. Fierce rivalry in production and marketing continued, and the price of salt dropped even more. No respite from the downward spiral, which had begun during the final months of the existence of Hewitt, Ruffner and Company, would occur unless the Kanawha salt makers combined.

9

The Kanawha Producers and the Salt Tariff

Shielded by the almost impenetrable Allegheny Mountains and the southward-flowing Ohio and Mississippi rivers, the Kanawha salt producers for more than a decade were not affected by substantial importations of salt to the East Coast and to New Orleans. Before the 1820s tariff rates on salt little concerned Kanawha manufacturers. The steamboat, which conquered the currents that protected Kanawha markets from importations, destroyed this geographic security. Liverpool, Turk's Island and numerous other varieties of foreign salt could compete with the Kanawha product at any location. Kanawha salt makers therefore joined the debate about national tariff policy.

After the development of the western Virginia saltworks, the population of the emergent West grew rapidly. By 1822 Indiana, Illinois, and Missouri had become states. Westerners as salt consumers, however, had economic interests contrary to those of Kanawha producers. These western capitalist desires eventually joined other political interests and vented themselves in national legislative halls.

From the establishment of the new government under the Constitution, salt bore a tariff because it was a commodity that had market characteristics attractive to revenue officials. Alexander Hamilton, first secretary of the Treasury, declared salt to be "one of those objects, which, being consumed by all, will be most productive and yet, from the smallness of the quantity in which it is consumed by any, and of the price, will be least burthensome."[1] During the Federalist administrations, the salt tariff rose from six cents to twenty cents per bushel.[2] Antitariff men and westerners constantly opposed this impost.

Despite philosophical opposition to high tariffs, the Jefferson administration could not initially change the salt impost because of the reluctance of Secretary of the Treasury Albert Gallatin to yield the half million dollars of revenue. He was attempting to reduce the national debt inherited from the Federalists and to meet the financial burdens imposed by the Louisiana Purchase and the Barbary War. Republican philosophy and the general unpopularity of the tariff in western Republican strongholds overcame the policy of retrenchment, though, and the salt duty was repealed on March 3, 1807.[3]

The various embargo acts and the War of 1812 so disrupted the international salt trade that existing American factories could not meet internal demand. As a result, domestic salt establishments east and west of the mountains developed and prospered. Possible future commercial disruptions occasioned by Great Britain led nationalistic Americans to protect manufacturers of necessary articles and supplies with legislation.[4] Wartime expenditures and postwar debt ensured the increase of tariff rates, the principal source of federal revenue. The national debt had risen from $55,963,000 in 1812 to $127,334,000 by the end of 1815. Protection of vital infant domestic industries, the achievement of some measure of solvency, and the fear of another conflict with Great Britain enabled the framers of the Tariff of 1816 to extend the 1813 duty of twenty cents per bushel of salt.[5]

At the same time that the steamboat intruded on western waters and a salt-consuming political constituency grew in the West, annual federal revenue surpluses in the late 1820s ranged from $6,000,000 in 1825 to $9,700,000 in 1830. Arguments of financial expediency would not be an adequate defense against advocates of the repeal of tariff duties on salt. In the first session of the Nineteenth Congress (1826), Senator Levi Woodbury of New Hampshire initiated the first serious questioning of the necessity of the salt tariff. As chairman of the Committee on Agriculture, he maintained that the agricultural interests of the United States sustained the burden of the oppressive salt tariff.[6] In the second session of the same Congress, a full-scale debate on the merits of the salt impost occurred in the Senate. The proponents of full or partial repeal, repeating Woodbury's argument, contended that the domestic salt industry did not require protection, that the wartime duty inhibited agricultural expansion and prosperity, and that the importation of foreign salt should be encouraged in peacetime. Opponents, especially those from New England, feared that the reduction of salt duty would destroy the bounty given to fisheries, because the two issues were interconnected. Moreover, they believed that low duties would not guarantee cheaper salt to the consumer, because salt was not a principal article of trade but was used for ballast or as a filler in incomplete cargoes. Importers would reap the benefits of tariff reduction because they could set their own price on the commodity.[7]

Senator William Henry Harrison of Ohio, posing as a cultivator of the soil, emerged as the spokesman of western consuming interests and as the main assailant on the business practices of Kanawha salt makers. He maintained that the combination of Kanawha producers aroused the exporters of pork and farmers in Ohio because it intended to preclude the importation of foreign salt while raising prices for its own product. Completion of the Ohio canal system would bring New York salt to Ohio, where it also would benefit from the import duty. Attributing all price rises of Kanawha salt to the combination, Harrison contended that the manufacture of salt required little investment. If the Kanawha salt-works were destroyed by tariff reduction, he believed that they could be rebuilt at once in the event of war. In the opening days of the Twentieth Congress, Harrison, introducing a bill reducing the existing salt duty, blamed a price increase on salt in southern Ohio on a combination of Ohio River capitalists. The people of Ohio, he claimed, were at the mercy of these speculators. Reduction of the duty would protect people from Kanawha associations, while supplies of imported salt could be cheaply obtained.[8]

In his last defense of the bill before resigning from the Senate to serve as minister to Columbia, Harrison pledged to counteract the efforts of the "wealthy" Kanawha monopolists to reap high profits at the expense of the West. The burden imposed on agriculture, he thought, was obvious. Livestock production from grazing to meat preservation required plentiful supplies of cheap salt, domestic or foreign. Reduction of the duty would prevent monopolists from increasing the price of domestic salt for farmers.[9]

Some Kanawha salt producers had anticipated renewal of the proposal to reduce salt duties and had made preparations in advance for the mobilization of opinion. Reaction to the Harrison bill by the producers was immediate. At a meeting of the manufacturers of Kanawha County held on January 9, 1828, Joel Shrewsbury, Sr., moved that a committee composed of himself, Lewis Summers, Andrew Donnally, James Bream, Joseph Lovell, Lewis Ruffner, and Isaac Noyes be appointed to consider and recommend to the assembly measures to be adopted on the proposed reduction of duty on foreign salt. The approved committee offered an extensive petition and accompanying documents, which were read and unanimously adopted. The committee was instructed to sign the petition on behalf of all manufacturers and to transmit it to Littleton Walker Tazewell and John Tyler to be presented to the United States Senate. An additional resolution urged the Virginia senators to block Harrison's proposal, which threatened to prostrate the salt industry in western Virginia.[10]

The petitioners urged that the duty on salt not be reduced and suggested that it could be raised if Congress desired to protect domestic manufacturing. The committee recounted the price history of salt from the time of first settlement in the West until 1827. While the price of imported salt on the East Coast increased during the War of 1812,

Kanawha producers furnished salt to western consumers at a reduced price of fifty to sixty-two and a half cents per bushel. The army of the Northwest was supplied with provisions preserved with Kanawha salt. After the Treaty of Ghent, a depression had overcome the Kanawha salt industry. Ignoring some other basic reasons, the petitioners attributed this economic occurrence to two causes: the establishment of competing saltworks throughout the West, which enjoyed transportation advantages in local markets; and the influx of foreign salt originally used as ballast in transoceanic trade at New Orleans and the carriage of the article from that point by the western steamboat to inland ports. On descending voyages, the steamboats carried full cargoes of bulky agricultural products, whereas on return trips, they brought more valuable but lighter goods. To complete their tonnage capacity, captains filled their holds with imported salt. The steamboat had aided in forcing the price of Kanawha salt down as low as twelve cents per bushel in 1827.[11]

Joseph Lovell and Lewis Ruffner compiled economic data concerning the Kanawha salt manufacturers. Of the sixty-five existing furnaces, nine were idle. The sixty-one brine wells could potentially supply one hundred furnaces. A 0.074-percent rate of return (not deducting interest on investment) was realized on a total investment of $585,000, which yielded a profit of $43,285. Enumeration of the labor force, the consumption of coal and agricultural products, and iron products employed in erection and repair of factories was forwarded as evidence of the economic importance of the industry.[12]

In describing salt production in the United States, the petitioners cited evidence attempting to prove the inadequacy of the salt tariff for protection. Appealing to patriotic motives, they noted that three-quarters of the imported salt came from Great Britain and its dependencies, which excluded American foodstuffs and levied high taxes on American tobacco. The threat of the discontinuance of the duty on New England fisheries was wisely emphasized for the purpose of securing political allies: "We are naturally brought to inquire, what influence will this measure exercise over our fisheries, that nursery of American seamen and important source of natural wealth?"[13]

The petitioners rebutted the proponents of reduction or repeal. The salt tariff was not a war tax: since the conflict, succeeding tariff enactments recognized the duty as a permanent part of the revenue system, and its permanency encouraged large domestic enterprises. The argument of denial that the western producer would be greatly affected by repeal or reduction was controverted by the revolutionary effect of the steamboat on internal commerce. The burden on agriculture was nonexistent, since the history of salt prices disclosed that the present duty was inadequate for protection of the domestic salt industry. An adequate domestic supply would ensure the absence of financial burden. Destruction of the American industry would not guarantee cheap imported salt. "To rely on mercantile patriotism for a supply on the terms to which the price of salt might be, in the first instance, reduced, would be as vain as to expect the revival of manufactories which foreign production might crush as soon as erected." Internal trade concentrated in Kentucky and Ohio, especially in Cincinnati, would suffer greatly with the further economic decline of the Kanawha salt factories. The Kanawha manufacturers viewed the question of repeal of the salt tariff as a controversy between shipping interests and home manufacturers. They hoped that the shipping interests would "not be further enriched by the spoils of the entire interest now invested in the home manufacture of salt."[14]

On his return from Washington in the summer of 1828, Kentucky senator Henry Clay traveled to Ashland by way of the James River and Kanawha Turnpike, after stopping at the fashionable White Sulphur Springs. On behalf of the salt manufacturers, Colonel Joseph Lovell greeted Clay on his arrival at Kanawha Salines with a short speech on a subject of mutual interest. He pointed out to Clay that he was surrounded by salt factories that the tariff had brought into existence and sustained. As a result of protective duties, the establishments supplied even western states with a cheap, abundant quantity of salt. Reaching his oratorical climax, Lovell emphasized: "It is here, Sir, that the most striking commentary is furnished upon that policy so recently urged, which would annihilate within this narrow valley nearly a million of capital, impoverish some hundreds of respectable and deserving families, under the pretext of cheapening salt to consumers by [delivering] them up to the rapacity of foreign manufactories, and foreign merchants." In his reply, Clay testified to the importance of Kanawha salt and revealed an awareness of the problems of the industry. Endearing himself to many Kanawha salt makers, he asserted that "the prosperous state of manufacturers of a necessary of life, in this neighborhood" illustrated his American system.[15]

In the Twenty-first Congress, Senator Thomas Hart Benton, after seizing the cudgel dropped by his fellow westerner William Henry Harrison, became the personified bête noire for the advocates of a salt duty and especially for Kanawha producers. In his memoirs, Benton claimed to have been a disciple of Nathaniel Macon, who viewed the salt duty with great hostility because it burdened an article of necessity. In recounting his senatorial career, he looked upon the salt tariff as a "curse," an "odious measure," a "political blunder," and "an impiety."[16]

Senator Benton's battle over the continuation of the salt duty and fishery bounties terminated only with his last term in the Senate and deserves to be compared with his well-known positions on hard money and the Second Bank of the United States.

Between February and May 1830, during the first session of the Twenty-first Congress, Benton, launching a crusade that was to occupy his attention for two decades, achieved partial success in his fight for repeal of the salt duty. Congress enacted a House-originated bill that reduced the salt duty to fifteen cents per weighed bushel after December 31, 1830, and to ten cents after the end of 1831.[17] Although legislative support for partial and full repeal was greater in the House of Representatives, the rationale behind the movement was best expressed by Benton in Senate debate.[18] The Magnificent Missourian's original bill not only provided for elimination of the salt impost but also proposed to abolish allowances to fishing vessels and bounties on exported fish.[19]

Benton was the first to risk the enmity of powerful domestic interests by linking the salt duty and the New England fishing bounty for their common destruction. Intensive study of the legislative history of the seemingly hallowed programs had revealed to him their mutual dependency. Since the salt tariff was the foundation of fishing bounties and allowances, the westerner thought that "they should sink and fall together." He wrote, "It is a heavy tax on the farmers of the West, who export provisions; and no tax at all, but rather a source of profit, to that branch of the fisheries to which the allowances of the vessels apply." Exporters of provisions (i.e., westerners) should also receive a bounty, as they had before 1807. The salt tariff renewed in 1813 had, Benton declared, made "fish of one and flesh of the other ever since."[20]

The primary reason why Benton favored repeal of the duty on imported alum salt was that the article was indispensable to the provision trade of the United States. "The Western county is the great producer of provisions; and there is scarcely a farmer . . . whose interest does not require a prompt repeal of the duty." The Missourian viewed the Union as consisting of three sections: the Northeast, the South, and the West. The salt duty and the fishery bounty only benefited the Northeast. The Northeast made solar salt that was used by the fisheries, while they drew money from the Treasury under laws intended to compensate them for the duty paid on imported salt employed in packing. The South, with few saltworks and no fisheries, was penalized by the duty. According to Benton, however, the West was the "true seat of the most oppressive operations of the salt tax." The West's prosperity depended on the exportation of many items preserved with salt. Salt was needed in raising hogs and cattle and was used in preparing beef, pork, bacon, cheese, and butter for market. Next to reduction of public land prices,

Benton considered the free trade in foreign salt as the most beneficial program that the federal government could enact for the West.[21]

Considering original cost, Benton charged that the tariff was exorbitant. Before exportation, foreign salt was worth around fifteen cents per measured bushel of eighty-four pounds. The American tariff substituted weight for measure for assessment purposes. Fifty-six pounds, by weight, was the standard bushel for which duty was paid. Retail merchants customarily sold salt at a weighed fifty-pound bushel unit. At retail, the consumer paid about three times the foreign cost for fifty pounds of imported salt.[22]

Kanawha manufacturers reacted to the attempts to reduce the salt duty with expected bitterness. They employed every means to place their case before the national legislative bodies. In 1829 the secretary of the Treasury had been instructed by the House of Representatives to take an inventory of American saltworks. With the submission of pertinent statistical data on the Kanawha industry in compliance with the secretary's request, a Committee on Behalf of the Manufacturers appended a statement of views on tariff reduction. For the most part the committee repeated previous arguments. It asserted that the insufficient tariff was one of the main reasons why the Kanawha factories could not produce at capacity or enlarge. Repeal of the existing duty would "circumscribe most if not all of the Western manufactories." The only economic hope for western producers would be wartime conditions. Domestic competition, said the committee, was the only way to ensure cheap prices while foreclosing the possibility of mercantile monopoly. The Kanawha industrialists also resubmitted to the House and Senate the same petition that they had presented to the Twentieth Congress.[23]

Editorial defense against the charges leveled by Senator Benton began appearing in a Charleston newspaper. The *Kanawha Banner* warned that the West, "for which Mr. Benton seems most to be concerned," would be liable to economic injury if it depended solely on New Orleans for its salt supply. A single, restricted geographic entrance to interior America would be sufficient ground for westerners to fear the possibility of the creation of a monopoly "much more fatal and much more to be dreaded in its consequences, than any that could be created among some fifteen or twenty domestic works." Arguments showed the dependence of the iron industry on salt furnace erection and repair, to encourage domestic iron manufacturers to oppose attempts to repeal the salt duty.[24]

Under the pseudonym Publius, rational refutations appeared to destroy Benton's claim to infallibility in debate on economic matters. The Missourian stated that the duty raised the price of imported salt over

200 percent of its original value and, therefore, constituted a tax on the consumer. Publius noted that Benton based his calculations on the price of salt at the country of origin and did not include transportation costs, which would have increased the price at the port of entry. Moreover, Benton added the merchants' markup for profit to reach his conclusion on the enormity of the tax. Publius observed that the merchant would gather a profit that the consumer would bear regardless of the size of the import tariff.[25]

Publius defended the association of salt manufacturers in forming a sales agency, which had been "christened with the name of *monopoly*" with "wilful perversion" by certain people. The agency created by the association abridged the expenses of sales and afforded different markets a constant and regular supply of salt. The factors appointed by the agency would make a monetary advance to the manufacturer, which enabled him to continue operations. The monetary advance was the only advantage enjoyed by the manufacturer. But Publius did add that "under this arrangement, the manufacturers have the regulation of the price of the article in all the markets, which the competition met with necessarily keeps down." He did not disclose the result in the absence of competition. The consumer benefited from the reduced charges of transportation brought about by the planned deliveries by the agency.[26]

Anticipating the upcoming session of Congress, the salt manufacturers and other interested parties met on November 22, 1830, at Terra Salis to prepare a petition urging the restoration of the twenty-cent duty on foreign salt. The petitioners reviewed the legislative history of the salt tariff, the domestic price history, and executive statements encouraging domestic manufacturing in presenting their case for restoration.[27] Since no petition had been presented in national legislative halls complaining of the salt duty as oppressive or injurious to economic interests and since no mention had been made of the salt duty in the tariff debates of 1824 and 1828, the "most timid relinquished fears of an oscillating policy on the part of the Government in relation to the manufacture of salt." The petitioners surmised that the act of May 29, 1830, reducing the duty not only injured the domestic salt industry but also produced "apprehensions and alarm in the minds of all who are engaged in the great business of manufacturing."[28]

Congress was serving up American industry to British manufacturers in return for the false hope of cheaper salt prices. The petitioners illustrated their point by relating that while Kanawha salt had been scarce in the Cincinnati and Louisville markets in the autumn of 1830 because of low water, an ample supply of the foreign product existed. After Kanawha salt had disappeared in the market, merchants raised the price of foreign salt by one-third. Supplies of imported salt would not guarantee cheap prices in the absence of domestic competition. The Kanawha producers also resented the false comparison of the salt tariff with the *grand gabelle* of France and the taxing system (called the *felo de se* by opponents) of Great Britain. They correctly informed Congress that these hated taxes were not levied on foreign importations or domestic exportations but on salt produced and consumed within the kingdoms.[29]

In reply to charges of domestic production of an impure product, the western Virginia petitioners admitted that the large number of manufacturing establishments meant varying degrees of perfection in preparation. "Time, competition, increasing experience, and wholesome inspection laws, are rapidly diminishing the production of impure salt, and must shortly banish all of that grade from the markets." The producers challenged the comparison of the purity of the Kanawha product with any other, domestic or foreign.[30]

They dismissed the charge of the existence of a monopoly among the western manufacturers of salt for the purpose of increasing prices. "A business carried on almost every tributary of the Ohio, and spread through seven or eight states, is not in its nature susceptible of concerted action or combined operation. So wild a project was never thought of, much less attempted." If this charge was directed at Kanawha producers, it was equally without foundation. The manufacturers in the area had met with great competition in all their markets and had been plagued with overproduction. Impending disaster and financial embarrassment compelled the manufacturers to sell their salt at reduced prices to capitalists who might have sold the commodity at high prices. The Kanawha producers were not a party to this action and did not share in the profits. Other economic reasons prevented a salt monopoly. Increases of price beyond what was "essential to carry on the business" would encourage production by minor western saltworks in weak brine fields and would attract more importations. In the opinion of the western Virginians, the national government had to patronize the domestic salt industry by tariff protection if American demand was to be met. Protection was also the only way to ensure technological progress in the industry. If Congress embarked upon a policy of free trade, the Kanawha entrepreneurs warned, western salt manufacture would become one of the first casualties.[31]

In the second session of the Twenty-first Congress, Senator Benton asked leave to introduce a bill to reduce the duty on alum salt to ten cents per bushel in April 1831 instead of on December 31, to make a second reduction effective on April 1, 1832, and to abolish the duty entirely in April 1833. He felt that the selection of the month of December as a date for the operation of the act was unrealistic because pork packing in the West had usually concluded by that time of the year. In April, salt could be brought to interior markets by the flooded rivers. In his lengthy supporting argument, the Missourian focused attention on testimony taken in 1818 before a committee of the British House of Commons on the repeal of the internal salt tax. He read extended extracts from the statements of Sir John Sinclair, Arthur Young, and ten other eminent British authorities who had testified about the beneficial results of a plentiful supply of cheap salt in manufacturing and agricultural enterprise. In preparation for the Senate session, Benton had circulated questionnaires throughout western states inquiring about the sale and consumption of impure domestic salt and the existence of monopolies in the domestic salt trade. The fifteen inquiries whose answers required the submission of a measure of opinion instead of fact on the part of the respondent were calculated to indict the business practices and the product of the Kanawha factories. Benton read responses to this questionnaire into the record. He also included an anonymous statement of a Kanawha County resident, with the names of the payers and receivers of dead rent deleted (it was Benton's stated objective to expose a system, not to condemn individuals).[32]

Benton then directed his oratorical condemnation at the Kanawha producers. Somewhat erroneously, he claimed that the interior salt trade depended on "one vast and cruel monopoly," and he declared the results to be "double price and scant measure; the whole country districted, allowanced, and stinted; ready money exacted; wells rented from their owners to lie idle; new wells prevented from being dug; overgrown fortunes to the monopolizes, privation, want, and suffering among the people and stock."[33]

The assault upon the salt tariff led many people in the Kanawha Valley to question their political principles in regard to states' rights and governmental economic policy. Dr. John J. Cabell, originally of Lynchburg, Virginia, provides an outstanding example of vested economic interest's affecting political views. Cabell owned a salt furnace on the Kanawha River and had moved to the area to supervise the furnace personally in an attempt to pay his outstanding debts. He also retained a part interest in a states' rights, low-tariff, anti-Ritchie Lynchburg newspaper with his son-in-law Richard K. Crallé, who served as editor and who would later edit the first collection of the papers of John C. Calhoun. Although aware of his son-in-law's views on free trade, Cabell had become alarmed at the attack of southern low-tariff advocates on the salt duty. Confiding his views to Crallé, the salt manufacturer revealed his philosophical plight. Cabell favored free trade in principle, but he thought that he would suffer economic ruin if the tariff on salt was eliminated.[34]

Thomas Hart Benton renewed his attack on the salt duty in the first session of the Twenty-second Congress by attempting to advance the effective date on the second stage of the duty reduction enacted in the previous Congress. Benton moved the referral of his bill to the sympathetic Committee on Finance, but Henry Clay successfully guided the measure to the Senate Committee on Manufactures, over the vehement objections of the Missourian and Senator Robert Y. Hayne.[35] In asserting the primacy of agricultural interests over manufacturing, Benton scored the Kanawha "monopolists" and their alleged business tactics:

Home made salt must be paid for in gold and silver, or their equivalent; foreign salt can be had for our productions, and thus the foreign salt maker is the encourager of domestic industry; the domestic salt maker gives no encouragement to the farmer. He must have the money. At Kenhawa, salt is silver; whatever it is sent, it is for silver; no produce is taken in return. The foreign importers at New Orleans go back freighted with the production of our farms; the agent of the domestic salt makers go back loaded with our money. They ask for the food which we have to spare; we ask for the salt which God and nature makes upon their islands. Shall the Federal Government get between, interdict the exchange, and compel us to give gold for the base salt which will not cure our provisions.[36]

He believed that a reciprocal trade in provisions could be maintained between the West and the British West Indies in exchange for alum salt imported at New Orleans.[37]

The Kanawha salt manufacturers, impressed by the gravity of Benton's accusations, formulated a letter of reply. James Bream, Joseph Lovell, Johnston Armstrong, Lewis Ruffner, Isaac Noyes, James C. McFarland, Richard E. Putney, Daniel Ruffner, Levi Welch, and Andrew Parks addressed their rebuttal to the Senate Committee on Manufactures. They did not regard the isolated remarks of Senator Benton as unusual, "but when viewed in connection with previous attempts to cast odium upon the works established in their county," the comments demanded a reply. Benton had charged that the salt duty was oppressive to the farmer, that it kept the domestic salt price inflated, and that it allowed the salt makers to combine to impose high prices on the consumer. To the manufacturers, the price history of domestic salt seemed to refute this charge. Low salt prices had benefited the farmer as a result of the increased domestic production stimulated by the tariff.[38]

The manufacturers considered Benton's accusation that domestic producers sold their commodity at exorbitant prices, through monopolies, as the most serious. Decreasing salt prices would again seem to have been an adequate refutation of the charge. The Kanawha producers thought that salt factories in twenty-two of the twenty-four states embraced "a diversity of interests and of operations too great to admit of concentrated action for any purpose." Salt production in the West was so widespread as to preclude monopolies. It seemed that the charge of monopoly was "ill-founded, if not paradoxical." As far as the industry in Kanawha County itself was concerned, the allegation of combination was erroneous. The salt manufacturers had sold their entire output to capitalists when they were threatened with economic ruin. Later a sales agency had been created to advance money on salt deliveries, but when it existed, the salt price was 15 to 20 percent lower than usual. "Yet this arrangement . . . has been represented a monopoly; and . . . the attempt was made, by means of misguided, unfair, and *ex parte* testimony, to load it with odium before the Senate of the United States." The signers pledged to prove any assertion that the Committee on Manufactures might desire. Furthermore, they looked to the committee "to detect and expose the misrepresentation and interested testimony with which the enemies of the protective system" sought to oppress them.[39]

The letter of the Kanawha proprietors was referred to the Senate Committee on Manufactures by consent. Benton believed the communication to be both encomiastic and disparaging. He particularly objected to its use as evidence. He wanted to obtain countervailing testimony by empowering the Committee on Manufactures to make examinations of witnesses in writing, under oath, on the salt industry and to report the evidence to the Senate.[40]

After some debate, the Senate, indulging Benton's wishes, agreed to his resolution, which instructed the Committee on Manufactures to ask, by letter, the Kanawha producers twelve questions concerning the price history of Kanawha salt for a ten-year period, transportation costs, restriction of production by combinations, dead rents, wholesale pricing, weighing procedure, and the establishment of sales agencies in western districts. Upon receipt of the replies, Senator Mahlon Dickerson's Committee on Manufactures recommended indefinite postponement of Benton's bill because the interest of the country would not be served by the proposal and because sufficient time had not elapsed to ascertain the effect of the act of May 29, 1830, upon the domestic salt trade.[41]

The storm of controversy that arose in the South in reaction to the tariff of 1832 accomplished what Thomas Hart Benton had never been able to do. The compromise tariff of 1833, which was intended to appease South Carolina, greatly affected the salt rate. Henry Clay's role in this controversy was not especially pleasing to his Kanawha sympathizers. The tariff of 1833 provided for a gradual ten-year decrease of all duties in excess of 20 percent of the value of the imported product. In 1842 a uniform ceiling of 20 percent on all tariff items was to be imposed. The salt rate, at ten cents per weighed bushel, was in excess of 80 percent of the value of imported alum salt. The immediate effect of the compromise was the reduction of the salt duty to eight cents. In 1843 it was to be approximately three cents per fifty-six-pound bushel.[42]

Congress did not debate the salt duty for a few years after the passage of the compromise tariff of 1833. In February 1837, in the second session of the Twenty-fourth Congress, Senator Silas Wright of New York renewed the issue by introducing a bill that proposed to reduce duties on certain imported items and to allow free importation of salt. Reaction to the bill was vehement, especially on the part of John C. Calhoun, because it raised the question of whether the Wright bill would violate the compromise. Ultimately, the Senate enacted the free salt bill, but the session expired before the House of Representatives could act.[43]

In his legislative conflicts before 1839, Benton had linked domestic salt manufacturers who supported a high tariff with New Englanders who favored the continuance of governmental bounties and allowances to fisheries, but never had he openly attacked both interests simultaneously as he did in the third session of the Twenty-fifth Congress. Most New England congressmen opposed the Missourian's salt crusade because of their suspicion of his ulterior motives regarding the fishery interests and because of the development of a coastal salt industry. With Benton's introduction of a bill, the same one that had been enacted in the Jefferson administration, proposing to abolish the salt duty and the fishery bounties and allowances, the advocates of the interests of King Cod assumed a belligerent legislative stance that prevented passage of the measure. Although New England cod fisheries received most of his attention, Benton also used the occasion to attack the monopolizers of the interior, whom he accused of depriving western America of a salt supply and of extorting exorbitant prices from the helpless farmer. "At the Kanawha, the old games of monopoly, with paying wells and furnaces to lie idle, that the few that worked might get double price, has again been renewed."[44]

Three days into the first session of the Twenty-sixth Congress, Senator Benton gave notice that he would introduce a bill abolishing salt duties and fishery bounties and allowances at the earliest opportunity. He concentrated his efforts in this session, however, on the formation of a propaganda base from which he could level his attacks. Included in his material were the responses to a Benton-framed questionnaire that was intended to indict Kanawha producers and statements by respectable Missourians condemning the connection between banks and the salt manufacturers. The proposed publication ran into stiff but temporary legislative resistance. When Benton reported the documents from the Committee on Finance and moved that they be printed, Henry Clay declared that he would oppose the printing of another "bundle of trash". Senator William Allen of Chillicothe, Ohio, goaded by Clay's satiric remark, noted that Clay had previously urged the public printing of all documents relating to the Second Bank of the United States but that the Kentuckian would readily disregard the condition of mechanics, farmers, and banks in favor of one rapacious monopoly. He warned that the salt associations were formed "to suppress, not to develope, the natural resources of the country." The Kanawhans create a triangular monopoly, he said: they control bank capital in the region, salt factories, and the sale of the article.[45]

Clay energetically scored the revolutionary tendency of Allen's remarks. Attacking monopoly was but a new way to destroy private property. "A man may not use his property in what form he pleases, even if sanctioned by the laws of the community in which he lives, without being denounced as a monopolist." Only the Virginia legislature should be concerned about state business operations. The dangerous agrarian leveling spirit that first attacked the Second Bank of the United States and then all banks, Clay warned, now threatened the domestic salt and fishing industries.[46]

Benton declared that he embarked upon this project with much more enthusiasm than he manifested in the cause of "the most glorious expunging resolution." He considered this crusade as an attack "upon an odi[o]us, infamous, and diabolical monopoly; a monopoly which would cover its authors and defenders with blushes, if the papers . . . could be printed." The Missourian regretted to hear the old Federalist monarchical cry of attack on private property. "A parcel of salt monopolizers who rent furnaces and wells to be idle—who hire owners of salt water not to dig for it—who poison their salt by adulteration—who stint the supply to the community—who district the country and allowance it, and allow it not half enough; their monopolizers, by their defenders on this floor," Benton asserted, "cry out that their property is attacked when we propose to prove their monopoly, and its abuses, and to repeal the salt duty which, by impeding the importation of foreign salt, enables them to monopolize all that is made at home." Eventually all objections to the printing of the materials relating to the salt industry were removed.[47] Senator Benton's intention was to defeat his opponents with the sheer weight—by poundage if not by logic—of statistical facts.

Leading the exposé was Benton's questionnaire and its anticipated responses. On September 1, 1839, the senator sent a letter to his constituents asking for testimony and facts on the salt trade for the next congressional session. He urged citizens to meet in public to frame responses. The thirty questions, revealing the usual assumptions of Benton and other westerners, were to elicit responses about matters on which Kanawha salt manufacturers were universally condemned: use of the fifty-pound bushel, short weight by drainage and drying of the product, inadequate supply, impurities, price fixing, and the propensity to combine to control production.[48]

On March 30, 1840, Senator Benton managed to have a select committee of three members appointed to produce a report on the origin and nature of the fishing bounties and allowances. The three were Benton, Alexander Outlaw Anderson, a James Knox Polk ally from Knoxville, Tennessee, and John Davis of Massachusetts. Since Anderson came from a section of Tennessee that had long been plagued by the lack of transportation facilities and the resultant high price of salt obtained at King's Salt Works on the Holston River in southwestern Virginia, Benton had a majority to uphold his views. In twenty days, the select committee reported its findings.[49] The majority, Benton and Anderson, presenting its case in great detail, asserting that the fishery bounties and allowances were based on the salt tariff, that there was no basis in reason, law, or the Constitution for the exactions, and that the free importation of foreign salt was necessary "to relieve the country from the oppressions of a salt monopoly in the west." It concluded that all duties on salt and all bounties and allowances to northeastern fisheries should be repealed.[50]

Davis, in the minority, cautioned that establishment of legislative motive for any statutory enactment was most difficult. Although he concentrated on the effects of repeal upon his New England constituency, Davis displayed a detailed understanding of the domestic salt trade. He did not believe that foreign salt could ever seriously affect Kanawha salt producers, because they could always undersell importers. The cause of occasional high prices of salt in the West was low water, but an importer could never incur the risk of accumulating a large quantity of foreign salt for fear of resumption of normal transport conditions. Only competition can break the effects of a monopoly, Davis said. Therefore the duty of six cents per bushel does not produce high prices for domestic salt, and its abolition would not bring relief. If the duty is repealed to injure "western monopolies, as they are styled, it will accomplish no such end, but will leave their power undiminished, and their control of the market unimpaired.[51]

The first session of the Twenty-sixth Congress marked the high point of Benton's fight against continuance of the salt tariff and fishery bounties and allowances.[52] The Missourian was to continue a token opposition until the end of his senatorial career, but he was never successful. The advent of a Whig administration immediately forestalled such efforts, and for the next two decades, change forced Benton himself, his political party, and his Jacksonian philosophy on matters regarding the Union, economics, and slavery into political obsolescence.

The Panic of 1837 caused a decrease in governmental revenues and, therefore, created a serious burden for those who advocated a decrease in any tariff rate. The embarrassed Treasury could provide a favorable argument for protectionists. A Whig administration, tempered by the accession of Tyler, put Clay and Whigs of various stripes in control of Congress. After difficulties between Clay and President Tyler over the distribution of income from the sale of public lands were resolved, the protective tariff of 1842 was enacted. The specific salt duty was established at eight cents per weighed bushel. The ad valorem rate, according to Senator Benton, was 50 percent on Liverpool blown, 100 percent on Turk's Island, 200 percent on St. Ubes, and 300 percent on Adriatic salt.[53]

In Polk's administration, the tariff controversy resumed under the direction of Robert J. Walker, secretary of the Treasury. When the Walker tariff was first proposed, salt appeared on schedule D, which provided for a 25-percent ad valorem rate. Opponents of the salt duty succeeded in removing the item from schedule D but could not place it on the free list. After the confusion of votes on many tariff articles in 1846, salt emerged as an unenumerated article, which placed it on the 20-percent ad valorem list.[54]

In 1850, in his last senatorial term, Thomas Hart Benton served notice that he was going to ask leave to introduce a bill to suppress the salt duty.[55] The Senate, however, faced more important questions. By the 1850s the salt tariff was also of questionable importance to Kanawha producers, who were more affected by domestic competition, by the transportation revolution, and by basic demographic alterations in the Midwest than by foreign importations. The growth of railroad systems solved the problem of the West's salt supply. The western economy had changed the Kanawha salt industry more in twenty-five years than had Senator Benton's perceptions of it.

10

White Labor, Subsidiary Industries, and Furnace Managers

The dramatic expansion of the saltworks catapulted the Great Kanawha Valley from hunting and trapping and agricultural economies. The Salines became a booming manufacturing and commercial area of noxious reputation, vastly different from the typical rurality of the West. The development fostered many auxiliary businesses and occupations that met the needs of the extractive enterprise. The commercial economy of the valley, remarkably diversified for its time and location, depended upon the cyclical salt industry, which reacted to domestic agricultural markets.

Travelers at Kanawha Salines invaribly commented on the scale of activity, the noise, dirt, dreary appearance, and the coarseness of the inhabitants. One experienced observer, noting the salt furnaces dotting the riverbanks for several miles, the smoke-saturated air, the rattling of coal trains, and the numerous steamboats and other craft, compared the area to a large city. The candid Anne Newport Royall described the place as "dismal," with "the sameness of the long low sheds; smoking boilers; men, the roughest that can be seen, half naked; hundreds of boat men; horses and oxen, ill-used and beat by their drivers; the mournful screaking of machinery, day and night."[1]

Economic opportunity attracted people who had various motives, sordid and honorable. The unenviable reputation of white laboring class caused the Salines to become notorious among respectable citizens. The judgment seemed to be justified, as the legal record of Kanawha County tells of a diversity of crime, carnal and otherwise, emanating from the saltworks. Contrasting the moral condition of Cincinnati, Henry Ruffner informed his father that "it is a pleasing sight to me just emerging from the prophanity drunkenness & other vices of

Kanawha to enter a place where scarce any thing of the kind is seen or heard." A Presbyterian missionary observed in 1819 that "the state of society" of the Salines was "deplorably immoral and irreligious." Conceding that a few honorable and genteel men whose manners and abilities would distinguish any community lived in the area, Royall generally found that the men of the Salines "gloried in a total disregard of shame, honour and justice, and an open avowal of their superlative skill in petty fraud." In contrast, she found that the women possessed "the domestic virtues in an exemplary degree; they are modest, discreet, industrious and benevolent."[2]

The salt industry, though fostering a rough-hewn citizenry, did support a mobile society that had access to western and international markets. It maintained a sizable retail trade in the Kanawha Valley that introduced trade goods from eastern and western domestic centers. The many salt company stores sold general merchandise, dry goods, and produce in order to acquire cash, to barter, and to supply the work force. Companies preferred to pay their white labor and independent artisans in merchandise so that they could gain the profit on the markup and could conserve their cash. The company stores did not exercise any substantial social and economic control over the labor force, except in individual cases. Many stores competed in the accessible Kanawha Salines, and in an economy characterized by labor scarcity, companies generally could not abuse their positions. Certainly owners encouraged their workmen to trade at their stores by extending credit in advance of wage payments. Individuals could spend in excess of their means and lose economic freedom. In 1825 a white blacksmith hired himself to a salt company for one year for a wage of $200.00; during the year, however, he accumulated a store account of almost $437.55.[3]

The transient laborers on the river contributed to the disorderly society. As early as 1816 several prominent Kanawha Count residents petitioned the Virginia General Assembly for the incorporation of a police district encompassing the saltworks and Charleston. They complained that statutes intended to accommodate a virtuous yeomanry could not cope with watermen and other laborers. The petition contended that "vice immorality and almost every kind of outrage which destroyes and interupts the peace tranquility and good order of civil society" characterized this group. Two civil cases support this claim. In 1833 two boatmen, who had entered a tavern, had broken bottles, glasses, and a pitcher, had smashed chairs, had severely beaten a visitor, and had assaulted the proprietor with two-pound weights in their hands, were arrested. Four years later, four thugs entered the cabin of a moored steamboat, the *Davy Crockett*, threatened to take possession of the boat, indicated an intention of cutting the wheel ropes, and sang vulgar songs. They also threw a tumbler at someone and threatened another passenger with a drawn knife.[4]

Individual flatboat pilots, conversely, enjoyed a reputation for dependability, as they had to possess a vast store of knowledge about the rivers they plied. The pilot was the absolute ruler on his craft from the time it left the Salines until it reached the place of delivery. He selected the crew of five to nine men, including a cook, and made all decisions about operations.[5] Sometimes he paid the crew and, if required, stayed at the final delivery place to sell the flatboat. The pilot's reputation with salt companies rested upon his accident rate (his record of losses). In recommending a pilot by the name of James Woodyard, a Pomeroy, Ohio, man noted that Woodyard had never suffered an accident and added: "He had been running the river from his infancy, I believe, and I consider him a better boatman than many who take boats out of Kanwha."[6]

If a cargo was sunk, the owner of the salt incurred the financial loss. W.S. Laidley, in his sometimes romantic history of Charleston and Kanawha County, asserted that the owner never questioned the pilot's handling of the boat in case of loss, because it was assumed that accidents were unavoidable, and the salt makers readily gave the pilot another load to guide to market. Irate businessmen, on the contrary, did not quickly forgive losses of salt. Donnally, Steele and Company sought two thousand dollars in damages from Thomas Russel, who sank 191 barrels of salt in the Kanawha River, but later dropped the suit. William Steele and Company sued a man hired to carry 90 barrels of salt over Johnston's Shoals who lost 22 of them in the Kanawha River. Steele, Donnally and Steeles loaded four flatboats directed by Samuel Moore with 1,568 barrels to be carried for fifty cents each to Nashville. When Moore lost one boat containing 490 barrels in the Ohio River, the salt company immediately brought suit for four thousand dollars in damages. One pilot lost several barrels on Elk Shoals in the Kanawha River after being warned by the manufacturer about overloading his craft. The salt maker later sued for the value of the lost cargo. Donnally and Noyes sued Thompson Trackwell for losing 450 barrels of salt and a flatboat in the Ohio River, but the jury in the circuit superior court found for the defense.[7]

One salt maker, informing his partner of the perils that their flatboats faced from an Ohio River ice floe, revealed his true concerns. An informant had told him that on one salt boat "the hands was upon Top the Boats imploring assistance from God, that man could give them none." The manufacturer wrote, "The whole River is in a bustle some about their Children Brothers & Husbands and Rest of us about our Salt."[8]

Another court case reveals the individual initiative required of a pilot on a voyage and the unappreciative responses of a salt company. In 1841 Stephen Rooks piloted a flatboat loaded with salt from Donnally and Noyes to Maysville, Kentucky. Rooks received a salary of $1.25 per day, and the hands earned 62.5 cents per day plus $3.00 each to pay for the return home. When Rooks's boat entered Thirteen Mile Chute in the Kanawha River, it struck a log and ran into the side of the chute. The boat following, steered by Elisha Bell, unavoidably crashed into Rooks's vessel, breaking its corner studding. All provisions for the journey were ruined, along with sixty barrels of salt. The men present unloaded the damaged flatboat and removed the log from the chute. Rooks repaired and reloaded the vessel.[9] On his trip to Maysville, he attempted to purchase bacon, potatoes, and onions with salt but had to pay cash. Rooks's total expenditures for wages, repairs, and provisions were $160.58. The salt company refused to pay $54.58 because of the lost salt, and the pilot had to bring an inconclusive suit to recover the balance.[10]

Pilots and hands were usually paid at the point of delivery. Generally the agent or merchant receiving the salt would pay a lump sum to the pilot, who would in turn pay the hands. Usually, if a commission merchant paid the boatman, the amount would be credited to the cash advance and purchase price on the salt delivered. Allowances were made for the number of days in transit and the cost of the return home.[11]

Dependence upon semi-independent workmen and flatboats for transportation of their product to market prevented salt makers from achieving complete control over deliveries. Salt companies, pilots, and boatmen had to share mutual trust. Boatmen could disregard instructions. Unscrupulous watermen could peddle salt as their own in distant river towns. Misunderstandings among parties hampered efficient deliveries. Ruffner, Donnally and Company experienced difficulties with boatmen who would not go beyond certain towns on the Ohio.[12]

An important subsidiary activity was the cooperage industry. Before the advent of the cardboard box, trade goods were shipped in wooden crates and barrels. Cooperage imparted some value to the forests bordering waterways that led to the Salines and furnished employment to craftsmen and farmers. In 1828 the industry consumed 130,000 barrels, worth $32,000. In 1850, 421,196 barrels, appraised at $104,000, were used to pack Kanawha salt. The depression that affected the salt industry seriously struck the wood products enterprises: 1860 consumption of barrels dropped 53 percent from the 1850 levels to 199,160 barrels, valued at $55,360.[13]

Although independent white coopers supplied the industry with barrels throughout the antebellum period, many salt manufacturers integrated the packaging function into their factories, where they used mostly slave labor. In 1820 twelve independents with thirty-five men and eleven women and two salt makers with five men and one woman manufactured 41,000 barrels on the Kanawha.[14] In 1830 the salt producers estimated that the thirty-one firms employed two hundred coopers. In 1850 in Kanawha County, twenty-two independent barrel makers employed ninety-two men and seven women. From raw materials such as 3,787,000 pieces of cooper stuff worth $16,703 and 1,050,020 hoop poles worth $5,505, the independent coopers fabricated 184,500 barrels valued at $47,255. One independent manufacturer, John Williams, produced 800,000 pieces of cooper stuff and 100,000 hoop poles worth $3,600 with a steam mill and eleven workmen. He made 30,000 barrels with part of the materials and sold the surplus.[15]

The labor force in cooperage was mixed, slave and free white, but it is impossible to determine the percentages of each. Free white coopers who worked for salt companies usually were paid by the barrel, but a few received high monthly wages. In 1838 a cooper made thirty-three and a third dollars per month. Sometimes the white cooper who contracted his services to a salt maker held slave coopers. Andrew Donnally employed cooper George C. Adcock by promising him, his family, and his workmen board and lodging. In addition, the salt manufacturer undertook to provide the cooper with all raw materials and thirteen cents for each finished barrel. Adcock and five workmen produced 14,990 barrels in 1835 and 14,833 barrels in 1836.[16]

Some coopers agreed to supply barrels and to pack them in a company's salt house. Payment was based on the number of bushels of salt packed. Men who supplied barrels and packed salt in 1830 received board and lodging and four cents for each bushel packed.[17] Payment to white labor for packing salt, exclusive of furnishing the barrel, was three cents per barrel.[18]

Salt firms would pay cash for good salt barrels, but they adopted a policy of defraying part of the expense with goods from their stores. Armstrongs, Grant and Company advertised in 1827 that it would "give the highest price for 50,000 good merchantable Salt Barrels . . . one half in cash and the other in goods or supplies, payable on delivery." Coleman and Company paid a Kanawha County farmer nine dollars in cash and the remainder in store credit for two hundred salt barrels. Store owners and individuals would readily accept substantial salt barrels in promissory notes in lieu of cash. John Wilson promised to discharge his fifty-dollar store account in cash, salt, or salt barrels. In 1831 Larkin C. Roy agreed to pay on order three hundred good salt barrels for value received.[19]

Some farmers in the valley supplemented their incomes by manufacturing cooper stuff (staves, headings, and hoop poles) from their forest land. In 1820 cooper shops used over 1,000,000 pieces of this material to fabricate salt barrels. One man floated 19,300 pieces of cooper stuff from Big Sandy Creek down Elk River to the Salines. In the 1830s John Greenlee and Stokes Prewitt delivered hoop poles at seven dollars per thousand.[20]

Flatboats were the single most economical method of transporting Kanawha salt to major markets. The steamboat never displaced the refined flatboat. The flatboat dominated the antebellum Ohio and Mississippi river basins in the downstream shipment of raw materials, bulky semimanufactured products, barreled items, and heavy manufactured goods such as iron. Although some risk was involved, flatboats offered advantages over steamboats that the salt producers could not disregard. A manufacturer without a steamboat investment could avoid paying higher shipping charges by purchasing flatboats in the neighborhood. Individualistic entrepreneurs enjoyed market flexibility and controlled the destination of flats to a degree that was impossible with commercially operated steamboats. Besides representing a cheaper freight cost, the flatboat had value in reuse or as lumber after it reached the market. It could reach towns on shallow water that was impassable for steamboats. Also, local carpenters could quickly assemble flatboats in response to transportation needs. Flatboats were elastic to productive capabilities and market demands, and they did not require a high fixed investment.[21]

The adaptation of the flatboat to salt hauling was rapid. The first boats to carry Kanawha salt were pirogues fashioned from large poplar trees, that were sixty to eighty feet in length. Salt manufacturers preferred large boats that bore large payloads, although a few smaller boats were needed to serve some tributary river markets. The favored craft was one at least sixteen feet in width and sixty feet in length, with sides in excess of four feet. The ideal boat had sweeps and oars of natural size (not sawed), had poplar planking at least one and three-fourths inches in thickness (if oak, the planking to be one and a half inches thick), and was well caulked with hemp and flax.[22]

The construction of numerous flatboats fostered the growth of a lumber industry on the Kanawha River and its tributaries. Water-powered and steam sawmills developed to cut the planking needed. Salt companies for the most part depended upon these mills and independent carpenters to construct boats. In 1820 six independent builders and three salt makers, employing forty-seven men and thirteen women, manufactured 93 boats worth between $150 and $200 each. In 1850 eight independent boat builders employing twenty-one workmen built 104 craft, and three sawmill operators built an additional 24.[23]

Prices paid for boats varied with the condition and quality of construction. Payment was made by the foot, so larger flats commanded a higher price. Boat prices were also seasonable, with the highest prices being offered in spring and summer, when most salt was floated to market. Salt makers who purchased boats in winter incurred great risks of possible damage by freezing or complete loss when the ice broke up on the river.[24]

Extremely specialized occupations developed to meet the demands of salt furnace operators for skilled labor and for certain types of equipment. Although some salt firms drilled wells with their own workmen and tools, one man emerged as a specialist. Jabez Spinks and various associates contracted drilling work in the Salines. He drilled new wells, rebored and deepened old ones, and performed other tasks to secure increased brine production. In 1823 Spinks and his associate Middleton Harman, using a spring pole bored wells four hundred feet deep for one to three dollars per foot (the price increased with the depth). In 1844 Spinks and another cohort used a steam engine to drill more than one thousand feet and tubed the well with copper pipe.[25]

The use of noncorrosive copper in well tubing created the trade of coppersmithing. In 1850 two firms in Kanawha Salines specialized in the manufacture of tubing and copper repair work: Doyle and Kline and H.W. Reynolds and Company. In one year H.W. Reynolds and Company consumed 300 pounds of solder, 200 pounds of tin, and 1,000 bushels of charcoal, brass, and other miscellaneous materials worth $701. Two workmen fabricated 9,840 pounds of copper tubing that had a finished value of $3,936. The firm's yearly repair work netted $2,000. Deducting a plant investment of $300, a raw material bill of $3,558, and an annual average wage for two workmen of $1,200, the copper shop cleared $878 in one year.[26]

Although slaves owned and hired by a company sometimes performed the skilled work necessary to erect and repair furnaces, manufacturers generally contracted with individual white laborers for such jobs as stonemasonry, bricklaying, and carpentry. Carpenters received compensation by the foot for the erection of graining and settling cisterns and well frames. Stonemasons and bricklayers furnished all materials necessary for construction and were compensated for the finished products. In 1835 Henry B. Saunders charged salt makers two dollars for each perch of stone erected and seven dollars per thousand for bricks furnished and laid.[27]

Constructing and maintaining a salt furnace required considerable amounts of iron. Before the advent of the steam evaporation process, the construction of a salt furnace capable of producing one hundred bushels per day demanded 8 tons of cast iron and 0.5 ton of bar iron for kettles, pans, grates, and bars. In 1830 operators estimated that 36 tons of wrought iron and 149 tons of cast iron were annually required to maintain all factories on the Kanawha River. Iron products came from Pittsburgh, Ohio, and Kentucky. Kanawha producers even transported pig iron by wagon over mountainous terrain from Wythe County, Virginia.[28]

Although foundries at Pittsburgh and Cincinnati furnished most specialized products and steam engines, some indigenous foundries and machine shops appeared in the Kanawha Valley to meet the needs of the salt industry.[29] In 1849–50 three foundries and engine-building shops— Watson and Jones, Robert F. Hudson, and Abram E. Sargent—produced sixteen steam engines, hundreds of tons of castings, and brass fittings. In one year, the largest establishment, Abram E. Sargent, employed eighteen workmen, constructed eleven steam engines worth $6,775, and performed tasks for the salt industry worth more than $7,000.[30]

The furnishing of fuel to furnaces occupied most of the labor in the Kanawha salt industry. Wood was the initial fuel source, and every salt maker attempted to procure a plentiful supply. Early leases for the construction and operation of furnaces invariably contained provisions concerning timber-cutting rights. Donnally and Steele and Company leased extensive areas of timberland in order to ensure a sufficient fuel supply. Cord wood was cut on the hilltops and rolled down troughs to the river, where it could be taken by boat to the furnaces.[31] Salt companies employed woodchoppers and contracted with individuals for deliveries. In 1815 a man undertook to deliver 6.5 cords daily to a salt furnace in return for a monthly payment of 675 bushels of salt. Another person agreed to chop wood for 1 bushel of salt for each cord delivered.[32] The insatiable appetite of the furnaces speedily stripped the forests accessible to waterways and gave the mountains a "bare, rugged, inhospitable," and "gloomy appearance."[33] The depletion of a nearby wood supply and the obvious heating advantages of coal compelled the manufacturers to seek a solution to the problem of ash removal, so that coal could replace wood in the furnaces.

Several coal seams were readily accessible to Kanawha Salines. William Barton Rogers and Dr. S.P. Hildreth, in their investigations of the area in the 1830s noted that salt makers were mining two seams, one five to six feet thick and another three and a half to four feet thick. In his geological reconnaissance of Virginia in 1839, Rogers labeled the thicker vein number 2 bituminous coal and the smaller number 6 bituminous coal.[34] The clumsy, preliminary attempts to identify the coals then in use can be misleading, because the location of the sample strata on the Kanawha River was not specified. The most productive and best-quality vein in the George's Creek and Campbell's Creek area was the Campbell's Creek or number 2 gas coal (identified by Rogers as number 6 bituminous). High upon the hillsides, a smaller seam, three and a half to four feet thick, was mined extensively. This source could have been the Point seam or the Coalburg (Brooks) coal, depending on location.[35]

The mountainous lands behind the river bottoms where the furnaces stood had been worthless to their owners after the removal of timber. After the success of David Ruffner in 1817, this land became valuable and necessary to every furnace operation because of the bituminous coal it contained. The search for coal deposits immediately began, and one producer retained a prospector to discover coal on his land. Contractual arrangements had to be formulated and altered before exploitation. When copartners had divided the bottomlands for furnace and well sites, they had neglected to consider mineral rights in the steep adjoining lands. Also, in the early 1820s the separation of mineral ownership from surface possession began. Isaac and Bradford Noyes held a two-hundred-acre tract of land on the southeast side of the Kanawha River in common with Andrew Donnally and his wife. In 1823 the partners agreed to divide one vein of coal into six sections, while reserving one-half of a seventh section in the bottom to be held in common "for the purpose of draining coal banks, erecting buildings for coal diggers &c." Some lands could not be conveniently divided by lines of demarcation. Andrew Donnally, James Wilson, John Ruffner, James Bream, and Joseph Lovell jointly owned 160 acres of coal land. They agreed that all parties could take coal to burn in their respective homes; that Donnally and Wilson, who held a one-half interest, could extract enough fuel for two furnaces for each of them; that Bream, who had a one-quarter interest, could have sufficient coal for two furnaces; and that Lovell and Ruffner, who held a one-quarter interest, had the right to mine enough coal for one furnace apiece.[36]

The monetary value of bituminous coal was not known by salt manufacturers when they first converted their furnaces to its exclusive use. No precedent existed on which they could estimate the costs of mining, although they realized that coal was a superior fuel source and that using it would cost less than obtaining wood from a distant forest. In 1823 William Steele and Andrew Donnally leased some coal land to a man who was constructing a salt furnace, but they hesitated to set a charge for the coal consumed because they had no basis on which to formulate a price. They simply delayed valuation of the coal with a provision for a future accord. In case the respective parties could not agree on a price, they named two impartial men who would set the amount that would bind all signatories.[37] Experience soon enabled a manager to estimate the cost of bushel of coal. A bushel of unmined coal on the Kanawha

River came to be appraised at one cent per bushel or twenty-five cents per ton. In 1837 a reporter for the *Cincinnati Chronicle* estimated that a salt manufacturer spent from one and a half to two and a half cents per bushel to mine and transport coal to a furnace.[38] If this appraisal was correct, then salt makers valued a net ton delivered between sixty-two and a half and seventy-seven and a half cents.

Transportation of the coal from the mines to the furnaces in the Salines was inexpensive because of the proximity of the source of production. Initially, wagons carried the mineral from the mine. Later, railroads with wooden rails were laid so that coal cars with flanged cast-iron wheels could be pulled directly by mules and horses from mine openings on lower elevations. Coal mined in seams high up on the mountainsides tumbled from the opening down plank slides onto a receiving platform, where it was loaded into coal cars and transferred to the furnace.[39]

Before midcentury, Kanawha coal mining, which was a completely integrated function of salt manufacturing, experienced a meteoric rise in output and consumption.[40] In 1850 only two independent coal producers existed in the county, and one of these mined cannel coal. Before 1850 nearly all coal produced in Kanawha County fueled salt furnaces. In 1827 it was estimated that the salt industry burned 1,695,000 bushels (67,800 net tons) of coal annually, but the estimate declined to 1,580,000 bushels (63,200 net tons) in 1830.[41] In 1849–50 the thirty-three salt companies in Kanawha Salines consumed 5,658,250 bushels (226,330 net tons) of bituminous coal, valued at $56,664.[42] By 1860 the coal consumption of the nine remaining salt firms dropped a startling 69 percent to 1,769,850 bushels (70,794 net tons), worth $60,616.[43]

Although salt companies generally operated their own coal mines, some manufacturers leased them to individual contractors who assumed responsibility for managerial tasks at the site, for labor, and for deliveries. The lease contracts of these "captive" mines usually provided for exclusive delivery of the coal to the lessor. Daniel Ruffner employed Conrad Myers to open a mine on his land and then contracted for delivery of all coal production to his furnaces. Myers agreed to furnish all labor and to deliver the entire output to Ruffner at the mine mouth for fourteen cents per bushel.[44]

Mine leases and contracts offered by salt companies varied greatly. John Thomas agreed to provide coal for the two furnaces of a salt firm for a one-year term if the company would furnish "five good able bodied work hands and all tools which shall be deemed necessary for the purpose of digging hauling and delivering the Coal at the mouth of the pit." The company also had to pay Thomas five hundred dollars each quarter and to furnish board, lodging, and laundering services. James and Woodford G. McDowell, proprietors of Truro Furnace, retained a miner to provide all the coal necessary to run a salt furnace and fuel a steam pump engine. The McDowells agreed to supply the miner with an enclosed garden, candles, lamps, oil for lights, all blacksmith work, planking and timbering props, and eleven dollars per month for coal deliveries.[45]

Salt manufacturers confronted a twofold problem in coal mining: labor costs incurred in mining constituted the most expensive item in the use of bituminous coal, and free white miners were difficult to secure on a long-term basis. Initially, furnace operators attempted to employ experienced white men in their mines. In the late summer of 1821 Richard E. Putney advertised in the Charleston newspaper for "10 to 20 steady and industrious men, who understand digging coal." Applicants who desired high wages could contact Putney or any manufacturer who used coal. It became apparent that salt producers could obtain free men only as independent contractors for coal deliveries, and even then whites demanded very favorable terms. Records reveal only one known case of a minor working for a wage: William Williams worked at a salt company's coal mine at Brownstown (Marmet) for one dollar and twelve and a half cents per day in 1836.[46] In an economy of labor scarcity, free white labor did not have to accept or endure the hardships of mining. No immigrants or native refugees from marginal agricultural lands were available to exploit. Also, the production of the coal mines did not have to meet extraordinary demands of outside markets. Mine operators turned to cheaper and more dependable slave labor to meet manpower needs and to technological innovation to reduce fuel costs.

Salt makers could have employed natural gas to reduce manufacturing costs. Kanawha Valley drillers constantly encountered gas reservoirs while boring into the salt sands for brine. Considering the potential energy a nuisance, they dispelled it into the atmosphere. Some of the strikes were quite explosive. While drilling at 1,400 feet, William Tompkins struck a trapped reservoir that tossed the auger and iron sinker, weighing 500 pounds, and a pole 1,500 feet long from the well into the air.[47] In his locally famous "salt water or hell" well, Nathaniel V. Wilson touched a powerful source 1,200 feet deep that blew his boring tools out of the hole. Wilson spent several months and much money to control the gas before the well finally choked itself off.[48]

Primitive attempts were made to harness natural gas for use in furnaces. The pressure of gas emission from the ground forced brine through pipe logs to the cistern without pumping. When ignited at the furnace, the natural gas evaporated the water. In 1842–43, when William Tompkins struck a natural gas reservoir while boring a brine well, he initially ignited the gas so that it illuminated his saltworks. A visitor noted that a newspaper could be read at night thirty yards from the wellhead. Later Tompkins cut coal costs in half by using the natural gas fuel to crystallize salt. In 1844 Warth and English used gas pressure to force water without a pump and the gas itself as the sole energy source to generate steam for crystallization. The well produced a quantity of brine that overwhelmed the single furnace, and the firm had to construct another facility.[49]

Kanawha salt producers were as prodigal as their descendants in the use of natural gas. Effective utilization of natural gas could have eliminated labor costs incurred in fueling furnaces, but salt makers hardly thought of gas as a fuel source, although they used it in producing brine. One reason was that corrosion from brine restricted dependable and continuous gas flow through the small-diameter tubing that was used.[50] Also, the availability of large quantities of easily mined coal did not compel salt firms to develop their technical skill to ensure continuous gas employment.

As the enterprise grew, a separation occurred between what Alfred D. Chandler, Jr., called the entrepreneurial and operational functions in some salt firms. The division of function was widespread, but not universal, with the large, multifurnace factories creating a premodern hierarchy. Distance between the place of manufacture and the market as well as scale completed this development. Also, the owner's residence and preferred life-style dictated approach. Some owners acted as general superintendents or handled sales, while others delegated responsibility and traveled extensively to the springs or to Cuba. The size of the managerial hierarchy required to operate a salt furnace varied considerably in the Kanawha Salines. In a completely integrated manufacturing operation, a manager, boss kettle tender, coal-bank manager, and well tender composed the supervisory staff in the production process.

From the beginning of the industry, furnace owners relied on managers to attend to manufacturing details. Managers and superintendents made decisions within a general policy framework set by owners. General policy encompassed one basic goal—economical optimum production. Nathaniel S. Brooks said tersely: "My manager, is my *factotum*, has general Supervision & control of all hands engaged in the Manufacture of Salt—including the Bank Manager & Boss Kettle tender." Describing his duties as manager for Lewis Ruffner, Benjamin S. Smithers deposed that he "hired and paid off all the hands, attended to the procuring of supplies, & had the general superintendance & management of the furnaces etc." James Cowey, a professional manager for fourteen years, supervised two submanagers at two different furnaces, which employed forty-eight slaves and six white hands. Cowey stated: "I have the whole management of the entire concern, hiring negroes, occasionally, draw bonds, pay them off, I keep the books, give receipts, and manage the business entirely, out and out."[51]

Generally, experienced general managers enjoyed considerable freedom, good salaries, and safety. On occasion, though, tensions existed between owners and managers. One superintendent accused his superior of retarding output by constantly meddling. Salaries ranging from $1,000 to $1,500 annually in the 1850s were respectable. Often a house and fuel were furnished. Although the task of the general manager could not be considered hazardous, one young supervisor of Van B. Donnally's furnace slipped to his death in a boiling cistern.[52]

The degree of competence of a manager often spelled the financial success of a manufacturing operation. John J. Cabell, attempting to revive his fortunes in the 1830s, reopened his salt property on the Kanawha River. At first he could not secure a manager, but he finally convinced a Moses Penn, a native of Lynchburg, Virginia, to move his family to Kanawha Salines. Cabell had spent several months acquainting the new manager with the manufacturing process. Penn, after inheriting an estate in eastern Virginia, became sullen and less attentive to Cabell's directions and during a cholera epidemic, he returned with his family to Lynchburg. Loss of a supervisor was not the only problem that plagued Cabell. Penn had allowed the slave work force to impose demands upon him and had failed to make necessary contracts when directed. Cabell estimated that Penn's ignorance and temper had cost two thousand dollars.[53]

The head or boss kettle tender supervised the actual salt-making process and kept the furnace in repair. Nathaniel S. Brooks said that his boss kettle tender "has charge of the hands engaged in Boiling the furnace, and has exclusive command of the repairs etc done on the furnace." In the 1850s this position paid five hundred dollars annually. Kettle supervisors were often blamed for breaking pans and kettles. Crockett Ingles accused Jacob May of allowing an incompetent person to tend the furnace while he played cards for four hours. As a result, a salt pan was broken, and the furnace had to be closed ten weeks for repairs. Lewis Ruffner charged his boss kettle tender with carelessness and negligence for salt-pan damages that required one month for repair. Brayton Allen sued Walker J.L. Sanford for the same wrongdoing.[54]

Outside the furnace itself, some operations used a coal-bank supervisor and a manager of wells and engines. In factories that supplied their own fuel, a coal-bank manager who earned from five to six hundred dollars annually supervised all coal production, loading, and transportation on the tramway.[55] If wells were over four hundred yards apart and if brine was scarce, an overseer of engines prevented possible damage. Under these conditions, steam engines pumped at regular intervals after sufficient water had accumulated in the wells. The normal annual salary for a well and engine tender was four hundred dollars.[56]

Of the total work force connected with the Kanawha salt industry, free white laborers usually worked as supervisors and managers, distributors, or independent contractors in factory construction and operation. In actual production, where only a few whites were workmen, free labor was usually semiskilled or skilled. Kanawha salt production thus depended upon the institution of slavery for a stable and adequate work force.

11

Slavery in the Kanawha Salt Industry

From the War of 1812, Kanawha manufacturers, not having sufficient white labor available, relied primarily upon slaves for their work force. The phenomenal growth of the salt industry and its economic opportunities attracted slave owners as both furnace proprietors and lessors of chattels. The resultant slave society made the Malden area unique in the antebellum South: bondsmen located in the Appalachian Mountains produced an extractive commodity for interstate commerce. This chapter details the usage, adaptability, and adjustment of slavery in the Kanawha salt industry, thereby amplifying recent historiography on the subject.[1]

Initially slaves came to the Great Kanawha Valley from Kentucky and Piedmont Virginia, but as time passed, most slaves originated in eastern Virginia.[2] The western Virginia salt industry drew labor from the commonwealth's tobacco economy, which was in decline.[3] Most slaves were hirelings, as some large eastern slaveholders had leasing agents on the Kanawha and many salt companies annually sent representatives to the Piedmont to rent slaves.[4] Legal agreements between eastern Virginia entrepreneurs who entered the salt business often provided for shared furnishing of slave labor.

Keeping pace with the growing demands of the salt industry between 1810 and 1850, the slave population of Kanawha County grew very rapidly. From 1810 to 1820 the number of slaves in the county more than tripled, growing from 352 to 1,073. In succeeding decades the growth rate was slower. From 1820 to 1830 slave numbers increased 60 percent to 1,717. In the decades 1830–40 and 1840–50 the rate slowed to increases of 49 and 22 percent respectively. In 1850 the slave population reached its peak, at 3,140 slaves. The rate of demographic increase of slave inhabitants was more impressive when compared with the growth of the white citizenry, which was much slower: from 1810 to 1820, the population grew from 3,468 to 5,297, a 53-percent increase; 1820 to 1830 saw a 42-percent increase; the number from 1830 to 1840 grew 44 percent to 10,910; and from 1840 to 1850 the rate slowed to 10 percent with 12,001 white inhabitants in 1850.[5]

Although slave numbers were substantial, the population figures representing slaves are not absolute: the numbers of slaves associated with the Kanawha industry far exceeded fixed census figures. Slaves were often transient, passing in and out of the valley individually and in groups. Many furnace operators moved their owned or leased chattels at will (usually on an annual basis) by redeployment to other occupations, nonrenewal of leases, or sale. When Harry Heth, a well-known Manchester, Virginia, coal operator, his son-in-law Beverley Randolph, and Samuel G. Adams entered the salt business with high hopes in December 1814, Heth and Randolph agreed to furnish thirty-six "Negroe men," and Adams would augment the number as required.[6] Within four months, Randolph, who acted as resident manager and overseer, saw that the partnership had entered an economic quagmire and started extricating it from the business. The slaves who had been reluctant to come to the Kanawha were eager to return to the Richmond area. In reply to Heth's expressed desire for a group of ten to remain and for the others to return, Randolph warned, "No 10 will be more willing to stay than any other 10. They all despise this place as much as I do, & more they can not." On the other hand, William Dickinson and Joel Shrewsbury, a Piedmont Virginia partnership, in January 1814 moved owned and leased slaves to their salt property, where owned slaves and their offspring that were retained remained until the Civil War.[7] Although hired slaves could be transferred quickly, many remained on the Kanawha for years or even decades, usually with several different manufacturers.

Salt makers employed slaves in all phases of the manufacturing process and in all subsidiary activities necessary to support a salt furnace. Most tasks performed by hired and company-owned slaves were routine, but some required a high degree of skill. One completely integrated salt furnace operation that did not contract for coal and barrel deliveries required twenty-three to thirty-three slaves. A two-furnace factory needed approximately double that number. In 1854 James Cowey, a manager of two salt furnaces, deposed that of sixty-four laborers under his control, fifty-eight were slaves. Testifying in 1853, veteran salt maker Richard C.M. Lovell estimated the employment of hands at two salt furnaces as fourteen coal diggers, five wheelers (they wheeled coal from the interior of the mine to its mouth), four haulers (they hauled coal by team on the railroad tramway from the mine mouth to the furnace), three kettle tenders, one or two "cat-hole" cleaners (they cleaned the coal ash repository), six engineers (they ran steam engines to pump brine from the well), two salt lifters and wheelers (they lifted the salt from the pan after evaporation and wheeled the product to the packing shed), seven "jim arounds" and packers ("jim arounds" were general laborers, and firemen and packers placed salt into barrels for shipment), two blacksmiths, one "negro man sort of manager," and one cook.[8]

To attain optimum production capabilities and return on plant investment, salt makers ran their furnaces twenty-four hours per day and, if they chose to incur the risk of arrest and overproduction, seven days per week. Although police regulations forbade labor on Sunday and established six days as the legal length of the work week, producers usually disobeyed this laxly enforced prohibition. At times depressed salt prices occasioned by overproduction forced Kanawha manufacturers to agree mutually to "blow out" their furnaces on Sunday. In these periods, community pressure caused the justices of peace to enforce the law. In 1841 Nathaniel Hatch, a justice who held court in the Terra Salis Presbyterian Church, fined a number of producers for breaking the Sabbath by working themselves and forcing their slaves to work.[9]

Salt manufacturers offered monetary incentives to factory slaves (except coal diggers) to work without days of rest, and these payments became recognized by custom. The firms paid both hired and owned slaves an extra amount for Sabbath labor. The manager carried the accumulated amounts on the books during the year and paid the whole sum to the slave on Christmas Day. A former coal-bank manager noted: "The coal diggers generally dug their coal for Sunday's run on Saturday; but it was paid for extra. It was generally hauled to the furnace on Sunday. The other hands . . . were actually employed on Sunday." Over a five-year period Thomas Friend paid between $1,200 and $1,482 annually for extra Sunday work to thirty-five to forty hands.[10] When Joel Shrewsbury in 1816 returned leased slaves to Bedford County, Virginia, he asked his partner to furnish the slaves certain items of clothing. He also said, "You will let Reuben & Frank have the amt set against each of their names in Store goods it being for Cord Wood cut by them of Nights & C." Shrewsbury expected one and a half cords of wood per slave per day. For the 1818 year, Shrewsbury made similar requests to his Bedford partner: "Please pay the negroe boys in Store Goods as follows Viz Spence Nine & half Dollars Tom Six & half Dollars & Abram Four Dollars for labour of Sunday & Christmas & C." Manufacturers frequently operated their furnaces during the Christmas season. Slaves received direct extra payment for this holiday work.[11]

Owners and managers could project the production of a furnace for a certain operating period, barring breakdowns and accidents. They knew the amount of fuel and the number of barrels that were needed for efficient operation, and they could set production goals for labor. A stable and predictable labor supply and work system met these requirements and goals. Kanawha manufacturers universally adopted the task system in the Salines to measure production and to reduce managerial costs. John D. Lewis, who had manufactured salt since 1832, testified in 1854 in a court case that, on the Kanawha, "we operate a furnace by task work, a coal digger has a prescribed quantity of coal to dig, a hauler, a salt packer a prescribed quantity to pack, and engineer, and kettle tender a certain time to be on watch."[12]

Despite the use of the task system, owners maintained a managerial hierarchy. In an integrated salt manufacturing facility, a manager (overseer), boss kettle tender, coal-bank manager, and, in some cases, a well tender composed the supervisory personnel. Resident owners acted as general superintendents and handled sales but left the active management to overseers. Managerial personnel were responsible for meeting the goals of production and for repairing the machinery and equipment.[13] Usually white men occupied supervisory positions, but there is evidence that slaves sometimes performed managerial functions. In the furnaces operated by Thomas Friend, two slaves held the important positions of boss kettle tender and overseer. In an inventory of hands, Tom, the boss kettle tender, was adjudged as very skillful in maintaining and repairing the furnace. Simon, age thirty-three, was appraised: "Kean, stout; salt well tuber, engine repairer, salt-maker and overseer—experienced, skilful, and industrious."[14]

Slave ownership and leasing reached a high point in the Kanawha salt industry in 1850, as demonstrated by 1850 census data (see table 1). Unfortunately several limitations are inherent in the content of table 1. The census schedule listing products of industry gives thirty-three salt companies, but only twenty-seven appear as possessors of slaves in the schedule of slave inhabitants in Kanawha County. The six missing companies—Gleason and Downward, C.W. Atkinson, Norton and Kline, William and Jones, Shrewsbury and Fitzhugh, and Warth and English—reported a combined average monthly total of 133 male workers. We can assume that at least 100 of these workers were slaves because the proportion would be consistent with the number of slaves in the total work force of other enumerated firms. The census schedules of slave inhabitants also do not denote whether the slaves in the possession of salt companies were leased or owned. The accuracy of the reporting of the slaves' ages in the census returns cannot be assured, although experienced hirers and users who enumerated slaves in their possession would be approximately correct. Factors such as physical condition and work skill of slaves are not recognized. For example, a fifty-year-old slave who was a kettle tender or blacksmith might have been more desirable for a salt company to retain than a twenty-five-year-old laborer. Generalizations about prime hands are hazardous, but it could be conceded that slaves between fifteen and thirty-nine years old were in greater demand, since most labor around the salt furnace was physically rigorous.

In trans-Allegheny Virginia, Kanawha County had the highest total slave population in 1850: 3,140 persons. Of this total, 1,902 were male, and 1,238 were female.[15] Salt firms controlled and possessed at least 1,497 of the total number. Adding the 100 slave hands presumed to have been controlled by the six salt companies mentioned above, one can conclude that over one-half of all slaves in Kanawha County were controlled by the salt industry centered at Kanawha Salines. Basing our calculations on the data presented in table 1, we can see that salt manufacturing firms retained 60 percent of all male slaves and 29 percent of all female slaves in Kanawha County. Of the total number of slaves possessed by salt firms, 76 percent were male. Of the total number of male slaves held by the salt manufacturers, 34 percent were between the ages of twenty and twenty-nine, and 21 percent were from thirty to thirty-nine. Hence, 55 percent of all male slaves were in the prime labor age category. If one extended the prime male slave category to include the group aged fifteen to nineteen, 64 percent of all male slaves held by salt companies would be considered prime workmen. Of the total number of slaves, both male and female, retained by the salt companies, 49 percent were males between the ages of fifteen and thirty-nine.

Slave family units did exist to some extent. Female slaves had limited uses in the domestic establishment of the enterprise: some worked as cooks. Women over fifteen years numbered only 186 and composed 51 percent of the female slave population in the salt business. Of the total number of slaves held by the salt companies, 364, or 24 percent, were males and females under fifteen. As in the southern slave population as a whole, the numbers of males and females in the under fifteen group on the Kanawha were approximately equal. The male-to-female ratios in the other age groups differed markedly: fifteen to nineteen, 3.5:1; twenty to twenty-nine, 5.5:1; thirty to thirty-nine, 6.8:1; forty to forty-nine, 5.3:1; fifty to fifty-nine 4.1:1; and over fifty-nine, 1.9:1.[16] There is a definite correlation between the largest salt firms and manufacturers, measured both in total production and in total slave possession, and the control of slave women and children. The largest salt companies, which included the oldest in the industry, held most of the slave women and children. The top seven firms in slave possession controlled 57 percent of all slaves held by salt manufacturers in 1850 and 50 percent of the males over fourteen. These same firms held 69 percent of

Table 1. Slaves Owned or Leased by Salt Firms in Kanawha County in 1850

Firm	Under 15		15-19		20-29		30-39		40-49		50-59		Over 59		Total by Sex		Grand Total
	M	F	M	F	M	F	M	F	M	F	M	F	M	F	M	F	
Dickinson & Shrewsbury	29	15	15	8	76	5	36	3	31	4	7	1	1	1	195	37	232
John N. Clarkson	39	26	10	5	28	16	14	2	6	2	3	—	2	—	102	51	153
Andrew Donnally & Co.	11	21	8	7	26	6	16	3	11	1	8	3	—	1	80	42	122
Joseph Friend	25	18	7	3	22	8	14	3	—	1	3	2	1	2	72	37	109
John D. Lewis	16	27	6	1	9	7	12	3	8	1	13	3	2	1	66	43	109
Samuel H. Early	7	12	8	—	21	3	4	4	2	4	6	—	—	2	48	25	73
Henry H. Wood	5	7	7	1	12	3	10	4	3	—	2	1	—	—	39	16	55
W.C. Brooks & Co.	3	3	3	—	24	1	10	1	5	1	1	—	1	—	47	6	53
James S.O. Brooks	3	—	3	2	19	1	16	1	6	—	1	—	1	—	49	4	53
E.V. Cox & William Hedrick	11	9	6	—	5	1	4	2	3	3	1	—	2	1	32	16	48
Lewis Ruffner	4	5	1	—	11	2	12	1	3	—	4	2	3	—	38	10	48
William D. Shrewsbury	2	3	4	1	12	4	8	2	7	—	2	—	—	—	35	10	45
Frederick Brooks	7	6	2	—	4	—	8	2	6	1	1	—	—	—	28	9	37
John P. Hale	3	4	—	—	11	—	6	—	6	2	2	1	—	—	28	7	35
Nathaniel V. Wilson	2	—	—	1	10	1	8	—	5	—	3	2	1	—	29	4	33
Spicer Patrick	—	1	1	—	10	—	6	—	8	1	2	—	2	—	29	2	31

Firm	Under 15		15-19		20-29		30-39		40-49		50-59		Over 59		Total by Sex		Grand Total
	M	F	M	F	M	F	M	F	M	F	M	F	M	F	M	F	
Ira Hurt & Son	2	1	3	—	10	—	9	1	2	1	1	—	—	—	27	3	30
R.C.M. Lovell & Co.	2	1	5	—	10	—	7	—	2	—	1	—	2	—	29	1	30
Franklin Noyes	3	2	—	—	7	2	11	1	1	—	1	—	—	—	23	5	28
Henry Chappel	4	6	3	—	6	2	5	—	1	—	—	—	—	—	19	8	27
Joseph Ruffner	—	—	1	—	15	1	5	—	3	1	—	—	—	—	24	2	26
George H. Warth	2	2	2	—	6	1	3	1	3	1	2	1	1	—	19	6	25
Enos S. Arnold	—	—	3	—	9	—	6	—	6	—	—	—	—	—	24	0	24
William A. McMullin	2	4	2	—	7	1	1	—	2	1	3	—	—	—	17	6	23
Jacob S. Darneal	3	1	1	—	3	1	7	—	1	1	1	—	—	1	16	4	20
Coleman & Ingles	2	2	—	—	9	2	—	—	1	—	—	—	—	—	12	4	16
James H. Fry	1	—	1	—	4	2	1	1	—	—	1	—	—	1	8	4	12
Total	188	176	102	29	386	70	239	35	132	26	69	16	19	10	1,135	362	1497

Sources: Schedule 2, Slave Inhabitants, County of Kanawha, State of Virginia, vol. 7, United States Census of 1850; schedule 5, Products of Industry, County of Kanawha, State of Virginia, vol. 2, pp. 13-20, United States Census of 1850.

all females and 71 percent of the slaves, of both sexes, under the age of fifteen. Operators of single furnaces could not support many slaves under fifteen or many family units. Newer companies and short-term entrepreneurs had not been in operation long enough, nor had they the resources, to accumulate slave families. Firms or manufacturers on leased property would rent prime labor in order to maximize profits, to maintain annual flexibility, and to withdraw easily upon expiration of the lease. For example, James S.O. Brooks leased a furnace from Luke Willcox in 1845 for an eight-year term.[17] In 1850 he possessed forty-nine male and four female slaves, and all the females were between fifteen and thirty-nine years old.

In 1850 Dickinson & Shrewsbury, one of the two oldest salt manufacturing companies, was the largest slave user, holding 232 slaves, 195 males and 37 females. In 1855, when the partnership dissolved, it owned or had an interest in 128 slaves, 93 males and 35 females. The relatively constant number of female slaves suggests that family units existed. The 104 fewer slaves, almost all male, displayed the level of slave leasing in 1850 and some attrition by sale and death. Analysis of the 1855 Dickinson & Shrewsbury slave inventory reveals the existence of family units. The list gives ages for only one group of sixteen slaves and does not indicate male kinship ties, only noting relationships between mother and child and grandmother and grandchild.[18]

Of the 128 slaves held by Dickinson & Shrewsbury in 1855, 68 are associated with nine separate common female ancestors; 55 are single men, though several may be related to one or more of the common female ancestor groups; and 5 are single women. The best-documented family group descended from a woman named Fann. The partnership had purchased a half interest in Fann on April 14, 1814, from John Lacy of Franklin County, Virginia. Joel Shrewsbury traveled to Guilford County, North Carolina, where he individually purchased the other half interest. He noted that "the wench is heavy with child."[19] Fann bore ten children, six boys and four girls, who in 1855 ranged in age from twenty-five to forty-five. The two oldest were described as "mulatto," and the remainder, "black." The oldest female was sold, and the youngest male had died. Two daughters, Rachel and Elija, had borne respectively two and four grandchildren, aged from a few months to eighteen years. Of Fann's descendants living in 1855, ten were male, and four were female. Of the remaining eight maternal ancestors, three women account for thirty-five of the fifty-four slaves in family groups. Four of the women had surnames: Jane Turner, Lucinda McCommas, Marcella Sharpe, and Sally Burke (deceased). Few other slaves on the list had last names. Of the 128 Dickinson & Shrewsbury slaves in 1855, at least 38 males and 20 females were part of the nine family groups.

Most salt firms exclusively employed their chattels in the salt furnace and allied activities. Dickinson & Shrewsbury's effective integration of manufacturing with an extensive agricultural enterprise, however, probably made it the most efficient user of slave labor of all the salt companies. From the time of Joel Shrewsbury's arrival in the Salines in 1814, the firm acquired some of the best agricultural land in the valley. Besides vertically integrating its own furnace operations by cutting its own wood (and later mining its own coal), it sold its surplus to others. It constructed its own factories, buildings, barns, outbuildings, and houses. It established a blacksmith shop (with slave labor) that performed all the firm's work and much for other producers. Its slaves cleared land, raised livestock (the firm speculated in hogs and cattle), and engaged in extensive cultivation of the bottomlands. After a few years Dickinson & Shrewsbury annually raised four thousand bushels of corn. Management shifted its slaves from factory to farm as needed. In 1820 Shrewsbury wrote that he ran two salt furnaces, five or six plantations, a sawmill and gristmill, and a blacksmith shop.[20]

Many slaves held by the Kanawha salt industry were hirelings, but the exact number cannot be determined. In his pioneering work on industrial slavery, Robert S. Starobin concluded that four-fifths of industrial bondsmen in the Old South were company owned. On the Kanawha, the proportion of owned slaves was much lower, as demonstrated by Dickinson & Shrewsbury, which controlled 232 slaves in 1850 but owned only 128 in 1856, when the partnership was dissolved. One could assume that about 100 slaves were leased, as Dickinson & Shrewsbury was an active producer until its dissolution. Frequently 30-45 percent of a salt company's slave labor force was leased, and in some cases the proportion was as high as 90 percent. One physician-manufacturer stated: "The larger proportion is hired, taking all the furnaces."[21] Leased slaves in the Kanawha salt industry would exceed 50 percent of all slave labor controlled by manufacturers in any given year.

Hire or lease agreements between bailor and bailee in the leasing of slave labor in the salt industry were as diverse as the desires of the contracting parties and reflect the adjustment of the institution to an industrial situation.[22] In the typical hire agreement, verbal or written, the bailee agreed to treat the property humanely, to provide a certain standard of clothing and medical attention, and to pay all taxes. Slaves were usually hired for the period from January to December 25. Hired slaves, by custom, were usually returned to their owners on Christmas or the day before with a blanket and winter clothing. A general slave holiday lasted from Christmas to New Year's Day.

Some slaveholders enhanced their investment by arranging for the instruction of their slaves in trades or occupations useful in the salt industry. Samuel Hannah hired a young slave to a blacksmith for a four-year term for a yearly rent of fifty dollars. The blacksmith bound himself "to teach & learn the said Boy Preston to the best of his skill & judgment The Blacksmiths trade in all its various branches of business and to keep the said boy employed at no other business of work." Three slaves were hired to salt maker Samuel H. Early "to be allowed a Reasonable time to learn to cooper." If they could not become coopers, the slaves could be employed at other labor. A slave named Tom was hired by his master to a producer "to spend part of his time learning the Coopers trade."[23]

One of the safest and most common employments for slaves at the Salines was in the manufacture of barrels for packing salt. The standard slave task was the assembling of 7 barrels per day or 2,142 barrels in a year.[24] William H. Alpin hired two slave coopers, Henry and Ananias, on an incentive basis from the trustees of the estate of L.C. Lett. In addition to paying for medical bills, clothing, taxes, and food, Alpin promised to pay "ten cents for each and all barrels they shall have made over forty two each week" to the slaves. Several bailors prevented the overexertion of their slaves in manufacturing barrels by inserting restrictive provisions in the lease agreement. Richard, a cooper owned by Samuel B. Brown, was required to assemble only six barrels per day. Of course, such a provision could be interpreted as a requirement for a minimum level of performance. John Waid agreed not to demand hired slaves "when they labor to make more than six barrels per day each."[25] Many lease contracts specified that certain slaves would be employed only in the cooperage trade so that owners or managers of salt furnaces could not force the slave cooper to work in a more dangerous job.[26]

With the exception of coopering, occupations in the salt industry were hazardous. Coal mining was the most dangerous of all nineteenth-century employments. Slaves were the laborers in the coal banks that supplied the fuel for salt furnaces, and many black coal miners met savage accidents and deaths. Luke Willcox in 1844 wrote in his diary that his slave Isam had his "Arm Broke by Slate and coal falling on him." The master immediately sent for medical aid, but he later tersely noted the outcome: "Isam died about 7 o'clock in the Evening." In a court case in which a doctor was suing a salt manufacturer for a medical fee, a physician's assistant related a gruesome accident. The slave treated was injured in a roof fall, "a very bad one." His thigh was broken, his arm was fractured in two places, one above and one below the elbow, and crushed, and one hand was mangled, with two fingers removed.[27] Aware of the inherent dangers of mining, some slaveholders stipulated that a lessee could not work the valuable property in coal mines. George W. Summers forced the salt company that leased his slave Jim to agree to several prohibitions: "The negro man Jim is not to be worked in Coal Bank or as a kettle-tender, nor to be compelled to work on Sundays."[28]

Prohibitions forbidding slaves from working in unsafe pursuits did not restrain salt makers or managers. A woman sued Lewis Ruffner for eight hundred dollars in damages when her slave was killed in a roof fall in Ruffner's mine. The plaintiff contended that Ruffner had agreed not to employ the slave in his coal mines. On January 1, 1832, Charles G. Reynolds hired two slaves, Lewis and Harry, from Ann Pollard for one hundred dollars apiece. During the term of bailment, the slave Lewis was "suffocated, crushed, and killed" in Reynolds's coal bank. Pollard said that her slave was killed in September 1832. She asserted that Reynolds had promised that he intended to use the slaves to tend kettles. Lewis was appraised at seven hundred dollars, and as a result of being deprived of "divers great gains and profits" by his death, the plaintiff sued for one thousand dollars in damages. The defendant entered a general demurrer to each count of the declaration and pleaded non assumpsit.[29]

In a separate case, Pollard again sued Reynolds for the two hundred dollars in rent for Lewis and Harry. Reynolds showed that Lewis was killed in the coal mine on January 18, 1832, seventeen days after his hiring, without any fault on the defendant's part. Declaring that he was willing to pay for the hire of Harry, the defendant claimed a credit for ninety-five dollars for the loss of services caused by the death of Lewis for the remainder of the term of hire. The jury upheld the claims of Reynolds and awarded Pollard $105 and costs.[30] Although this case leaves much unsaid, it is instructive. The distance between owner and slave when the bondsman was hired to a salt manufacturer is apparent. Pollard, though she lived in Kanawha County, did not know when her slave was killed or the circumstances of his demise.

The machinery and highly heated brine of a salt furnace provided many inherent dangers for the unwary novice and the careless workman. Loss of balance around the grainer pan could result in a fall into nearly boiling water. One of Luke Willcox's slaves, Mid, was so severely scalded and burned in such an accident that he died.[31] Boiler explosions around the steam engines occurred frequently. In 1845 James Cowey and Company hired a slave named Frank to haul coal from its mines to its salt furnace. When the company later used the slave in tending a steam engine, the boiler exploded and killed him. The owner, Edward C. Murphy, sued for the value of the slave plus damages, contending that the boiler was defective. The accident occurred on Sunday and thus when the slave was working contrary to law, since salt evaporation was not a household duty "of daily necessity." After litigation lasting from 1848 to 1852, the jury in the circuit superior court found for the plaintiff, awarding him $739.75 in damages plus interest from December 4, 1852.[32]

Wiley P. Woods, the hiring agent for the plaintiff, stated that he had hired the slave, Frank, to Stuart Robinson of James Cowey and Company during the Christmas holidays of 1844 for one hundred dollars a year. The agent had never seen this particular slave before, and Frank was the last slave hired by the agent in the Kanawha Salines that year. Woods understood that the slave had been in Kanawha County only one year and had been employed by George Warth as a car driver in his coal banks. Warth had refused to give the agent the full price of the hire for the young man because he considered him an inexperienced hand. In the lease to James Cowey and Company, Woods secured no written contract but understood that Frank would be used as a driver of a coal car. The agent described the slave as a young Negro of small size, "rather below ordinary . . . delicate looking." He estimated his value at $500-$550 in 1847.[33]

Edward Turnbull, a native of Great Britain and a "practical Engineer of Locomotive & Stationary Engines," managed James Cowey and Company manufacturing operations from 1845 to 1848. He controlled all slave labor at the furnace. Turnbull employed Frank at hauling coal, packing salt, and wheeling salt, but he found him too weak to perform these tasks efficiently. The manager then placed Frank on the steam engine as an operator, where the work was lighter. He attended the steam engine until the boiler explosion. On Sunday morning, March 7, 1847, at four or five o'clock, the steam engine was stopped because Frank's slave partner, John, had boiled the boiler dry, melting the lead rivets in the bottom. Turnbull worked from the time that the engine stopped until one o'clock in the afternoon replacing the rivets. He then started the engine again. Turnbull ran the engine for one hour before placing John on duty, as it was his turn. (John and Frank had alternate six-hour shifts through a twenty-four-hour period.) He remained with John for five minutes and then left. Fifteen minutes after his departure, the boiler exploded. In the interval before the explosion, John had left the scene, and Frank had entered the engine house, where he was killed by the blast. The manager, upon hearing the explosion, ran back to the site and saw Frank dead, but he did not find John immediately. Turnbull testified that the slaves stayed in a cabin one hundred feet from the engine when not on duty but that the company did not confine them there.[34]

The location of the salt industry on the Great Kanawha River, which furnished so many advantages for transportation, was a mixed blessing for slave owners. The westward-flowing Kanawha River furnished an avenue of escape for bondsmen to the free state of Ohio, and accidental drowning was an ever-present threat, since the manufacturing center straddled the Kanawha River. Ann and Martin P. Brooks hired a slave named Lewis to Hewitt, Ruffner and Company to be used as a blacksmith, kettle tender, or coal digger or in any other work connected with salt manufacture. The company promised to use Lewis in a "reasonable and moderate manner." The Brooks family alleged that the company forced the slave to board a steamboat to labor "without the knowledge or consent of the owners." After completing blacksmith work aboard the *Tuckahoe*, Lewis became intoxicated, fell overboard, and drowned. His owners sued the company. John Hays, a clerk of the steamboat, maintained that Lewis was not on the boat when he became intoxicated and drowned. Upon being cross-examined by the plaintiff's counsel, Hays could not definitely establish the departure of the slave from the boat, as thirty blacks whom he could not identify were working around the steamer. This point determined the decision of the jury, which awarded the owners one thousand dollars in damages for the full value of the slave.[35]

The overland flight of slaves from the saltworks to Ohio occurred frequently. In 1827 Joel Shrewsbury surmised that a slave belonging to William Brooks, Isaac, had received advice and provisions from a bondsman of James Gilbert's. Both slaves, he guessed, had fled to Ohio. He thought that two discreet men could capture them if they spent enough money, but he warned that "neither fools nor Misers will ever be able to get runaway Negroes in the corrupted S[tate of] Ohio." After the holiday season in 1834, there was a rash of escapes. Judge Lewis Summers reported to his brother in January 1835 that "there seems to be some restlessness among the slaves of the salt works, and I thought more uneasiness in relation to that species of property than usual." Two slaves had fled from a Mr. Fitzhugh. "On the happening of this occurrence, he shiped all the residue of his slaves to Natches and the lower markets." Moses M. Fuqua "lost three of his black boys," but two were recovered and "pretty efficient measures adopted for the recovery" of the other one. In 1844 Lewis Ruffner advertised the escape of Gatewood, "supposed to be 25 or 26 years old, about 5 feet 7 inches high, tolerably black, speaks gruff when spoken to." Gatewood had run away from Ruffner's coal mine. "There is reason to suppose that he is lurking about in the neighborhood, but may if not soon taken up, make for Ohio." A Monroe County, Virginia, resident advised the law firm to which he was sending a slave to be sold to meet legal expenses to lodge the bondsman "in jail for greater Security and that no notice Should be given him as I think he will be disposed to run."[36]

Salt maker John J. Cabell experienced much difficulty with one slave who desired to secure his freedom by escaping to Ohio. Black Jack ran away from the Cabell furnace to Ohio, but he was captured and placed in jail at Point Pleasant. After paying seventy dollars in expenses to retake Jack from the Mason County jail, Cabell tried to sell him on the Ohio River, but no one wanted to buy a slave who was likely to flee. On the first night of the journey back to the Salines, Jack escaped again. He was soon captured a second time in Ohio. After expending another eighty-five dollars, Cabell lodged Black Jack in the Kanawha County jail, "awaiting an opportunity to Selling him to be carried to New Orleans."[37]

One slaveholder in Kanawha County protected his property from drowning or escape by water by inserting a restrictive clause in lease agreements. Salt producers who leased his slave promised "not [to] suffer s[ai]d Negro or go on the river in any kind [of] Craft for employment." Other slave owners were not so cautious. Francis Thompson leased a slave girl for service on the steamboat *Daniel Webster*.[38]

The steamboat, the primary vehicle of transportation of people and goods other than salt, was a corrosive influence on the institution of slavery at the Salines. Steamers frequently employed slaves as stewards and cooks. Such slaves enjoyed a degree of freedom unavailable to laborers at salt furnaces. The steamboat transported ideas as well as merchandise. Contacts with "liberated" slaves who transferred knowledge of distant Ohio ports could erode discipline. To fleeing slaves, boats furnished the possibility of quick mobility that overland flight did not. The presence of steamboats provided another motive for owners to keep their chattels away from river craft.[39]

The Great Kanawha that so advantageously carried the produce of the Salines down its current brought an ascending, unwelcome visitor when the steamship eased two-way intercourse with Ohio River towns. The unwelcome visitor was Asiatic cholera, a dreaded scourge in the nineteenth century. Caused by the bacterial toxin *Vibrio cholerae*, the waterborne infectious disease, which inflicted upon its victims violent diarrhea and spasmodic vomiting, muscular cramps, dehydration (often cyanosis), and eventual collapse, was a serious threat to life. Its effects ranged from extreme illness to death within a few hours or days.[40]

The first major epidemic of Asiatic cholera occurred in the United States and in the Kanawha Salines in 1832. The disease was introduced into Atlantic seaports and passed to the Ohio River via the Great Lakes and the Ohio Canal.[41] Diary and manuscript accounts indicate that slaves were more affected by the epidemic than white residents of the Salines. In October 1832 a Charleston newspaper reported that three slaves had died of the disease. Joel Shrewsbury reported the same three deaths at the same furnace. He had heard that three steamboats had attempted to land with cholera victims at Charleston and that municipal authorities had refused to permit them to stop. Commenting on the presence of cholera in mid-November, John J. Cabell, salt maker and physician, lamented the loss of one of his slaves and reported that the effect of the disease was abating somewhat, since the new cases appeared to be milder and many slaves were recovering. At the end of the month Cabell wrote that there had not been any new cases for several days.[42]

In the summers of 1833 and 1834 cholera again arrived at the Salines. In July 1833 Dr. Cabell, who would himself succumb to the disease in a later year, wrote to his wife in Lynchburg, Virginia, that "the people dying around us everyday more or less with that fatal Epedimic the Cholera." Business was suspended at the saltworks and the towns along the Ohio. Over half of the salt furnaces had stopped production because of the desertion of the labor force. Cabell reported that five or six of his slaves, including his carriage driver, had the disease. In the summer of 1834 the *Kanawha Banner* noted that cholera had killed a number of Negroes at the Salines.[43]

The most serious epidemic of Asiatic cholera spread to Kanawha County in 1849. This attack claimed an estimated three hundred lives in the county between April and August 1849. During May, diarist and salt producer Luke Willcox counted forty-five deaths in the Salines alone. Willcox departed for a timely vacation at Blue Sulphur Springs on June 22, and in a seven-day interval between his departure and his receipt of a letter from home, thirty people had expired. In mid-July, Willcox estimated that approximately a hundred people had died from cholera just in the Salines.[44]

During the 1849 epidemic, a clerk in the John R. Smith and Company store in Malden kept a cholera death register in which he recorded all expirations that occurred on the Great Kanawha from Elk River to the upper saltworks (about a ten-mile stretch). He noted that the first phase of the scourge began on May 1 at Tinkersville and lasted four weeks. Thirty-nine deaths resulted. His register encompassed the second phase, which began on June 19 and ended on August 23 with the death of prominent salt manufacturer, Levi Welch. The clerk recorded the place of death, sometimes the victim's name or occupation, the victim's race, whether the victim was an adult or a child, and the sex of adults only. Including Charleston, seventy-eight people died, thirty-one whites and forty-seven blacks. Excluding Charleston, where no salt was made and sixteen white and four blacks died, all other deaths occurred in the salt-manufacturing district. Of these fifty-eight deaths, fifteen of the victims were white, and forty-three were slaves.[45]

The existence of cholera and its effects caused some litigation and adaptation of slave-hire agreements. On behalf of Zalinda L. Davis, agent John McConihay hired a slave named Jack to Crockett Ingles, a salt maker, for the year 1849. Ingles had agreed to return the slave to his owner in the event of a cholera epidemic. When the disease struck the locality in the late spring of 1849, Ingles refused to surrender Jack. Jack contracted cholera and expired on July 10. Upon this slave's death, Ingles's other hired slaves fled to their homes in eastern Virginia. Jack's owner successfully sued Ingles in the circuit court because of noncompliance with the verbal agreement.[46]

After the 1849 outbreak, agreements for hire almost invariably contained provisions for slave safety in case of a cholera epidemic. Martha Stone of Bedford City, Virginia, hired out two slaves, Jim and John, for $325 for the year 1850 with a reservation: "It is further understood that if the cholera should reappear in the salt works during the present year that Mrs. Stone or her agent has permission to withdraw the said negroes deducting for the time so lost at the rate of $325 a year." Warth and English promised to remove a hired slave "should the cholera prevail," with the owner's deducting the time lost from the rent.[47]

In the summer of 1850 Asiatic cholera again struck the Salines. During ten days ending on July 5, a salt maker recorded that eighteen people died in the Salines. The clerk who kept the 1849 register kept an identical tabulation in 1850. Between June 27 and September 2 he recorded sixteen deaths, all in the Salines: five white males and eleven slaves, of which eight were men and three were women. Again slaves suffered more. During the brief visitation, Green, a slave belonging to John Potter of Franklin County, Virginia, ran away to his home from the salt firm of Warth and English. Advising the owner to retain Green because of the possibility of future flight to Ohio, the firm minimized the alarm of disease as a motive by asserting that the runaway "only used it as a pretext to make a call on his old friends in Franklin."[48]

In all phases of slave life on the Kanawha, what the individual slave thought is difficult to determine. We can consider only acts. No words exist. Correspondence among the salt makers reveals that owned and hired slaves from Piedmont Virginia who did not wish to move from their homes to the Kanawha resisted however they could. In 1819, when Harry Heth marched a coffle from Manchester under the care of an overseer to hire to salt makers, three slaves escaped their chains in Buckingham County.[49] Resistance was usually more subtle. William Dickinson warned his partner, who in 1814 was gathering hired slaves in Franklin County for the trek to the Kanawha, that his father was willing to lease two "if they are Wiling to go, but they dont seem quite Wiling to go, but perhaps you could influence them." Having difficulty convincing another group that he had hired from William Terry, Shrewsbury commented that they "were very loath to go but have had no trouble with them." In 1820 Dickinson wanted to send more of his slaves to the Kanawha, but he had to arrange to overpower one slave who objected. The owner observed, "Jim & Will concluded to frustrate the design & seem to fein them sick, first one & then the other—& Will has hinted that [he] would not go. I have had pr hand Cuffs made & shall put Will & Washington together." Dickinson & Shrewsbury always had an overseer with owned or hired slaves when they traveled westward from the Piedmont, but when hired slaves were to return at the end of their hire periods to Franklin or Bedford counties, the firm often allowed them to travel unaccompanied. At Christmas in 1819 Shrewsbury sent Tom, Spencer, and Abram home with a pass and expense money "As they are sensible negroes & desireous to get home," Shrewsbury wrote, he "thought it not necessary to be at the expense of hiring a hand to go with them."[50]

A subtle system of control imposed discipline upon the slaves in the Kanawha salt industry. Most tasks, including skilled ones, could be routinized, thus minimizing management costs and establishing a common discipline. Goals for production of coal, barrels, and packed barrels were easily set. Slaves in positions requiring skill and attention, such as kettle tenders and machinery operators, worked on a time basis. If slaves met measured work requirements, they enjoyed considerable freedom to roam at large, although the task size restricted this possibility to some degree. Owners and managers tendered incentives to encourage production. Payments for Sunday and holiday work caused slaves to endure continuous daily labor. Deferring payment until year's end discouraged misbehavior and flight, since the slave had accumulated something of value that was possessed by the manager and subject to his whim. A recalcitrant slave who refused to meet production goals could be employed in a wet room in the coal mine and subjected to the ridicule of fellow workers. Salt makers fostered a sense of pride and rivalry among the work force of the different furnaces. Veteran salt manufacturer Henry H. Wood observed that overestimation of furnace output was quite common, "particularly by the hands," because they try "to excel other furnaces—and to gain reputation."[51]

The goals of production had priority over the interests of the slave. At most furnaces, a superintendent or manager oversaw operations. Since assessments of his performance were based on production and efficiency, his primary concern was probably not the condition of the labor force unless output was inhibited. Economic self-interest did encourage kindness to the extent that the protection of property required the humane treatment of personally owned slaves. If a hired slave was abused physically or died from an industrial accident, the result would be nonrenewal of the lease, or the operator might entertain the fear of an unsavory reputation and perhaps a costly legal controversy with a distant owner.[52]

The food and clothing of Kanawha slaves were substantial and plentiful. The nature of the work required ample food and durable apparel, and the presence of company stores that regularly traded with Cincinnati ensured the availability of a variety of articles. Clothing, "stout and coarse, suitable for rough work," consisted of summer cloth (pants and shirt), a blanket, one hat, one winter coat and pants, one winter shirt, socks, and three to six pairs of shoes and tacks. Bacon and cornbread were the basic dietary staples, but flour, sugar, coffee, molasses, and vegetables accompanied this fare. Tea and rice were available to the sick. Allotments of food to slaves were not strict. Thomas Friend, operator of two furnaces, tried to give his slaves what they would eat, as "they labored very hard," although he restricted meat to one and one-fourth pounds of side bacon and one and a half pounds of shoulder per day to each slave.[53]

With the extensive employment of hired slaves, the salt producers separated the owners from their chattel. The producer gained the supervision of the bondsmen away from the knowledge and watchful eyes of the owners. Distance would tend to result in the harsher use of the bondsmen. This separation, especially apparent with slaves from eastern Virginia, is revealed by comments entered in the inventories of estates in Franklin County. Before his death, Samuel Patterson leased a slave to a salt company. The appraisers of his estate reported that the "Negro Man Amos (Known to us but now in Kanawha County, Va if in health)" was worth nine hundred dollars. The administrators of another estate represented "that Man Squire who is now hired at the Kanawha that from the best information that we have we suppose to be worth" four hundred dollars.[54]

Although salt makers hired slave labor for both skilled and unskilled jobs in their factories, most leased bondsmen were employed in the unskilled, dangerous occupations of coal mining and wheeling. Most labor at a furnace worked in the mine. The skilled slaves were often owned by the manufacturers, and the higher rents paid for skilled workmen ensured their usage at their trades. Thomas Friend, who owned a higher percentage of his hands than was usual, rented from five to fifteen slaves per year from 1846 to 1850. He employed every leased slave in his coal mine as a digger or wheeler.[55]

Bailors and bailees recognized that higher rents prevailed for slaves employed in the salt industry of the Kanawha Valley than elsewhere in the Upper South because of the increased possibility of accident or escape to Ohio. In a court case heard by the Supreme Court of Appeals of Virginia in the 1830s, the fact that slaves taken from Wood County to the Kanawha Salines hired for rates that were 25 to 30 percent higher than elsewhere was introduced as evidence. In 1838 slaves hiring for $90 per year in eastern Virginia could be leased for $150 in Kanawha County. A resident of Louisa County wrote a friend, a salt maker who had inquired about the slave market, that "in relation to hire likely men can be had at $90 & from that downwards but I discover the people of this country dont like to hire to the Kanawha people, it is a long distance & near the state of Ohio." Some Kanawha petitioners to the Virginia General Assembly blamed the high lease prices on the activity of Ohio abolitionists.[56]

Rentals varied greatly with the knowledge and skill of the individual slave in the salt business. Experienced and skilled workmen hired at higher rates than common labor. Age, sex, and physical condition would affect a slave's rental value. A first-rate boss kettle tender or blacksmith would lease for double the amount paid for a common laborer, such as a coal hauler, salt packer, salt lifter, or salt wheeler. A good coal digger would bring a premium of twenty-five dollars over the rent of a common laborer.[57]

Hire rents for slaves, although they were on an upward trend throughout the antebellum period, fluctuated widely and were quite sensitive to the economic condition of the Kanawha salt industry. In 1937 Thomas Senior Berry conducted an important, comprehensive study of commodity prices in the antebellum Cincinnati market. Basing his findings on sources then available, Berry plotted salt prices in that emporium and related these to Kanawha production. Despite the limitations of his sources that marred his narrative about the development of the Kanawha salt industry, Berry's production figures and price charts are accurate. He charted the monthly purchasing power of Kanawha salt using general prices in the Cincinnati market from 1816 to 1860. Chart 1 shows the correlation of the hire rates of common slave labor with the annual purchasing power of Kanawha salt in the Cincinnati market for the period 1844–54. This time period is the only extensive span for which sufficient slave-hire data exist. It should be emphasized that the slaves were hired for common, not skilled labor. Also, the changes in purchasing power of salt were not as precipitous in fact or on Berry's chart. The abrupt changes are caused by the use of annual percentages.

A close correlation existed between common slave hire prices and the annual purchasing power of Kanawha salt in the Queen City market. This correlation would be even closer if the rent for each year was cast in the preceding year, when the contracts of hire were actually consummated. For example, the rate for the year 1847 could be placed in December 1846, eliminating the lag. The diverse factors affecting salt

Chart 1. Relationship of Average Annual Hire Rates for Common
Slave Labor in the Kanawha Salt Industry to the Annual
Purchasing Power of Kanawha Salt in the Cincinnati Mar-
ket, 1844–1854

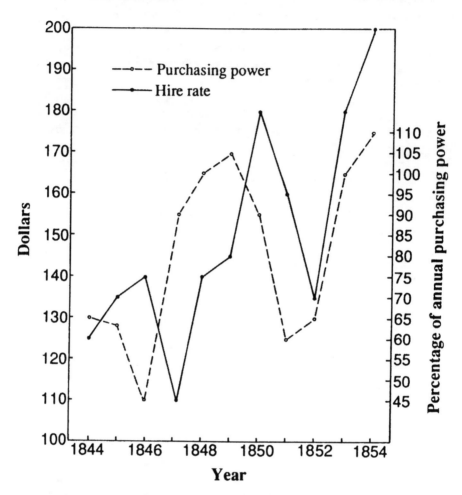

Sources: Berry, *Western Prices,* chart 27, p. 304; Hale, "Salt," 303; deposition of Robert Blaine, [n.d.], in *Early* v. *Friend* (1857), 1: 222-23; deposition of John N. Clarkson,
Feb. 28, 1855, in *Thomas R. Friend* v. *William J. Stephens, Abraham Williams, et al.,* CSC,
MCCR (1853). Luke Willcox Diary, Jan. 1, 11, and 16, 1844, vol. 1, p. 1; Jan. 1, 1845,
vol. 1, p. 17; Dec. 5 and 30, 1847, vol. 1, pp. 54[64]–55[65]; Dec. 25 and 26, 1848, vol.
2. p. 10; Dec. 31, 1849, vol. 2, p. 25; Dec. 31, 1851, vol. 2, p. 55; Dec. 27, 1853, vol.
3, p. 5.

production are ignored here, although total production affected the annual purchasing power of the commodity. High production begot lower purchasing power, and low production produced higher purchasing power, which in turn affected rents. This is not to suggest that the purchasing power of salt was the sole influence on hire prices. Undoubtedly the cholera epidemic of 1849 had some impact on hire rates for 1850.

Between 1850 and 1860 the salt industry of the Great Kanawha Valley suffered a severe decline unrelated to the labor system. Only nine salt manufacturing establishments existed in 1860. The surviving companies only employed an average of 285 male and 10 female hands in a month of operation. Annual salt production was approximately a third what it had been a decade before. While Kanawha County's white population increased between 1850 and 1860, to become second only to that of Ohio County in the area of present-day West Virginia, the slave population dropped dramatically because of the demise of the salt industry (see table 2).[58] The total slave population decreased 30 percent, and the male and female slave populations decreased 35 percent and 23 percent respectively. The adjustment is more meaningful when one views the decreases in the prime age groups for male labor: ages fifteen to nineteen, 37 percent; twenty to twenty-nine, 56 percent; and thirty to thirty-nine, 49 percent. In fact, in Kanawha County there were fewer slaves in 1860 than in 1850 in every age and sex category except for males and females over fifty-nine.

Contemporary salt manufacturers believed that slave labor was superior for their industrial needs because of cheapness, supply, and stability. Salt makers who petitioned the Virginia General Assembly asserted: "Slave labor is usually cheaper than free and for the business in which we are engaged it is believed to be the best."[59] A comparison of costs of hired common slave labor and free white labor in the period 1850–54 reveals that slave labor was cheaper than free white (see table 3). The comparison assumes that the latter was available, but free labor was actually scarce. The operation of the hire system eliminates questions about the cost of rearing slaves and care for the infirm and elderly. The average hire for common slave labor for the period, a time of high rents, was $170 per year. In 1855 John N. Clarkson estimated that board, clothes, taxes, and medical treatment for each leased slave cost a bailee approximately $100 annually above the rental cost. Table 3 uses a higher estimate. The major extra cost was board, but furnace operators customarily furnished board to white laborers as they did for slave labor. The slave lease always provided for the rental payment at the end of the hire period. This was, in fact, the loan of capital and labor for a one-year term. The employment of free labor could not be executed with this ad-

Table 2. Slave Inhabitants of Kanawha County in 1850 and 1860

Year	Under 15		15-19		20-29		30-39		40-49		50-59		Over 59		Total by Sex		Grand Total
	M	F	M	F	M	F	M	F	M	F	M	F	M	F	M	F	
1850	600	574	172	126	498	209	316	137	175	104	98	51	43	37	1,902	1,238	3,140
1860	507	424	108	101	221	165	160	118	113	66	77	39	48	37	1,234	950	2,184
Increase or decrease	−93	−150	−64	−25	−277	−44	−156	−19	−62	−38	−21	−12	+5	0	−668	−288	−956

Sources: Table 1, "Population by Counties—Ages, Color, Condition," State of Virginia, in U.S. Bureau of the Census, *Seventh Census,* 252–56; table 1, "Population by Age and Sex," and table 2, "Population by Color and Condition," State of Virginia, in U.S. Bureau of the Census, *Eighth Census,* 510–11.

Table 3. Comparative Costs of Hired Common Slave Labor and Free White Labor, Kanawha Salt Industry, 1850–1854

	Hired slave	Free white
Rent or wage	$170.00	$450.00
Board	75.00	75.00
Clothing	24.00	—
Medical care	5.00	—
Taxes	1.00	—
Deferred interest on rental at 6%	—	53.48
Total cost	$275.00	$578.48

Sources: Luke Willcox Diary, Dec. 27, 1853, vol. 3, p. 5; depositions of John N. Clarkson, Feb. 28, 1855, and R.C.M. Lovell, Sept. 5, 1854, in *Thomas R. Friend v. William J. Stephens, Abraham Williams, et al.*, CSC, MCCR (1853); deposition of Robert Blaine, [n.d.], in *Early v. Friend* (1857), 1: 222–23.

vantage, and therefore a 6-percent interest rate (a low estimate of the cost of money) on the monthly wage must be charged to free labor in calculating costs. Management costs would be about the same. John J. Cabell reported to his son-in-law in 1832 that the few white hands that he had hired required more supervision than all his slaves. On the Kanawha, it was commonly assumed that a salt furnace operated at least three hundred days annually. In 1854 Richard C.M. Lovell deposed that the cost of free labor in the Kanawha Salines was $1.50–$2.00 per day.[60] Taking the lower figure results in a yearly wage of a free white laborer of $450.00. One can readily see that hired common slave labor was cheaper than free labor. If one assumed the free labor to be skilled, the hire of the common slave can be doubled, as in the case of a boss kettle tender, and a marked differentiation remains. The wage of the free laborer could be reduced to one-half, and the result is the same.

Kanawha salt makers preferred to lease slaves because they could maintain lower costs and flexibility. Less capital could be invested in human property, and manufacturers could adjust their labor needs annually. The payment of rents in December came at a convenient time, since salt makers were often short of operating capital and the greatest salt sales occurred in autumn, before the slaughtering season. In 1833 John J. Cabell wrote that it was an established rule on the Great Kanawha River that if an able-bodied young male slave could be hired at 20 percent or less of his value per year, then that slave would be cheaper to lease than to purchase.[61] Incompetent workmen could be returned on the basis of misrepresentation, or they could be allowed to find other bailees at the expiration of the lease term. Loss in case of accident could be minimized by leasing slaves, because one's own property was not being killed or maimed. The only threat was a lawsuit, but an adverse result could be defeated on appeal, delayed, or avoided when the plaintiff resided in a distant locality.

In light of recent debates of historians concerning the question of the economic efficiency and function of slave labor, the Kanawha salt industry provides an interesting case. Historians usually inquire about the alternative use of free white or slave labor, a choice not confronted by western Virginia entrepreneurs. In the Salines there never was enough free labor available for employment in all phases of the salt industry. The real alternative was between no or insufficient labor or slave labor, and the manufacturers did not hesitate to make the necessary choice. The evidence indicates that Kanawha producers preferred slave labor. There is no sign of ethical opposition or question in the matter. Transient free labor could not be depended upon for salt production. Slave workmanship was adequate in an enterprise where most jobs were routine. Slaves learned to tend kettles, cooper, dig coal, haul and pack salt, load boats, and drive teams as well as free labor. Incentive was not a problem, since subtle rewards were provided and production was easily measurable. What was most needed at a salt furnace was a stable supply of workmen, and slaves fulfilled the requirement. In a court case in Mason County in 1853, expert testimony on the cost of erection and operation of salt furnaces was required in order to settle a controversy between the developers of the West Columbia saltworks. Kanawha salt makers consistently deposed that the Kanawha manufacturing establishments operated more cheaply than those on the Ohio River because of the lower cost and stability of the slave labor supply.[62] The West Columbia saltworks could not retain free white labor for long periods, as it hired workers by the day or month.[63]

Slavery in the Great Kanawha Valley salt industry differed greatly from the institution that prevailed in agricultural or urban situations in the Old South. This microcosmic investigation does not lend itself to extensive, broad generalizations about the larger questions of political economy in the Old South. After all, Kanawha slavery at its peak involved only a few thousand slaves and a few hundred whites, whereas southern slavery as a whole affected millions. On the eve of the Civil War, Virginia's slave population approached a half million. The extractive salt business, depending upon surplus Virginia chattels for its labor and having its product's major market on the Ohio River and its southern and midwestern tributaries, was an exceptional phenomenon resting upon the effective functioning of a hire system. The Kanawha salt industry's rise and fall, essentially unrelated to its labor system, were induced by the market. The institution of slavery did not restrict the entry of entrepreneurs, nor did it inhibit technological progress. The salt enterprise could not have expanded or flourished as it did without slave labor and the hire system. The Kanawha system displayed a remarkable ability to meet the industrial requirements of salt manufacturers. Their success in harnessing the institution for their use suggests what might have occurred in southern Appalachian extractive industries had slavery continued to exist.

12

The Kanawha Salt Association and Ruffner, Donnally & Company, 1847–1855

During 1846, when total production levels reached the all-time high of 3,224,786 bushels, Kanawha salt prices in the Cincinnati market deteriorated to the lowest point since the development of the industry. The disastrous financial results forced valley producers to attempt to solve their common problems. In November, the manufacturers tried to create a joint stock company. After failing in this scheme, they considered the possibility of forming a sales agency or "making a purchase." A major reason for the failure of these proposals was that the largest independent company in the industry, Dickinson & Shrewsbury, refused to surrender its autonomous position. In January 1847 several manufacturers successfully petitioned the Virginia General Assembly for an act of incorporation of a company to manufacture and vend Kanawha salt.[1] If the producers could not raise capital or cooperate in the formation of a joint stock company, the probability of their launching a corporation to control the industry was slight.

During January and February 1847 the salt producers organized the Kanawha Salt Association, primarily a sales agency, to exert some central control over the marketing of their commodity. Persons actively manufacturing salt, owners of salt property, and those who controlled salt on the Kanawha composed the association. In the preamble to their agreement, the manufacturers declared their objectives as "relieving our business from its present grevious embarrassments, which, as we believe, have arisen from an over production of salt, from excessive competition in the markets, and from a general want of confidence in ourselves." They swore a supposedly binding pledge to promote union among themselves in order to avoid ruin by division.[2] The agreement provided for two types of meetings: stated and special. Stated meetings were to be held once each month "for consultation and the transaction of business." The president of the association or, in his absence, the vigilance committee could call special meetings whenever it was necessary.

Each member had one vote for each twenty-five thousand bushels of salt he manufactured in the quarter preceding the meeting. The inspectors' returns determined the actual amount manufactured. Regardless of production, however, each member had one vote. Two-thirds of the votes, in person or by proxy, constituted a quorum for conduct of business. A majority vote determined all matters brought before the association except those dealing with association articles or "fundamental principles." A two-thirds vote was necessary to amend or to abolish association bylaws.

At the February stated meeting and annually thereafter, the membership selected a president and a secretary. The presiding officer and secretary could succeed themselves and could serve until successors were selected. The key governing group was the committee of vigilance, which consisted of nine persons: seven resident members of the association and two agents, commission merchants, or members who resided elsewhere. The committee was elected annually at the regular February meeting, but if for any reason that meeting did not choose a new committee, the old committee continued to act until successors were selected.

The committee of vigilance was the primary day-to-day governing body of the Kanawha Salt Association. The committee had general supervision and control "of the furnaces at home and the markets abroad." Besides setting prices for sales, it had to approve, license, and grant permission to all traveling agents and commission merchants who handled the salt of any association member. Unless otherwise provided, the committee possessed final authority to decide all questions involving violation of association articles, resolutions, and rules and to set appropriate penalties.

Individual association members had the responsibility to aid the committee of vigilance in the performance of its duty and to report to it all violations of the articles, resolutions, or pledges. In addition to securing the prior approval of all traveling agents, members had to "exact from each agent" and file with the association secretary a signed pledge, in which the agent promised to conform to Kanawha Salt Association regulations under threat of dismissal for violations. Each member and his agent had to secure upon the delivery of salt to a commission merchant signed duplicate receipts, one of which they had to file with the association secretary, in which the merchant promised and bound himself "to sell strictly in accordance with the prices fixed from time to time by the Kanawha salt association, and to confirm to all the regulations they have adopted, or may adopt for the sale of salt." Furthermore, the merchant agreed that the vigilance committee could remove salt from his possession if he had intentionally violated association pricing policy and regulations. All approved and qualified traveling agents and commission merchants could appoint other traveling agents and merchants if they secured the appropriate duplicate pledges and receipts. They were to retain one copy and forward the other to the association secretary so that the committee of vigilance could approve their appointments. Pending final approval, the previously qualified agent and merchant were responsible for their appointees' fidelity.

Each association member who sold salt on the Kanawha River for shipment had to obtain a receipt whereby the purchaser agreed to abide by all association rules in the sale of salt. The member had to file the receipt promptly with the association secretary. If he failed to secure or file the receipt or if the purchaser violated the conditions, the seller would "in all respects, be liable for any violations in the salt thereof, as fully as if he had sold and committed the violation himself."

At the end of each inspection quarter, the manufacturer had to deliver to the committee of vigilance 3 percent of the total amount that he produced. These deliveries were the collateral intended to secure the adherence of members to all rules. The committee enjoyed full discretion to sell the salt. After deduction of the current expenses of the association and any penalties, the committee annually paid the net proceeds from such salt sales to the producer, if he had complied with the association rules during the year.

Each association member agreed to maintain set sales prices and a standard grading scale. To reduce production, the members ceased all manufacturing activities on the Sabbath. Also, each member who sold, leased, or transferred his salt property had to obligate the receiver to association rules and articles.

If a purchaser violated the stipulations of a receipt, the committee of vigilance would, upon reasonable notice, conduct a trial. If the purchaser was convicted of an infraction, the committee would inform association members in writing of the name of the violator and would report the same at the next stated meeting. The committee would also enter an order in the association books prohibiting any member from trading with the party. Members who violated the order would incur a penalty.

If a member willfully and voluntarily contravened the articles, resolution, or pledge of the association, two-thirds of the members at a stated meeting could expel him after previously informing him of the causes. It "shall be duty of each member to withhold all offices of good neighborhood and kindness, and to decline all business intercourse with each expelled member, so far as those offices and such business intercourse may directly or indirectly aid him in making, vending or shipping salt." Members also agreed to shun persons who might aid the expelled member in the salt trade until the violator made restitution for his wrongdoing and agreed to abide by the regulations of the association.

If persons in any market refused to comply with the terms of the association, the committee of vigilance had the power to employ other agents at association expense and to charge the owner of the salt for the usual sales commissions. In this way, the committee could directly control market sales if necessary.

At the first association meeting in February 1847, the members selected Colonel William Dickinson as president and James Norton as secretary. The committee of vigilance consisted of William Dickinson as chairman, John D. Lewis, Henry H. Wood, Joseph Friend, Samuel H. Early, Nathaniel V. Wilson, John Rogers, Job English, and Lewis Ruffner. Joel Shrewsbury, Sr., served as an alternate for his business partner, William Dickinson, while George H. Warth served as an alternate for Job English. After selecting its officers, the association enacted eight resolutions concerned with the conduct of its business and with the sale of salt.[3] It set a regular monthly meeting time, the first Thursday after the second Monday. It required that only written questions could be submitted to the association. Also, no member who appeared at a meeting could depart before adjournment without leave of the president. If any merchant, trader, or other person outside the association acquired Kanawha salt and sold it at less than the established price, the members of the association had the duty to "withdraw all patronage in way of business" from him. Any salt maker who offered any price advantage to the purchaser was guilty of violating the established price. Enumerated violations included the granting of credit without interest, the delivery of salt free of charges for drayage from landings or warehouses, the reduction of the price of boats, and reweighing. The seller and purchaser could not resort to any device to reduce the price of salt. No commission merchant could include inspection fees as part of the fixed salt price. The granting of cash advances did not authorize a commission merchant to violate the established prices or otherwise to alter his obligations to the association.

No violation by commission merchants or agents authorized or excused violations by others. All persons who subscribed to pledges had the responsibility to report violations, along with names and all other evidence, to the association secretary or to the vigilance committee. The committee of vigilance ordered the articles of association and all resolutions printed for general distribution and obtained sufficient quantities of blank pledges and receipts so that the new venture could begin.

The Kanawha Salt Association, in addition to attempting to centralize all sales, did attack, with partial success, the problem of overproduction. The members agreed that the fires in the furnaces be raked out, that the engines for pumping water be stopped, and that all labor be suspended from daylight on Sunday until daylight on Monday each week. The Episcopal rector, riding on Sunday to his parish at Malden, rejoiced that he saw clear skies and intimated a theological connection between working on the Sabbath and the economic plight of the producers.[4] This prohibition would have reduced production from existing furnaces by 15 percent, but it did not allow for the increased output arising from new, enlarged, or rebuilt furnaces. James Norton later testified that the organization arranged to dead rent some furnaces in order to reduce production. The active manufacturers delivered 10 percent of their quarterly production to the association, which in turn used the salt to discharge dead rents.[5]

The association had trouble controlling agents and commission merchants with the use of pledges and consignment agreements. The vast number of manufacturers and merchants involved ensured the presence of some dishonest individuals. Richard C. M. Lovell asserted that commission merchants would sometimes sell salt secretly, undercutting association prices, for the purpose of raising capital for the manufacturer. He secured the conviction of a Madison, Indiana, dealer on this charge by the vigilance committee when he bought salt from the merchant at two cents less than the regular association price.[6]

Although the Kanawha Salt Association lacked the power of complete control and the capital strength to solve the major problems confronting the decentralized industry, it succeeded in raising the profit margins of the producer on his vended salt. After it diminished the amount of surplus salt remaining after the banner production year of 1846, the association gradually raised the bushel price in the Cincinnati market from twenty cents in March 1847 to thirty-one and a half cents in September 1848. In September 1849 it set the Cincinnati price at thirty-five cents.[7] The association paid a high per-barrel commission to agents to encourage them to remain honest and to maintain prices in depressed periods. Whereas the usual commission was twenty to twenty-five cents, the association at times offered up to forty-five cents to commission merchants who guarded the set price.[8]

Price violations became more widespread in 1850. As sales margins widened over production costs, manufacturers appeared more willing to violate association prices to consummate sales and to acquire capital.

When complaints became frequent, the vigilance committee appointed an investigatory group to meet all the salt commission merchants in Maysville, Kentucky. The group found that rules were universally violated, some transgressed by the merchants' free will and others "by colleaguing" with the producer. The investigators originally intended to discharge all guilty parties, but they changed their minds upon learning of the situation and agreed "to let them off if they promised to do better hereafter." The committee discovered the same state of affairs at other river markets.[9]

In November and December 1850 commission merchants, instructed by individual salt manufacturers, undercut the established price of thirty cents in the Cincinnati market. They often deducted up to 25-50 percent from association prices.[10] In defense, a salt maker instructed his Cincinnati agent to adhere to association prices if possible, but if others reduced their prices, he was to do likewise.[11]

Sometime in the last quarter of 1850 the temptation to capital-starved manufacturers to violate the Kanawha Salt Association agreement became too intense. The high prices offered short-term opportunities of gain to producers and fostered the beginning of the accumulation of a salt surplus in markets. Discretionary consumers, seeing the buildup and anticipating the expiration of the association, delayed purchases. Producers, well knowing the inevitable result of a surplus, ran for the economic exits with whatever capital they could acquire. In its final year the cooperative Kanawha Salt Association could not effectively regulate production and markets. At the time of the association's dissolution on December 31, 1850, manufacturers estimated that one million bushels of surplus Kanawha salt remained in the distribution network.[12]

With these conditions, manufacturers had to exert every effort to conclude a new arrangement to succeed the Kanawha Salt Association. According to Richard C.M. Lovell, the salt makers had to "devise some way to or means to make a living—to keep them from utter ruin." As early as January 1850 the producers had begun negotiations to form a new salt company.[13] In February 1851 they created Ruffner, Donnally and Company, a joint stock venture.

Unlike the association, the centralized Ruffner, Donnally and Company directly controlled the production and marketing of salt. In the preamble to their agreement, the salt makers observed that the condition of their industry rendered an arrangement necessary to lessen output, to reduce competition, and to secure a more efficient shipping and marketing system. The several stated objectives of the copartners were to buy and deal in salt manufactured in Kanawha County, to buy and lease coal and salt properties, to purchase "all articles and provisions necessary to be had and used or vended in carrying out objects of this co-partnership, and for the further purpose of shipping of, and vending said Salt in such markets as may be deemed expedient [in] The Western & South Western states."[14]

The company was to operate until January 1, 1856, when it would expire by limitation. In order to avoid the disastrous results incurred by Hewitt, Ruffner and Company in the aftermath of the Panic of 1837, however, the stockholders reserved the option of dissolving the concern on December 31, 1851, or at the end of any calendar year upon sixty days' previous notice. The stockholders refused to guarantee profitable set prices and leases to manufacturers and lessors in future economic adversity as Hewitt, Ruffner and Company had.

The company had a capitalization of two hundred thousand dollars, divided into two thousand shares of capital stock of one hundred dollars par value. The copartnership consisted of twenty-two individual manufacturers and thirteen producers associated in six firms. The stockholders were John N. Clarkson (221 shares); William C. Brooks (170); John D. Lewis (152); Andrew F. Donnally, Lewis F. Donnally, and William Donnally, doing business as Andrew F. Donnally and Company (149); Samuel H. Early (125); John P. Hale (103); William D. Shrewsbury (100); Lewis Ruffner (80); Nathaniel V. Wilson and Henry H. Wood (70 each); William D. Shrewsbury, Henry H. Wood, John D. Lewis, George H. Warth, John A. Warth, and Job English, doing business as G.H. Warth and Company, and George H. Warth and Job English, doing business as Warth and English (67) each; William A. McMullin (56); John D. Lewis and William D. Shrewsbury, doing business as Lewis and Shrewsbury (52); Frederick Brooks, James S.O. Brooks, James H. Fry, Richard C.M. Lovell, and Samuel A. Miller (50 each); Gustavius B. Quarrier (45); Crockett Ingles (44); Henry Chappell (42); E.S. Arnold and William I. Rand, doing business as Arnold and Rand, and Ira Hurt and Richard A. Hurt, doing business as Ira Hurt and Son (40 each); Franklin Noyes (30); Leonora C. Rogers (12); Nathaniel S. Brooks (10); and William A. Brigham (5). Thus 2,000 shares were sold.

To encourage the purchase of stock and to ease the burden of raising capital, the agreement spread the payment for subscribed shares over twenty months. Subscribers paid 6-percent installments over the first ten months of company operations and 4 percent over the next ten months. Stockholders who rented dead furnaces to the company could have the monthly installments deducted from the quarterly rental payments. Also, subscribers could deduct their payments for stock from their three-month notes for salt. If any subscriber failed to pay the installment for his stock within twenty days of the due date, the principal agents had to sell the defaulted stock at public auction at the company's counting room, after advertising the delinquency and posting a notice on the door of the room thirty days in advance. The purchaser had to pay the total amount of his bid. If the sale price was less than the delinquent amount and the remaining installments, the subscriber owed the deficiency to the company. The company retained the money from the auction and the right to sue the subscriber for the deficiency.

Transfers of stock could be made on the company's books, but several conditions regulated changes in ownership. The person proposing to transfer ownership could not have an outstanding debt or claim due to the company. The recipient of the stock was not entitled to vote unless he was an original shareholder in the enterprise. In order to acquire voting rights and to receive dividends, the recipient had to submit his salt property to the jurisdiction of Ruffner, Donnally and Company. If possible transfer of stock resulted from a copartner's death, the same conditions applied.

General meetings for stockholders were held twice a year, on the first Mondays in March and April. Unless otherwise provided, voting was by shares. A majority of voting stock had to be represented to create a quorum. Proxies could be voted if they were filed in the company office.

The copartners vested management of Ruffner, Donnally and Company in the hands of five "resident principal agents." The stockholders chose these officers after all contracts creating the company were concluded. One of the principal agents would be the "Office Agent, Book keeper and financier," to be "entrusted with the custody of the funds, papers, vouchers &C &C. of the company." Unlike the other principal agents, he did not have to be a manufacturer of salt or the owner of salt property in Kanawha County. His yearly compensation was $2,500. Two other principal agents would be "shipping and active agents" at a yearly salary of $1,500 each. The remaining two would be "consulting and advising agents," paid $500 each per year. Collectively, the principal agents had great power, but sometimes stockholders could intervene. The five agents could appoint, remove, and fix the compensation of all subagents. They oversaw the company store and furnished the store manager with necessary funds. They could borrow up to $250,000 when they deemed it prudent. They could declare dividends, and they enjoyed complete freedom to lease salt property when the interest of the company required it. The principal agents completely supervised the two agents in Cincinnati and Louisville who managed all company affairs in downriver markets, and they authorized those agents to use the company name in conducting business.

The office agent conducted the correspondence of the company, employing such clerks and assistants as he thought necessary. He had to keep all books in the usual mercantile method. He had to make all correspondence and books accessible to the examination of any stockholders who might desire to see them. Usually the office agent had the authority to sign the name of the firm, but three principal agents could authorize, in writing, a principal agent or shareholder to sign or endorse the firm's name for a limited time and for a specific purpose.

The two shipping agents had "actively, industriously and with an eye single to the true interests of the company" to conduct the "out door" business of the firm in Kanawha County. The two consulting agents were to be in the counting room whenever their associates required their presence and at appropriate times to confer and advise in the conduct of business.

Three of the principal agents, excluding the office agent, were selected by the stockholders as a standing committee of stockholders. This committee was to meet at least quarterly at the company's counting room to investigate every transaction and account. It had to demand quarterly balance sheets from the office agent. The committee had the power to examine every agent's accounts. It had to keep a record of its proceedings and report them to the next meeting of the stockholders with appropriate remarks and recommendations. The committee could call special stockholders' meetings with five days' notice. Each committee member earned an extra annual remuneration of one hundred dollars.

The stockholders could intervene in company affairs. Shareholders who were manufacturers annually selected two salt inspectors by a majority of voted shares. They also elected one of their number as the manager of the company store to work under the supervision of the principal agents. The stockholders had the authority to discharge any principal agent, any member of the standing committee of stockholders, any inspector, or the store manager for any reason at any time. It was expected that the principal agents would declare dividends, but a majority of stockholders could declare dividends if the manager refused and if financial conditions warranted. Also, stockholders had to assent by vote to the markets in which Kanawha salt was to be sold.

The stockholders agreed that none of their group, except those who were principal agents, could sign the name of the firm unless specifically authorized by the agents. If any stockholder violated this prohibition to the loss of the company, he was liable for the deficiency to the extent of his stock, dividends, and the value of his individual property. Stockholders who acquired salt property not controlled by the company agreed to lease the wells and furnaces to the company on the same general terms as all other rented facilities. If a stockholder refused to submit an acquisition to company control, the company was empowered to occupy the property until a lease was concluded or until an injunction restraining operation was obtained. The stockholders and the company retained the privilege of maintaining actions of law against each other.

The company had to maintain "a Dry Goods & Grocery store" in Kanawha Salines for use by stockholders and others. The store had to charge an uniform price for goods sold to stockholders and to earn an uniform rate of profit. The store could deduct store debts from the proceeds of the manufacturers' salt sales and dead rents.

The company paid manufacturers sixteen cents per bushel for first-quality salt and fourteen cents for second-quality salt in negotiable notes payable at the bank in equal amounts, due three, six, and nine months from the delivery date. The company paid dead rents in cash on a quarterly basis. Manufacturers had to deliver their salt, drained for at least three days, in good, well-seasoned, well-nailed lined barrels. All salt had to be delivered, but producers could take salt for their own consumption or for sale to their salt packers.

The two salt inspectors, before assuming office, had to swear before a Kanawha County justice of the peace "impartially and honestly to weigh and inspect all the salt made or to be made for the company, marking and branding all the barrels in plain letters with their true weight and quality, and the names of the makers." The company or manufacturer could appeal an inspector's decision to five impartial men, two selected by each party and the fifth chosen by the four, for final resolution. The manufacturer paid the inspection fee and charges in all cases.

With the exception of the saltworks of one partnership, Ruffner, Donnally and Company exercised complete control of all salt properties in Kanawha County. In cases where manufacturers did not subscribe to the articles of agreement creating Ruffner, Donnally and Company, the company rented the properties with the use of the lease and re-lease clauses and with other contractual stipulations that allowed reentry and collection of damages by the company in case of contract violations. The agreement with Richard C.M. Lovell was typical. Lovell leased to Ruffner, Donnally and Company his salt property "with the Coal Mines Rail Roads, furnaces, Salt Wells, Salt House, and other houses, fixtures, and appurtenances" for a five-year term until January 1, 1856. The company retained the option of annulling the agreement at the end of any calendar year after issuing sixty days' written notice. Lovell agreed that if he should acquire other salt interests, he would lease them to the company on similar terms. The joint stock company granted Lovell permission to occupy the property until the expiration of the organization or until Lovell or his legal representatives failed to comply with contract provisions. Ruffner, Donnally and Company reserved the right to reenter the property upon the failure of any part of the agreement.[15]

For the privilege of occupancy, Lovell agreed to deliver all salt manufactured at his furnace to the company's salt inspector at the end of
each month. The salt had to meet the general specifications provided in
the original copartnership agreement of stockholders, and Lovell received identical compensation. Lovell promised not to "Sell, Carry away
or Ship, or in any Manner Cause to be Sold, Carried away, or shipped
by or to any other persons other than to said Ruffner Donnally & Co., or
their authorized agents any Salt whatever." If Lovell violated this prohibition, the company enjoyed the right of reentry, and Lovell had to
pay ten cents for each bushel involved. Ruffner, Donnally and Company
could obtain damages from funds owed to Lovell or from dividends on
his capital stock, or it could recover damages by legal suit.

The contract also restricted production and prevented plant expansion. If Lovell ran his furnace on Sunday, he would be liable to a penalty
of ten dollars for each hour of operation. Lovell also agreed not to increase the boiling capacity of the existing furnace or to erect any new
furnace on the property during the existence of the company. If he violated this covenant, Ruffner, Donnally and Company could reenter the
property, collect ten cents for each bushel of salt manufactured on the
new or enlarged facilities, and discount the amount from obligations
outstanding to Lovell or sue for damages.

Ruffner, Donnally and Company did not gain control of Dickinson
& Shrewsbury, the largest single company in the Kanawha salt industry. In 1850 thirty-three salt companies existed. The firms had $889,400
total capital invested in real and personal property in the Kanawha enterprise, and of this Dickinson & Shrewsbury held $103,400. Of the total
annual product of 3,104,898 bushels, Dickinson & Shrewsbury produced 252,202.[16] As the dominant organization, Dickinson & Shrewsbury was in an advantageous position in the negotiations for the
creation of the joint stock company. A circuit judge later stated that
"many & great efforts were Made to induce them to become Members of
the Company." The other manufacturers offered to pay the firm a premium of two to three cents per bushel for its salt in order to secure its
agreement, but Dickinson & Shrewsbury refused. Nevertheless, the
firm agreed to vend its product at the Ruffner, Donnally and Company
price in all markets. It would not be regulated by production controls or
by assignment of markets for vending. Thus Dickinson & Shrewsbury,
maintaining its independence, benefited fully from the sacrifices of the
other manufacturers.[17]

The Ruffner, Donnally and Company arrangement, a blend of
shareholder democracy and managerial centralization, and its contracts
with manufacturers represent the application of legal and practical business experience gained by the Kanawha salt makers and their lawyers

from previous agreements. Management was centralized, but the stockholders directly selected the principal agents, the manager of the company store, and the salt inspectors and held extensive powers of removal. Stockholders could intervene in management by declaring dividends and by approving markets. They could also terminate the arrangement upon notice, so that they could avoid continued financial losses during depressed economic circumstances, when lessors and manufacturers who were not shareholders were profiting from the guaranteed delivery prices. No limitation on production restrained operating furnaces. Therefore, a producer could efficiently employ his labor and mechanical resources without suspending operations. The prohibition against plant expansion or modernization or new construction prevented manufacturers from increasing their productive capacity under guaranteed purchase agreements and upsetting the company's production calculations in dead renting other salt properties. The company could regulate output with relative certainty, and it could avoid, as Hewitt, Ruffner and Company was unable to do, additional expenditures for further reduction of production.

Ruffner, Donnally and Company surmounted the problem of internal control of the production area, although it did not control Dickinson & Shrewsbury. The test for the company would be how successfully it would confront competition, marketing, the changing western transportation system and economy, and national economic conditions.

13

Ruffner, Donnally & Company and the External Economy

Extant correspondence permits a detailed view of the day-to-day operations and managerial decisions of Ruffner, Donnally and Company that is not possible for other antebellum salt agencies, joint stock companies, or individual Kanawha manufacturers.[1] Ironically, the absence of other financial and legal sources prevents an accurate appraisal of the profits and success of Ruffner, Donnally and Company. Therefore, less is known about its overall impact than about the profitability of other central sales agencies and joint stock ventures.

In its first year of operation, Ruffner, Donnally and Company had to overcome some severe marketing problems throughout the West. The collapse of the Kanawha Salt Association left the salt business completely prostrated. Over one million bushels of surplus salt reposed in major western markets. Outside speculators held much of the surplus, and knowing of the creation of Ruffner, Donnally and Company, they awaited an opportunity to sell the appreciated commodity.[2] The company planned to maintain low supplies and prices until the disposal of outside stocks.[3] In February 1851 it set the bushel price at twenty-five cents in the Cincinnati market and maintained the quotation until July 1, 1852. Although the company refused to consummate large sales in order to purge the market of outside salt, it did sell some at twenty-one to twenty-two cents per bushel to packers on four-month notes.[4] To accomplish its objective, Ruffner, Donnally and Company incurred large initial expenses. The liabilities of its Cincinnati agency in the first twelve and a half months of operation were $10,424.28, excluding interest charges and the traveling expenses of agents. Added to the costs of the first year was the loss of salt boats sunk by the breakup of early ice on the Great Kanawha River in December 1851.[5]

Ruffner, Donnally and Company had an extensive production, distribution, and marketing organization. The home agency at Kanawha Salines determined policy and controlled the conduct of the company's affairs. Samuel A. Miller, an attorney, was the general business manager. The company had primary downriver offices at Cincinnati and Louisville. Joseph H. Rogers, the Cincinnati agent, managed all sales between the mouth of the Great Kanawha River and Louisville. Lewis Ruffner and John B. Smith managed the Louisville agency, which handled all transactions on the Ohio River below Louisville, on the Mississippi, and on the various tributaries, including the White, Wabash, Cumberland, Tennessee, Osage, Forked Deer, and Hatchie. The commission merchants of Hewitt, Roe and Company aided the Louisville agency in distributing from St. Louis. After the company purchased most of the salt produced in Meigs County, Ohio, and Mason County, Virginia, it appointed James Mitchell as its agent to receive the commodity at the various Ohio River furnaces. Two men supervised the transportation and actual distribution of the salt on the river and made collections from commission merchants and individual agents. William A. Lewis replaced O.F. Jackson as the supervisor of operations on the Ohio River and its tributaries above Louisville after Jackson lost $3,998.97 of company money in his gambling den.[6] N.B. Cabell handled all distributions and collections on the Ohio River and tributary rivers between Louisville and Cairo, Illinois.

The home agency operated the large company store that furnished mercantile credit to salt manufacturers and that lessened the immediate capital needs of the company. The company refused to use its downriver facilities or the salt makers' receipts in its possession to obtain supplies for individual producers. All purchases had to be made at the home agency, which regularly used store accounts to discharge obligations to manufacturers for delivered salt or for furnace rentals. The major demands of the store's customers were for pork products, dry goods, and hardware.[7]

The home agency had to coordinate a large flotilla of steamboats and flatboats to transport and distribute salt to river markets. Ruffner, Donnally and Company relied upon its own fleet of four steamboats— the *Artella Wood*, the *Salem*, the *Return*, and the *Stella*—to deliver salt on tributary streams between the Falls of the Ohio and St. Louis and to convey freight and supplies to Kanawha Salines. Flatboats distributed salt on the Ohio River and its tributaries above Louisville. In some years the number of flatboats exceeded four hundred.[8]

The Cincinnati agent, located in the strategic marketing center, coordinated much of the flatboat traffic. Ruffner, Donnally and Company wanted to send the flatboats in fleets so that labor would be available in extenuating circumstances and for ease of supervision and handling. The home agency forwarded a list of boats dispatched to the Cincinnati agent, who then knew each boat's number, its pilot, the quantity of barrels carried, and who had manufactured the salt on board. The agent arranged for unloading the boat in the Queen City or redirected it to another point downriver.[9]

After the flatboat was unloaded, the agent either sold it or made arrangements to have it towed back to the Salines. An extensive market in flatboats existed in river towns. The Cincinnati and Louisville agents also purchased other flatboats to be towed to Ohio River salt furnaces for loading. The company steamboat or an independent boat towed eight flats upriver at a time.[10]

Joseph H. Rogers must have thought that flatboat shipments descended in torrents from the production area. In June 1853 he informed the home agency that he would need approximately ten thousand barrels of salt to add to his twelve-thousand-barrel stock to prepare for the winter season. By September, company distributors from the Kanawha to Louisville were oversupplied.[11] Because Rogers had filled his storage space, twenty-three loaded flatboats accumulated at Columbia, the Queen City's mooring area. He pleaded with the home agency to suspend shipments while he reduced the quantity price at the river in order to unload the boats. Nevertheless, by November 30 thirty vessels were docked at Columbia and were in danger of sinking by waves from large passing steamboats. The frozen Ohio finally stopped salt arrivals during the packing season.[12]

The Cincinnati and Louisville agents of Ruffner, Donnally and Company faced the difficult task of distributing salt at market towns. Fluctuating water levels affected river markets. If they placed a surplus of salt in one location, setting prices would be difficult, storage costs would escalate, and mercantile risks would increase. Shortages would raise prices and attract competition, but the company could not sell something it did not have. Generally in May and June each year, the agents estimated the quantities of salt needed in each market area. The company sent laden steamboats to supply the towns on swollen tributary streams before stocking the Ohio River markets. In the spring, steamboats could carry salt on these normally smaller and shallower streams.[13] Upon taking orders, the Cincinnati agent would warn distributors that the company would not deliver on low water and that sufficient quantities should be ordered for the winter season while the water was high.[14] Many merchants, perhaps because of the payment necessary upon receipt of salt, refused to take adequate supplies. When the river level dropped, the merchants, being short, would demand supplies from Cincinnati.[15]

The merchantable characteristics of salt caused financial losses if a particular market was oversupplied. Besides incurring possible storage costs, the salt would dry over a period of time and become much lighter in weight. Because the wooden staves in barrels became brittle, cooperage repairs were frequent and necessary. Customary handling procedures became impossible. Salt stored in warehouses for extended periods also might be lost owing to fire, flood, or other causes.[16]

Although Ruffner, Donnally and Company directly controlled the Cincinnati and Louisville agencies, it depended upon independent commission merchants to vend its product outside these market centers. To obtain dealerships, prospective vendors had to comply with several conditions. Upon receiving the salt, the merchant had to advance one dollar for each barrel to cover freight charges. He had to forward the balance as the barrels were sold, after deduction of a twenty-cent-per-barrel commission, which paid all charges for selling, drayage, and storage. The merchant also had to sign a receipt in which he agreed to abide by company instructions and to keep the salt from "waste and exposure to the weather."[17]

The company had difficulty controlling the commission merchants. Sheer numbers prevented effective supervision. For example, in 1853 Joseph H. Rogers in Cincinnati was responsible for 102 merchants in Virginia, Ohio, Kentucky, and Indiana. A Portsmouth, Ohio, agent deducted excess commissions when prices were high, and Rogers chided: "We did not ask our Agents to reduce the Commission for Selling Salt when the price was reduced & we do not advance the Commission with the price." A rival agent in Ripley, Ohio, charged his competitor with deducting commissions from the purchase price, warning a prospective buyer that the price was being advanced, and retaining a supply of company salt on his own account after the price was increased. After confronting the merchant with the charges and expressing the hope that innocence might be established, Rogers warned: "No one that would do so with the article he had on Commission would be worthy of Confidence." The Queen City manager constantly had to warn agents of the consequences of handling independent salt. He exerted pressure on many agents to expand their storage space for Kanawha salt.[18]

A bitter controversy arose between the Cincinnati agency and White, Cunningham and Company, commission merchants of Madison, Indiana, over the purchase of independent salt. Another agent in Madison possessed two thousand barrels of independent salt that Ruffner, Donnally and Company desired to control because it was being sold cheaper. Also, the company wanted to advance prices and prevent the independent from benefiting. Rogers instructed White, Cunningham and Company to purchase the barrels on the salt company's account without mentioning the real purchaser. After buying the outside salt at Rogers's instruction, the Madison firm maintained that it had been directed to purchase it for itself.[19]

The company insisted, as was customary with Kanawha salt manufacturers, that barreled salt be sold in the original package at "lick
weight," the weight of the product at inspection. Since the salt subse-
quently drained and became lighter, merchants could falsely report the
weight of the salt sold in market if the package was opened. A Lexington, Kentucky, commission merchant attempted to cheat on his returns
to the Cincinnati agency on the basis of weights of Pomeroy salt. Joseph
H. Rogers informed him that disinterested parties weighed the barrels:
"We had a Clerk standing by the Scale & So they had. We know the Salt
was Weighed Correctly."[20]

Ruffner, Donnally and Company also encountered the difficulty of
agents' selling large quantities of salt to people who intended to speculate in the commodity. The company continually warned agents of the
sale of large lots to persons other than packers and other large users,
but speculation was difficult to prevent. Agents were tempted to sell
huge quantities in order to receive the commission. Regraters could always benefit from the company's price advances. When informed by
the home agency of a possible speculation in Nashville, the Louisville
manager outlined the difficulties of prevention: "Salt is like any other
article of Comerce liable to be bought up and when the price is once
fixed parties Can buy If they choose in Small ways so no agent Can Sus-
pect them and When all is Sumed up it amounts up."[21] The Cincinnati
agent had to combat the regrating efforts of Frederick F. Brooks, who
had been his predecessor as Queen City agent in the first year of the
company. Being knowledgeable about the business, Brooks had purchased one thousand barrels of salt from the company agent in Madison, Indiana, in August 1853, to hold until the price was advanced for
the packing season.[22] Keeping track of Brooks's whereabouts, Rogers
detected when the speculator was going to Madison to sell his salt. He
immediately informed his Madison agent and advised him to consummate all large pending sales.[23]

The management of Ruffner, Donnally and Company exercised an
extensive and remarkable grasp of the economic conditions of the salt
trade in the Ohio and Mississippi river basins. The firm's adjustment to
competitive factors, internal and external, in the domestic and foreign
spheres of salt commerce was always rapid and calculated. From 1851
through 1855 Ruffner, Donnally and Company had five interrelated organizational goals for dominating its sales area. First, the company
sought exclusive control of the salt trade in the market area on the Ohio
River and tributary streams between the mouth of the Great Kanawha
and Louisville and on the Ohio River tributaries below Louisville of the
Wabash, the Green, and, to a lesser extent, the Cumberland. The firm
devoted especial attention to the largest salt consumers in the area, the

pork packers. Second, it managed Ohio River markets below Louisville and Mississippi River markets to foreclose, to the greatest extent possible, the penetration of imported salts shipped from New Orleans into the primary market area. Third, Ruffner, Donnally and Company exercised vigilance on the Ohio River above Point Pleasant, Virginia, to prevent penetration of the primary market by Ohio and Pennsylvania salt manufacturers. It eventually dominated markets up the river to Wheeling. Fourth, the company constantly monitored the cost and competitiveness of New York salt in order to adopt strategies to minimize its incursion into market areas. Finally, after 1852 the Kanawha producers attempted to achieve complete control of all salt manufactured by the new Ohio River salt furnaces, in Mason County, Virginia, and Meigs County, Ohio.

The largest single market for Kanawha salt was the pork-packing industry at Maysville, Cincinnati, and Louisville. The Cincinnati and Louisville agents tried to contract for salt deliveries at fixed prices to major packers in their districts during April and May before the packing season. Commission merchants handling Kanawha salt outside these packing centers were to do likewise. Concluding arrangements early enabled agents to plan orderly deliveries, made speculation by independent merchants more difficult, and discouraged packers from ordering imported salt from New Orleans. The contract price was based on the cost of foreign salt freighted from New Orleans.[24] The company delivered the salt to packers between June and September. The firm promised to complete all deliveries before the commencement of the packing season. In 1854 low water prevented Ruffner, Donnally and Company from fulfilling supply contracts to Louisville packers at thirty-seven and a half cents per bushel. The firm had to "buy off" at fifty cents per bushel.[25]

Ruffner, Donnally and Company used brand recognition to coax packers to use its best salt instead of Liverpool blown. Consumers and packers often preferred the Liverpool salt because of its very white appearance. Contracts signed with packers often provided for the delivery of stated quantities of the better (very white) Kanawha salts: that produced by Joseph Lovell, James S.O. Brooks, Henry H. Wood, or Andrew F. Donnally and Company. Packers used these salts to cure hams.[26]

Ruffner, Donnally and Company constantly monitored the importation of salt at New Orleans and upriver freight rates in order to assess the impact of foreign salt on sales on the lower Ohio and Mississippi rivers. To control the salt price, company agents manipulated their salt deliveries to the St. Louis area, keeping surplus supplies at that point so that low prices would deter steamboat captains from carrying imported salt. If foreign salt penetrated the prime market area above Louisville, company agents exerted every effort to purchase substantial quantities of Liverpool, Turk's Island, and Mediterranean salt to resell.[27] The threat of importations made the Mississippi River markets extremely precarious. Commenting on the possibility of sales in the Memphis area, the Louisville agent noted: "These Markets we will avoid this year as we did last & if any Salt sent there we will make the sales at once deliver the Salt at Memphis & take paper at 6 or 8 m/d with at least one good endorser." Ruffner, Donnally and Company tried to avoid sales on the lower Mississippi, especially the Forked Deer and Hatchie rivers, since, as the Louisville agent put it, they "do not pay overly well." Kanawha salt quantities furnished from year to year to the Missouri market varied greatly. The Louisville agency of Ruffner, Donnally and Company would sometimes rush salt to Hewitt, Roe and Company of St. Louis when no imported salt was on the upper reaches of the Mississippi or downstream.[28]

In the spring of 1854 Ruffner, Donnally and Company began negotiations with the New Orleans commercial house of Cobb, Martin and Company to formulate a plan to speculate in and maintain high, mutually profitable price levels in imported sack salt. Both firms could profit from control of the foreign salt, and Ruffner, Donnally and Company could obtain higher profit margins on Kanawha salt sales. Cobb, Martin and Company estimated that the two firms would have to purchase 150,000 bags in order to control the market to any extent but that purchases of over 100,000 bags would tend to advance prices. The New Orleans firm proposed that the necessary funds be raised by both parties. Owing to the stringency in money matters at New Orleans and St. Louis, Lewis Ruffner deduced that only the salt company could ultimately raise the necessary amount. In April, Ruffner traveled to New Orleans to investigate the speculative possibilities. After a week, he concluded that a speculation by the salt company would be imprudent. Huge stocks of foreign salt were stored, and more was arriving from England. High freight rates into the interior of the United States accounted for the large quantity in storage and would deter shipments into the Kanawha market area. The deflated money market compelled Cobb, Martin and Company to decline entering a speculation. Ruffner concurred in this decision, concluding, "Our main interest looked at Keep. g up the rates—This will I think be accomplished without us." In late summer Ruffner's assumption appeared to be correct.[29]

Ruffner, Donnally and Company's operations reached into the Muskingum River area of Ohio and northward to Pittsburgh on the upper Ohio River. The company used this area, much like the St. Louis area, to dump excess salt from the Cincinnati market and to meet competition from New York, the Muskingum River factories, and western

Pennsylvania. The Cincinnati agent often shipped surplus salt to Wheeling when cheap freight rates were available on ascending steamers. In the summer of 1853 the firm's agent on the upper Ohio, Frederick Brooks, purchased the entire production of the Muskingum River salt furnaces and sold the commodity in Ohio to meet competition from New York State. In 1854 he again acquired most of the thirty-thousand-barrel output of Muskingum furnaces for $1.50 per 280-pound barrel. After surmising that twenty thousand barrels would be sold on the Ohio River above Marietta, Brooks reported to the home agency that he had purchased all Muskingum salt" with the exception of two furnaces that produce about 4000 Barrels which I think may yet be obtained by suitable *address & appliances.*"[30]

Besides facing the competition from New York in the upper Ohio Valley, Ruffner, Donnally and Company had to adjust prices to meet those of the salt of the Conemaugh and Kiskiminetas river areas of western Pennsylvania. In 1853 Brooks entered a price-fixing arrangement with the Keystone State producers with ease, because all sales were consummated at Pittsburgh. The two groups attempted to partition markets, but the Pennsylvanians desired exclusive control of the Wheeling market. A counterproposal by Ruffner, Donnally and Company provided for a division of markets at Wheeling with competition to be maintained at that city. The Kanawha company would control the area below, and the Pennsylvanians would dominate all territory above. James H. Stout, the Kanawha firm's commission merchant in Wheeling, supplied regular information on salt commerce in western Pennsylvania.[31]

Salt manufactured in Onondaga County, New York, furnished a major source of domestic competition for the Kanawha product. In their economic characteristics, the Kanawha and Onondaga industries were very similar. The two factors affecting the price of salt from New York or the Great Lakes in what the Kanawha manufacturers considered their market area were the original cost at the furnace and freight charges. The Kanawha industry had the advantage of cheap fuel costs for manufacturing fine-grained salt. Until the construction of railroads into the Pennsylvania coal region, New York salt production depended for fuel on wood, a diminishing resource that was increasingly distant from the production site. Solar evaporation, however, did produce some coarse-grained New York salt.

The officials of Ruffner, Donnally and Company kept abreast of the economic conditions of the New York industry. The company reviewed sale prices in Onondaga County; the transportation rates on the Erie Canal and freight costs from Buffalo and Oswego to Lake Erie ports; market prices in lake ports, especially Sandusky, Cleveland, and Toledo; freight rates on the Ohio canal system; and general indicators of supply and demand. In August 1853 Joseph H. Rogers advised the home agency that "the Price at Sandusky Cleveland etc depends on the Freight from Works to the points on the Lake they Selling just what it Cost them Sometimes More Sometimes Less."[32] On the eve of the 1853 packing season, Rogers wrote commission merchants in Cleveland, Sandusky, Toledo, and Chicago requesting information about New York salt without mentioning his connection with Ruffner, Donnally and Company.[33] He asked the Toledo merchant to tell him "the present price of N. York salt—the Supply on hand—the probable price of Salt during the Winter & the probable Supply—the price of Freight to this point & to Dayton." After gathering the necessary information, the Cincinnati agent advised the Louisville agency that "New York Salt is now Selling . . . at 162 cts per bbl at Cleveland & 60 cts per bbl Freight to Indianapolis you will See that they will Cut us off of a Very large portion of the Sales to the Country in both Indiana & Ohio—as the Salt is much Cheaper."[34]

As early as 1842, Kanawha producers had visited the New York saltworks and inspected the economic and technical condition of the industry. In June 1854 Lewis Ruffner and Joseph H. Rogers explored the Onondaga furnaces and interviewed many persons. They examined everything from furnace construction and capacity, total production quantities, fuel problems, and marketing methods to freight rates in their report to the home agency. Rogers summarized current price factors affecting New York salt in the Cincinnati market: "Cost of Salt $1.43 Freight to Oswego 10 cts bbl Freight from Oswego to Tolledo 10 to 12 cts per bbl Frt from Toledo here 43 to 50 cts per bbl. Say Cost here not over $215 per bbl or 38 ½ cts per bushel."[35]

Ruffner, Donnally and Company, in keeping abreast of salt developments in the Empire State, paid an informer residing in the area. During 1854 George Stephens, a secretary in the New York salt superintendent's office, voluntarily reported general industry conditions on a monthly basis to the Kanawha company. In February 1855 the Louisville agent sent Stephens a New York draft for one hundred dollars. Stephens replied, "I can assure you [it] was entirely unexpected, which must leave me largely indebted to you which you must command my services when I can be of use to you." John B. Smith informed the home agency that Stephens would furnish monthly statements throughout 1855.[36]

In February 1853 Ruffner, Donnally and Company altered the size of the customary barrels in order to compete with New York salt in interior Ohio. New York salt was distributed in 280-pound barrels, whereas Kanawha salt had always been packed in 350-pound barrels, containing seven or more bushels. The retail trade and small consumers preferred the smaller containers. When the plan was being formulated, Joseph H.

Rogers observed: "We are in hopes to introduce them on the Canal & Rail Road & will do what we Can to introduce them with the Retail trade in the City." He further suggested that "the packages ought to be good & neat, to Come in Competition with New York Salt & the Weight Uniform & ought to be put on with a brand made for the purpose." The company packed the premium Lovell brand salt in the smaller barrels to meet Onondaga competition. In April the Cincinnati agent began extensive distribution efforts in interior Ohio, where acceptance of the smaller barrels was almost immediate.[37]

Dealers located on the Ohio River tried to obtain salt in the small containers, but the company initially refused to place the limited quantities in a noncompetitive location. Rogers informed a Maysville merchant: "The quantity of Salt put up in Small bbls will be Very Small & the Company do not propose distributing any out on Commission along the river it is intended to be put in Competition with the New York Salt on the Rail Roads & Canals."[38] Later Rogers advised modification of the Ohio River ban in order to furnish small barrels to Portsmouth, where the Ohio Canal brought Onondaga salt from Cleveland. Eventually, when sufficient quantities of 280-pound barrels quenched demand in interior Ohio, Rogers liberalized distributions, because the company realized a ten-cent-per-bushel premium on salt sold in small containers.[39]

When the company was contemplating the introduction of the small barrels, Joseph H. Rogers began negotiations with the superintendent of the Little Miami Railroad for a reduction of freight rates. The Cincinnati agent informed the official of the new barrel size and suggested, "If you put the price of Freight at a Low ratio (as low in proportion to distance as the Lake Salt is brot this Way) we can in Crease the shipments Very much on your Road." The railroad increased the competitive possibilities of Kanawha salt by adjusting rates to twenty-five cents per barrel for each carload of fifty containers to any place between Cincinnati and Springfield. Rogers then began encouraging an Urbana, Ohio, commission merchant to induce the Mad River and Lake Erie Railroad to reduce transportation rates on Kanawha salt north of Springfield.[40]

In 1850 brine deposits were discovered on the Ohio River at Ice's Creek in Mason County, Virginia. In the following decade, salt furnaces mushroomed on both sides of the river, and production capabilities expanded. In 1851 and 1852 three small salt companies in Mason County, Virginia, and Meigs County, Ohio, competed with the Kanawha product. In January 1853 Ruffner, Donnally and Company concluded agreements with William J. Stephens of West Columbia, Virginia, the Pomeroy Salt Company of Pomeroy, Ohio, and the Coalport Salt Company of Ohio to purchase their entire production for 1853. The three firms received nineteen cents per bushel for their salt.[41]

In 1854 and 1855 Ruffner, Donnally and Company purchased the output of all Ohio River salt factories except one. The West Columbia Mining and Manufacturing Company, the Pomeroy Salt Company, and the Coalport Salt Company sold their entire output for nineteen cents per bushel, but the Coal Ridge Salt Company's single furnace remained outside the Kanawha company's control.[42] The Coal Ridge Salt Company, located near Pomeroy, Ohio, operated independently throughout the tenure of Ruffner, Donnally and Company, although the Kanawha company constantly attempted to purchase its output.[43]

Acting outside the Kanawha combination, Lemuel H. Sargent, the Cincinnati sales agent of the Coal Ridge Salt Company, sometimes purchased the salt outright on his own account. Sargent paid twenty-one cents per bushel—two cents more than Ruffner, Donnally and Company— one-third in cash, one-third in twenty-four-month notes, and the remainder in thirty-six-month notes with security.[44] Generally, he sold the Coal Ridge product at the same price as Kanawha and other controlled salt, but when sales were not forthcoming, Sargent would intentionally sell large quantities at profitable rates to the Kanawha company. Joseph H. Rogers purchased three thousand barrels of Coal Ridge salt in May 1855 for thirty-five cents per bushel because he "did not wish it to get into other hands."[45]

The agents of Ruffner, Donnally and Company reacted to the presence of Coal Ridge salt in various ways. In June 1854, when packers began to purchase their salt stocks for the winter, the Cincinnati agent frantically requested more boats: "Sargent had 334 bbls by Steam last week & has to day 600 Bbls & he is making great Efforts to Sell & is Selling Considerable of it he being the only one that has it at the River." At times the company secretly acquired Sargent salt through third parties. John B. Smith, the Louisville agent, obtained control of a boatload of 884 barrels for thirty-six cents per bushel without Sargent's knowledge. Smith explained, "Sargents Boat was to go below the Falls, this I did not want & Kept a Constant watch on it to prevent it & in that way had to use a friend to Make the purchase." On another occasion, the Louisville agent resorted to cruder tactics. He negotiated unsuccessfully for three days with Sargent's boatman to purchase salt while "one of our agents was before him & one behind so I think he will find he had a hard road to travel."[46]

Setting prices for salt in the various markets was an extremely delicate matter. The Louisville and Cincinnati agents enjoyed autonomy in fixing price levels, but they sought general agreement with the home agency. Special situations arose when the agent had to reduce prices immediately to meet competition. In January 1855, near the end of the packing season, an independent brought four barges loaded with salt to Cincinnati. Joseph H. Rogers contemplated reducing the bushel price on Kanawha salt, as he did "not want him to finish furnishing the Packers." The later arrival of Liverpool and Turk's Island salt compelled him to reduce prices.[47]

Generally, Kanawha salt was slightly cheaper in Cincinnati than elsewhere because of competitive possibilities. In the Queen City three different prices existed: the wholesale price for purchases of twenty barrels or more out of storage, the wholesale price for quantity purchases at the river (the cheapest rate, as the company saved drayage and storage costs), and the retail price for purchases of fewer than twenty barrels. Maintaining a higher price outside Cincinnati presented some problems. In July 1853 Rogers advised the increase of the Queen City price because consumers outside the city would be dissatisfied and agents would become displeased.[48]

Timing price advances required canniness. Increasing prices in the early season, while rivers were open to navigation, could have disastrous effects. Joseph H. Rogers stated: "There is no doubt but the high prices Encourages much larger importations into this part of the Country & in that way reduced Sales of Kanawha." When Lewis Ruffner considered advancing the salt price in September 1853, the Cincinnati agent warned the home agency that dealers would have time to secure salt from elsewhere. In October, Rogers reported: "We find the imports of Lake Salt had Very Much increased the past two weeks which would be Natural from the great advance in Kan[a] & bringing all that Could be had on the Lake."[49]

Ruffner, Donnally and Company had to prepare the market for price increases. The company agents would warn commission merchants against contracting sales for future deliveries except at future current prices.[50] Also, sales in large quantities had to be avoided in order to realize better future profit margins and to prevent others from speculating on predictable price increases. The Cincinnati agent informed the home agency in August 1853: "There is Some Other talking of purchasing—I will not Sell any more than possible although Cannot refuse to Sell Some to Pork Men if they want although will not Sell say one more than 500 bbls." Purchases of independent salt had to be consummated to exercise market control and to prevent competitors from making profits from the increase. The Cincinnati agent instructed a commission merchant, who was to purchase independent salt secretly, to "Purchase it as Soon as you get this as we are advancing the price." Ultimately the company had to decide whether the total profits would be greater with increased margins or with increased volume. Joseph H.

Rogers complained to the home office in January 1855: "Salt is Entirely to[o] high & has been all the Season the Sales would have been much larger if the price had been lower."[51]

Dickinson & Shrewsbury, the only firm on the Kanawha outside the control of Ruffner, Donnally and Company, initially agreed to maintain its price levels at the set rate. Ruffner, Donnally and Company was to inform Dickinson & Shrewsbury agents of any price increases in any market.[52] In all other aspects the two organizations remained vigorous competitors. The initial compact occasionally collapsed. In October 1853 negotiations between the two firms failed to produce an agreement on the timing of price increases. The home agency telegraphed the Cincinnati agent: "Cannot do anything with D & S act accordingly." In August 1854 Dickinson & Shrewsbury advanced its salt prices on the Ohio River without informing Ruffner, Donnally and Company. The precipitous action prompted consumers to purchase salt in other markets because of the certain knowledge that prices would eventually be increased. The company would thus be robbed of potential profits on tributary rivers. John B. Smith hoped that the early indication of price levels would not be disastrous: "I hope all will go well yet but much fear Wabash, as RR from Cincinnati all over Indiana in So short a time." Joseph H. Rogers worried: "I fear the loss of the Company & theirs also Will be large on the Wabash & other Rivers owing to the advance on the Ohio & this price quoted in the papers before the advance on the Rivers below."[53]

The price of salt in the Cincinnati market during the first two years of the company was quite nominal, at twenty-five to twenty-seven cents per bushel. The company gradually raised the price to forty-eight cents in January 1854, but the level rapidly declined to thirty-five to thirty-nine cents. In January 1855 the combination increased the price to a record high of fifty to fifty-five cents, but upon expiration of Ruffner, Donnally and Company, the price eroded to thirty-five cents. The *Cincinnati Price-Current* in December 1855 reported sparing and cautious purchases because of the dissolution of the Kanawha company: "There is some doubt that the partnership will be renewed, and should it not be, it is anticipated prices of the kind of Salt will materially decline." In April 1856 the Cincinnati agent sold Ruffner, Donnally and Company's remaining stock of 6,170 barrels for thirty-five cents per bushel plus thirty-five cents per barrel.[54]

An accurate assessment of the financial success and profitability of Ruffner, Donnally and Company is impossible because of the lack of records and testimony. One could surmise that the company and its stockholders achieved some margin of profit, as market prices for salt were maintained at reasonable levels and the company did not dissolve on the renewal anniversaries. The company probably was not as profitable as Armstrongs, Grant and Company (1827–30) and Hewitt, Ruffner and Company (1836–41) had been. The inability to secure the cooperation of Dickinson and Shrewsbury, the payment of a premium price for Ohio River salt while being unable to control its production quantities, the lack of success in securing possession of all Ohio River furnace output, and the rapidly mounting incursions of New York salt and imported salt into primary markets made the trade an increasingly risky and less profitable business.

Individual manufacturers who were not stockholders certainly did not profit from the existence of Ruffner, Donnally and Company, but they lost less than they would have without the company. For manufacturers who held interests, it is questionable whether the dividends from stock ownership offset production losses. Intelligent Kanawha salt makers estimated that under optimum operating conditions, salt cost fourteen cents per bushel to manufacture.[55] The company paid only sixteen cents for the first-quality product. A margin of two cents under optimum production was hardly enough to guarantee adequate profit. In 1853 Richard C.M. Lovell, recounting the circumstances of the formation of the company, recalled that the producers were desperate and that "it was conceded by many of the salt-makers that 16¢ per bushel would not pay for the manufacture of salt; and, from what we have seen since I believe it to be a fact. We thought that we had better take 16¢ as we thought we would not get 10¢ by Fall, and our credit was nearly exhausted." Lovell added, "The simple fact of the salt-makers forming an association did their credit more good than their pockets." Mercantile creditors, however, eventually would demand financial satisfaction. In the same year Dr. Spicer Patrick observed: "The manufacture of salt gives one a present capital, whereby the manufacturer can get credit; yet when the manufacturer attempts to wind up his business he will, as far as my observation goes, find that his salt operations have been a losing business to him."[56] Before Ruffner, Donnally and Company expired, economic realities were winnowing the ranks of the Kanawha salt manufacturers.

14

Kanawha Salt Loses Its Economic Savor

Before the dissolution of Ruffner, Donnally and Company on January 1, 1856, the Kanawha salt manufacturers had attempted and failed to consolidate their production and marketing functions under the aegis of another organization. After extended negotiations, all efforts to combine collapsed in February. The decline of Kanawha salt prices in Cincinnati was not immediate because of low water on the Ohio River throughout 1856. Sometime in the late summer the Kanawha manufacturers created a central sales agency called Ruffner, Hale and Company. This new association did not control production quantities but simply transported and marketed the salt of all factories.[1] This weak organization could not meet the economic challenges facing the Great Kanawha River salt industry.

In the relatively short span from 1850 to 1857, the output of Kanawha furnaces and investment in factories precipitously declined. In 1850 thirty-three operating companies had a total of $889,400 invested in real and personal property and manufactured an estimated 3,104,898 bushels of salt per year. In 1860 nine factories with a total capital investment of $175,000 annually produced an estimated 1,262,915 bushels.[2] One year earlier, in April 1859, the *Kanawha Valley Star* reported the quarterly production of seven furnaces owned by five different firms. In 1861 eleven furnaces raised potential annual production to 1,500,000 bushels. In 1857 an eastern Virginia traveler in the Kanawha Valley noted upon passing the Salines, "Here there are a number of dismantled and deserted engines and houses." After surmising that competition destroyed the once profitable industry, the visitor heard from several sources that there were "no new investments in this element of Kanawha's wealth." The local newspaper editor asserted that any person "who shall hereafter hazard capital or credit in a salt furnace—unless under consolidation—will give evidence of his fitness for a straight-jacket."[3]

With the general decline, the value of salt property and real estate along the Great Kanawha greatly depreciated. In December 1859 several property owners petitioned the Virginia General Assembly for equalization of real estate assessments on dilapidated furnaces. They complained that "the value of their estates [had] depreciated to a degree hardly to be appreciated" and that most salt makers had "been reduced to a state of unexampled embarrassment if not total ruin." Property assessments had occurred when the industry was prosperous, but circumstances had greatly altered. To buttress their contention, the petitioners attached a list of assessments of certain properties and their depreciated sale prices. Some assessments were three and four times market values. Nelson B. Coleman, a commissioner appointed to reassess lands in the Salines, received a request to consider immediately the old Bradford Noyes furnace. One of the four owners informed Coleman that the property was assessed at twenty thousand dollars but that the market value was under three thousand. The four proprietors had offered it to each other for four thousand dollars, but none would purchase.[4]

Although expressions of interest from outside investors surfaced in 1856, by 1860 investors in Kanawha County's natural resources were more interested in the potentials of cannel coal, natural gas, and oil than in salt production. In October 1856 a group of eastern Virginia businessmen had considered acquiring all Kanawha River salt property for the purpose of consolidating into one company all manufacturing and marketing. The owners of the salt interest would take one-fourth the valuation of their property in capital stock in the proposed company, while the outside investors would subscribe for three-fourths of the shares and control the enterprise. Nothing came of this proposal, and dilapidated brine wells and salt properties were leased for natural gas and oil exploration.[5]

Only one salt company was large enough and possessed the means to consolidate the Kanawha salt business in the 1850s, but the partners in the firm were too old to undertake the immense task of managing and adapting the enterprise to new economic realities. Besides, Dickinson & Shrewsbury had become prosperous by steering an independent course and by using the sacrifices of other manufacturers to obtain maximum prices for its uncontrolled output. Since before 1820 its predisposition was not to sacrifice its production quantities or sale prices to achieve combination or unity. In December 1856 William Dickinson, then eighty-six years old, instituted dissolution and partition proceedings against his brother-in-law and partner since the early 1800s, Joel Shrewsbury, Sr., who was eighty-three. Upon dissolution, Dickinson & Shrewsbury owned four salt furnaces and fifty-nine separate parcels of land ranging in size from three-quarter-acre lots in Malden to tracts of five or six thousand acres in Kanawha County. Other real property was located in other Virginia counties, Kentucky, and Tennessee. Had Dickinson and Shrewsbury been younger, their operational attitudes likely would have prevented them from undertaking a centralizing tact. Even that approach, however, would not have altered the economic prognosis for the industry.[6]

Many factors accounted for the demise of the Kanawha salt industry. The immediate causes would have created hardship for the enterprise under any condition, but when combined with the basic alteration of the agricultural economy of the West, the results proved fatal. The competitive transportation environment of the 1850s offered little promise to Kanawhans. Certainly competition between domestic producing areas became more severe with the transportation revolution. More imported salt arrived at New Orleans as ballast, with the low tariffs and with the great increase in cotton exports in the late 1850s. Despite a growing population in the Mississippi basin to consume the imported salt, underutilization of steamboats during the 1850s encouraged captains to haul cheaply any article upstream to Ohio River ports.[7]

Foremost among the domestic competitors was the Ohio River production field, located approximately seventy miles from Kanawha Salines in Meigs County, Ohio, and Mason County, Virginia. The Ohio River industry enjoyed all the advantages that the Kanawha industry did except for a plentiful labor supply. Slavery could not exist on a large scale in Mason County, Virginia, because of its proximity to Ohio. Obviously slaves could not work around the furnaces on the Ohio side of the river. Ohio River entrepreneurs solved their problem of labor scarcity by sending agents to Wales to recruit a work force. Within a decade, however, the outcome of the Civil War made the relative advantage of slaves a moot economic question.[8]

The Ohio River brine area possessed some positive economic advantages. The salt manufacturing operations were subsidiary to the main goal of profitable bituminous coal production. Salt furnaces consumed the slack coal not preferred in downriver markets and supplemented the efficient management of mines. The prosperity of the Ohio River companies thus did not depend solely upon the fortunes of the salt trade. The coal industry attracted investors before the Civil War from Philadelphia, New York, and New England. Infusions of capital into mining caused the erection of new, efficient salt factories for economic use of the fuel resource.[9] The Ohio River furnaces were located along the same commercial artery as the Kanawha industry, and their superior location closer to markets made transportation costs to Cincinnati for their output one-half that for the Kanawha product.[10]

When the Ohio River field first developed, Ruffner, Donnally and Company obtained market control over the salt produced at most furnaces. This dominance exacted a great price from Kanawha manufacturers. To control, Ruffner, Donnally and Company paid a higher price to Ohio River manufacturers than to Kanawha producers: a premium of three cents per bushel. Also, Ohio salt makers never agreed to production controls. Therefore, any reduction in output made by Ruffner, Donnally and Company fell in the Kanawha field. While Kanawha furnaces closed and decayed, Ohio River furnaces expanded in number and output. The Kanawha industry's grip on the salt trade loosened, and eventually Ohio River producers formed their own marketing organizations to dominate Kanawha manufacturers. In 1859 Mason City salt drove New York salt completely from the Cincinnati market. In the same year Ohioan Charles Cist declared that salt had "undergone more changes" in the Cincinnati market "in price, quality, and source of supply, than perhaps any other [article] that can be named." A short time ago, he wrote, "the Kanawha Salines were our principal sources of supply, but the best quality and largest quantity are now derived from our own state—salt being extensively made in and adjacent to Pomeroy, Meigs County."[11]

The fluctuations of the economic cycle always had an immediate effect on the Kanawha salt business. The western financial disturbance of 1854, occasioned by the failure of two Indiana free banks, resulted in a monetary contraction and high rates of discount. The three principal private Cincinnati banking houses suspended payments in November 1854. Although confidence was restored early in 1855, Ruffner, Donnally and Company had experienced difficulties in making collections. The Louisville agent reported that he had "seen a Number of Phila C New York Merchants who have visited the west and all Complain Severely about Collections."[12]

Much more serious was the Panic of 1857. The Ohio Life Insurance and Trust Company of Cincinnati (OLITC), an Ohio bank with a New York City office, suspended operations on August 24, 1857, and triggered a recession that reached directly to Kanawha Salines. After the Panic of 1837 and its aftermath, many western banks had begun depositing their specie in New York banks and merely used drafts for commercial transactions. The OLITC borrowed specie through the New York office for use in its western business. With the contraction in commercial conditions throughout 1857, the banks in the West withdrew their specie from New York. In turn, New York houses had to liquidate their loans and other liabilities. The failure of the OLITC's New York office, a minor prop in the national financial structure, had serious consequences for residents of the Kanawha Valley.[13]

The OLITC had strong financial ties with Kanawha commerce. The Ohio institution, originally incorporated in 1834, acquired ownership of the Bank of Kanawha at Kanawha Salines. When the main office failed in August 1857, Kanawha County citizens began a run on the local office, demanding specie. Finally, in the first week of October, the Bank of Kanawha suspended specie payments after redeeming 60 percent of its outstanding circulation. Since Ruffner, Donnally and Company had used the offices of the Bank of Kanawha and the Cincinnati outlet of the OLITC almost exclusively, it is probable that some salt manufacturers maintained the connection. The extent of the effect of suspension and failure upon salt makers is impossible to determine, but it was substantial. Seven hundred lawsuits were initiated in the first nine months of 1857 in Kanawha County.[14]

Natural events did not allow the Kanawha Valley to repose peacefully in its economic misery. In September 1861 a fifty-three-foot perpendicular rise in the water level flooded the entire valley floor. Floodwaters washed away dilapidated furnaces and factory structures and filled the deteriorated brine wells with salt. This event cleared the river bottom of almost all visible evidence of a once booming enterprise.[15]

During the fifteen years before 1857, a rapid change took place in the American West, especially in the Ohio Valley. Trade patterns and the population of the West moved northward and westward from the Ohio River commercial axis. In 1840 the Ohio Valley states of Ohio, Indiana, and Kentucky had 72.26 percent of the population of the Midwest, and the Mississippi Valley states of Illinois, Missouri, Iowa, and Wisconsin had 22.61 percent. By 1860 the respective percentages were 47.29 and 42.40. Ohio's proportion in the same period fell from 36.78 to 22.83 percent, while Illinois's grew from 11.53 to 16.71 percent.[16] The evolution of the railroad network in the West altered old trade patterns and forged new ones. These basic changes ensured the demise of Kanawha salt's market position.

The early railroads extending from the Ohio River inland, like the first canals, initially expanded the market for Kanawha salt, but the completion of the interstate, east-west lines signaled the transformation of the commercial pattern of the western economy and, hence, the beginning of the end of a distant river-based enterprise. In 1854 the Louisville agent of Ruffner, Donnally and Company realized the railroad's impact at New Albany and Jeffersonville, Indiana. He reported, "Summer stock sales at both of the latter places will be greatly increased over any former year owing to their Rail Road facilit[i]es through Indiana but Sales May be lessened by this at Madison of this the future will determine however."[17]

Railroads in the Old Northwest multiplied. A railroad map of 1850 showed only one completed track across Ohio from Lake Erie to Cincinnati. Ten years later an extensive rail network crisscrossed the Buckeye State. In 1850 Ohio had 299 miles of track, but by 1853 it had 1,383 miles. By 1858 this figure had jumped to 2,788 miles. Growth in Indiana and Illinois occurred almost as rapidly. Between 1850 and 1858, 1,942 miles of railroad were constructed in Indiana. From 1852 through 1856, 2,307 miles of track were laid in Illinois.[18]

Demographic and transportation changes affected the location of the pork-packing centers that furnished the major market for Kanawha salt. Swine raising, like the population, moved westward and northward from the Ohio River basin in the two decades before the Civil War. Illinois surpassed Ohio in the number of swine, while production declined south of the National Road in Ohio and Indiana.[19] The editor of the Cincinnati Price-Current noted in 1852 that "for three year past [Cincinnati] . . . has been a considerable distance from the geographical centre, and with each year the distance is increasing." "It is evident," he asserted, "that the producing business is rapidly extending Westward . . . the trade must increase at various points in the West."[20]

Railroads affected the pork-packing industry in two ways: by moving packing points away from the riverine system and by shipping live swine to the East. Both results had adverse effects on the Kanawha salt industry. As early as 1845 railroads transported hogs to Pittsburgh and Wheeling for seaboard customers. In 1858 Ohio railroads carried 1,200,000 live swine, mostly to eastern markets.[21]

Although several western towns profited from Cincinnati's static position in the packing industry, Chicago benefited most. Cincinnati continued to pack substantial numbers of hogs throughout the 1850s, but growth did not occur. The highest annual number packed in the decade was 431,000 in 1854, and the Queen City pack would not again reach that height until Civil War demand stimulated activity. In the 1861–62 season, Chicago surpassed Cincinnati in the number of hogs packed.[22] In 1848, when the first railroad reached Chicago, the city packed only 10 percent of all hogs butchered in Illinois. By 1859 that proportion had grown to 47 percent. By 1861 the thirteen railroads, with tracks covering 4,500 miles, and the growing population of the upper Mississippi Valley assured the dominance of the Windy City in all phases of the national packing industry. Besides pork, Chicago packed extensive amounts of beef and transshipped large numbers of livestock. For the first time in the economic history of the United States, the packing industry tended toward centralization in a single city.[23]

Change in western salt commerce occurred so rapidly that some experienced difficulty in understanding the basic nature and permanence of the alteration. At least one long-time Cincinnati salt dealer understood. In 1859 Lemuel H. Sargent was asked whether the Cincinnati market was the foremost in the West. He replied, "Some do not so regard it."[24] The salt market on the Ohio River and in Cincinnati remained static until hostilities during the Civil War stilled importations of foreign salt from New Orleans and created a temporarily high demand for domestic salt.[25]

Concurrent with the shift of the packing industry toward the Great Lakes was the discovery of a new source of western salt. Stimulated by a Michigan legislative bounty, in 1859 the East Saginaw Salt Manufacturing Company was organized to explore for brine deposits. Early in 1860 the company successfully began to produce salt. Immediate, rapid expansion of the Saginaw Valley salt industry occurred. In the first year 4,000 barrels of Michigan salt were produced. In 1864 sixty-seven firms with an invested capital of $2,269,500 manufactured 529,073 barrels of salt. Besides having the advantage of a location near major centers of demand, the Michigan industry also benefited from the presence of the lumber enterprise. Soon the salt factories were operating in conjunction with lumber mills. Cheaper than mined coal, the refuse lumber, slabs, and sawdust became the fuel of Michigan salt furnaces. One chronicler boasted that the production of the Saginaw Valley industry in five years equaled nearly fifty years of Kanawha Valley production and sixty-seven years of Onondaga, New York, output.[26] The market area available to Kanawha manufacturers could never be extended.

15

Perspectives

The place of the antebellum western Virginia salt manufacturers in United States economic, business, and legal history remains elusive, as much basic research on other industries and businesses of the time must still be conducted. Nevertheless, within the context of what is known, the Kanawha producers' activities and responses to market imperatives make them both similar to and unlike contemporary producers and their mercantile ancestors. Their quest for control of production and marketing of their commodity in response to cutthroat competition and decentralized, inefficient distribution launched them as progenitors of post–Civil War legal and business organizations and methods. As a result, the employment of stage theory of economic development as a way of placing the Kanawha salt industry in perspective is somewhat useful but does not fully elaborate the meaning of salt makers' activities in historical development. To state simply that they were merchant capitalists operating on the eve of the period of industrial capitalism or that they were incipient industrial capitalists at the end of the era of merchant capitalism is to ignore more complex implications. The inevitable final question about the Kanawha industry will be whether, in its time, its manifold activities were unique and distinctive.[1]

Although the economic actions of Kanawha manufacturers after 1814 certainly demonstrate the application of Adam Smith's dictum that "people of the same trade seldom meet together, even for merriment and diversion, but the conversation ends in a conspiracy against the public, or in some contrivance to raise prices," it does not conceptually explain in economic terms the salt makers' continual plight. Applying the economic concept of cutthroat competition to the textile industry of the twentieth-century United States, the classic essay by Lloyd G. Reynolds could have been as easily written about the post-1814 western Virginia salt industry. Reynolds based the existence of cutthroat competition upon the presence of excess capacity in an industry: "Excess capacity may be said to exist, if all plants in the industry were to be used to capacity, the profit ratio of the industry would be below normal. Under pure competition, subnormal profits indicate the presence of excess capacity."[2] He distinguished between excess capacity and unused capacity. The former refers only to an entire industry, while the latter may refer to an industry or to an individual factory. Unused capacity of a plant or industry is the difference between actual output and the capacity output over time. Unused capacity does not necessarily indicate excess capacity. Excess capacity is the amount that can be withdrawn from production to cause a rise in prices to restore normal profits. Under pure competition, the term *cutthroat competition* is synonymous with *excess capacity.*

If producers can prevent the use of excess capacity, its existence does not necessarily lead to subnormal profits. Cutthroat competition arises when producers cannot control production or prices. If producers fail to achieve control of prices with excess capacity, profit margins shrink, some firms will fail, and eventually capacity will reduce. This does not necessarily result in permanent closure of factories, as many will continue to produce as long as their fixed assets have any value.

Reynolds suggested that the problem of excess capacity would continue as long as the exploitation of labor through low wages was possible. Low labor costs beget excess capacity by encouraging factory construction and expansion to an extent greater than if labor costs were higher. If an exploitable labor supply remains over time, the problem of excess capacity becomes chronic. Reynolds applied his concept to a free labor situation, but if one applied it to an industry based on slave labor, the suggestive conclusions for Kanawha entrepreneurs are inescapable. A critique of the salt-slave economy would not rest upon slavery's adaptability, immediate profitability, or efficiency but upon its overall impact on salt's industrial environment.[3]

In marketing their commodity, Kanawha salt makers anticipated what later nineteenth-century manufacturers would encounter if they were to control the price and distribution of their product. Glenn Porter and Harold C. Livesay, in their study of nineteenth-century marketing, contend that most manufactured goods were sold by sedentary merchants unconnected to manufacturers and that the pattern continued until the 1870s. Merchants were the merchandisers as well as the financiers of economic growth. This result arose because of the generic nature of most manufactured goods and the diffuse markets. Producers replaced merchants in the wholesale distribution of goods whenever they could vend their own products at a lower unit cost than other merchants and when deficiencies in the ability and willingness of independent wholesalers to sell goods developed. Generally, these conditions did not evolve until the last decades of the nineteenth century.[4]

The example of Kanawha producers cannot alter the general interpretive conclusions of Porter and Livesay. The attempts of Kanawha manufacturers to control distribution, among other objectives, through combination occurred somewhat earlier than their generalization indicates, however. Despite producing a generic good, but a necessary one, the salt makers, from the beginning of the industry, understood the destructive and uneconomic effects of competition between manufacturers' commission merchants and between producers who might use the same commission merchant. Also, vendors often speculated on their own account in salt. Major salt firms often placed one of their own partners or a paid agent in major markets before 1820. Individual partnerships usually concentrated in one town or area where they were familiar with all merchants. The early centralizing partnerships and joint stock ventures had their own agents (usually major partners or stockholders) in Cincinnati, Louisville, and Nashville. They worked as distributors and vendors, handling all sales in the city and closely supervising vendors in the surrounding area. Collectively, the Kanawha producers themselves centralized sales in major markets as early as 1836. Control of sales and distribution reached its zenith with Ruffner, Donnally and Company between 1851 and 1856. The antebellum distribution system used by most manufacturers and sellers as portrayed by Porter and Livesay did not prevail at all times among Kanawha salt makers. That was the distribution system that the Kanawhans who formed combinations were trying to evade.

The Kanawha salt makers' attempts to control production, prices, and distribution of their product led them to negotiate and adopt various legal forms that made them unique among antebellum industrialists by antedating similar nineteenth-century combinations such as pools and sales agencies. James Willard Hurst has asserted that the legal forms of business organization arise because they are required by law, because they are required by the functional needs of the business, or because the forms' "availability or their limitations expand or restrict the range of choice and creative opportunities for entrepreneurs."[5] The first category had little effect on the Kanawhans' legal approach to their economic problems. To put their activities in a historical context, one must explore briefly the state of knowledge about early nineteenth-century legal forms.

Although we can identify the lawyer who drafted the earliest combination agreements, including the one organizing the Kanawha Salt Company in 1817, we have no evidence about the legal preparation of Joseph Lovell in addition to his assumed practice-apprenticeship in Richmond. With his Tidewater Virginia upbringing, he could have learned at the feet of one or more legal luminaries, and with his British birth and the London connections of his wealthy stepfather and his father's noble family, education in England could have been possible. The legal arrangements that Lovell and his fellow salt makers created in 1817 were adjusted to meet succeeding manufacturers' individual and collective economic and political requirements over four decades. Until now, scholars have had no detailed knowledge of the specific agreements and their content.

Historigraphic development in United States legal history on the question of the importance of the role of the corporation in raising funds and managing enterprise in the antebellum period falls into two schools. One emphasizes the importance of legislative or state grants of charters to corporate endeavor, while the other argues that the transfer of present-day thinking backward in searching for modern corporate origins has led scholars to miss the significance of the partnership, voluntary association, and joint stock venture in serving as the antecedent to the corporation. The latter position rests upon the telling premise that in the early nineteenth century, except for the existence of a legislative grant of charter, substantial legal differences between a corporation and a joint adventure did not exist. Change and difference came later. Writings in the first historigraphic school are much more extensive than in the second.[6]

The major work that emphasizes the importance of the rich diversity of business conducted by private associations, whose documents, incidentally, are more hidden than the public record, is Shaw Livermore's *Early American Land Companies*.[7] In his brilliant survey of American law, Lawrence M. Friedman follows Livermore's trail in his account of antebellum legal form: "The general corporation did not evolve from the special charter system; rather, it reflected the richness of business practice in private associations, operating without charters. These associations were similar to later full-blown business corporations because they were functionally so much alike . . . the old law of corporations provided nothing but words and forms."[8] Although Hurst in various works on the economy and the law has emphasized the importance of freedom, spontaneity, and drift in legal evolution, he sides with the traditional argument about the relative importance of the chartered corporation of the early national period. Despite acknowledging the insights of Livermore and others, he warns: "We lack evidence to compare the use of the corporation with the resort to the nearest informal analogue, the unincorporated joint stock company. But there is no solid evidence that such unincorporated ventures set the norm for associated enterprise or that corporate charters merely copied what private contract had thus already accomplished."[9]

The various copartnership and joint stock ventures of the Great Kanawha salt manufacturers clearly substantiate Livermore's interpretive approach on the evolution of American law before the democratization of the granting of corporate charters by general state statute. This investigation suggests that additional studies of basic American industries will furnish the evidence that Hurst decried.

The Kanawha salt makers' legal activities, operating under contemporary contract and partnership law, demonstrate the economic freedom of the antebellum period, when commercial men, merchants, and manufacturers wrested the economic and legal system from intrusive state and public interference and control. The associative legal arrangements of Kanawha producers ran counter to common law notions of a paternalist law and state intervention to ensure fair and just prices to consumers. Their agreements illustrate Morton J. Horwitz's contention that commercial contracts have evolved from those that must demonstrate private and public fairness to be valid to those that simply represent a "meeting of the minds" of contracting parties. The procedural conditions that were present when a contract was formulated, rather than the contract's content, became the basis of action.[10]

Influenced by the emergence of will theory and by market ideas, the salt makers' agreements emerged in the golden age of contractual freedom. The consensual theory of contract, with weight given to the common intention of the parties, became the essence of contractual agreements and spread throughout Jacksonian America. This principle as a legal test went beyond traditional factors such as consideration, offer, and acceptance. The notion emerged that men had the right to formulate any contracts they pleased so long as they did not agree as a result of fraud or force. The subject matter, the particulars of subject matter, and the identity of contracting parties were of no judicial concern. Subjective determination of intention, not adequacy of consideration or public policy, was the legal test. Later nineteenth-century legal doctrines that sprang from the position of subjective concurrence of intention were mistake, undue influence, and duress. This freedom allowed Kanawha enterpreneurs and their lawyers to innovate in order to solve their industrial problems. Their empirical legal arrangements created the basis of later legal adaptations by corporate America.[11]

Therein the very freedom to act without legislative or judicial interference from the state, however, in a way worked against Kanawha manufacturers. Their attempts to preserve future contractual freedom by surrendering their individual autonomy and destiny only temporarily to collective efforts to secure individual profit caused them to limit their joint ventures to five or fewer years. Therefore, no permanent resolution or response to their industry's problems through centralized administration was possible. At least one major company, Dickinson & Shrewsbury, never surrendered its independent position. The temporary nature of the salt makers' combinations also prevented extensive

capital accumulation in good times to allow one or a few firms to centralize in bad ones. The economic and legal theme for Kanawha salt
makers was simple and repetitive. Individuals and partnerships produced without collective effort until excess capacity created a commodity surplus and economic desperation. These results forced them to
organize to achieve prosperity. When salt makers negotiated as a group
to achieve a joint venture agreement, they would be concerned about
whether manufacturers selling the salt to the joint venture or prospective renters of idle property who did nothing had the best of the deal,
while the future joint stockholders had the same question. All parties
would opt for a short-term agreement that would obviate a long-term
solution to industry-wide problems and would make immediate business success more difficult. One side or the other, stockholders or manufacturers, would achieve the better of the arrangement, causing the
other group not to seek renewal of existing agreements and to want another, more favorable arrangement. The salt industry would again
plunge into the effects of excess capacity. When manufacturers resorted
to pools or sales agencies that passed profits and losses directly to producers, the absence of effective central control or general economic conditions caused some individuals to violate sales agreements, thus
disrupting the legal approach and ensuring failure.

In his pioneering study of post-1860 consolidation and concert in
sixteen industries, including the formation of the National Salt Company, Arthur Stone Dewing formulated a generalized schematic outline
of what businessmen legally do to achieve industrial consolidation. The
most elementary form of cooperation was the gentleman's agreement to
prevent economic ruin. After violations of gentleman's agreements in-
evitably occurred, industrialists formed pools with clauses in their
agreements to exact financial penalties from offending parties. Because
of deceptions and other weaknesses of a pool, the producers created legal trusts. When the state interfered, they formed corporations and,
later, holding corporations.[12] Dewing's accurate, evolutionary classification of post-1860 consolidation in various enterprises was anticipated by
similar developments in the Kanawha salt industry. The Kanawha salt
makers certainly entered the first two phases as early as 1816, broached
the idea of a trust in the late 1820s, and achieved their highest legal refinement with joint stock companies, analogous to the corporate form,
also in the late 1820s. They ineffectively sought corporate charters from
the Virginia legislature, but the acrimonious individualism that characterized the Kanawha manufacturers as a group mitigated against what
basically was a political as well as an economic solution to their industrial circumstances.

In combining to restrict production and to set prices of Kanawha salt, the western Virginia manufacturers anticipated what became common and formal in the post–Civil War business methods of many enterprises in manufacturing and transportation to ensure profits. Scholarly studies normally date these approaches in the United States to the cordage pool of 1860, the Michigan Salt Association in 1868, and the 1871 anthracite coal combination.[13] Calling the Kanawha combination agreements the first in the United States would doom the proclaimer to inevitable, eventual refutation, but to view them as distinctive, as the earliest presently known, or as a corrective to previously held scholarly assumptions about nineteenth-century United States combination is to be prudent while claiming scholarly consideration.

No doubt exists that the antebellum western Virginia salt industry holds a distinctive position in nineteenth-century American economic and legal development. The Kanawha Valley was a much different place on the eve of the Civil War than it had been when the first salt producers confronted the heavily forested bottom during the War of 1812 era. When the industry faded at midcentury, the inheritors of deteriorated Great Kanawha salt properties with extractive, industrial, and commercial experience looked to newer extractive enterprises, not farming, for their economic futures. When the railroads penetrated the valley in the late 1860s, a boom in the extraction of timber and coal began, which would lead to an economic environment similar to that previously confronted by the Kanawha salt makers. Oil and natural gas exploration, production, and transportation contributed to prosperity in the construction of the infrastructure and the enhanced economic possibilities. When these resources combined with the discredited salt brine to create a chemical industry, the economic salvation of the inheritors gradually appeared.

Notes

Abbreviations

CC, KCCR   County Court, Kanawha County Court Records, West Virginia and Regional History Collection, West Virginia University Library, Morgantown, West Virginia

Clerk, KCCH   Office of the Clerk of the County Commission, Kanawha County Courthouse, Charleston, West Virginia

CSC, KCCR   Circuit Superior Court, Kanawha County Court Records, West Virginia and Regional History Collection, West Virginia University Library, Morgantown, West Virginia

CSC, MCCR   Circuit Superior Court, Mason County Court Records, West Virginia and Regional History Collection, West Virginia University Library, Morgantown, West Virginia

Early v. Friend (1857)   *Early & Wife v. Friend et al.* In *An Appeal from the Circuit Court of Kanawha.* 2 vols.; Lewisburg, Va.: William F. Farish, printer, 1857

Reynolds v. McFarland et al. (1846)   *Ellicott Reynolds, next friend of James and Henry William Reynolds v. James C. McFarland, Joel Shrewsbury, Sr., Levi Welch, Andrew Donnally, William Dickinson, John D. Lewis, William Tompkins, Benjamin H. Smith, and Alexander W. Quarrier,* Circuit Superior Court of Law and Chancery (1846), Kanawha County, West Virginia Department of Archives and History, Charleston, West Virginia

1. Kanawha Salt's Savor

1. Thomas Childs Cochran, *Frontiers of Change: Early Industrialism in America* (New York: Oxford Univ. Press, 1981).

2. Alan Dawley, *Class and Community: The Industrial Revolution in Lynn* (Cambridge, Mass.: Harvard Univ. Press, 1976); Anthony F. C. Wallace, *Rockdale: The Growth of an American Village in the Early Industrial Revolution* (New York:

Knopf, 1978); idem, *St. Clair: A Nineteenth-Century Coal Town's Experience with a Disaster-Prone Industry* (New York: Knopf, 1987).

3. For the consideration of relationships between law and the economy undertaken by Stuart Bruchey in preparation for his book *Enterprise: The Dynamic Economy of a Free People* (Cambridge, Mass.: Harvard Univ. Press, 1990), see Bruchey, "Law and Economic Change in the Early American Republic," in *American Industrialization, Economic Expansion, and the Law,* ed. Joseph R. Frese and Jacob Judd (Tarrytown, N.Y.: Sleepy Hollow Press and Rockefeller Archive Center, 1981), 85-111.

4. No attempt is made to review comprehensively the historiography of law and the economy, but several works and articles substantiate this viewpoint. For a nonlegal but intelligent methodological approach to economic history, consult Margaret Walsh, "The Dynamics of Industrial Growth in the Old Northwest, 1830–1870: An Interdisciplinary Approach," in *Business and Economic History Papers Presented at the Twenty-first Annual Meeting of the Business History Conference, 28 February–1 March 1975,* ed. Paul Uselding, 2d ser., vol. 4 (Urbana, Ill., 1975), 12-29. For critiques of legal-economic approaches, see James Willard Hurst, "Perspectives upon Research into Legal Order," *Wisconsin Law Review* (May 1961): 356-67; Harry N. Scheiber, "At the Borderland of Law and Economic History: The Contributions of Willard Hurst," *American Historical Review* 75, no. 3 (Feb. 1970): 744-56; Morton Keller, "Business History and Legal History," *Business History Review* 53, no. 3 (Autumn 1979): 295-303. For reviews of legal-economic literature, see Harry N. Scheiber's articles: "Government and the Economy: Studies of the 'Commonwealth' Policy in Nineteenth-Century America," *Journal of Interdisciplinary History* 3 (Summer 1972): 135-57; "Federalism and the American Economic Order, 1789–1910," *Law and Society Review* 10 (Fall 1975): 58-67; "State Law and 'Industrial Policy' in American Development, 1790–1987," *California Law Review* 75, no. 1 (Jan. 1987): 415-44. For external surveys of American legal development, see Lawrence M. Friedman, *A History of American Law* (New York: Simon and Schuster, 1973), and Morton J. Horwitz, *The Transformation of American Law, 1780–1860* (Cambridge, Mass.: Harvard Univ. Press, 1977). No one can work in the field without acknowledging the various works of James Willard Hurst, especially his magisterial book *Law and Economic Growth: The Legal History of the Lumber Industry in Wisconsin, 1836–1915* (Cambridge, Mass.: Harvard Univ. Press, 1964), in which Hurst examines external federal and state public policy and judicial intervention.

5. A sophisticated synthesis of issues of the Jacksonian Era is Edward Pessen, *Jacksonian America: Society, Personality, and Politics,* rev. ed. (Homewood, Ill.: Dorsey Press, 1978). See particularly his dissection of Benton and Missouri Democrats as well as techniques of mobilizing public opinion (230-31, 291).

6. Thomas Senior Berry, "The Effect of Business Conditions on Early Judicial Decisions Concerning Restraint of Trade," *Journal of Economic History* 10, no. 1 (May 1950): 30-44.

7. Harry N. Scheiber comments that many important studies of the law and economy "have confined their attention to Massachusetts, New York, Pennsylvania, and Wisconsin"; Scheiber, "Regulation, Property Rights, and Definition of 'The Market': Law and the American Economy," *Journal of Economic History* 41, no. 1 (March 1981): 107-8. See also David J. Bodenhamer and James W. Ely, Jr., eds., *Ambivalent Legacy: A Legal History of the South* (Jackson: Univ. Press of Mississippi, 1984), particularly Lawrence M. Friedman's "The Law Between the States: Some Thoughts on Southern Legal History," 30-46; and Margaret Walsh,

The Manufacturing Frontier: Pioneer Industry in Antebellum Wisconsin, 1830–1860 (Madison: State Historical Society of Wisconsin, 1972), v-xi.

Suggestive essays analyzing the antebellum southern and midwestern economies deplore this shortcoming: see Fred Bateman, James D. Foust, and Thomas Weiss, "Large-Scale Manufacturing in the South and West, 1850–1860," *Business History Review* 45, no. 1 (Spring 1971): 1-17; Fred Bateman and Thomas Weiss, "Market Structure before the Age of Big Business: Concentration and Profit in Early Southern Manufacturing," *Business History Review* 49, no. 3 (Autumn 1975): 312-36; and Raymond L. Cohn, "Local Manufacturing in the Antebellum South and Midwest," *Business History Review* 54, no. 1 (Spring 1980): 80-91. Most studies of southern industry logically focus upon slavery's effects on enterprise; however, a different and corrective approach is found in Fred Bateman and Thomas Weiss, *A Deplorable Scarcity: The Failure of Industrialization in the Slave Economy* (Chapel Hill: Univ. of North Carolina Press, 1981).

Though a decade old, Cochran's *Frontiers of Change* is still the best summary of early national industrial development. Other scholarly exceptions are Norman Crockett, *The Woolen Industry of the Midwest* (Lexington: Univ. Press of Kentucky, 1970), and Margaret Walsh, *The Rise of the Midwestern Meat Packing Industry* (Lexington: Univ. Press of Kentucky, 1982). A noteworthy article about coal mining and coal oil in Virginia's Great Kanawha Valley is Otis K. Rice, "Coal Mining in the Kanawha Valley to 1861: A View of Industrialization in the Old South," *Journal of Southern History* 31, no. 4 (Nov. 1965): 393-416.

Much scholarly work since Cochran's survey still emphasizes the bias: see Paul G. Faler, *Mechanics and Manufacturers in the Early Industrial Revolution: Lynn, Massachusetts, 1780–1860* (Albany: State Univ. of New York Press, 1981); Philip Scranton, *The Textile Manufacture at Philadelphia, 1800–1885* (New York: Cambridge Univ. Press, 1982); Paul F. Paskoff, *Industrial Evolution: Organization, Structure, and Growth of the Pennsylvania Iron Industry, 1750–1860* (Baltimore: Johns Hopkins Univ. Press, 1983); Jonathan Prude, *The Coming of Industrial Order: Town and Factory Life in Rural Massachusetts, 1810–1860* (New York: Cambridge Univ. Press, 1983); Barbara M. Tucker, *Samuel Slater and the Origins of the American Textile Industry, 1790–1860* (Ithaca, N.Y.: Cornell Univ. Press, 1984); and Cynthia J. Shelton, *The Mills of Manayunk: Industrialization and Social Conflict in the Philadelphia Region, 1787–1837* (Baltimore: Johns Hopkins Univ. Press, 1986).

8. See Alfred D. Chandler, Jr., "The Railroads: Pioneers in Modern Corporate Management," *Business History Review* 39, no. 1 (Spring 1965): 16-40; idem, *Strategy and Structure: Chapters in the History of Industrial Enterprise* (Cambridge Mass.: MIT Press, 1962), 8-12; and idem, *The Visible Hand: The Managerial Revolution in American Business* (Cambridge, Mass.: Harvard Univ. Press, 1977), 9-10. Also see Barbara M. Tucker, "The Merchant, the Manufacturer, and the Factory Manager: The Case of Samuel Slater," *Business History Review* 55, no. 3 (Autumn 1981): 297-313.

9. See Ronald L. Lewis, "From Peasant to Proletarian: The Migration of Southern Blacks to the Central Appalachian Coalfields," *Journal of Southern History* 55, no. 1 (Feb. 1989): 77-102.

10. Though he mentions the antebellum Kanawha industry and others, Ronald D Eller basically emphasizes southern Appalachia's nonindustrialized aspect; Eller, *Miners, Millhands, and Mountaineers: Industrialization of the Appalachian South, 1880–1930* (Knoxville: Univ. of Tennessee Press, 1982), xv-xxvi, 3-38.

11. Franklin F. Mendels, Proto-Industrialization: The First Phase of the Industrialization Process," *Journal of Economic History* 32, no. 1 (March 1972):

241-61. See also L.A. Clarkson, "Proto-Industrialization: The First Phase of Industrialization?" in *The Industrial Revolution: A Compendium*, ed. L.A. Clarkson (Atlantic Highlands, N.J.: Humanities Press International, 1990, 149-209.

12. No attempt is made here to detail the many participants in the domestic debate or their interpretations and extensive writings. A perceptive summary is Allan Kulikoff, "The Transition of Capitalism in Rural America," *William and Mary Quarterly*, 3d ser. 46, no. 1 (Jan. 1989): 120-44. A recent monograph treating the subject is Christopher Clark, *The Roots of Rural Capitalism: Western Massachusetts, 1780–1860* (Ithaca, N.Y.: Cornell Univ. Press, 1990).

13. On Kanawha land speculation and its effects, see John Edmund Stealey III, "George Clendinen and the Great Kanawha Valley Frontier: A Case Study of the Frontier Development of Virginia," *West Virginia History* 27, no. 4 (July 1966): 278-95.

2. Early Development and Expansion

1. Frederick Jackson Turner, in an early interpretation of the significance of frontier salt licks, suggested that salines made eastern settlement possible and began to free frontiersmen from dependence upon the Tidewater; Turner, *The Frontier in American History* (New York: Henry Holt and Co., 1920), 17-18. Isaac Lippincott adhered to the same view in "The Early Salt Trade of the Ohio Valley," *Journal of Political Economy* 20, no. 10 (Dec. 1912): 1029-30. More recent findings, resulting in a modification of Turner's observations, emerged in a detailed study by a geographer: John Allais Jakle, "Salt and the Initial Settlement of the Ohio Valley," Ph.D. diss., Indiana University, 1967. Jakle's conclusions are conveniently condensed in his article "Salt on the Ohio Valley Frontier, 1770–1820," *Annals of the Association of American Geographers* 59, no. 4 (Dec. 1969): 687-709.

2. S.P. Hildreth, "Observations on the Bituminous Coal Deposits of the Valley of the Ohio . . . ," *American Journal of Science and Arts* 29 (Jan. 1836), 117.

3. James Morton Callahan, *Semi-Centennial History of West Virginia* (N.p.: Semi-Centennial Commission of West Virginia, 1913), 12-13; Henry Ruffner, "Origin of the Kanawha Salt-works," 1-2, William Henry and Henry Ruffner Papers, Historical Foundation of Presbyterian and Reformed Churches. Also see Hildreth, "Bituminous Coal Deposits," 117; Anne Newport Royall, *Sketches of History, Life, and Manners in the United States* (New Haven, Conn.: Privately printed, 1826), 46. J.P. Hale, *Trans-Allegheny Pioneers*, 2d ed. (Charleston, W.Va.: Kanawha Valley Publishing Co., 1931), 22-30; idem, "Salt," in *Resources of West Virginia*, ed. M.F. Maury and William M. Fontaine (Wheeling, W.Va.: Register Co., 1876), 278.

4. See Reuben Gold Thwaites and Louise P. Kellogg, eds., *Documentary History of Dunmore's War, 1774* (Madison: State Historical Society of Wisconsin, 1905), for detailed accounts of Dunmore's campaign. Hale, "Salt," 279.

5. Deed Book A, 102-3, Clerk, KCCH.

6. Ruffner, "Origin of the Kanawha Salt-works," 2-3, 21-21; extract from Ruffner Family Bible, Ruffner-Kanawha Valley Scrapbook, 2-4, Roy Bird Cook Collection, West Virginia and Regional History Collection, West Virginia University Library.

7. Deed Book A, 168, Clerk, KCCH; Ruffner, "Origin of the Kanawha Salt-works," 21-22; extract from Ruffner Family Bible, Ruffner-Kanawha Valley Scrapbook, 2.

8. Bonds of Joseph Ruffner to John Dickinson, June 11, 1793, in *Adam Dickinson, Joseph Kincaid, and John and Samuel Shrewsbury, executors of John Dickinson, deceased* v. *David and Joseph Ruffner, executors of Joseph Ruffner, deceased,* CSC, KCCR (hereinafter cited as *Dickinson v. Ruffner,* CSC, KCCR).

9. Bond of John Dickinson to Joseph Ruffner, June 11, 1793, in *Dickinson v. Ruffner,* CSC, KCCR.

10. Ruffner, "Origin of the Kanawha Salt-works," 3-4; J.P. Hale, "Historical and Descriptive Sketch of the Great Kanawha and New River Valleys from Point Pleasant to Hinton," *West Virginia Historical Magazine Quarterly* 1, no. 2 (April 1901): 18.

11. Last Will and Testament of Joseph Ruffner, Sr., Feb. 4, 1803, in *Dickinson v. Ruffner,* CSC, KCCR.

12. Superior Court Minute Book, 1809-13, pp. 29-30, Clerk, KCCH.

13. Deposition of William Dupuy, Oct. 11, 1808, in *Dickinson v. Ruffner,* CSC, KCCR.

14. Deed Book C, 130-31, Clerk, KCCH.

15. Ruffner, "Origin of the Kanawha Salt-works," 12-13, 21-24; Henry Ruffner to Samuel Williams, Feb. 9, 1816 (typescript), Henry Ruffner Papers, Roy Bird Cook Collection.

16. Ruffner, "Origin of the Kanawha Salt-works," 5-6.

17. Ibid., 6-9.

18. Ibid., 9-12.

19. Deed Book C, 294-95, Clerk, KCCH; Ruffner, "Origin of the Kanawha Salt-works," 5-6.

20. Ruffner, "Origin of the Kanawha Salt-works," 17-18.

21. Ibid., 19-20; extract from Ruffner Family Bible, Ruffner-Kanawha Valley Scrapbook, 2; Hildreth, "Bituminous Coal Deposits," 117-18.

22. *Dickinson v. Ruffner,* CSC, KCCR; Superior Court Minute Book, 1809-13, pp. 22-24, Clerk, KCCH.

23. Superior Court Minute Book, 1809-13, pp. 17, 18, 19, 28-31, Clerk, KCCH.

24. Ibid., 5-6, 7-8, 9, 10, 17, 81, 95.

25. Henry Ruffner to Samuel Williams, Feb. 16, 1808 (typescript), Henry Ruffner Papers, Roy Bird Cook Collection.

26. Ibid.; [Virgil A. Lewis, ed.], "Lewis Summers' Journal of a Tour from Alexandria, Virginia, to Gallipolis, Ohio, in 1808," *Southern Historical Magazine* 1, no. 2 (Feb. 1892): 61.

27. Henry Ruffner to Samuel Williams, Jan. 1, 1810 (typescript), Henry Ruffner Papers, Roy Bird Cook Collection.

28. Elizabeth Cometti, ed., "The Memorandum of William Whitteker," pt. 2, *West Virginia History* 1, no. 4 (July 1940): 287, 288-89; Henry Ruffner to Samuel Williams, Jan. 1, 1810 (typescript), Henry Ruffner Papers, Roy Bird Cook Collection.

29. Cometti, "Memorandum of William Whitteker," pt. 2, pp. 283-86; George Wesley Atkinson, *History of Kanawha County.* . . . (Charleston: West Virginia Journal, 1876), 277-78.

30. Cometti, "Memorandum of William Whitteker," pt. 2, pp. 288-90; Deed Book C, 410-13, Clerk, KCCH.

31. Agreement of Isaac Noyes with William and Levi Whitteker, Sept. 6, 1809, CC, KCCR (1809); Cometti, "Memorandum of William Whitteker," pt. 2, pp. 291-92.

32. Zadok Cramer, *The Navigator.* . . . 7th ed. (Pittsburgh: Cramer, Spear and Eichbaum, 1811), 94-95.

33. Ibid., 96; Jakle, "Salt on the Ohio Valley Frontier," table 1, p. 700.

34. John Leander Bishop, *A History of American Manufactures from 1608 to 1860*, 3 vols. (Philadelphia: Edward Young and Co., 1866), 1: 134, 156-67, 292-95; Curtis P. Nettels, *The Emergence of a National Economy, 1755–1815*, vol. 2 of *The Economic History of the United States* (New York: Holt, Rinehart and Winston, 1962), 283; Lippincott, "Early Salt Trade," 1029-46.

35. Lippincott, "Early Salt Trade," 1036-37; Thomas Senior Berry, *Western Prices before 1861: A Study of the Cincinnati Market* (Cambridge, Mass.: Harvard Univ. Press, 1943), 288-91; U.S. Congress, Senate, *Memorial of the Manufacturers of Salt, in the County of Kanawha, Virginia, against the Repeal of the Duty on Imported Salt*, 20th Cong., 1st sess., 1828, S. Doc. 47, pp. 3-4.

36. Cramer, *Navigator*, 95.

37. Ibid., 12-20, 95.

38. [Lewis], "Lewis Summers' Journal," 61.

3. Growth, Chaos, and Combination, 1811–1824

1. U.S. Congress, Senate, *Memorial of the Manufacturers of Salt*, S. Doc. 47, p. 4; Lippincott, "Early Salt Trade," 1029; *Niles' Weekly Register*, July 16, 1814, p. 330.

2. Cramer, *Navigator*, 94-95, and *Niles' Weekly Register*, April 22, 1815, p. 135. The date of the David Ruffner letter was misprinted as November 8, 1815, but owing to the date of publication, it must have been written in 1814.

3. See depositions of Daniel Ruffner and Allen Baxter, Jan. 4, 1826, and other case papers, in *Edward Burgess and wife, Jane v. William Nickle, Sr., and William Nickle, Jr.*, CC, KCCR (1825).

4. For contemporary economic conditions, see Richard C. Wade, *The Urban Frontier: The Rise of Western Cities, 1790–1830* (Cambridge, Mass.: Harvard Univ. Press, 1959), 161-89; Walter Buckingham Smith and Arthur Harrison Cole, *Fluctuations in American Business, 1790–1860* (Cambridge, Mass.: Harvard Univ. Press, 1935), 18-21; Ralph C. H. Catterall, *The Second Bank of the United States* (Chicago: Univ. of Chicago Press, 1902), 1-21; Bray Hammond, *Banks and Politics in America from the Revolution to the Civil War* (Princeton, N.J.: Princeton Univ. Press, 1957), 227-50.

5. Petition dated Nov. 1, 1817, Legislative Petitions of Kanawha County, Virginia State Library and Archives.

6. Auditor's Item 86, Virginia State Library and Archives.

7. Joel Shrewsbury to Col. William Dickinson, Dec. 20, 1814, letterbook, 56-58 (copy), Dickinson & Shrewsbury Papers, James E. Morrow Library, Marshall University.

8. W. S. Laidley, *History of Charleston and Kanawha County, West Virginia, and Representative Citizens* (Chicago: Richmond-Arnold Publishing Co., 1911), 389.

9. Steele Family Genealogy File and Shelby County Marriage Papers, Kentucky Historical Society. I am indebted to Dr. James C. Klotter, state historian of Kentucky, for his timely assistance on a long-standing genealogical problem. Steele family genealogical material is located in *Genealogies of Kentucky Families: From the Register of the Kentucky Historical Society, O-Y* (Baltimore: Genealogical

Publishing Co., 1981), 276-94. See particularly "Thomas Steele, Pioneer," 282-85, "Supplement to the 'Steele Genealogy,' " 286-87, and "Mrs. Martha McKamie Steele," 288-94. On John Steele, see Clarence Edwin Carter, ed., *The Territory of Mississippi, 1798–1817*, vol. 5 of *The Territorial Papers of the United States* (Washington, D.C.: Government Printing Office, 1937), 29 n. 15, and Hale, *Trans-Allegheny Pioneers*, 201.

10. Deed Book D, 105-6, Clerk, KCCH.

11. Deed Book C, 406-13, Book D, 41-42, Clerk, KCCH; agreement of Charles Brown with William Steele, Oct. 15, 1812, CC, KCCR (1812). In his generally outstanding, brief account of the Kanawha salt industry, Thomas Senior Berry viewed the amount of salt paid by Whitteker to Donnally and Steele and Company and the crediting of the amount of surplus salt delivered to Whitteker's account at one dollar per bushel as evidence of a rent and re-lease agreement to control production (*Western Prices*, 293-94). Actually, the payment in salt by Whitteker was in accordance with his simple lease agreement with Charles Brown and the subsequent arrangement with Steele. Evidently Donnally and Steele and Company encouraged Whitteker to discharge his debt faster than the contract provided and merely carried the amount delivered in excess of the contract specifications on the accounts at one dollar per bushel. See Donnally and Steele and Company, Kanawha Salt Works Account Book, 1813–15, p. 35, West Virginia and Regional History Collection, West Virginia University Library. Whitteker's seven-year, two-hundred-bushel-per-month rent payments were to expire in 1818, but he completely discharged the obligation to William Steele in September 1815. See the endorsed receipt on the Brown-Steele contract in the loose court papers, agreement of Charles Brown with William Steele, Oct. 15, 1812, CC, KCCR (1812). There is no evidence to indicate that the partnership attempted to control production.

12. Donnally and Steele and Company, Kanawha Salt Works Account Book, 1813–15, pp. 2, 3, 5, 7, 29.

13. Deed Book D, 259-60, 270-71, 314, Clerk, KCCH.

14. Ibid., 50, 353, 403-6.

15. Ibid., 459-61, 461-62, 462-63.

16. Deed Book E, 88-89, Clerk, KCCH.

17. The rough, conservative estimate of the percentage of Donnally and Steele and Company production in the industry is based on a comparison of the estimated individual furnace output times the number of furnaces rented and owned plus the salt deliveries received with the total production of all furnaces on the Kanawha.

18. Dudley Woodbridge to Donnally, Steele and Co., Nov. 15, 1813, and Dudley Woodbridge to Woodbridge and Pierce, Nov. 20, 1813, letterbook no. 2, Woodbridge Mercantile Company Records, West Virginia and Regional History Collection, West Virginia University Library.

19. This standard interpretation is based on the assertions of Kanawha chroniclers William S. Laidley, George W. Atkinson, and John P. Hale and frequent journalistic claims of Charleston newspapers. See Charles Henry Ambler and Festus Paul Summers, *West Virginia: The Mountain State*, 2d ed. (Englewood Cliffs, N.J.: Prentice-Hall, 1958), 128-29; Elizabeth Cometti and Festus Paul Summers, eds., *The Thirty-fifth State: A Documentary History of West Virginia* (Morgantown: West Virginia University Library, 1966), 198; Elizabeth J. Goodall, "The Manufacture of Salt—Kanawha's First Commercial Enterprise," *West Virginia History* 26, no. 4 (July 1965): 242-44. The one scholarly exception is Louis C.

Hunter, *Studies in the Economic History of the Ohio Valley* (Northhampton, Mass.: Smith College, 1934), 53.

20. Joel Shrewsbury to Col. William Dickinson, March 5 and April 22, 1817, letterbook, 149-52, 153-58 (copy), Dickinson & Shrewsbury Papers.

21. Allan Nevins, *John D. Rockefeller: The Heroic Age of American Enterprise,* 2 vols. (New York: Scribner's, 1940), 1: 602-17; idem, *Study in Power: John D. Rockefeller, Industrialist and Philanthropist,* 2 vols. (New York: Scribner's, 1953), 1: 382-97.

22. The literature on combination is quite extensive, especially during the Progressive Era and the New Deal period. For the best work, see William H.S. Stevens, "A Classification of Pools and Associations Based on American Experience," *American Economic Review* 3, no. 3 (Sept. 1913): 545-75; idem, ed., *Industrial Combinations and Trusts* (New York: Macmillan, 1913), 1; William Z. Ripley, ed., *Trusts, Pools and Combinations,* rev. ed. (Boston: Ginn and Co., 1916), xi-xix; and Henry R. Seager and Charles A. Gulick, Jr., *Trust and Corporation Problems* (New York: Harper and Brothers, 1929), 1-85.

23. H. Heth to Beverley Randolph, Jan. 24, 1815, Heth Family Papers, Alderman Library, University of Virginia; Henry Ruffner to Samuel Williams, July 10, 1816 (typescript), Henry Ruffner Papers, Roy Bird Cook Collection.

24. See Deed Book F, 90-3, 199-202, 310-B, Clerk, KCCH.

25. Joseph Lovell to James Bream, June 29, 1817, Joseph Lovell Papers, West Virginia Department of Archives and History; Joel Shrewsbury to Col. William Dickinson, March 5 and April 22, 1817, letterbook, 149-52, 153-58 (copy), Dickinson & Shrewsbury Papers.

26. *Genealogies of Kentucky Families,* 286-87; "Col. Joseph Lovell (1793–1835)," Charleston Scrapbook, 76, Roy Bird Cook Collection; Laidley, *Charleston and Kanawha County,* 277-78; W.S. Laidley, "Col. Joseph Lovell," *West Virginia Historical Magazine Quarterly* 4, no. 4 (Oct. 1904): 295-98.

27. Joseph Lovell to James Bream, June 29, 1817, Joseph Lovell Papers.

28. Ibid.

29. Laidley, *Charleston and Kanawha County,* 277-78; *Kanawha Republican,* Jan. 15, 1842.

30. Joseph Lovell to James Bream, June 29, 1817, Joseph Lovell Papers.

31. Joel Shrewsbury to Col. William Dickinson, Oct. 28, Nov. 12 and 18, 1817, letterbook, 168-69 169-73, 174-76 (copy), Dickinson & Shrewsbury Papers.

32. "Articles of Agreement Association and Co-partnership Made and Entered Into," Nov. 10, 1817, West Virginia Department of Archives and History. A printed copy is in Lorena Andrews Anderson, "Salt Industry of the Kanawha Valley," M.A. thesis, Marshall College, 1942, but it is dated November 13. Fragments of the agreement appear in Cometti and Summers, *Thirty-fifth State,* 198-203.

33. *Macker Cheek* v. *John B. Genatte* (Jenatte, Jenat), CSC, KCCR (1818).

34. *John B. Jenatte* (Jenat, Genatte) v. *Andrew Donnally,* CSC, KCCR (1818).

35. Petition dated 1818, Legislative Petitions of Kanawha County.

36. Joel Shrewsbury to Col. William Dickinson, Feb. 5, 1818, April 7 and 20, May 2 and 25, and July 6, 1819, letterbook, 188-90, 220-22, 225-26, 227-30, 232-34, 235-41 (copy), Dickinson & Shrewsbury Papers.

37. *William Steele, Adam Steele, Richard Steele, Robert M. Steele and Andrew Donnally, doing business as Steele, Donnally and Steeles* v. *Philip G. Todd,* CSC, KCCR (1823).

38. See Murray N. Rothbard, *The Panic of 1819: Reactions and Policies* (New York: Columbia Univ. Press, 1962); Hammond, *Banks and Politics*, 253-59; Catterall, *Second Bank*, 51-67; Berry, *Western Prices*, 380-400; Wade, *Urban Frontier*, 170-72, 174-77; William M. Gouge, *The Curse of Paper-Money and Banking* . . . . (London: Mills, Jowett, and Mills, 1833), 54-87, 88-94. For a detailed microeconomic view, see Marilynn Melton Larew, "The Cincinnati Branch of the Second Bank of the United States and Its Effect on the Local Economy, 1817–1836," Ph.D. diss., University of Maryland, 1978; see esp. 124, 159, and 170, for Steele, Donnally and Steeles' use of "race horse bills."

39. Thomas H. Greer, "Economic and Social Effects of the Depression of 1819 in the Old Northwest," *Indiana Magazine of History* 44, no. 3 (Sept. 1948): 229-30; Harold M. Somers, "The Performance of the American Economy, 1789–1865," in *The Growth of the American Economy*, ed. Harold Francis Williamson, 2d ed. (Englewood Cliffs, N.J.: Prentice-Hall, 1951), 31-34.

40. Records of the 1820 Census of Manufactures, County of Kanawha, State of Virginia, Records of the Bureau of the Census, Record Group 29, National Archives Microfilm Publication M279, roll 18, frame 107.

41. Joel Shrewsbury to Col. William Dickinson, Feb. 1, 7, and 15, March 7 and 26, and April 21, 1820, letterbook, 254-63, 270-78 (copy), Dickinson & Shrewsbury Papers; quotation from Feb. 15, 1820, letterbook, 259-63.

42. Wm. S. Summers to Lewis Summers, Nov. 24, 1820, Summers Family Papers, West Virginia College of Graduate Studies, Glenwood; James C. McFarland to Sam'l Hait, Aug. 22, 1821 (typescript), James C. McFarland Papers, Roy Bird Cook Collection.

43. Articles of Agreement of William and Robert M. Steele with John J. Cabell and Walter Trimble, March 18, 1822, in *Robert M. Steele, surviving partner of William and Robert M. Steele, for use of Andrew Donnally v. Cabell and Trimble*, CSC, KCCR (1826).

44. Articles of Agreement of William and Robert M. Steele with William Tompkins, March 23, 1822, in *Steele v. Cabell and Trimble*, CSC, KCCR (1822).

45. Articles of Agreement of William and Robert M. Steele with Aaron Stockton, March 21, 1822, in *Steele v. Cabell and Trimble*, CSC, KCCR (1822).

46. Articles of Agreement of William and Robert M. Steele with John D. Shrewsbury and John B. Crockett, April 25, 1822, in *John D. Shrewsbury and John B. Crockett v. William and Robert M. Steele*, CSC, KCCR (1824). In this case, Crockett and Shrewsbury brought an inconclusive suit against the Steeles for breach of contract as a result of alleged infiltration of the restricted area.

47. Hale, *Trans-Allegheny Pioneers*, 288; entry for Jan. 13, 1834, p. 160, David Ruffner Weather Register, 1832-34 (copy), West Virginia Department of Archives and History.

48. Deed Book F, 90-91, Clerk, KCCH.

49. Ibid., 91-92.

50. Ibid., 92-93.

51. Ibid., 199-202.

52. Ibid., 310-12.

53. Several sources offering early examples of relationships between salt makers and merchants are *Oliver Ormsby and William Stanley v. Claudius Buster and John Reynolds*, CSC, KCCR (1813); deposition of Robert Munn, March 29, 1825, in *John Armstrong and Philip Grandin, surviving partners of themselves of themselves and John H. Pratt, deceased, doing business as John H. Pratt and Company v.*

Aaron Stockton, CSC, KCCR (1829); agreement of John Reynolds with William Hogue and Nicholas Flanagan, April 12, 1816, CC, KCCR (1816).

54. Berry, *Western Prices*, table 37, p. 578; David Ruffner to Henry Ruffner, Oct. 10, 1823, Ruffner Family Papers, West Virginia and Regional History Collection, West Virginia University Library.

4. Kanawha Salt's Use and Its Pre-1850 Markets

1. The standard treatise on salt is Robert P. Multhauf, *Neptune's Gift: A History of Common Salt* (Baltimore: Johns Hopkins Univ. Press, 1978); see pp. 3-7 on culinary consumption. For a regional view of salt consumption by people who subsist on a pork diet, see Sam Bowers Hilliard, *Hog Meat and Hoecake: Food Supply in the Old South, 1840-1860* (Carbondale: Southern Illinois Univ. Press, 1972), 40-45, 56-59, 92-111, 213-24.

2. West Virginia University Agricultural Experiment Station, *Occurrence of Barium in the Ohio Valley Brines and Its Relation to Stock Poisoning*, by C.D. Howard, Bulletin 103 (Morgantown, W.Va., June 1906), 282-83, 288-89.

3. Ibid., 282-83; *Niles' Weekly Register*, June 15, 1844, p. 245; J.D.B. DeBow, *The Industrial Resources, etc., of the Southern and Western States*, 3 vols. (New Orleans, 1853), 1: 376; Rudolf Alexander Clemen, *The American Livestock and Meat Industry* (New York: Ronald Press Co., 1923), 116-18 (hereinafter cited as Clemen, *Meat Industry*).

4. The most important work on the antebellum packing industry is Margaret Walsh's: "Pork Packing as a Leading Edge of Midwestern Industry, 1835–1875," *Agricultural History* 51, no. 4 (Oct. 1977): 702-17; "The Spatial Evolution of the Mid-Western Pork Industry, 1835–1875," *Journal of Historical Geography* 4, no. 1 (1978): 1-22; "From Pork Merchant to Meat Packer: The Midwestern Meat Industry in the Mid Nineteenth Century," *Agricultural History* 56, no. 1 (Jan. 1982): 127-37; *Rise of the Midwestern Meat Packing Industry*. On the decentralized nature of the industry, see Walsh, "Spatial Evolution," 10. For older, yet still important works, see Berry, *Western Prices*, 225-26; John G. Clark, *The Grain Trade in the Old Northwest* (Urbana: Univ. of Illinois Press, 1966), 143-46; Paul W. Gates, *The Farmer's Age: Agriculture, 1815–1860*, vol. 3 of *The Economic History of the United States* (New York: Holt, Rinehart and Winston, 1960), 221; Rudolf Alexander Clemen, "Waterways in Livestock and Meat Trade," *American Economic Review* 16, no. 4 (Dec. 1926), 642-43, 656-47; Howard Copeland Hill, "The Development of Chicago as a Center of the Meat Packing Industry," *Mississippi Valley Historical Review* 10, no. 3 (Dec. 1923): 265.

5. Berry, *Western Prices*, 218, 226-28; Hill, "Development of Chicago," 254-55; Walsh, "Spatial Evolution," 10; *Niles' Weekly Register*, Jan. 11, 1834, p. 331.

6. Clark, *Grain Trade*, 138; Berry, *Western Prices*, 225; Charles Cist, *Sketches and Statistics of Cincinnati in 1851* (Cincinnati: William H. Moore and Co., 1851), 279.

7. *Niles' National Register*, Feb. 7, 1846, p. 359, and March 14, 1846, p. 21; [*DeBow's*] *Commercial Review of the South and West*, July 1848, pp. 65-67; Clark, *Grain Trade*, 28, 44-45; Clemen, *Meat Industry*, 100-101. The standard work on the swine industry in Ohio is Robert Leslie Jones, *History of Agriculture in Ohio to 1880* (Kent, Ohio: Kent State Univ. Press, 1983), 120-38.

8. Berry, *Western Prices*, 229, 239-46; Clark, *Grain Trade*, 138-39; Clemen, *Meat Industry*, 110-11.

9. For a sample of hog-market predictions, see *Niles' Weekly Register,* Feb. 23, 1839, p. 403; March 10, 1838, pp. 22-23; Nov. 25, 1843, p. 208; Nov. 2, 1844, p. 131; Dec. 13, 1845, p. 240; and Feb. 7, 1846, p. 359.

10. Louis C. Hunter, *Steamboats on the Western Rivers* (Cambridge, Mass.: Harvard Univ. Press, 1949), 21, 35; Bishop, *History of American Manufactures* 2: 262. When writing from Parkersburg in 1840, Judge Lewis Summers reported: "Upwards of 4,000 barrels of salt is Vended here this year—mostly carried off by the N. West road—mostly from Pittsburgh & Muskingum"; Lewis Summers to George W. Summers, Sept. 3, 1840, George W. and Lewis Summers Papers, West Virginia and Regional History Collection, West Virginia University Library.

11. *Francis Tiernan and Michael Tiernan, doing business as Francis Tiernan and Company v. Andrew Donnally, Isaac Noyes, and George White,* CC, KCCR (1827); *Joseph W. Ray v. Andrew Donnally, Isaac Noyes, partners of George White, deceased,* CSC, KCCR (1829); Laidley, *Charleston and Kanawha County,* 196-97.

12. Hildreth, "Bituminous Coal Deposits," 72; Howard N. Eavenson, *The First Century and a Quarter of American Coal Industry* (Pittsburgh: Privately printed, 1942), 173-74 (hereinafter cited as Eavenson, *American Coal Industry*).

13. S.P. Hildreth, "Observations on the Saliferous Rock Formation, in the Valley of the Ohio," *American Journal of Science and Arts* 24, no. 1 (July 1833): 48-51; Lippincott, "Early Salt Trade," 1040-42.

14. William M. Talley, "Salt Lick Creek and Its Salt Works," *Register of the Kentucky Historical Society* 64, no. 2 (April 1966): 85-100; Eavenson, *American Coal Industry,* 301.

15. Lippincott, "Early Salt Trade," 1043-44; Logan Esarey, *A History of Indiana,* 2 vols. (Indianapolis: B.F. Bowen and Co., 1918), 1: 881-82.

16. The best general treatment of the Erie Canal within its political context is Ronald E. Shaw, *Erie Water West: A History of the Erie Canal, 1792–1854* (Lexington: Univ. of Kentucky Press, 1966); see chap. 8, pp. 140-63. On consumer preferences, see New York State Museum, *Salt and Gypsum Industries of New York,* by Frederick J.H. Merrill (Albany: Univ. of the State of New York, 1893), 39-43. For economic comparison, see *Merchants' Magazine and Commercial Review,* April 1843, p. 360.

17. The best work on the Ohio canal system is Harry N. Scheiber, *Ohio Canal Era: A Case Study of Government and the Economy, 1820–1861* (Athens, Ohio: Ohio Univ. Press, 1969). See *Niles' Weekly Register,* Oct. 20, 1832, p. 117; DeBow, *Industrial Resources* 2: 346; U.S. Congress, House, *Reports on the Trade and Commerce of the British North American Colonies and upon the Trade of the Great Lakes and Rivers,* by Israel D. Andrews, 32d Cong., 2d sess., 1853, H. Exec. Doc. 136, pp. 306-7; Arthur H. Hirsch, "The Construction of the Miami and Erie Canal," *Proceedings of the Mississippi Valley Historical Association* 10, pt. 2 (1919-20): 348.

18. Hirsch, "Construction," 349, 357-58; U.S. Congress, House, *Reports on the Trade,* H. Exec. Doc. 136, pp. 313-14; Francis Phelps Weisenburger, *The Passing of the Frontier, 1825-1850,* vol. 3 of *The History of the State of Ohio,* ed. Carl Wittke (Columbus: Ohio State Archaelogical and Historical Society, 1941), chap. 4, pp. 89-118; John H. Krenkel, *Illinois Internal Improvements, 1818–1848* (Cedar Rapids, Iowa: Torch Press, 1958).

19. Scheiber, *Ohio Canal Era,* 196-97; Elbert Jay Benton, *The Wabash Trade Route in the Development of the Old Northwest* (Baltimore: Johns Hopkins Univ. Press, 1903), 102; *Niles' National Register,* Jan. 27, 1844, p. 341.

20. *Buffalo Commercial Advertiser*, quoted in *Niles' Weekly Register*, Jan. 16, 1841; *Niles' Weekly Register*, Sept. 11, 1841, p. 21. See also Charles M. Snyder, *Oswego: From Buckskin to Bustles* (Port Washington, N.Y.: Ira J. Friedman, 1968, 83-96.

21. Ernest L. Bogart, "Early Canal Traffic and Railroad Competition in Ohio," *Journal of Political Economy* 21, no. 1 (Jan. 1913): 62.

22. *Merchant's Magazine and Commercial Review*, May 1845, p. 454.

23. Scheiber, *Ohio Canal Era*, 256-58.

24. L. Welch to Geo. W. Summers, Feb. 4, 1844, Summers Family Papers (Glenwood).

25. Caroline E. MacGill et al., *History of Transportation in the United States before 1860* (Washington, D.C.: Carnegie Institution, 1917), 498-99, 652; U.S. Congress, House, *Reports on the Trade*, H. Exec. Doc. 136, p. 308.

5. The Manufacturing Process and Technological Progress

1. Hildreth, "Saliferous Rock Formation," 55-56; Hildreth, "Bituminous Coal Deposits," 120. Compare the early Kanawha manufacturing procedure with the similar New York method: U.S. Department of Interior, Bureau of Mines, *Technology of Salt-Making in the United States*, by W.C. Phalen, Bulletin 146, Mineral Technology, no. 20 (Washington, D.C.: Government Printing Office, 1917), 52-55.

2. A stimulating discussion of some causes of technological innovation is H. J. Habakkuk, *American and British Technology in the Nineteenth Century: The Search for Labour-Saving Inventions* (Cambridge: Cambridge Univ. Press, 1967). See also Paul Uselding, "Studies of Technology in Economic History," in *Research in Economic History, Supplement 1-1977: Recent Developments in the Study of Business and Economic History: Essays in Memory of Herman E. Kroos*, ed. Robert E. Gallman (Greenwich, Conn: JAI Press, 1977), 159-219.

3. Eugene David Thoenen, *History of the Oil and Gas Industry in West Virginia* (Charleston, W.Va.: Education Foundation, 1964), 5, 10.

4. West Virginia Geological Survey, *Iron Ores, Salt and Sandstones*, by G.P. Grimsley, vol. 4 (Morgantown, W.Va.: Acme Publishing Co., 1909), 331-32; West Virginia Geological Survey, *Kanawha County*, by Charles E. Krebs and D.D. Teets, Jr. (Wheeling, W.Va.: Wheeling News Litho. Co., 1914), 599-600; West Virginia Geological Survey, *Salt Brines of West Virginia*, by Paul H. Price et al., vol. 8 (Morgantown, W.Va.: Morgantown Printing and Binding Co., 1937), 35-36, 38-40, 73-75.

5. John Bradbury, *Travels in the Interior of America in the Years 1809, 1810, and 1811*, vol. 5 of *Early Western Travels, 1748–1846*, ed. Reuben Gold Thwaites (Cleveland: Arthur H. Clark Co., 1904), 277. Anne Newport Royall's graphic description of the drilling process, written on her trip in the Kanawha Valley in 1823–24, demonstrates that the process had not changed from the Ruffner techniques of 1808–9; Royall, *Sketches*, 44-46.

6. Hildreth, "Saliferous Rock Formation," 54.

7. Ibid., 54-55; Cometti "Memorandum of William Whitteker," pt. 2, pp. 290-91; Hale, "Salt," 285-86.

8. Hale, "Salt," 286-87.

9. Hale, "Historical and Descriptive Sketch," 19; William Henry Ruffner, "The Ruffners: Part III, David," *West Virginia Historical Magazine Quarterly* 1, no. 4 (Oct. 1901): 53 (hereinafter cited as Ruffner, "David").

10. *Niles' Weekly Register*, April 22, 1815, p. 135.

11. Joel Shrewsbury to Col. William Dickinson, June [13], 1815, letterbook, 91-93 (copy), Dickinson & Shrewsbury Papers.

12. Articles of Agreement between Beverley Randolph and Co. and N. Bosworth (copy), March 29, 1815, Heth Family Papers.

13. Nath'l Bosworth to Harry Heth, April 22, 1815; Beverley Randolph to Maj. Harry Heth, May 9, 23, and 30, and June 13, 1815; H. Heth to Beverley Randolph, June 15, 1815; B. Randolph to Maj. Henry Heth, July 10, 1815; Bevy Randolph to Maj. Harry Heth, July 15, 1815, all in Heth Family Papers.

14. Joel Shrewsbury to Col. William Dickinson, June [13], 1815, letterbook, 91-93 (copy), Dickinson & Shrewsbury Papers.

15. Ruffner, "David," 53; Hildreth, "Bituminous Coal Deposits," 119; Lewis Ruffner to E. Meriam, Jan. 17, 1842, in *Kanawha Republican*, Nov. 12, 1942.

16. Hildreth, "Saliferous Rock Formation," 55; Hildreth, "Bituminous Coal Deposits," 119-20.

17. Hildreth, "Bituminous Coal Deposits," 119-20; Carroll W. Pursell, Jr., *Early Stationary Steam Engines in America: A Study in the Migration of a Technology* (Washington, D.C.: Smithsonian Institution Press, 1969), 82-83, 73.

18. Agreement of George H. Patrick with Andrew Donnally, Isaac Noyes, and Bradford Noyes, Feb. 14, 1832, CC, KCCR (1832).

19. *Kanawha Banner*, Oct. 11, 1832. The technical description of the manufacturing process was reprinted in *Niles' Weekly Register*, Oct. 27, 1832, p. 143.

20. U.S. Department of Interior, Bureau of Mines, *Technology of Salt-Making*, 77; U.S. Department of Interior, "Salt-Making Processes in the United States," by Thomas M. Chatard, in *Seventh Annual Report of the United States Geological Survey to the Secretary of the Interior, 1885–86* (Washington, D.C.: Government Printing Office, 1888), 522-23, 526.

21. The manufacturing process and furnace described would represent a typical factory; however, the dimensions varied between individual furnaces. This process evolved over a century with the use of new materials in construction and configurations of the vats. For a description of the process in the 1880s and before World War I, see U.S. Department of Interior, Bureau of Mines, *Technology of Salt-Making*, 77-80; U.S. Department of Interior, "Salt-Making Processes," 522-27.

22. Depositions of Lewis Ruffner, Aug. 19, 1845, and William Tompkins, July 24, 1845, in *Reynolds* v. *McFarland et al.* (1846), 336, 284.

6. Manufacturers and State Intervention

1. *Acts Passed at a General Assembly of the Commonwealth of Virginia*, Oct. 10, 1814, chap. 4, pp. 23-30; petition dated Nov. 1, 1817, Legislative Petitions of Kanawha County.

2. *Acts Passed at a General Assembly of the Commonwealth of Virginia*, Oct. 10, 1814, chap. 4, pp. 23-30.

3. Joel Shrewsbury to Col. William Dickinson, Jan. 7, 1815, letterbook, 59 (copy), Dickinson & Shrewsbury Papers; note dated May 25, 1815, attached to Bevly Randolph to Maj. Harry Heth, May 23, 1815, Heth Family Papers; quarterly returns of the commissioners of revenue of Kanawha County, May 1815–Feb. 1816, Auditors Item 86.

4. Noted dated May 25, 1815, attached to Bevly Randolph to Maj. Harry Heth, May 23, 1815, Heth Family Papers.

5. Bevy Randolph to Maj. Harry Heth, Aug. 22, 1815, and H. Heth to Beverly Randolph, Sept. 5, 1815, Heth Family Papers.

6. "Statement shewing the quantity of Salt manufactured on the Eastern border of the commonwealth from returns made to this office," report of Auditor's Office attached to petition dated Nov. 1, 1817, Legislative Petitions of Kanawha County.

7. "An abstract of the Taxes now charged to the manufacturers of Salt on Kanawha River between the 10th day of Feby 1816 with notes of the Situation of the parties charged with the Tax. made out by Van B. Reynolds & Robt. Hamilton Deputies of William Cottle Sheriff of Kanawha," attached to petition dated Nov. 1, 1817, Legislative Petitions of Kanawha County (hereinafter cited as "An Abstract of Taxes Charged Manufacturers, Feb. 10, 1815–Feb. 10, 1816").

8. Petition dated Nov. 1, 1917, Legislative Petitions of Kanawha County.

9. "An Abstract of Taxes Charged Manufacturers, Feb. 10, 1815–Feb. 10, 1816"; petition dated Nov. 1, 1817, Legislative Petitions of Kanawha County.

10. Petition dated Dec. 17, 1813, Legislative Petitions of Kanawha County.

11. *Acts Passed at a General Assembly of the Commonwealth of Virginia*, Dec. 6, 1813, chap. 65, pp. 126, 128-29, 130.

12. Ibid., 126-27.

13. Ibid., 127-28.

14. Ibid., 129.

15. Ibid., 128, 130.

16. Ibid., 129.

17. Ibid., 129-30.

18. *Star of the Kanawha Valley*, Feb. 3, 1856. The history of the salt-inspection legislation was written by a person using the pseudonym Kanawha.

19. *Acts Passed at a General Assembly of the Commonwealth of Virginia*, Dec. 4, 1826, chap. 31, pp. 28-29. The entire text of the statute is presented in the *Western Virginian*, March 3, 1827.

20. *Acts Passed at a General Assembly of the Commonwealth of Virginia*, Dec. 4, 1826, chap. 31, p. 29.

21. Ibid., 30.

22. Ibid.

23. Ibid., 30-31, 29, 31.

24. *Acts Passed at a General Assembly of the Commonwealth of Virginia*, Dec. 7, 1829, chap. 50, p. 49.

25. *Acts Passed at a General Assembly of the Commonwealth of Virginia*, Dec. 6, 1830, chap. 200, pp. 282-83.

26. *Acts Passed at a General Assembly of the Commonwealth of Virginia*, Dec. 5, 1831, chap. 191, pp. 259-60.

27. *Acts Passed at a General Assembly of the Commonwealth of Virginia*, Dec. 3, 1832, chap. 176, pp. 144-45.

28. Ibid., 145; *Acts of the General Assembly of Virginia, Passed at the Session of 1836–37, Commencing 5th December 1836, and Ending 31st March 1837*, chap. 74, p. 51.

29. *Western Virginian*, June 27, 1827.

30. Petition dated [1830], Legislative Petitions of Kanawha County.

31. *Acts Passed at a General Assembly of the Commonwealth of Virginia*, Dec. 6, 1830, chap. 48, p. 117; *Kanawha Banner*, May 3, 1832.

32. Lewis Summers to George W. Summers, Dec. 15, 1831, and Jan 2 and 6, 1832, George W. and Lewis Summers Papers.

33. *Acts of the General Assembly of Virginia, Passed at the Session of 1836–37, Commencing 5th December 1836, and Ending 31st March 1837*, chap. 191, pp. 182-84; *Kanawha Republican*, Dec. 4, 1841.

34. Petition dated Dec. 1837, Legislative Petitions of Kanawha County.

35. Ibid.

36. Petition dated [Dec. 1838], Legislative Petitions of Kanawha County.

37. *Acts of the General Assembly of Virginia, Passed at the Session Commencing 7th January and Ending 10th April 1839*, chap. 87, pp. 53-55.

38. Petition dated Jan. 1840, Legislative Petitions of Kanawha County.

39. Petition dated [Winter 1840], Legislative Petitions of Kanawha County.

40. *Acts of the General Assembly of Virginia, Passed at the Session Commencing December 2, 1844, and Ending 26th March 1845*, chap. 69, p. 59.

41. Petition dated Jan. 28, 1842, Legislative Petitions of Kanawha County; *Acts of the General Assembly of Virginia, Passed at the Session Commencing 6th December 1841, and Ending 26th March 1842*, chap. 169, p. 103.

42. A work that deals with state policy during this period is James Roger Sharp, *The Jacksonians versus the Banks: Politics in the States after the Panic of 1837* (New York: Columbia Univ. Press, 1970), 215-73. A newer work with a different approach to policy and regulation is Larry Schweikart, *Banking in the American South from the Age of Jackson to Reconstruction* (Baton Rouge: Louisiana State Univ. Press, 1987); for Virginia, see 34-37, 120-27, 274-75.

43. Petition dated Feb. 4, 1841, Legislative Petitions of Kanawha County.

44. Petition dated March 14, 1842, Legislative Petitions of Kanawha County.

45. See Stealey, "George Clendinen," 278-95.

46. The standard account of the James River-Kanawha River connection is Wayland Fuller Dunaway, *History of the James River and Kanawha Company* (New York: Columbia Univ., 1922), esp. 7-72; see also Carter Goodrich, "The Virginia System of Mixed Enterprise," *Political Science Quarterly* 64, no. 3 (Sept. 1949): 355-87. A convenient synthesis of the internal improvement problem in the Kanawha Valley is Louis McNeill Pease, "The Great Kanawha in the Old South, 1671–1861: A Study in Contradictions," Ph.D. diss., West Virginia University, 1959, chap. 10, pp. 270-307.

47. Petition dated Nov. 1, 1815, Legislative Petitions of Kanawha County.

48. Petition dated [1817], Legislative Petitions of Kanawha County.

49. Ibid.

50. Petition dated [1818], Legislative Petitions of Kanawha County.

51. For a discussion of the general objectives and problems of the reorganization, see Dunaway, *History of the James River and Kanawha Company*, 66-91.

52. *Acts Passed at a General Assembly of the Commonwealth of Virginia*, Dec. 6, 1819, chap. 56, pp. 42-44; Dec. 6, 1820, chap. 46, pp. 48-49.

53. *Western Virginian*, Nov. 15, 1826.

54. Ibid., Nov. 21, 1827.

55. *Acts Passed at a General Assembly of the Commonwealth of Virginia*, Dec. 3, 1827, chap. 78, pp. 49-50.

56. *Commonwealth v. James River Company*, CSC, KCCR (1828).

57. *James River Company, use of Commonwealth of Virginia v. William Armstrong, Johnston Armstrong, James S. Armstrong, Gilbert Adams, William B. Phillips, Peter Grant, and James Hewitt, doing business as Armstrongs, Grant and Company*, CC, KCCR (1828); *Western Virginian*, July 30, 1828.

58. *Acts Passed at a General Assembly of the Commonwealth of Virginia*, Dec. 1, 1828, chap. 73, pp. 50-53.

59. Petition to the president and directors of the Baltimore and Ohio Railroad Company, July 20, 1827 (copy), West Virginia and Regional History Collection, West Virginia University Library.

60. Charles Henry Ambler, *Sectionalism in Virginia from 1776 to 1861* (Chicago: Univ. of Chicago Press, 1910), 125.

61. Ibid., 180.

62. L. Summers to John J. Cabell, Dec. 29, 1828, John J. Cabell Papers, Robert Muldrow Cooper Library, Clemson University; Dunaway, *History of the James River and Kanawha Company,* 92-122; *Kanawha Banner,* May 24 and 31, and July 19, 1832.

63. Lewis Summers to George W. Summers, Feb. 28, 1832, George W. and Lewis Summers Papers.

64. Andrew Parks to Lewis Summers, Jan. 12, 1843, George W. and Lewis Summers Papers.

65. *The James River and Kanawha Company* v. [*Hewitt, Ruffner and Company*], CSC, KCCR (1841).

66. *William A. McMullin* v. *The James River and Kanawha Company,* CSC, KCCR (1846).

67. This line of reasoning can be seen in a petition dated Jan. 14, 1847, Legislative Petitions of Kanawha County.

7. Merchant Capitalists, Independent Manufacturers, and Local Economic Developments, 1825–1835

1. U.S. Congress, Senate, *Memorial of the Manufacturers of Salt,* S. Doc. 47, p. 5; U.S. Congress, Senate, *Report of the Committee on Manufactures,* 22d Cong., 1st sess., 1832, S. Doc. 105, p. 8; *Niles' Weekly Register,* Aug. 26, 1826, p. 445; *Star of the Kanawha Valley,* Feb. 3, 1856; Thomas Green Diary, Aug. 23, 1826, p. 16, Virginia Historical Society.

2. U.S. Congress, Senate, *Memorial of the Manufacturers of Salt,* S. Doc. 47, p. 5; U.S. Congress, Senate, *Report of the Committee on Manufactures,* S. Doc. 105, p. 7.

3. *Western Virginian,* Dec. 6, 1826.

4. *Reynolds* v. *McFarland et al.* (1846), 2-3; Andrew Donnally and John Lewis with Adam Berger, Dec. 12, 1826, CC, KCCR (1826); U.S. Congress, Senate, *Memorial of the Manufacturers of Salt,* S. Doc. 47, p. 16.

5. Agreement of Armstrongs, Grant and Company with Walter Trimble, Dec. 19, 1826, in *Armstrongs, Grant and Company* v. *Walter Trimble,* CSC, KCCR (1830).

6. Agreement of Armstrongs, Grant and Company with Littleberry and Joel Leftwich, Dec. 29, 1826, in *William Armstrong, Johnston Armstrong, James S. Armstrong, Peter Grant, Gilbert Adams, James Hewitt, and William B. Philips, doing business as Armstrongs, Grant and Company,* v. *Joel and Littleberry Leftwich,* CSC, KCCR (1831); also in Deed Book G, 172-73, Clerk, KCCH.

7. Deed Book G, 173, Clerk, KCCH; Atkinson, *History of Kanawha County,* 305-7; Laidley, *Charleston and Kanawha County,* 498; Ruffner-Kanawha Valley Scrapbook, 192, Roy Bird Cook Collection. Peter Grant, half-brother of President Grant's father, Jesse Root Grant, was a prosperous tanner, leather manufacturer, and merchant in Maysville, Kentucky. One traveler knew him as "a man of fine,

natural good sense with a very clear perception of the best adaptation of means to ends"; *Roland Trevor; or, The Pilot of Human Life, Being an Autobiography of the Author Showing How to Make and Lose a Fortune, And Then to Make Another* (Philadelphia: Lippincott, Grambo, and Co., 1853), 260. President Grant remembered him as "one of the wealthy men of the West" and he drowned at the mouth of the Great Kanawha. Grant said that he died in 1825, but it must have been later. U.S. Grant, *Personal Memoirs of U.S. Grant*, 2 vols. (New York: Charles L. Webster and Co., 1885), 1: 19. James Hewitt, who married Peter Grant's daughter and whom a contemporary called "one of the most thriving and wealthy merchants of the West," established his prosperous seat on the Ohio River above Louisville (*Roland Trevor*, 261-62). See John Y. Simon, ed., *The Personal Memoirs of Julia Dent Grant* (New York: Putnam's, 1975), 56.

8. *Western Virginian*, Jan. 13, 1827; U.S. Congress, Senate, *Memorial of the Manufacturers of Salt*, S. Doc. 47, p. 16; U.S. Congress, House, *Salt Works—United States*, 21st Cong., 1st sess., 1830, H. Doc. 55, p. 31.

9. Laidley, *Charleston and Kanawha County*, 400; deposition of Frederick Brooks, May 15, 1845, in *Reynolds v. McFarland et al.* (1846), 211-12, 213; *Reynolds v. McFarland et al.* (1846), 3, 133.

10. Joel Shrewsbury to Pleasant Dickinson, March 27, 1828, letterbook [301]-3 (copy), Dickinson & Shrewsbury Papers.

11. U.S. Congress, Senate, *Report of the Committee on Manufactures*, S. Doc. 105, pp. 8, 10.

12. *Reynolds v. McFarland et al.* (1846), 3; *Roland Trevor*, 261.

13. U.S. Congress, Senate, *Report of the Committee on Manufactures*, S. Doc. 105, p. 7; U.S. Congress, House, *Salt Works*, H. Doc. 55, pp. 36-37.

14. Lewis Collins, *History of Kentucky*, rev. by Richard H. Collins, 2 vols. (Louisville: John P. Morton and Co., 1924), 1: 34; *Maysville Eagle*, quoted in *Western Virginian*, Feb. 17, 1827.

15. *Western Virginian*, Feb. 25, 1829.

16. Ibid.

17. Bill of complaint of Ellicott Reynolds et al., in *Reynolds v. McFarland et al.* (1846), 3; John J. Cabell to Henry Ann Cabell, Dec. 26, 1829, Jubal A. Early Papers, Library of Congress.

18. Bill of complaint of Ellicott Reynolds et al., in *Reynolds v. McFarland et al.* (1846), 3.

19. Deposition of Bradford Noyes, Aug. 22, 1845, in *Reynolds v. McFarland et al.* (1846), 397-98.

20. Ibid., 398; bill of complaint of Ellicott Reynolds et al., in *Reynolds v. McFarland et al.* (1846), 3; U.S. Congress, House, *Duty on Imported Salt*, 21st Cong., 2d sess., 1831, H. Rept. 70, p. 23.

21. U.S. Congress, Senate, *Report of the Committee on Manufactures*, S. Doc. 105, p. 5; John J. Cabell to Richard K. Crallé, Jan. 7, 1832, John J. Cabell Papers, Robert A. Brock Collection, Henry E. Huntington Library and Art Gallery; deposition of Bradford Noyes, Aug. 22, 1845, in *Reynolds v. McFarland et al.* (1846), 398-400.

22. John J. Cabell to Richard K. Crallé, July 7, 1831, John J. Cabell Papers, Robert A. Brock Collection; bill of complaint of Ellicott Reynolds Et al., in *Reynolds v. McFarland et al.* (1846), 4; Lewis Summers to George W. Summers, Dec. 15, 1831, George W. and Lewis Summers Papers.

23. John J. Cabell to Richard K. Crallé, July 7 and Nov. 13, 1831, and Jan. 7, 1832, John J. Cabell Papers, Robert A. Brock Collection.

24. Lewis Summers to George W. Summers, Jan. 6, 1832, George W. and Lewis Summers Papers.

25. *Reynolds* v. *McFarland et al.* (1846), 4, 134, 347.

26. Bill of complaint of Ellicott Reynolds et al., and answer of James C. McFarland, in *Reynolds* v. *McFarland et al.* (1846), 4, 134.

27. Deposition of James Norton, July 28, 1845, in *Reynolds* v. *McFarland et al.* (1846), 281.

28. Agreement of Reuben Roy with Donnally, Bream and Company, Aug. 21, 1833, in *Dickinson, Ruffner and Company* v. *Donnally, Bream and Company,* CSC, KCCR (1834).

29. Berry, *Western Prices,* table 39, p. 579; chart 26, p. 298; chart 27, pp. 304, 312-13. Deposition of Lewis Ruffner, Aug. 20, 1845, in *Reynolds* v. *McFarland et al.* (1846), 347; Lewis Summers to George W. Summers, Jan. 8, 1835, George W. and Lewis Summers Papers.

30. Lewis Summers to George W. Summers, Jan. 17 and 25, 1835, George W. and Lewis Summers Papers.

31. Petition dated [Jan. 1835], Legislative Petitions of Kanawha County.

32. Ibid.

33. Counterpetition dated [Jan. 1835], Legislative Petitions of Kanawha County.

34. Ibid. An analysis of the signatories suggests that the opponents of the incorporation proposal were substantially correct in their assessment of the proponents. In his cover letter to the Kanawha County delegate, James Craik stressed the haste with which the document was circulated: "Time has not been allowed to present the memorial to the manufacturers on the lower side of the river, where it is believed that the measure is as generally approved as it is evidently upon the upper side, the foregoing list containing the names of nearly all the proprietors of Salt property, between Charleston and the upper end of the Salines." James Craik to George W. Summers, Jan. 27, 1835, attached to petition dated [Jan. 1835].

35. Lewis Summers to George W. Summers, Feb. 18, 1835, George W. and Lewis Summers Papers.

36. Ibid.

8. Hewitt, Ruffner & Company and Depression, 1836–1846

1. Depositions of William Tompkins, July 21, 1845, and Charles G. Reynolds, Oct. 7, 1845, in *Reynolds* v. *McFarland et at.* (1846), 243, 318.

2. Lewis Summers to George W. Summers, Feb. 22, 1836, George W. and Lewis Summers Papers. Depositions of Lewis Ruffner, Aug. 19, 1845; William Tompkins, July 21, 1845; and Charles G. Reynolds, Oct. 7, 1845, in *Reynolds* v. *McFarland et al.* (1846), 331, 243, 318-19.

3. Articles of Agreement of Richard E. Putney, William Shrewsbury, Charles L. Shrewsbury, Joel Shrewsbury, Jr., and John Rogers, Jr., doing business as William Shrewsbury and Co.; John Lewis, William R. Cox, Frederick Brooks, Andrew Donnally, John D. Lewis, Moses M. Fuqua, Henry Fitzhugh, James Hewitt, and Luke Willcox, doing business as Hewitt and Willcox; James C. McFarland, Samuel Shrewsbury, Jr., Henry H. Wood, Levi Welch, William Tompkins, Daniel Ruffner, Lewis Ruffner, John D. Lewis, and William D. Shrewsbury, doing business as Lewis and Shrewsbury; Bradford Noyes, Jr.,

Benjamin H. Smith, and William I. Rand, doing business as Noyes, Rand and Smith; Isaac Ruffner, Samuel Q. Anderson, Robert Anderson, and Robert N. Anderson, doing business as Samuel Q. Anderson and Company; and Crockett Ingles, Nathaniel Hatch, John Warth, George H. Warth, and Job English, doing business as Warth and English with James Hewitt, Feb. 16, 1836, in *Reynolds* v. *McFarland et al.* (1846), 41, 49 (hereinafter cited as Articles of Agreement of Putney et al. with Hewitt, Feb. 16, 1836).

    4. Ibid., 41-42.

    5. Deposition of Samuel Hannah, May 15, 1845, in *Reynolds* v. *McFarland et al.* (1846), 222.

    6. Articles of Agreement of Putney et al. with Hewitt, Feb. 16, 1836, pp. 42, 45-46.

    7. Ibid., 50-51, 49-50.

    8. Ibid., 51, 52-53.

    9. Ibid., 46-47, 48.

    10. Depositions of William Tompkins, May 14, and July 21 and 24, 1845, in *Reynolds* v. *McFarland et al.* (1846), 192, 243, 282.

    11. Articles of Agreement of Putney et al. with Hewitt, Feb. 16, 1836, pp. 48-49.

    12. Ibid., 51-52.

    13. Ibid.

    14. Depositions of Samuel Hannah, May 15, 1845; William Tompkins, July 21, 1845; and Lewis Ruffner, Aug. 19, 1845, in *Reynolds* v. *McFarland et al.* (1846), 223, 244-45, 332.

    15. Deposition of Charles G. Reynolds, Oct. 7, 1845, in *Reynolds* v. *McFarland et al.* (1846), 320-21, 323.

    16. Articles of Agreement of Putney et al. with Hewitt, Feb. 16, 1836, pp. 42-45.

    17. Bill of complaint of Ellicott Reynolds et al., *Reynolds* v. *McFarland et al.* (1846), 5.

    18. Answer of Levi Welch; depositions of Samuel Hannah, May 15, 1845, and John M. Laidley, Aug. 19, 1845, in *Reynolds* v. *McFarland et al.* (1846), 16, 219, 386-87.

    19. Depositions of William Tompkins, May 14, 1845; Frederick Brooks, May 15, 1845; James Norton, July 28, 1845; Charles G. Reynolds, Oct. 7, 1845; Lewis Ruffner, Aug. 19, 1845; and John M. Laidley, Aug. 19, 1845, in *Reynolds* v. *McFarland et al.* (1846), 191, 213, 293, 321, 334, 343, 386.

    20. Depositions of William Tompkins, July 21, 1845, and Lewis Ruffner, Aug. 19, 1845, in *Reynolds* v. *McFarland et al.* (1846), 244, 332.

    21. Depositions of William Tompkins, May 14, 1845; Lewis Ruffner, Aug. 19, 1845; and John M. Laidley, Aug. 19, 1845, in *Reynolds* v. *McFarland et al.* (1846), 191, 334, 386.

    22. Answer of Levi Welch; and depositions of Samuel Hannah, May 15, 1845; John M. Laidley, Aug. 19, 1845; and Frederick Brooks, May 15, 1845, in *Reynolds* v. *McFarland et al.* (1846), 161, 219, 386, 213.

    23. Answer of Levi Welch; and depositions of William Tompkins, May 14, 1845; Brayton Allen, May 14, 1845; Frederick Brooks, May 15, 1845; Samuel Hannah, May 15, 1845; and Lewis Ruffner, Aug. 19, 1845, in *Reynolds* v. *McFarland et al.* (1846), 162, 192, 207-8, 213, 218, 334-35.

    24. Answer of Levi Welch; depositions of Samuel Hannah, May 15, 1845, and William Tompkins, July 21, 1845, in *Reynolds* v. *McFarland et al.* (1846), 162, 221, 246.

25. Answer of Levi Welch; and depositions of William Tompkins, May 14 and July 21, 1845; Brayton Allen, May 14, 1845; and Lewis Ruffner, Aug. 19, 1845, in *Reynolds* v. *McFarland et al.* (1846), 162, 192, 207-8, 246, 334-35.

26. S[amuel] Hannah to James C. McFarland, July 7, 1836, James C. McFarland Papers, Roy Bird Cook Collection; deposition of Samuel Hannah, May 15, 1845 in *Reynolds* v. *McFarland et al.* (1846), 219-20; *Kanawha Republican*, Dec. 4, 1841.

27. Deposition of Charles G. Reynolds, Oct. 7, 1845, in *Reynolds* v. *McFarland et al.* (1846), 320; Nelson B. Coleman to J. P. Hale, [Aug.] 1891, Nelson B. Coleman Papers, West Virginia Department of Archives and History.

28. Deposition of Thomas Friend, May 15, 1845, in *Reynolds* v. *McFarland et al.* (1846), 231-32.

29. Berry, *Western Prices*, table 39, p. 579.

30. Statement of Account of Hewitt, Ruffner and Company with James River and Kanawha Company, CC, KCCR (1836). The figures are calculated on an annual basis, from February 15 to February 15.

31. Deposition of Charles G. Reynolds, Oct. 7, 1845, in *Reynolds* v. *McFarland et al.* (1846), 320.

32. *Andrew Donnally, Isaac Noyes, and George H. Patrick, doing business as Donnally, Noyes and Patrick, for use of George H. Patrick* v. *Henry Smith French*, CSC, KCCR (1838).

33. Deposition of William Tompkins, July 24, 1845, in *Reynolds* v. *McFarland et al.* (1846), 276.

34. Depositions of Thomas Friend, May 15, 1845, and Charles G. Reynolds, Oct. 7, 1845, in *Reynolds* v. *McFarland et al.* (1846), 226, 319.

35. Berry, *Western Prices*, chart 26, pp. 298, 297, 299, 437; chart 27, p. 304.

36. For more detailed and specific treatment of this economic crisis, see the revisionist account, Peter Temin, *The Jacksonian Economy* (New York: Norton, 1969), and the traditional accounts, Reginald Charles McGrane, *The Panic of 1837: Some Financial Problems of the Jacksonian Era* (New York: Russell and Russell, 1965); Hammond, *Banks and Politics*, 451-548; Arthur H. Cole, "Business Fluctuations, 1820-45," in Smith and Cole, *Fluctuations in American Business*, 338-46. For a discussion of the impact on Cincinnati and the West, see Berry, *Western Prices*, 432-69.

37. Depositions of Samuel Hannah, May 15, 1845, and William Tompkins, July 24, 1845, in *Reynolds* v. *McFarland et al.* (1846), 218, 278; *Kanawha Republican*, Jan. 15, 1842; John D. Lewis to John J. Dickinson, Feb. 5, 1846, Lewis Family Papers, West Virginia and Regional History Collection, West Virginia University Library.

38. Bill of Complaint of Ellicott Reynolds et al., and deposition of Thomas Friend, May 15, 1845, in *Reynolds* v. *McFarland et al.* (1846), 6, 232.

39. Depositions of William Tompkins, July 21 and 24, 1845; Bradford Noyes, Aug. 22, 1845, in *Reynolds* v. *McFarland et al.* (1846), 248, 277-78, 400; deposition of Levi Welch, May 2, 1849, in *Early* v. *Friend* (1857), 1: 138.

40. Depositions of William Tompkins, July 24, 1845, and Bradford Noyes, Aug. 22, 1845, in *Reynolds* v. *McFarland et al.* (1846), 277, 400-401; deposition of Levi Welch, May 2, 1849, in *Early* v. *Friend* (1857), 1: 138.

41. Deposition of Lewis Ruffner, Aug. 19, 1845, in *Reynolds* v. *McFarland et al.* (1846), 344, 345.

42. Lewis Summers to George W. Summers, Feb. 18, 1838, George W. and Lewis Summers Papers; Henry Ruffner to David Ruffner, Dec. 31, 1840, Ruffner

Family Papers; Lewis Summers to George W. Summers, Dec. 2, 1840, George W. and Lewis Summers Papers.

43. Deposition of Thomas Friend, May 15, 1845 in *Reynolds* v. *McFarland et al.* (1846), 227; deposition of James A. Payne, Sept. 15, 1849, in *Early* v. *Friend* (1857), 1: 145; Berry, *Western Prices*, chart 26, p. 298, chart 27, p. 304, and table 39, p. 579.

44. Deposition of John B. Crockett, July 23, 1845, in *Reynolds* v. *McFarland et al.* (1846), 269, 270-71.

45. Depositions of William Tompkins, July 24, 1845, and Lewis Ruffner, Aug. 19, 1845 in *Reynolds* v. *McFarland et al.* (1846), 284-85, 336.

46. Depositions of Brayton Allen, May 14, 1845, and Samuel Hannah, May 15, 1845, in *Reynolds* v. *McFarland et al.* (1846), 208, 223; deposition of R.C.M. Lovell, Oct. 13, 1853, in *Early* v. *Friend* (1857), 2: 54-55.

47. Deposition of William Graham, [Oct. 9, 1849?], in *Early* v. *Friend* (1857), 1: 290.

48. Lewis Summers to George W. Summers, Jan. 11, March 20, May 7, and June 7, 1842, George W. and Lewis Summers Papers.

49. Lewis Summers to George W. Summers, July 20, 1842, George W. and Lewis Summers Papers. Examples of such payments are in A.M. January and Son to S. Shepperd, Aug. 1, 1842, and July 6, 1843, in *A.M. and Wm. January, doing business as A.M. January and Son* v. *Stephen Shepherd and David C. Kline, doing business as Stephen Shepherd and Co.*, CSC, KCCR (1846), and in Joseph Friend, by James S. Carr, attorney in fact, to James C. McFarland, Jan. 26, 1843, in *James C. McFarland* v. *Joseph Friend*, CSC, KCCR (1845).

50. Lewis Summers to George W. Summers, June 7, 1842, and Jan. 3, 1843, George W. and Lewis Summers Papers.

51. L. Welch to Geo. W. Summers, Feb. 4, 1844, Summers Family Papers (Glenwood).

52. Lewis Ruffner to Henry Ruffner, Jan. 19, 1845, William Henry and Henry Ruffner Papers; *Kanawha Republican*, March 26, 1845.

53. John D. Lewis to John J. Dickinson, March 17 and 21, 1846, Lewis Family Papers.

9. The Kanawha Producers and the Salt Tariff

1. No. 9, "State Debts," Walter Lowrie and Matthew St. Clair Clarke, comps., in *American State Papers*, III, *Finance*, vols. 1-4 (Washington: Gales and Seaton, 1832–59), 1: 43-44.

2. Edward Stanwood, *American Tariff Controversies in the Nineteenth Century*, 2 vols. (Boston: Houghton Mifflin, 1903), 1: 110; Davis Rich Dewey, *Financial History of the United States*, 12th ed. (New York: Longmans, Green and Co., 1934), 112-13.

3. Dewey, *Financial History*, 119-21, 122; Stanwood, *American Tariff Controversies* 1: 113.

4. The general feeling of many Americans owing to international disruptions of salt imports can be seen in no. 345, "Encouragement of Manufacturers," in *American State Papers, Finance* 3: 482.

5. William J. Shultz and M.R. Crane, *Financial Development of the United States* (New York: Prentice-Hall, 1937), 140, 165; Dewey, *Financial History*, 165;

Stanwood, *American Tariff Controversies* 1: 112; Norris W. Preyer, "Southern Support of the Tariff of 1816—A Reappraisal," *Journal of Southern History* 25, no. 3 (Aug. 1959): 306-7, 311-15.

6. Shultz and Crane, *Financial Development*, 216; Dewey, *Financial History*, 170; *Register of Debates*, 19th Cong., 1st sess., vol. 2, pt. 2, March 17, 1826, appendix, p. 142; U.S. Congress, Senate, *Report on the Repeal of the Salt Duty*, 19th Cong., 1st sess., 1826, S. Doc. 61.

7. *Register of Debates*, 19th Cong., 2d sess., vol. 3, Feb. 1, 1827, pp. 228-30; Feb. 2, 1827, pp. 230-32, 243-45, 253-54; Feb. 5, 1827, pp. 254-66.

8. Ibid., Feb. 5, 1827, pp. 256, 260; 20th Cong., 1st sess., vol. 4, Dec. 12, 1827, pp. 3-4.

9. U.S. Congress, House, *Biographical Directory of the American Congress, 1774–1927*, 69th Cong., 2d sess., 1927, H. Doc. 783, p. 1069; *Register of Debates*, 20th Cong., 1st sess., vol. 4, April 7, 1828, pp. 591-95.

10. U.S. Congress, Senate, *Memorial of the Manufacturers of Salt*, S. Doc. 47, pp. 3-5.

11. Ibid., 5-6, 16.

12. Ibid.

13. Ibid., 6-7, 12.

14. Ibid., 14, 12-15, 16.

15. *Western Virginian*, July 16, 1828. Also see Robert Seager II, ed., *The Papers of Henry Clay*, vol. 7 (Lexington: Univ. Press of Kentucky, 1982), 348-50, 384.

16. Thomas Hart Benton, *Thirty Years' View*, 2 vols. (New York: Appleton and Co., 1858), 2: 143, 154-55. See William M. Meigs, *The Life of Thomas Hart Benton* (Philadelphia: Lippincott, 1904), 156.

17. There is no report of the Senate's action on this measure in the official *Debates*. See Stanwood, *American Tariff Controversies* 2: 365; *Register of Debates*, 21st Cong., 1st sess., vol. 6, pt. 2, appendix, p. 43.

18. *Register of Debates*, 21st Cong., 1st sess., vol. 6, pt. 2, May 11, 1830, pp. 965, 966; May 12, 1830, pp. 966-76, 979; May 13, 1830, p. 986; May 15, 1830, p. 994; May 17, 1830, p. 1016; May 18, 1830, p. 1037; May 21, 1830, pp. 1120-21; May 27, 1830, p. 1139; May 19, 1830, p. 1049. For a brief summary of the bill's history, see Stanwood, *American Tariff Controversies* 2: 362-65.

19. *Register of Debates*, 21st Cong., 1st sess., vol. 6, pt. 2, Feb. 23, 1830, pp. 172-76.

20. Ibid., 177, 178, 179.

21. Ibid., 178; May 11, 1830, pp. 429, 430, 432.

22. Ibid., Feb. 23, 1830, p. 178.

23. "Letter from the Secretary of the Treasury transmitting a Report of the Number and Nature of the Salt Works established in the United States, &C. &C.," in U.S. Congress, House, *Salt Works*, H. Doc. 55, pp. 30-35; U.S. Congress, Senate, *Memorial of the Manufacturers of Salt in the County of Kenhawa, Virginia, against the Repeal of the Duty on Imported Salt*, 21st Cong., 1st sess., 1830, S. Doc. 134.

24. *Kanawha Banner*, Sept. 10 and Oct. 8, 1830.

25. Ibid., Nov. 12, 1830.

26. Ibid., Nov. 26, 1830.

27. Ibid.; "Memorial of the Manufacturers of Salt in Kanawha County, Virginia, Praying for a Restoration of the Duty on Imported Salt," in U.S. Congress, House, *Duty on Imported Salt*, H. Rept. 70, pp. 10-13. This petition also

appears in the *Register of Debates*, 21st Cong., 2d sess., vol. 7, appendix, pp. 125-31.

28. U.S. Congress, House, *Duty on Imported Salt*, H. Rept. 70, pp. 14-15.

29. Ibid., 17-18.

30. Ibid., 20.

31. Ibid., 22, 24.

32. *Register of Debates*, 21st Cong., 2d sess., vol. 7, Feb. 8, 1831, pp. 120, 147, 120-23, 126, 127-34, 136.

33. Ibid., 138-39.

34. John J. Cabell to Richard K. Crallé, Sept. 16, 1831, John J. Cabell Papers, Robert A. Brock Collection.

35. *Register of Debates*, 22d Cong., 1st sess., vol. 8, Dec. 29, 1831, p. 32; Dec. 30, 1831, pp. 32, 33-41.

36. Ibid., Dec. 30, 1831, p. 38.

37. Ibid., 36-39.

38. U.S. Congress, Senate, *Report of the Committee on Manufactures*, S. Doc. 105, pp. 2-5.

39. Ibid., 4-5.

40. *Register of Debates*, 22d Cong., 1st sess., vol. 8, Jan. 26, 1832, p. 181; Jan. 27, 1832, p. 182.

41. Ibid., Feb. 1, 1832, pp. 223-24; March 19, 1832, p. 591; U.S. Congress, Senate, *Report of the Committee on Manufactures*, S. Doc. 105, pp. 1-2.

42. *Register of Debates*, 24th Cong., 2d sess., vol. 8, pt. 1, pp. 884, 896, 930, 936.

43. Ibid., Feb. 21, 1837, pp. 872-93; Feb. 23, 1837, pp. 894-911, 920-32; Feb. 24, 1837, p. 939; Feb. 25, 1837, pp. 967-81.

44. *Congressional Globe*, 25th Cong., 3d sess., vol. 7, appendix, p. 135; Feb. 14, 1839, p. 182; Feb. 16, 1839, p. 188; appendix, p. 135.

45. Ibid., 26th Cong., 1st sess., vol. 8, Dec. 5, 1839, p. 17; Feb. 12, 1840, p. 186; Feb. 14, 1840, p. 198; appendix, pp. 177, 178.

46. Ibid., appendix, p. 178.

47. Ibid., 180, 179, 182.

48. U.S. Congress, Senate, *Documents Relating to the Trade in, and Manufacture and Uses of, Salt*, 26th Cong., 1st sess., 1840, S. Doc. 196, pp. 1, 2-4.

49. U.S. Congress, Senate, *Reports of the Majority and Minority of the Select Committee on the Origin and Character of Fishing Bounties and Allowances*, 26th Cong., 1st sess., 1840, S. Doc. 368, p. 2; Charles Sellers, *James K. Polk*, 2 vols. (Princeton, N.J.: Princeton Univ. Press, 1957–66), 1: 384, 396, 402, 403, 411, 435, 451; *Congressional Globe*, 26th Cong., 1st sess., vol. 8, April 10, 1840, p. 318.

50. U.S. Congress, Senate, *Reports of the Majority and Minority of the Select Committee on the Origin and Character of Fishing Bounties and Allowances*, S. Doc. 368, p. 59.

51. Ibid., 72, 73.

52. For the last and best major speech by Benton on this problem and for a summary of his arguments, see *Congressional Globe*, 26th Cong., 1st sess., vol. 8, April 22, 1840, pp. 345-48; appendix, pp. 390-401.

53. Dewey, *Financial History*, 237-39; *Congressional Globe*, 27th Cong., 2d sess., July 5, 1842, appendix, p. 661.

54. The best general treatments of the Walker tariff of 1846 are Sellers, *James K. Polk* 2: 343-44, 349-50, 445-46, 450-75, 477-80, 484-86; Dewey, *Financial History*, 249-52; and Stanwood, *American Tariff Controversies* 2: 74-75. For congressional

debate on the salt duty, see *Congressional Globe*, 29th Cong., 1st sess. pp. 190, 304-5, 538-49, 1193-94; appendix, pp. 968-69.

55. *Congressional Globe*, 31st Cong., 2d sess., vol. 23, Dec. 3, 1840, p. 7.

10. White Labor, Subsidiary Industries, and Furnace Managers

1. Hildreth, "Bituminous Coal Deposits," 121; Royall, *Sketches*, 46-47.

2. Royall, *Sketches*, 47; Henry Ruffner to Col. D[avid] Ruffner, Feb. 17, 1815, Ruffner Family Papers; Isaac Reed, *The Christian Traveller* (New York: J. and J. Harper, 1828), 34-35; Royall, *Sketches*, 47-48.

3. Articles of Agreement of Willis and Ruffner with John H. Hull, Feb. 12, 1825, in *John H. Hull v. Notley Willis and Charles Ruffner, doing business as Willis and Ruffner*, CSC, KCCR (1826).

4. Petition dated Nov. 16, 1816, Legislative Petitions of Kanawha County; *Smith French v. John Mushrush and Fleming Scott*, CSC, KCCR (1833); *Jefferson Donnally, Levi Welch, Henry Wood, Solomon K. Grant, Samuel J. Cabell, James Hewitt, William Tompkins, and Lewis Ruffner v. James Neale, Scott St. Clair, Milburn Johnston, and George Hix*, CSC, KCCR (1837).

5. Laidley, *Charleston and Kanawha County*, 195-96. For names of antebellum pilots, also see Louis A. Martin, "The Great Kanawha Valley in 1850," *West Virginia Historical Magazine Quarterly* 2, no. 3 (July 1902): 68-69.

6. J.H. Rogers to Weyer and McKee, Aug. 26, 1853, letterbook, 554, and William A. Lewis to S.A. Miller, May 5, 1855, Ruffner, Donnally and Company Papers, West Virginia and Regional History Collection, West Virginia University Library.

7. Laidley, *Charleston and Kanawha County*, 195-96; *Andrew Donnally, Jr., William Steele, Robert Steele, and Jacob Darneal, doing business as Donnally, Steele and Company v. Thomas Russel*, CSC, KCCR (1813); *William Steele and Company v. Thomas Reynolds*, CC, KCCR (1815); *Steele, Donnally and Steeles v. Samuel Moore*, CSC, KCCR (1818); *Levi Hungerford v. James Brown*, CSC, KCCR (1820); *Andrew Donnally and Isaac Noyes, doing business as Donnally and Noyes v. Thompson Trackwell*, CSC, KCCR (1846).

8. Joel Shrewsbury to Col. William Dickinson, Feb. 15, 1820, letterbook, 259-60, Dickinson & Shrewsbury Papers.

9. Deposition of Elisha Bell, June 4, 1842, in *Stephen Rook v. Andrew Donnally and Isaac Noyes, doing business as Donnally and Noyes*, CSC, KCCR (1844).

10. *Stephen Rook v. Andrew Donnally and Isaac Noyes, doing business as Donnally and Noyes*, CSC, KCCR (1844).

11. *William Christy v. Andrew Donnally*, CSC, KCCR (1844); J.H. Rogers to Weyer and McKee, July 2, 1853, and Taylor to James Mitchell, Aug. 26, 1853, letterbook, 507, 550, Ruffner, Donnally and Company Papers.

12. *Andrew Donnally, Jr. v. John Jones and Samuel Smith*, CSC, KCCR (1819); John B. Smith to Ruffner, Donnally and Co., June 21, 1854, Ruffner, Donnally and Company Papers.

13. U.S. Congress, Senate, *Memorial of the Manufacturers of Salt*, S. Doc. 47, p. 5; Schedule 5, Products of Industry, County of Kanawha, State of Virginia, vol. 2, pp. 13-20, United States Census of 1850, Virginia State Library; Schedule 5, Products of Industry, County of Kanawha, State of Virginia, pp. 214-16, United States Census of 1860, Virginia State Library.

14. Computed from County of Kanawha, State of Virginia, Records of the 1820 Census of Manufactures, Records of the Bureau of the Census, Record Group 29, National Archives Microfilm Publication M279, roll 18, frames 96-105, 107 (hereinafter cited as NA RG 29, M279 18).

15. U.S. Congress, House, *Salt Works*, H. Doc. 55, pp. 36-37; Schedule 5, Products of Industry, County of Kanawha, State of Virginia, vol. 2, pp. 18-20, 15, United States Census of 1850.

16. *Marcellus W. Petitt, for benefit of John Rogers and Joel Shrewsbury, doing business as Rogers and Shrewsbury v. Bradford M. Noyes, William J. Rand, and Benjamin H. Smith, doing business as Noyes, Rand and Company; George C. Adcock v. Andrew Donnally*, both CSC, KCCR (1838).

17. *Nelson Priddy v. Frederick Brooks*, CSC, KCCR (1830); agreement between Charles Ruffner and Joseph Malcolm, Nov. 29, 1830, CC, KCCR (1830).

18. *William Gardner v. R.C.M. Lovell and Brothers*, CSC, KCCR (1849); *Charles and Henry Ferrell v. John D. Lewis*, CSC, KCCR (1851).

19. *Western Virginian*, May 12, 1827; agreement between Coleman and Company and Samuel Rucker, May 10, 1833, Nelson B. Coleman Papers; *James Hogue, surviving obligee of William Hogue, deceased v. John Wilson*, CC, KCCR (1825); *William Atkinson v. Larkin C. Roy*, CSC, KCCR (1833).

20. NA RG 29, M279, 18/95-99, 101-5; *William Schoonover v. Matthew Geary and David Enoch*, CSC, KCCR (1836); *John Greenlee and Stokes Prewitt, doing business as Greenlee and Prewitt v. Charles G. Reynolds*, CSC, KCCR (1835).

21. Hunter, *Steamboats*, 54-55. Antebellum inland water transportation has received scholarly treatment in recent years. A perceptive and succinct study of the economic aspects of flatboat use is Harry N. Scheiber, "The Ohio-Mississippi Flatboat Trade: Some Reconsiderations," in *The Frontier in American Development: Essays in Honor of Paul Wallace Gates*, ed. David M. Ellis (Ithaca, N.Y.: Cornell Univ. Press, 1969), 277-98. Several articles by Eric F. Haites, James Mak, and Gary M. Walton, the most relevant to flatboat use being James Mak and Gary M. Walton, "On the Persistence of Old Technologies: The Case of Flatboats," *Journal of Economic History* 33, no. 2 (June 1973): 444-51, culminated in an analytical study: Haites, Mak, and Walton, *Western River Transportation: The Era of Early Internal Development, 1810-1860* (Baltimore: Johns Hopkins Univ. Press, 1975).

22. Atkinson, *History of Kanawha County*, 188; *William Dickinson, Joel Shrewsbury, Sr., James C. McFarland, Andrew Donnally, Jno. Lewis, Isaac Noyes, Bradford Noyes, James Hewitt, James S. Armstrong, and James Bream, doing business as Dickinson, Armstrong, and Company v. John Frail*, CSC, KCCR (1836).

23. NA RG 29, M279, 18/95-97, 100-105; Schedule 5, Products of Industry, County of Kanawha, State of Virginia, vol. 2, pp. 15-18, United States Census of 1850.

24. Deposition of William V. Hutt, March 18, 1839, in *William F. and William W. Whittaker, for use of Thomas Whittaker v. Noyes, Rand and Company*, CSC, KCCR (1838).

25. Articles of Agreement of Aaron Stockton with Jabez Spinks and Middleton Harman, Nov. 3, 1823, in *Jabez Spinks and Julius Breach v. Aaron Stockton*, CSC, KCCR (1825); Articles of Agreement between Jabez Spinks and George Montgomery and Bradford Noyes and James M. Thompson, May 16, 1844, in *John R. Humphries v. Bradford Noyes*, CSC, KCCR (1848).

26. Schedule 5, Products of Industry, County of Kanawha, State of Virginia, vol. 2, pp. 14, 20, United States Census of 1850.

27. *John R. Humphries v. Bradford Noyes*, CSC, KCCR (1848); *Henry B. Saunders, for benefit of David Farrier, John Goshorn, Francis Thompson, and Frederick Brooks v. Daniel Ruffner*, CC, KCCR (1835).

28. *Kanawha Banner*, Oct. 8, 1830; U.S. Congress, Senate, *Memorial of the Manufacturers of Salt*, S. Doc. 47, p. 6; U.S. Congress, House, *Salt Works*, H. Doc. 55, pp. 32, 36-37.

29. Donnally and Steele and Company, Kanawha Salt Works Account Book, 1813–15, p. 15; John J. Cabell to Henry Ann Cabell, Jan. 10, 1830, Jubal A. Early Papers; Pursell, *Early Stationary Steam Engines*, 82.

30. Schedule 5, Products of Industry, County of Kanawha, State of Virginia, vol. 2, pp. 15, 19, 20, United States Census of 1850.

31. Donnally and Steele and Company, Kanawha Salt Works Account Book, 1813–15, pp. 2, 5; Reed, *Christian Traveller*, 34-35; *Bartholemew Henry, for use and benefit of Samuel Gillespie v. John A. Duke*, CC, KCCR (1824).

32. Donnally and Steele and Company, Kanawha Salt Works Account Book, 1813–15, pp. 52, 71; *John Brown, Ansel Wood, and James Harris v. James Shepherd*, CSC, KCCR (1816); *William Toney v. Alexander and Martin Warth*, CSC, KCCR (1817).

33. Royall, *Sketches*, 47.

34. Hildreth, "Bituminous Coal Deposits," 104, 108; Virginia Geological Survey, *Report of the Progress of the Geological Survey of the State of Virginia for the Year 1839*, by William Barton Rogers, in *A Reprint of Annual Reports and Other Papers on the Geology of the Virginias*, by William Barton Rogers (New York: Appleton and Co., 1884), 380-81.

35. For a sample of nineteenth-century stratigraphy of the Salines area, see Hildreth, "Bituminous Coal Deposits," 104. For a discussion of the characteristics and locations of the various coal seams in Kanawha Salines, see West Virginia Geological Survey, *Levels above Tide; True Meridians; Report on Coal*, by I. C. White, vol. 2 (Morgantown, W.Va.: Morgantown Post Co., 1903), 500-600; West Virginia Geological Survey, *Kanawha County*, 454-566.

36. *Robert Young v. Walter Trimble*, CSC, KCCR (1822); agreement of Andrew Donnally and his wife with Isaac and Bradford Noyes, Jan. 7, 1823, CC, KCCR (1828); agreement of Andrew Donnally, James Wilson, John Ruffner, James Bream, and Joseph Lovell, Aug. 28, 1822, CC, KCCR (1822).

37. Articles of Agreement of Andrew Donnally and William Steele with Stephen Radcliff, Jan. 2, 1823, Deed Book F, 283-84, Clerk, KCCH.

38. James C. McFarland to Representative William Hunt [1845], quoted in the *Charleston Gazette*, June 17, 1951, Ruffner-Kanawha Valley Scrapbook, Roy Bird Cook Collection; *Cincinnati Chronicle*, quoted in *Niles' Weekly Register*, Aug. 19, 1837, p. 386.

39. *Andrew L. Alden v. John B. Crockett*, CSC, KCCR (1822); Hildreth, "Bituminous Coal Deposits," 108.

40. All estimates and calculations of coal tonnage are based on the assumption that a bushel of bituminous coal weighed eighty pounds. See Berry, *Western Prices*, 151, and Eavenson, *American Coal Industry*, 11.

41. Schedule 5, Products of Industry, County of Kanawha, State of Virginia, vol. 2, pp. 18, 20, United States Census of 1850; U.S. Congress, Senate, *Memorial of the Manufacturers of Salt*, S. Doc. 47, p. 16; U. S. Congress, House, *Salt Works*, H. Doc. 55, pp. 36-37.

42. Schedule 5, Products of Industry, County of Kanawha, State of Virginia, vol. 2, pp. 13-20, United States Census of 1850. Professor Otis K. Rice es-

timated Kanawha County coal output in 1850 at 6,284,200 bushels (Rice, "Coal Mining," 396). Adding the production of the independent operators, Jackson Ritter and Aaron Stockton, Kanawha County output in 1849–50 was 5,748,250 bushels. Schedule 5, Products of Industry, County of Kanawha, State of Virginia, vol. 2, pp. 18, 20, United States Census of 1850. Computation of coal production on the basis of salt production is hazardous, because the saturation of brine, the productive efficiency of individual furnaces, and the temperature capabilities of different coals varied. Eavenson's estimate of Kanawha County production in 1850 at 213,700 net tons is slightly low, as he surmised (*American Coal Industry*, 425, 508).

43. Schedule 5, Products of Industry, County of Kanawha, State of Virginia, pp. 214-16, United States Census of 1860.

44. Depositions of James McDowell and Singleton Farmer, Nov. 26, 1824, in *Conrad Myers v. Daniel Ruffner*, CC, KCCR (1824).

45. Articles of Agreement of John Lewis, Samuel Moore, and Charles Reynolds with John Thomas, May 21, 1821, CC, KCCR (1821); *Moses W. Keeney v. James and Woodford G. McDowell*, CSC, KCCR (1834).

46. *Western Courier*, Aug. 21, 1821; *William Williams v. Thomas Fowler*, CSC, KCCR (1838).

47. *Niles' National Register*, Oct. 4, 1845, p. 67.

48. D.L. Ruffner to W.H. Ruffner, Sept. 28, 1887, William Henry and Henry Ruffner Papers.

49. Ibid.; Maxwell Pierson Gaddis, *Foot-Prints of an Itinerant* (Cincinnati: Methodist Book Concern, 1856), 313; *Kanawha Republican*, Feb. 8, 1844. The same account of Warth and English appeared in *Niles' Weekly Register*, March 2, 1844, p. 6.

50. D.L. Ruffner to W.H. Ruffner, Sept. 28, 1887, William Henry and Henry Ruffner Papers.

51. Donnally and Steele and Company, Kanawha Salt Works Account Book, 1813–15, pp. 74-93. Depositions of Nathaniel S. Brooks, Feb. 23, 1855, Benjamin S. Smithers, Sept. 5, 1854; and James Cowey, Aug. 31, 1854, in *Thomas R. Friend v. William J. Stephens, Abraham Williams, et al.*, CSC, MCCR (1853).

52. Deposition of Jacob Runyon, Feb. 9, 1858, in *George W. Clarkson v. David J. W. Clarkson*, CC, KCCR (1858). Depositions of James Cowey, Aug. 31, 1854; Benjamin S. Smithers, Sept. 5, 1854; Nathaniel S. Brooks, Feb. 23, 1855; and John N. Clarkson, Feb. 28, 1855, in *Thomas R. Friend v. William J. Stephens, Abraham Williams, et al.*, CSC, MCCR (1853). *Kanawha Republican*, Dec. 4, 1841.

53. Richard K. Crallé to John J. Cabell, Dec. 13, 1831, John J. Cabell Papers, Robert A. Brock Collection; John J. Cabell to Henry Ann Cabell, June 27, Nov. 16, Dec. 30, 1832, and Jan. 17, 1833, Jubal A. Early Papers; John J. Cabell to Richard K. Crallé, Dec. 30, 1832, John J. Cabell Papers, Robert A. Brock Collection.

54. Deposition of Nathaniel S. Brooks, Feb. 23, 1855, in *Thomas R. Friend v. William J. Stephens, Abraham Williams, et al.*, CSC, MCCR (1853); *Crockett Ingles v. Jacob May* (1838), *Lewis Ruffner v. Thomas Neale* (1843), and *Brayton Allen v. Walker J.L. Sanford* (1843), CSC, KCCR. The threat to boss kettle tenders was not too significant, as the jury found for the defense in all three cases.

55. Depositions of Nathaniel S. Brooks, Feb. 23, 1855, and John N. Clarkson, Feb. 28, 1855, in *Thomas R. Friend v. William J. Stephens, Abraham Williams, et al.*, CSC, MCCR (1853); *George Nevill v. Andrew Donnally and Isaac Noyes, doing*

business as Donnally and Noyes, CSC, MCCR (1842); *James Casken* v. *George Warth and Job English, doing business as Warth and English,* CSC, MCCR (1849).

56. Deposition of Nathaniel S. Brooks, Feb. 23, 1855, in *Thomas R. Friend* v. *William J. Stephens, Abraham Williams, et al.,* CSC, MCCR (1853).

11. Slavery in the Kanawha Salt Industry

1. The extensive number of studies of slavery defies brief bibliographical citation. A convenient starting point is John David Smith, comp., *Black Slavery in the Americas: An Interdisciplinary Bibliography, 1865–1980,* 2 vols. (Westport, Conn.: Greenwood Press, 1982). The encyclopedic, yet comprehensive and contemporary, introductions with bibliographies contained in Randall M. Miller and John David Smith, eds., *Dictionary of Afro-American Slavery* (Westport, Conn.: Greenwood Press, 1988), are quite useful: see "Diet," by Kenneth F. Kiple, 190-92; "Economics of Slavery," by Gavin Wright, 201-9; "Slave Family," by Allan Kulikoff, 227-33; "Health Care," by Todd L. Savitt, 312-17; "Hiring Out," by Orville Vernon Burton, 321-26; "Historiography of Slavery," by John David Smith, 326-36; "Industrial Slavery," by Robert H. McKenzie, 359-64; "Profitability of Slavery," by Harold D. Woodman, 592-97; "Task System," by Philip D. Morgan, 715-16; "Slavery in West Virginia," by John E. Stealey III, 806-9.

Several studies are directly relevant to the present work. Robert S. Starobin produced three: "Disciplining Industrial Slaves in the Old South," *Journal of Negro History* 53, no. 2 (April 1968): 111-28; "The Economics of Industrial Slavery in the Old South," *Business History Review* 44, no. 2 (Summer 1970): 131-74; and *Industrial Slavery in the Old South* (New York: Oxford Univ. Press, 1970). Also, one should consult Ronald L. Lewis, *Coal, Iron, and Slaves: Industrial Slavery in Maryland and Virginia, 1715–1865* (Westport, Conn.: Greenwood Press, 1979), and James E. Newton and Ronald L. Lewis, eds., *The Other Slaves: Mechanics, Artisans and Craftsmen* (Boston: G.K. Hall and Co., 1978). The only published volume treating slavery in western Virginia offers a superficial account: Charles Embury Hedrick, *Social and Economic Aspects of Slavery in the Transmontane prior to 1850* (Nashville: George Peabody College for Teachers, 1927). Hedrick did not recognize the existence of slavery in the Great Kanawha salt industry.

2. Articles of Agreement between Charles Brown and William Cathey, Nov. 14, 1808, CC, KCCR (1808); petition of Jesse B. Boone, dated [1812], Legislative Petitions of Kanawha County; Joel Shrewsbury to Col. William Dickinson, Dec. 22, 1815, letterbook, 115 (copy), Dickinson & Shrewsbury Papers.

3. Avery Odelle Craven, *Soil Exhaustion as a Factor in the Agricultural History of Virginia and Maryland, 1606–1860* (Urbana: Univ. of Illinois, 1926).

4. *William Cobbs* v. *David Ruffner, Lewis Ruffner, Daniel Ruffner, and Richard E. Putney, doing business as David Ruffner and Company,* CSC, KCCR (1828); *George M. Woods* v. *Andrew Donnally,* CSC, KCCR (1844); *Martha Stone* v. *William D. Shrewsbury and Henry H. Wood,* CSC, KCCR (1852); deposition of Jacob Runyon, Feb. 9, 1858, in *George W. Clarkson* v. *David J.W. Clarkson,* CC, KCCR (1858).

5. Table 2, "Population by Counties, 1790–1870," State of West Virginia, in U.S. Bureau of the Census, *Ninth Census of the United States* (Washington, D.C.: Government Printing Office, 1872), 1: 72. Formations of new counties would affect the growth rate of the white population more than the slave, since few bondsmen were located in portions of Kanawha County territory incorporated

into new counties. Most slaves were concentrated in the Kanawha Salines area, which remained within the boundaries of Kanawha County.

6. Memorandum of an agreement between Harry Heth, Samuel G. Adams, and Beverley Randolph, Dec. 3, 1814, Heth Family Papers.

7. Note dated May 25, attached to Bevly Randolph to Maj. Harry Heth, May 23, 1815, Heth Family Papers; "A List of Negros belonging to Dickinson & Shrewsbury, November 1855," in *William Dickinson v. Joel Shrewsbury*, CSC, KCCR (1856).

8. Depositions of Nathaniel S. Brooks, Feb. 23, 1855; John N. Clarkson, Feb. 28, 1855; and James Cowey, Aug. 32, 1854, in *Thomas R. Friend v. William J. Stephens, Abraham Williams, et al.*, CSC, MCCR (1853). Depositions of R.C.M. Lovell, Oct. 13, 1853, in *Early v. Friend* (1857), 2: 62.

9. *Commonwealth v. Joseph Friend, Commonwealth v. Joel Shrewsbury and William Dickinson, Commonwealth v. Andrew Donnally and Isaac Noyes*, CC, KCCR (1841).

10. Depositions of Obediah Crow, [n.d.], and Robert Blaine, [n.d.], in *Early v. Friend* (1857), 1: 276, 245.

11. Joel Shrewsbury to Col. William Dickinson, Nov. 26, 1816, Feb. 14, 1814, and Jan. 2, 1819, letterbook, 137-39, 61-64, 219 (copy), Dickinson & Shrewsbury Papers; depositions of Robert Blaine, [n.d.], and Obediah Crow, [n.d.], in *Early v. Friend* (1857), 1: 245, 277; Luke Willcox Diary, Dec. 31, 1844, vol. 1, p. 17, West Virginia and Regional History Collection, West Virginia University Library.

12. Deposition of John D. Lewis, Aug. 31, 1854, in *Thomas R. Friend v. William J. Stephens, Abraham Williams, et al.*, CSC, MCCR (1853).

13. Depositions of James Cowey, Aug. 31, 1854; Nathaniel S. Brooks, Feb. 23, 1855; John N. Clarkson, Feb. 28, 1855; and John D. Lewis, Aug. 31, 1854, in *Thomas R. Friend v. William J. Stephens, Abraham Williams, et al.*, CSC, MCCR (1853).

14. Deposition of Robert Blaine, [n.d.], in *Early v. Friend* (1857), 1: 228.

15. Table 2, "Population by Counties, 1790-1870," State of West Virginia, in U.S. Bureau of the Census, *Ninth Census*, 1: 72; table 1, "Population by Counties—Age, Color, Condition," State of Virginia, in U.S. Bureau of the Census, *Seventh Census of the United States* (Washington, D.C.: Robert Armstrong, public printer, 1853), 252-56.

16. Professor Carl. N. Degler notes that the ratio between the sexes in the slave population in the United States was approximately equal in the so-called breeding and consuming regions of the South. He asserts that the existence of this ratio was conducive to the development of family units in slave society and eased the exertion of control over slaves. See Degler, "Slavery in Brazil and the United States: An Essay in Comparative History," *American Historical Review* 75, no. 4 (April 1970): 1017. The disparity between the sexes of slaves in Kanawha County demonstrates the impact of the salt industry in making the local slave system unique in the South. Consequently, if Degler's observations are correct, then one can conclude that in the Kanawha the family unit would not exist to a great extent and that there were obstacles to the maintenance of discipline.

17. Luke Willcox Diary, Aug. 29, Sept. 1, Oct. 27, and Nov. 1, 1845, vol. 1, pp. 27, 30.

18. "A List of Negros belonging to Dickinson & Shrewsbury, November 1855," in *William Dickinson v. Joel Shrewsbury*, CSC, KCCR (1856). This narrative owes much to Herbert G. Gutman's two works: *The Black Family in Slavery and Freedom, 1750-1925* (New York: Pantheon Books, 1976), pt. 1, pp. 3-350, and *Slav-*

ery and the Numbers Game: A Critique of Time on the Cross (Urbana: Univ. of Illinois Press, 1975, esp. 88-164.

19. "A List of Negros, the Children and Grand Children of Negro Woman Fann," in *William Dickinson* v. *Joel Shrewsbury*, CSC, KCCR (1856); Joel Shrewsbury to Pleasant Dickinson, March 14, 1814, letterbook, 33-35 (copy), Dickinson & Shrewsbury Papers.

20. Joel Shrewsbury to Col. Wm. Dickinson, March 7, 1820, letterbook, 270-74 (copy), Dickinson & Shrewsbury Papers.

21. Starobin, "Economics of Industrial Slavery," 132; idem, *Industrial Slavery*, 12; *William Dickinson* v. *Joel Shrewsbury*, CSC, KCCR (1856); deposition of Dr. Spicer Patrick, Nov. 4, 1853, in *Early* v. *Friend* (1857), 2: 71.

22. For the purposes of this study, a *bailor* is a party who bails or delivers goods, such as slaves, to another under a contract of bailment, expressed or implied. Conversely, the *bailee* is the party to whom personal property is delivered under an expressed or implied contract of bailment.

23. *Samuel Hannah* v. *Lewis Billings*, CSC, KCCR (1844); *James S. Turner* v. *Samuel H. Early*, CSC, KCCR (1848); *James A. Lewis* v. *John C. Ruby and Enos S. Arnold*, CC, KCCR (1857).

24. Deposition of John Waid, Sept. 1, 1859, in *Henry C. Sisson* v. *John P. Waid*, CC, KCCR (1858).

25. Articles of Agreement between Calvin Armstrong, Spicer Patrick, and R.C.M. Lovell, and William H. Alpin, Dec. 29, 1859 (1859); *Samuel B. Brown* v. *Thomas Potts and William Tompkins* (1828); *Timothy B. Taylor* v. *John P. Waid* (1859), all CC, KCCR.

26. *William Cobbs* v. *John D. Shrewsbury, Sr., and John D. Shrewsbury, Jr.* (1826); *William Gillison, for use of James Y. Quarrier and Brothers* v. *William F. Whitteker* (1837); *Joseph Agee, Sr.* v. *Van B. Donnally, Ebenezer Baines, and Andrew Donnally, doing business as V.B. Donnally and Company* (1839); *George W. Summers* v. *Henry and Robert M. Sims* (1845), all CSC, KCCR.

27. Luke Willcox Diary, Jan. 9, 1844, vol. 1, p. 1; deposition of Arthur Train, Dec. 18, 1852, in *Milton Parker* v. *William A. McMullin*, CSC, KCCR (1851).

28. *William Witcher, Administrator of Charles A. Gill* v. *Henry Robinson, Thomas Scott, and George Nevels*, CSC, KCCR (1846); *George W. Summers* v. *John R. Humphries and William Graham, doing business as Humphries and Graham*, CC, KCCR (1856).

29. *Elizabeth Beeson* v. *Lewis Ruffner*, CSC, KCCR (1846); *Ann Pollard* v. *Charles G. Reynolds*, CSC, KCCR (spring term 1833).

30. *Ann Pollard* v. *Charles G. Reynolds*, CSC, KCCR (fall term 1833).

31. Luke Willcox Diary, Sept. 19, 1844, vol. 1, p. 13.

32. *Edward C. Murphy* v. *James Cowey and Stuart Robinson, late partners in James Cowey and Company*, CSC, KCCR (1853).

33. Deposition of Wiley P. Woods, Sept. 28, 1852, in *Edward C. Murphy* v. *James Cowey and Stuart Robinson, late partners in James Cowey and Company*, CSC, KCCR (1853).

34. Deposition of Edward Turnbull, Nov. 21, 1852, in *Edward C. Murphy* v. *James Cowey and Stuart Robinson, late partners in James Cowey and Company*, CSC, KCCR (1853).

35. Deposition of John Hayes, May 30, 1840, in *Martin P. and Ann Brooks* v. *James Hewitt et al., doing business as Hewitt, Ruffner and Company*, CSC, KCCR (1839, 1840).

36. *Kanawha Banner*, April 2, 1835; Luke Willcox Diary, June 18, 1848, vol. 2, p. 2; Joel Shrewsbury to Pleasant Dickinson, July 12, 1827, letterbook, 288-89 (copy), Dickinson & Shrewsbury Papers; Lewis Summers to George W. Summers, Jan. 8, 1835, George W. and Lewis Summers Papers; *Kanawha Republican*, July 23, 1844; J.M. Byrnside to Summers and Miller, Dec. 17, 1846, George W. and Lewis Summers Papers.

37. John J. Cabell to Henry Ann Cabell, June 26, 1832, Jubal A. Early Papers; John J. Cabell to Richard K. Crallé, July 2, 1832, John J. Cabell Papers, Robert A. Brock Collection.

38. *Lindsey Thomas, Administrator of John Thomas v. Matthew Thomas and Levi Welch*, CSC, KCCR (1825); *Lindsey Thomas, Administrator of John Thomas v. Van Bibber Reynolds and Robert M. Steele*, CSC, KCCR (1825); *Francis Thompson v. Daniel Ruffner, Lewis Ruffner, Andrew L. Ruffner, Frederick Brooks, and Jefferson Donnally*, CC, KCCR (1835).

39. One case revealed the result when a slave worked on a steamboat. Solomon hired himself to the clerk of the *Ark* as a cook without the permission of his master, John Capehart of Coalsmouth (Saint Albans). Later, in 1845, Capehart talked with the captain of the *Ark* and gave him permission to employ Solomon provided that the slave shared his wages with him. Solomon quit working on the *Ark* and hired himself to another steamboat, the *Lelia*, as steward. He grew dissatisfied with his job on this boat and went on the *Medium* at Cincinnati. One of the owners of the *Medium*, Moses Norton, thought that Solomon was a free Negro. After he leased the steamboat for a three-month term to other parties, he learned from an agent of the administrator of the estate of John Capehart that the new cook was a slave. In 1847, while on the *Medium* in the employ of the lessee of the vessel, Solomon escaped into Ohio. The administrator of Capehart's estate sued the owners of the steamboat for the value of the escaped slave. The jury found for the defense even though the plaintiff alleged that the boat owners knew that Solomon was a slave and had allowed him to labor on the steamboat. *Elizabeth Capehart, Administrator of John Capehart v. Moses Norton and Nelson B. Coleman*, CSC, KCCR (1846).

40. The standard work on the subject as the disease affected Virginia slaves is Todd L. Savitt, *Medicine and Slavery: The Diseases and Health Care of Blacks in Antebellum Virginia* (Urbana: Univ. of Illinois Press, 1978), 226-40.

41. Hunter, *Steamboats*, 431; Hale, *Trans-Allegheny Pioneers*, 288. For a national view of the epidemic, see Charles E. Rosenberg, *The Cholera Years: The United States in 1832, 1849, and 1866* (Chicago: Univ. of Chicago Press, 1962), 13-39.

42. *Kanawha Banner*, Oct. 25, 1832; Joel Shrewsbury to Pleasant Dickinson, Oct. 24, 1832, letterbook, 309-11 (copy), Dickinson & Shrewsbury Papers; John J. Cabell to Henry Ann Cabell, Nov. 16, and 25, and Dec. 4, 1832, Jubal A. Early Papers; John J. Cabell to Richard K. Crallé, Dec. 30, 1832, John J. Cabell Papers, Robert A. Brock Collection.

43. John J. Cabell to Richard K. Crallé, July 7, 1833, John J. Cabell Papers, Robert A. Brock Collection; Laidley, *Charleston and Kanawha County*, 718; *Kanawha Banner*, July 31, 1834.

44. Hale, *Trans-Allegheny Pioneers*, 288; Wyndham B. Blanton, *Medicine in Virginia in the Nineteenth Century* (Richmond: Garrett and Massie, 1933), 241. Luke Willcox Diary, Aug. 21, 1849, vol. 2, p. 20; May 30, 1849, vol. 2, p. 17; June 29, 1849, vol. 2, p. 18; July 13, 1849, vol. 2, p. 18.

45. "Register-Deaths by Cholera in 1849—District Mth of Elk River to Upr Salt Works, Kanawha Salines, Kanawha County, Virginia," West Virginia Department of Archives and History. No discrepancy exists between this register and the Willcox diary. Willcox's total estimate of three hundred deaths was for Kanawha County as a whole. His mid-July 1849 estimate for the saltworks only was approximately one hundred deaths. Willcox noted in his diary account that his numbers were estimates.

46. *Zalinda L. Davis* v. *Emiline Ingles, Administratrix of Crockett Ingles*, CSC, KCCR (1852).

47. *Martha Stone* v. *William D. Shrewsbury and Henry H. Wood*, and *John Holland* v. *George H. Warth and Job English, doing business as Warth and English*, both CSC, KCCR (1852).

48. Luke Willcox Diary, July 5, 1850, vol. 2, p. 33; "Register Deaths by Cholera from 1850 frm [*sic*] Elk River to Joel Shrewsburys by H.N. Goshorn," West Virginia Department of Archives and History; Warth and English to John Potter, July 24, 1850, in *John Potter* v. *George H. Warth and Job English, doing business as Warth and English*, CSC, KCCR (1851).

49. A detailed account is in Lewis, *Coal, Iron, and Slaves*, 134-35.

50. William Dickinson to Joel Shrewsbury, Jan. 2, 1814; Joel Shrewsbury to Col. William Dickinson, Jan. 23, 1814; Wm. Dickinson to Joel Shrewsbury, Feb. 24, 1820; and Joel Shrewsbury to Col. William Dickinson, Jan. 2, 1819, letterbook, 19-20, 21-22, 264-69, 216-18 (copy), Dickinson & Shrewsbury Papers.

51. Deposition of H.H. Wood, April 13, 1857, in *Thomas R. Friend* v. *William J. Stephens, Abraham Williams, et al.*, CSC, MCCR (1853).

52. A Bedford County, Virginia, resident complained to his attorney that everyone in his locality knew that "juries gotten up by Salt Makers and Men of influence at the Salines . . . never fail to hang the Jury or find against a fereighner." Pleasant Purton to Summers & Miller, Oct. 20, 1850, George W. and Lewis Summers Papers.

53. Depositions of Robert Blaine, [n.d.], and Obediah Crow, [n.d.], in *Early* v. *Friend* (1857), 1: 230, 243, 275.

54. Appraisal and inventory of the estate of Samuel Patterson, Nov. 22, 1839, Will Book 5, p. 190; and an appraisal of the personal property of the estate of Philemon Sutherland, Aug. 4, 1848, Will Book 6, p. 379, Office of the County Clerk of Franklin County, Rocky Mount, Virginia, on microfilm, Virginia State Library and Archives.

55. Deposition of Robert Blaine, [n.d.], in *Early* v. *Friend* (1857), 1: 227-29.

56. *Spencer* v. *Pilcher*, 8 Leigh 383 (1836); James Michie to William [Tompkins], Nov. 26, 1838, William Tompkins Papers, Roy Bird Cook Collection; petition dated Jan. 27, 1835, Legislative Petitions of Kanawha County.

57. Deposition of Robert Blaine, [n.d.], in *Early* v. *Friend* (1857), 1: 222-23, 229.

58. Schedule 5, Products of Industry, County of Kanawha, State of Virginia, pp. 214-16, United States Census of 1860; table 2, "Population by Counties, 1790–1870," State of West Virginia, in U.S. Bureau of the Census, *Ninth Census*, 1: 71-72.

59. Petition dated Jan. 27, 1835, Legislative Petitions of Kanawha County.

60. Deposition of John N. Clarkson, Feb. 28, 1855, in *Thomas R. Friend* v. *William J. Stephens, Abraham Williams, et al.*, CSC, MCCR (1853); account of Samuel Watson and Company with Samuel Watson, Nov. 1, 1844–Dec. 25, 1845, in *Charles G. Reynolds* v. *Samuel Watson*, CSC, KCCR (1847); John J. Cabell to Rich-

ard K. Crallé, May 16, 1832, John J. Cabell Papers, Robert A. Brock Collection; deposition of R.C.M. Lovell, Sept. 5, 1854, in *Thomas R. Friend* v. *William J. Stephens, Abraham Williams, et al.*, CSC, MCCR (1853).

61. John J. Cabell to Richard K. Crallé, Dec. 28, 1833, John J. Cabell Papers, Robert A. Brock Collection.

62. Depositions of R.C.M. Lovell, Sept. 5, 1854; Nathaniel S. Brooks, Feb. 23, 1855; and John N. Clarkson, Feb. 28, 1855, in *Thomas R. Friend* v. *William J. Stephens, Abraham Williams, et al.*, CSC, MCCR (1853).

63. See statement of account for evidence of payment of employees for very short terms and of the rapid turnover of personnel in *Thomas R. Friend* v. *William J. Stephens, Abraham Williams, et al.*, CSC, MCCR (1853).

12. The Kanawha Salt Association and Ruffner, Donnally & Company, 1847–1855

1. Berry, *Western Prices*, chart 26, p. 298, and table 39, p. 579; John D. Lewis to John J. Dickinson, Dec. 9, 1846, Lewis Family Papers; Petition dated Jan. 19, 1847, Legislative Petitions of Kanawha County; *Acts of the General Assembly of Virginia, Passed at the Session Commencing December 7, 1846, and Ending March 23, 1847*, chap. 198, pp. 188-91.

2. The complete text is "Kanawha Association, January 1, 1847–December 31, 1840," in *Early* v. *Friend* (1857), 2: 102-6.

3. Ibid., 106-7.

4. Henry Dana Ward Diary, March 29, 1847, West Virginia and Regional History Collection, West Virginia University Library.

5. Deposition of James Norton, May 16, 1854, in *Early* v. *Friend* (1857), 2: 28-29.

6. Deposition of R. C. M. Lovell, Oct. 13, 1853, in *Early* v. *Friend* (1857), 2: 64.

7. Deposition of James Norton, Sept. 27, 1849, in *Early* v. *Friend* (1857), 1: 154, 163-65.

8. Deposition of Frederick F. Brooks, Oct. 19, 1857, in *Spicer Patrick* v. *Ruffner, Donnally and Company; Spicer Patrick* v. *N.B. Wilson, S.A. Wilson, J.B. Smith, William Gillison, and B.S. Smithers*, CSC, KCCR (1857).

9. Deposition of R.C.M. Lovell, Oct. 13, 1853, in *Early* v. *Friend* (1857), 2: 65.

10. Deposition of L.H. Sargent, May 14, 1852, in *Lewis W. Langley and Miles Manser* v. *Snelling C. Farley*, CSC, KCCR (1852); testimony of John A. Warth, in *Joseph D. Kinkead, Lemuel H. Sargent, and Miles Manser, doing business as Kinkead, Sargent and Company* v. *Samuel H. Early*, CC, KCCR (1854).

11. J.H. Fry to F.F. Brooks, Dec. 2, 1850, in *Frederick F. Brooks* v. *James H. Fry*, CSC, KCCR (1851).

12. Deposition of Frederick Brooks [Oct. 9, 1859], in *Early* v. *Friend* (1857), 1: 252.

13. Deposition of R.C.M. Lovell, Oct. 13, 1853, in *Early* v. *Friend* (1857), 2; 66; J.H. Fry to F.F. Brooks, Jan. 18, 1850, in *Frederick F. Brooks*, v. *James H. Fry*, CSC, KCCR (1851).

14. "Articles of Agreement . . . 28th day of February Eighteen hundred fifty one," creating Ruffner, Donnally and Company, Festus P. Summers Collection, West Virginia and Regional History Collection, West Virginia University Library.

15. Articles of Agreement of Richard C.M. Lovell with Ruffner, Donnally and Company, Feb. 28, 1851, in *Spicer Patrick* v. *Ruffner, Donnally and Company; Spicer Patrick* v. *N.V. Wilson, S.A. Wilson, J.B. Smith, William Gillison, and B.S. Smithers*, both CSC, KCCR (1857).

16. Schedule 5, Products of Industry, County of Kanawha, State of Virginia, vol. 2, pp. 13-7, 19-20, United States Census of 1850.

17. Opinion of the Court, pp. 2, 4, 8, and deposition of Lewis W. Langley, Oct. 16, 1857, in *Spicer Patrick* v. *Ruffner, Donnally and Company*, CSC, KCCR (1857).

13. Ruffner, Donnally & Company and the External Economy

1. One book consists of the copies of the outgoing correspondence of the Cincinnati agency from February 1, 1853, to January 27, 1854. The other is a charred, fragmentary collection of the letters received by the home agency between February 1854 and June 1855. Ruffner, Donnally and Company Papers.

2. Deposition of S.A. Miller, Aug. 31, 1854, in *Thomas R. Friend* v. *William J. Stephens, Abraham Williams, et al.*, CSC, MCCR (1853). Depositions of Lemuel H. Sargent, Oct. 16, 1857; Lewis W. Langley, Oct. 16, 1857; and Frederick F. Brooks, Oct. 19, 1857, in *Spicer Patrick* v. *Ruffner, Donnally and Company*, CSC, KCCR (1857).

3. *Cincinnati Gazette*, March 14, 1851, quoted in Hunter, *Studies in the Economic History*, 59.

4. Depositions of Lewis W. Langley, Oct. 16, 1857, Frederick F. Brooks, Oct. 19, 1857; and Joseph H. Rogers, Oct. 19, 1857, in *Spicer Patrick* v. *Ruffner, Donnally and Company*, CSC, KCCR (1857).

5. Deposition of Frederick F. Brooks, Oct. 19, 1857, in *Spicer Patrick* v. *Ruffner, Donnally and Company*, CSC, KCCR (1857); R[achel] M. [Grant] Tompkins to Jennie [Tompkins], Dec. 30, 1851 (typescript), Ruffner–Kanawha Valley Scrapbook, 160, Roy Bird Cook Collection.

6. J.H. Rogers to Ruffner, Donnally and Co., Jan. 13 and 30, 1855; A.R.W. Quin[n] to Ruffner, Donnally and Co., May 5, 1855, Ruffner, Donnally and Company Papers.

7. [J.H. Rogers] to Ruffner, Donnally and Co., March 7, 1854; John B. Smith to Ruffner, Donnally and Co., May 2, 1855; J.H. Rogers to B.F. and H.P. Thomas, April 23, 1853, letterbook, 178, all in Ruffner, Donnally and Company Papers.

8. S.A. Miller to Lewis Ruffner, June 23, 1853; J.H. Rogers to Ruffner, Donnally and Co., Aug. 3, 1853, letterbook, 373, 376, 482-83; John B. Smith to Ruffner, Donnally and Co., Feb. 20, 23, and May 25, 1854, all in Ruffner, Donnally and Company Papers.

9. John B. Smith to Ruffner, Donnally and Co., June 3, 1954; J.H. Rogers to S.B. Poyntz, July 18, 1853, letterbook, 444, both in Ruffner, Donnally and Company Papers.

10. J.H. Rogers to Ruffner, Donnally and Co., July 11, 1853, letterbook, 425; J.H. Rogers to Ruffner, Donnally and Co., March 2, and June 13 and 9, 1854; John B. Smith to Ruffner, Donnally and Co., April 10, and June 1 and 3, 1854, all in Ruffner, Donnally and Company Papers. This description of the use of company-owned flatboats will augment the pioneering work of Scheiber, "Ohio-Mississippi Flatboat Trade," 277-98. The most recent econometric study

of the antebellum river transportation could have better emphasized the supplementary nature and intereconomic dependence of flatboats and steamers. Haites, Mak, and Walton, *Western River Transportation*, 120-22.

11. J.H. Rogers to Ruffner, Donnally and Co., June 7 and July 23, 1853, letterbook, 313, 464-65; J.H. Rogers to L. Ruffner, July 25 and Sept. 7, 1853, letterbook, 474, 589, all in Ruffner, Donnally and Company Papers.

12. J.H. Rogers to Ruffner, Donnally and Co., Sept. 17 and 20, Nov. 15, and Dec. 6, 1853, letterbook, 613, 617, 778, 828, Ruffner, Donnally and Company Papers.

13. John B. Smith to Ruffner, Donnally and Co., May 2 and June 5, 1854, Ruffner, Donnally and Company Papers.

14. J.H. Rogers to T.G. Warring, May 21, 1853; J.H. Rogers to B.F. and O.H.P. Thomas, June 8, 1853; J.H. Rogers to J.B. Poyntz, June 8, 1853, letterbook, 267, 318, 319, Ruffner, Donnally and Company Papers.

15. J. H. Rogers to Benj. Tiller, Aug. 25, 1853, letterbook, 548, Ruffner, Donnally and Company Papers.

16. John B. Smith to Ruffner, Donnally and Co., June 3, 1854; J.H. Rogers to L. Ruffner, Nov. 5, 1853, letterbook, 751; J.H. Rogers to Pollys and Butler, Nov. 5, 1853, letterbook, 753, all in Ruffner, Donnally and Company Papers.

17. J.H. Rogers to T.G. Warring, May 21, 1853, letterbook, 267, Ruffner, Donnally and Company Papers; Ruffner, Donnally and Company Receipt Form, Nelson B. Coleman Papers.

18. Letterbook, 306-8, 429-32; J.H. Rogers to C.A. Damarien, Nov. 16, 1852, letterbook, 780; J.H. Rogers to F.T. Liggitt, June 1, 1853, letterbook, 284; J.H. Rogers to Ruffner, Donnally and Co., June 9, 1854; J.H Rogers to Weyer and McKee, Aug. 27, 1853, letterbook, 555, all in Ruffner, Donnally and Company Papers.

19. J.H. Rogers to White, Cunningham and Co., Aug. 6, 1853, letterbook, 492-93, also 485, 521, Ruffner, Donnally and Company Papers.

20. J.H. Rogers to Swift and Robbins, June 8, 1853, letterbook, 323, Ruffner, Donnally and Company Papers.

21. [John B. Smith] to Ruffner, Donnally and Co., March 13, 1855, Ruffner, Donnally and Company Papers.

22. Deposition of Frederick F. Brooks, Oct. 19, 1857, in *Spicer Patrick* v. *Ruffner, Donnally and Company*, CSC, KCCR (1857). J.H. Rogers to L. Ruffner, Aug. 27 and 31, 1853; J.H. Rogers to Ruffner, Donnally and Co., Sept. 1, 1853, letterbook, 554, 566-67, 572, Ruffner, Donnally and Company Papers.

23. J.H. Rogers to Pollys and Butler, Dec. 3, 1853, letterbook, 823, Ruffner, Donnally and Company Papers.

24. J.H. Rogers to White, Cunningham and Co., Aug. 13, 1853, letterbook, 521; John B. Smith to Ruffner, Donnally and Co., April 23 and 27, 1855, Ruffner, Donnally and Company Papers.

25. John B. Smith to Ruffner, Donnally and Co., April 14, 1855, Ruffner, Donnally and Company Papers.

26. J.H. Rogers to Ruffner, Donnally and Co., Aug. 11 and Sept. 8, 1853, letterbook, 516, 595; J.H. Rogers to Ruffner, Donnally and Co., June 9, 1854; John B. Smith to Ruffner, Donnally and Co., June 13, 1854, all in Ruffner, Donnally and Company Papers.

27. J.H. Rogers to E.F. Wilson and Co., Dec. 1, 1853, letterbook, 816; J.H. Rogers to D. and C. Miller, Dec. 13, 1853, letterbook, 861; J. H. Rogers to Ruffner, Donnally and Co., May 16, 1854, all in Ruffner, Donnally and Company Papers. Also see *Cincinnati Price-Current*, Nov. 16, 1853, and the deposition

of Joseph H. Rogers, Oct. 19, 1857, in *Spicer Patrick v. Ruffner, Donnally and Company*, CSC, KCCR (1857).

28. John B. Smith to Ruffner, Donnally and Co., Jan. 13 and April 14, 1855; *St. Louis Price-Current*, Jan. 1, 1855, quoted in John B. Smith to Ruffner, Donnally and Co., Feb. 28, 1855; John B. Smith to Ruffner, Donnally and Co., June 5 and July 27, 1854, all in Ruffner, Donnally and Company Papers.

29. John B. Smith to Ruffner, Donnally and Co., Feb. 20, 1854; L[ewis] Ruffner to Ruffner, Donnally and Co., Louisville, April 3 and 22, 1854; John B. Smith to Ruffner, Donnally and Co., Aug. 1, 1854, all in Ruffner, Donnally and Company Papers.

30. J.H. Rogers to Ruffner, Donnally and Co., Dec. 6, 1853, letterbook, 828; F. Brooks to Ruffner, Donnally and Co., Aug. 4, 1853, and July, 6, 1854, all in Ruffner, Donnally and Company Papers.

31. F. Brooks to Ruffner, Donnally and Co., Aug. 4, 1853; Jas H. Stout and Co. to Ruffner, Donnally and Co., Aug. 7, 1854, and June 21, 1855, all in Ruffner, Donnally and Company Papers.

32. J.H. Rogers to Ruffner, Donnally and Co., Aug. 17, 1853, letterbook, 529, Ruffner, Donnally and Company Papers.

33. J.H. Rogers to W.C. Winslow, Nov. 2, 1853; J.H. Rogers to S.S. Hosmer, Nov. 2, 1853; J.H. Rogers to J.P. Norton, Nov. 2, 1853; J.H. Rogers to N.B. Iglehart, Nov. 2, 1853, letterbook, 736, 737, 738, Ruffner, Donnally and Company Papers.

34. J.H. Rogers to J.P. Norton, Nov. 2, 1853, and J.H. Rogers to L. Ruffner, Dec. 21, 1853, letterbook, 737, 898, Ruffner, Donnally and Company Papers.

35. Lewis Summers to George Summers, May 7, 1842, George W. and Lewis Summers Papers; J.H. Rogers to Ruffner, Donnally and Co., June 23, 1854, Ruffner, Donnally and Company Papers.

36. George Stephens to Ruffner, Donnally and Co., Louisville, Feb. 16, 1855, and John B. Smith to Ruffner, Donnally and Co., Feb. 21, 1855, Ruffner, Donnally and Company Papers.

37. J.H. Rogers to Ruffner, Donnally and Co., Feb. 15, 1853; J.H. Rogers to Coons and Matthews, Aug. 25, 1853; and J.H. Rogers to [?], April 4, 1853, letterbook, 29, 547, 153, Ruffner, Donnally and Company Papers.

38. J.H. Rogers to E.F. and P. Metcalfe, March 5, 1853, letterbook, 278; see also J.H. Rogers to J. Hemphill and Co., June 1, 1853, letterbook, 280, both in Ruffner, Donnally and Company Papers.

39. J.H. Rogers to Ruffner, Donnally and Co., May 31, 1853, and J.H. Rogers to Coons and Matthews, Aug. 25, 1853, letterbook, 277, 547, Ruffner, Donnally and Company Papers.

40. J.H. Rogers to W.H. Clements, March 11, 1853; J.H. Rogers to John Anderson, June 1, 1853; and J.H. Rogers to Mosgrove and Wiley, March 29, 1853, letterbook, 89, 282, 133, Ruffner, Donnally and Company Papers.

41. J.H. Rogers to Ruffner, Donnally and Co., Feb. 5 and Oct. 27, 1853, letterbook, 15-16, 718, Ruffner, Donnally and Company Papers; deposition of S.A. Miller, Aug. 31, 1854, and Articles of Agreement of Ruffner, Donnally and Company with William J. Stephens, Jan. 4, 1853, in *Thomas R. Friend v. William J. Stephens, Abraham Williams, et al.*, CSC, MCCR (1853).

42. J.H. Rogers to Ruffner, Donnally and Co., Sept. 13 and Oct. 27, 1853, and Jan. 7, 1854, letterbook, 607, 718, 948; J.H. Rogers to L. Ruffner, Nov. 2, 1853, all in Ruffner, Donnally and Company Papers. *Second Semi-Annual Report of the Board of Directors of the West Columbia Mining and Manufacturing Company, of*

Mason County, Va., to the Stockholders, February, 1854 (Cincinnati: Ben Franklin Book and Job Office, 1854), 29-30.

43. J.H. Rogers to Ruffner, Donnally and Co., Jan. 7, 1854, letterbook, 948; C.R. Pomeroy to [S.A. Miller], May 13, 1854, Ruffner, Donnally and Company Papers.

44. C.R. Pomeroy to [S.A. Miller], May 6, 1854, Ruffner, Donnally and Company Papers.

45. J.H. Rogers to Ruffner, Donnally and Co., May 15, 1855; John B. Smith to Ruffner, Donnally and Co., May 21, 1854, Ruffner, Donnally and Company Papers. *Cincinnati Price-Current*, June 28, 1854.

46. J.H. Rogers to Ruffner, Donnally and Co., June 9, 1854; [John B. Smith] to Ruffner, Donnally and Co., Jan. 13 and 21, 1855, Ruffner, Donnally and Company Papers.

47. J.H. Rogers to Ruffner, Donnally and Co., Jan. 6 and 13, 1855, Ruffner, Donnally and Company Papers.

48. J.H. Rogers to L. Ruffner, July 13, 1853, letterbook, 433, Ruffner, Donnally and Company Papers.

49. J.H. Rogers to Ruffner, Donnally and Co., Jan. 6, 1855; J.H. Rogers to Ruffner, Donnally and Co., Aug. 10, 1853, letterbook, 509; J.H. Rogers to L. Ruffner, Oct. 26, 1853, letterbook, 713, Ruffner, Donnally and Company Papers.

50. J.H. Rogers to B.F. and O.H. Thomas, June 8, 1853; J.H. Rogers to J.H. Sullivan, July 20, 1853; J.H. Rogers to S.B. Poyntz, July 22, 1853, letterbook, 318, 457, 462, Ruffner, Donnally and Company Papers.

51. J.H. Rogers to Ruffner, Donnally and Co., Aug. 19, 1853, letterbook 533; J.H. Rogers to Fee and Smith, July 14, 1853, letterbook, 437; J.H. Rogers to Ruffner, Donnally and Co., Jan. 6, 1855, all in Ruffner, Donnally and Company Papers.

52. J.H. Rogers to Ruffner, Donnally and Co., Aug. 2, 1854, Ruffner, Donnally and Company Papers; deposition of Lewis W. Langley, Oct. 16, 1857, in *Spicer Patrick v. Ruffner, Donnally and Company*, CSC, KCCR (1857).

53. J.H. Rogers to L. Ruffner, Oct. 13, 1853, letterbook, 666; John B. Smith to Ruffner, Donnally and Co., Aug. 1, 1854; J.H. Rogers to Ruffner, Donnally and Co., Aug. 2, 1854, all in Ruffner, Donnally and Company Papers.

54. *Cincinnati Price-Current*, Dec. 26, 1855; deposition of Joseph H. Rogers, Oct. 19, 1857, in *Spicer Patrick v. Ruffner, Donnally and Company*, CSC, KCCR (1857).

55. Deposition of William Tompkins, Oct. 6, 1853, in *Early v. Friend* (1857), 2:39. Lewis Ruffner called Tompkins, who manufactured salt from 1815 to 1845, "the most successful salt-maker," one who "was extremely vigilant and assiduous"; deposition of Lewis Ruffner, Oct. 7, 1853, in *Early v. Friend* (1857), 2: 46. Another estimate of costs is in the deposition of William Shrewsbury, Oct. 19, 1853, in *Early v. Friend* (1857), 2: 67.

56. Depositions of R.C.M. Lovell, Oct. 13, 1853, and Spicer Patrick, Nov. 4, 1853, in *Early v. Friend* (1857), 2: 66, 70.

14. Kanawha Salt Loses Its Economic Savor

1. N.S. Brooks to N.B. Coleman, Feb. 16, 1856, Nelson B. Coleman Papers; *Cincinnati Price-Current*, Sept. 10, 1856.

2. Schedule 5, Products of Industry, County of Kanawha, State of Virginia, vol. 2, pp. 13-17, 19-20, United States Census of 1850; schedule 5, Products of Industry, County of Kanawha, State of Virginia, pp. 214-16, United States Census of 1860.

3. *Kanawha Valley Star*, April 26, 1859, April 9, 1861, Oct. 6, 1857 (quoting the *Fredericksburg News*), and March 16, 1857.

4. Petition dated Dec. 1859, Legislative Petitions of Kanawha County; J.F. Hansford to N. B. Coleman, April 21, 1862, Nelson B. Coleman Papers.

5. The eastern Virginians' proposal is noted in the *Kanawha Valley Star*, Oct. 28, and Nov. 19, 1856. For interest in cannel coal, see Samuel H. Early to W.S. Rosecrans, Dec. 21, 1856, General William S. Rosecrans Papers, University of California at Los Angeles Library. See also James C. McFarland to Solomon Hart; S.S. Rex et al. to James A. Mason, both CC, KCCR (1861).

6. *William Dickinson v. Joel Shrewsbury*, CSC, KCCR (1856); Laidley, *Charleston and Kanawha County*, 749, 1003-5; Atkinson, *History of Kanawha County*, 323.

7. Petition dated Dec. 1859, Legislative Petitions of Kanawha County. On backhaulage, see Haites, Mak, and Walton, *Western River Transportation*, 33-160.

8. *Second Semi-Annual Report of the Board of Directors of the West Columbia Mining and Manufacturing Company*, 10-11; Sam¹ E. Mack to Elisha Mack, Feb. 27, 1855, in Howard N. Eavenson, ed., "Notes on an Old West Virginia Coal Field," *West Virginia History* 5, no. 2 (Jan. 1944): 98.

9. Eavenson, "Notes," 83-100; *DeBow's Review*, Jan. 1859, pp. 66-67; Eavenson, *American Coal Industry*, 262-63, 268-69.

10. Petition dated Dec. 1859, Legislative Petition of Kanawha County.

11. Sam. E. Mack to Elisha Mack, Nov. 29, 1854, in Eavenson, "Notes," 96-97; *Cincinnati Price-Current*, July 20, 1859; Charles Cist, *Sketches and Statistics of Cincinnati in 1859* (Cincinnati, n.d.), 362.

12. J. H. Rogers to Ruffner, Donnally and Co., June 26, 1854, and John B. Smith to Ruffner, Donnally and Co., June 5, 1854, Ruffner, Donnally and Company Papers.

13. Berry, *Western Prices*, 514-29; Smith and Cole, *Fluctuations in American Business*, 130-35; Hammond, *Banks and Politics*, 707-17. For contemporary analysis, see *Hunt's Merchants' Magazine*, Oct. 1857, p. 452, and J.S. Gibbons, *The Banks of New York, Their Dealers, the Clearing House, and the Panic of 1857* (1859; New York: Greenwood Press, 1968), 343-99. John Denis Haeger offers graceful renditions of the activities of the Ohio Life Insurance and Trust Company until the 1840s: "Eastern Financiers and Institutional Change: The Origins of the New York Life Insurance and Trust Company and the Ohio Life Insurance and Trust Company," *Journal of Economic History* 39, no. 1 (March 1979): 259-73, and *The Investment Frontier: New York Businessmen and the Economic Development of the Old Northwest* (Albany: State Univ. of New York Press, 1981).

14. *Kanawha Republican*, Oct. 6, 1857.

15. W.H. Ruffner to Harriet Ruffner, Dec. 23, 1865, William Henry and Henry Ruffner Papers.

16. Walsh, "Spatial Evolution," table 2, p. 6.

17. John B. Smith to Ruffner, Donnally and Co., July 27, 1854, Ruffner, Donnally and Company Papers.

18. Eugene H. Roseboom, *The Civil War Era, 1850-1873*, vol. 4 of *The History of the State of Ohio*, ed. Carl Wittke (Columbus: Ohio State Archaeological and Historical Society, 1944), 111; MacGill et al., *History of Transportation*, 488-502, 508; U.S. Congress, Senate, *Reports on the Trade*, H. Exec. Doc. 136, pp. 308-17;

Albert Fishlow, *American Railroads and the Transformation of the Ante-Bellum Economy* (Cambridge, Mass.: Harvard Univ. Press, 1965), table 16, p. 172.

19. Percy Wells Bidwell and John I. Falconer, *History of Agriculture in the Northern United States, 1620–1860* (Washington, D.C.: Carnegie Institution, 1925), table 61, pp. 436, 438, 440; Fishlow, *American Railroads*, 292. Margaret Walsh succinctly describes the transformation of the midwestern pork-packing industry: see "Pork Packing," "Spatial Evolution," "From Pork Merchant to Meat Packer," and *Rise of the Midwestern Meat Packing Industry*. For a study of the industry in a later period, see Mary Yeager, *Competition and Regulation: The Development of Oligopoly in the Meat Packing Industry* (Greenwich, Conn.: JAI Press, 1981).

20. *Cincinnati Price-Current*, Sept. 15, 1852.

21. Clark, *Grain Trade*, 141-43.

22. *Hunt's Merchants' Magazine*, Nov. 1854, p. 552; May 1862, pp. 543-44.

23. Hill, "Development of Chicago," 257-62; Bessie L. Pierce, *A History of Chicago*, 2 vols. (New York: Knopf, 1937–40), 2: 95-101; Clark, *Grain Trade*, 272-73.

24. Deposition of Lemuel H. Sargent, Oct. 16, 1857, in *Spicer Patrick v. Ruffner, Donnally and Company; Spicer Patrick v. N.V. Wilson, S.A. Miller, J.B. Smith, William Gillison, and B.S. Smithers*, CSC, KCCR (1857).

25. *Cincinnati Price-Current*, Sept. 9, 1857, and Sept. 5, 1858; William Smith, *Annual Statement of the Commerce of Cincinnati for the Commercial Year Ending August 31st, 1850* (Cincinnati: Gazette Co. Print, 1860), 38-39; idem, *Annual Statement of the Commerce of Cincinnati for the Commercial Year Ending August 31st, 1861* (Cincinnati: Gazette Co. Steam Printing Establishment, 1861), 43-44.

26. *Hunt's Merchants' Magazine*, June 1860, pp. 672-73; Aug. 1862, pp. 197-99; Sept. 1862, pp. 209-23; June 1865, p. 458. Michigan Geological and Biological Survey, *Mineral Resources of Michigan with Statistical Tables of Production and Value of Mineral Products for 1918 and Prior Years*, Publication 29, Geological ser. 24 (Fort Wayne, Ind., 1920), 119-25.

15. Perspectives

1. The pioneer in formulating the stage theory was N.S.B. Gras. See Gras, "Stages in Economic History," *Journal of Economic and Business History* 2, no. 3 (May 1930): 395-418; and idem, *Business and Capitalism: An Introduction to Business History* (New York: F.S. Crofts and Co., 1939). For a brief elaboration of this approach, see George Rogers Taylor and Lucius F. Ellsworth, eds., *Approaches to American Economic History* (Charlottesville: Univ. Press of Virginia, 1971), 25-36.

2. Adam Smith, *An Inquiry into the Nature and Causes of the Wealth of Nations*. Edited by Edwin Cannan. (New York: Modern Library, 1965), 128; Lloyd G. Reynolds, "Cutthroat Competition," *American Economic Review* 30, no. 4 (Dec. 1940): 736-47 (quotation on 737).

3. Peter Temin provocatively addresses the broader economic issue of slave labor use in *Causal Factors in American Economic Growth in the Nineteenth Century* (London: Macmillan, 1975), 53-63.

4. Glenn Porter and Harold C. Livesay, *Merchants and Manufacturers: Studies in the Changing Structure of Nineteenth-Century Marketing* (Baltimore: Johns Hopkins Univ. Press, 1971), 1-12, 228-31.

5. Hurst, *Law and Economic Growth*, 409.

6. For example of the state grant of charter school, see G.S. Callender, "The Early Transportation and Banking Enterprises of the State in Relation to the

Growth of Corporations," *Quarterly Journal of Economics* 17 (1903): 111-62; Oscar Handlin and Mary F. Handlin, "Origins of the American Business Corporation," *Journal of Economic History* 5, no. 1 (May 1945): 1-23; Committee of the Association of American Law Schools, comp. and ed., *Select Essays in Anglo-American Legal History* 3 vols. (Boston: Little, Brown, 1907-9), 3: 195-235; Joseph S. Davis, *Essays in the Earlier History of American Corporations, 2 vols. (Cambridge, Mass.: Harvard Univ. Press, 1917); James Willard Hurst, The Legitimacy of the Business Corporation in the Law of the United States, 1780-1970* (Charlottesville: Univ. Press of Virginia, 1970); and Ronald E. Seavoy, *The Origins of the American Business Corporation, 1784-1855: Broadening the Concept of Public Service during Industrialization* (Westport, Conn.: Greenwood Press, 1982).

7. Shaw Livermore, *Early American Land Companies; Their Influence on Corporate Development* (1939; New York: Octagon Books, 1968). Also, in an article, Livermore explores the similarities between corporations and nonchartered business associations: Livermore, "Unlimited Liability in Early American Corporations," *Journal of Political Economy* 42, no. 5 (Oct. 1935): 674-87.

8. Friedman, *History of American Law,* 177.

9. Hurst, *Legitimacy of the Business Corporation,* 14. See James Willard Hurst's books: *The Growth of American Law: The Lawmakers* (Boston: Little, Brown, 1950); *Law and Conditions of Freedom in the Nineteenth-Century United States* (Madison: Univ. of Wisconsin Press, 1956); *Law and Social Process in United States History* (1960; Buffalo, N.Y.: William S. Hein and Company, 1987).

10. Horwitz, *Transformation of American Law,,* esp. 160-266. A corrective assault on the Horwitz approach is Alfred William Brian Simpson, "The Horwitz Thesis and the History of Contracts," *University of Chicago Law Review* 46, no. 3 (Spring 1979): 533-61. The best summary of common law and British background is W.S. Holdsworth, "Industrial Combinations and the Law in the Eighteenth Century," *Minnesota Law Review* 18, no. 4 (March 1934): 369-90. Another survey of nineteenth-century United States application of common law to combinations is Frank J. Goodnow, "Trade Combinations at Common Law," *Political Science Quarterly* 12, no. 2 (June 1897): 212-45.

11. Keven M. Teeven, *A History of the Anglo-American Common Law of Contract* (Westport, Conn.: Greenwood Press, 1990), chap 6, pp. 173-216.

12. Arthur Stone Dewing, *Corporate Promotions and Reorganizations* (1913; New York: Harper and Row, 1969), 518-21.

13. See above, chap. 3, n. 22. For the most comprehensive review of consolidation, see Dewing, *Corporate Promotions.* Dewing's chapter 8 (203-26) is devoted to the National Salt Company. Also see Arthur Stone Dewing, *A History of the National Cordage Company* (Cambridge, Mass.: Harvard Univ. Press, 1913). For combination activities among railroads, see Charles S. Langstroth and Wilson Stitz, *Railway Co-operation* (Philadelphia, 1899). Two scholars recognized the significance of the associative nature of Kanawha producers and made the connection between the antebellum and postbellum combination movements, but they had little information about the specific legal arrangements. See Berry, *Western Prices,* 286-317, and idem, "Effect of Business Conditions," 30-44. In the article Berry argues that the general decline of salt prices during the period accounts for the lack of public interest in the Kanawhans' combination efforts. Also see Hunter, *Studies in the Economic History,* 50-77.

Works Cited

Primary Sources

Manuscripts

Alderman Library, University of Virginia, Charlottesville, Virginia
    Clement and Dickinson Family Papers
    Dickinson Family Papers
    Heth Family Papers
Henry E. Huntington Library and Art Gallery, San Marino, California
    Robert A. Brock Collection, John J. Cabell Papers
Historical Foundation of Presbyterian Reformed Churches, Montreat, North
    Carolina
    William Henry and Henry Ruffner Papers
James E. Morrow Library, Marshall University, Huntington, West Virginia
    Dickinson & Shrewsbury Papers
Kanawha County Courthouse, Charleston, West Virginia
    Deed Books A–G
    Superior Court Minute Book, 1809–13
Kentucky Historical Society, Frankfort, Kentucky
    Shelby County Marriage Papers
    Steele Family Genealogy File
Library of Congress, Washington, D.C.
    Jubal A. Early Papers
National Archives, Washington, D.C.
    Records of the 1820 Census of Manufactures, County of Kanawha, State of
        Virginia, Records of the Bureau of the Census, Record Group 29, Na-
        tional Archives Microfilm Publication M279, roll 18
    United States Census of 1850, State of Virginia, County of Kanawha, Sched-
        ule 2 (Slave Inhabitants), vol. 7
    United States Census of 1860, State of Virginia, County of Kanawha, Sched-
        ule 2 (Slave Inhabitants), vol. 4
Robert Muldrow Cooper Library, Clemson University, Clemson, South Caro-
    lina
    John J. Cabell Papers
University of California Library, Los Angeles, California
    General William S. Rosecrans Papers
Virginia Historical Society, Richmond, Virginia
    Thomas Green Diary

Virginia State Library and Archives, Richmond, Virginia
Auditor's Item 86, Returns of Salt, Lead, Iron and Cigars, 1814
Franklin County, Virginia, Will Books, nos. 5–6 (microfilm)
Legislative Petitions of Kanawha County, 1804–60
United States Census of 1850, State of Virginia, County of Kanawha, Schedule 5 (Products of Industry), vol. 2
United States Census of 1860, State of Virginia, County of Kanawha, Schedule 5 (Products of Industry)
West Virginia and Regional History Collection, West Virginia University Library, Morgantown, West Virginia
Donnally and Steele and Company, Kanawha Salt Works Account Book, 1813–15
Festus P. Summers Collection
George W. and Lewis Summers Papers
Henry Dana Ward Diary
Kanawha County Court Records, 1789–1867
Lewis Family Papers
Luke Willcox Diary
Mason County Court Records, 1850–66
Petition to the President and Directors of the Baltimore and Ohio Railroad Company, July 20, 1827
Roy Bird Cook Collection
Charleston Scrapbook
Henry Ruffner Papers
James C. McFarland Papers
Ruffner–Kanawha Valley Scrapbook
William Tompkins Papers
Ruffner, Donnally and Company Papers
Ruffner Family Papers
Woodbridge Mercantile Company Records
West Virginia College of Graduate Studies, Glenwood, Charleston, West Virginia
Summers Family Papers
West Virginia Department of Archives and History, Charleston, West Virginia
Articles of Agreement of November 10, 1817
David Ruffner Weather Register, 1832–34 (copy)
Ellicott Reynolds, next friend of James and Henry William Reynolds v. *James C. McFarland, Joel Shrewsbury, Sr., Levi Welch, Andrew Donnally, William Dickinson, John D. Lewis, William Tompkins, Benjamin H. Smith, and Alexander W. Quarrier,* Circuit Superior Court of Law and Chancery (1846), Kanawha County
Joseph Lovell Papers
Nelson B. Coleman Papers
Register—Deaths by Cholera in 1849—District Mth of Elk River to Upr Salt Works, Kanawha Salines, Kanawha County, Virginia
Register Deaths by Cholera 1850 frm Elk River to Joel Shrewsburys by H.N. Goshorn

Printed Sources and Contemporary Accounts

"Agreement to Make Salt: Laurence A. Washington and Benjamin F. Reeder." *West Virginia Historical Magazine Quarterly* 3, no. 3 (July 1903): 244–53.

Benton, Thomas Hart. *Thirty Years' View.* 2 vols. New York: Appleton and Co., 1858.

Bradbury, John. *Travels in the Interior of America in the Years 1809, 1810, and 1811.* Vol. 5 of *Early Western Travels, 1748–1846.* Edited by Reuben Gold Thwaites. Cleveland: Arthur H. Clark Co., 1904.

Carter, Clarence Edwin, ed. *The Territory of Mississippi, 1798–1817.* Vol. 5 of *The Territorial Papers of the United States.* Washington, D.C.: Government Printing Office, 1937.

Cist, Charles. *Sketches and Statistics of Cincinnati in 1851.* Cincinnati: William H. Moore and Co., 1851.

———. *Sketches and Statistics of Cincinnati in 1859.* Cincinnati, n.d.

Cometti, Elizabeth, ed. "The Memorandum of William Whitteker." *West Virginia History* 1, no. 3 (April 1940): 207–24 (pt. 1); 1, no. 4 (July 1940): 282–92 (pt. 2).

Cramer, Zadok. *The Navigator . . . .* 7th ed. Pittsburgh: Cramer, Spear and Eichbaum, 1811.

DeBow, J.D.B. *The Industrial Resources, etc., of the Southern and Western States.* 3 vols. New Orleans, 1853.

Eavenson, Howard N., ed. "Notes on an Old West Virginia Coal Field." *West Virginia History* 5, no. 2 (Jan. 1944): 83–100.

Gaddis, Maxwell Pierson. *Foot-Prints of an Itinerant.* Cincinnati: Methodist Book Concern, 1856.

Genealogies of Kentucky Families: From the Register of the Kentucky Historical Society, O–Y. Baltimore: Genealogical Publishing Co., 1981.

Gibbons, J.S. *The Banks of New York, Their Dealers, the Clearing House and the Panic of 1857.* 1859; New York: Greenwood Press, 1968.

Gouge, William M. *The Curse of Paper-Money and Banking; or, A Short History of Banking in the United States of America, with an Account of Its Ruinous Effects on Landowners, Farmers, Traders, and on All the Industrious Classes of the Community.* London: Mills, Jowett, and Mills, 1833.

Hildreth, S.P. "Observations on the Bituminous Coal Deposits of the Valley of the Ohio, and the Accompanying Rock Strata; with Notice of the Fossil Organic Remains and the Relics of Vegetable and Animal Bodies, Illustrated by a Geological Map, by Numerous Drawings of Plants and Shells, and by Views of Interesting Scenery." *American Journal of Science and Arts* 29 (Jan. 1836): 1–148.

———. "Observations on the Saliferous Rock Formation, in the Valley of the Ohio." *American Journal of Science and Arts* 24, no. 1 (July 1833): 46–68.

[Lewis, Virgil A., ed.] "Lewis Summers' Journal of a Tour from Alexandria, Virginia, to Gallipolis, Ohio, in 1808." *Southern Historical Magazine* 1, no. 2 (Feb. 1892): 49–81.

Reed, Isaac. *The Christian Traveller.* New York: J. and J. Harper, 1828.

Roland Trevor; or, The Pilot of Human Life, Being an Autobiography of the Author Showing How to Make and Lose a Fortune, and Then to Make Another. Philadelphia: Lippincott, Grambo, and Co., 1853.

Royall, Anne Newport. *Sketches of History, Life, and Manners in the United States.* New Haven, Conn.: Privately printed, 1826.

Seager, Robert, II, ed. *The Papers of Henry Clay.* Vol. 7. Lexington: Univ. Press of Kentucky, 1982.

Second Semi-Annual Report of the Board of Directors of the West Columbia Mining and Manufacturing Company, of Mason County, Va., to the Stockholders, February, 1854. Cincinnati: Ben Franklin Book and Job Office, 1854.

Simon, John Y., ed. *The Personal Memoirs of Julia Dent Grant*. New York: Putnam's, 1975.

Smith, Adam. *An Inquiry into the Nature and Causes of the Wealth of Nations*. Ed. Edwin Cannan. 1776; New York: Modern Library, 1965.

Smith, William. *Annual Statement of the Commerce of Cincinnati for the Commercial Year Ending August 31st, 1850*. Cincinnati: Gazette Co., 1860.

———. *Annual Statement of the Commerce of Cincinnati for the Commercial Year Ending August 31st, 1861*. Cincinnati: Gazette Co. Steam Printing Establishment, 1861.

Thwaites, Reuben Gold, and Louise P. Kellogg, eds. *Documentary History of Dunmore's War, 1774*. Madison: State Historical Society of Wisconsin, 1905.

Newspapers and Periodicals

Annual Reports of the Cincinnati Chamber of Commerce, 1848–69.

Cincinnati Price-Current, Oct. 5, 1853–Dec. 28, 1859.

Cincinnati Price-Current, Commercial Intelligence and Merchants Transcript, Sept. 3, 1851–Sept. 28, 1853.

DeBow's Review, New Orleans, Louisiana, Jan. 1846–June 1860. (Published under various titles.)

Kanawha Banner, Charleston, Virginia, Sept. 10, 1830–Dec. 30, 1831, and scattered issues from 1832 to 1835.

Kanawha Republican, Charleston, Virginia, Dec. 4, 1841–Dec. 25, 1844, and scattered issues from 1845 to 1861.

Kanawha Valley Star, Charleston, Virginia, Jan. 9, 1856–March 26, 1860, and scattered issues from 1860 and 1861.

Merchants' Magazine and Commercial Review [*Hunt's Merchant's Magazine*], New York, July 1839–Dec. 1870.

Niles' Weekly Register [*Niles' National Register*], Baltimore, 1813–49.

Star of the Kanawha Valley, Buffalo, Virginia, 1856.

Western Courier, Charleston, Virginia, 1821 (one issue), and June 11, 1822–July 1, 1823.

Western Register, Charleston, Virginia, July 24, 1829–Oct. 2, 1829, and Jan. 11, 1830–July 20, 1830.

Western Virginian, Charleston, Virginia, July 5, 1826–Dec. 31, 1828, Jan. 7, 1829–May 20, 1829, and 1852 (two issues).

Government Documents: National

American State Papers. III. *Finance*. Vols. 1–5. Washington D.C.: Gales and Seaton, 1832–59.

American State Papers. IV. *Commerce and Navigation*. Vol. 1. Washington, D.C.: Gales and Seaton, 1832.

Congressional Globe. 25th Cong., 2d sess. (1837)–31st Cong., 2d sess. (1851).

Register of Debates. 19th Cong., 1st sess. (1825)–25th Cong., 1st sess. (1837).

U.S. Bureau of the Census. *Seventh Census of the United States*. Washington, D.C.: Robert Armstrong, public printer, 1853.

———. *Eighth Census of the United States*. Washington, Government Printing Office, 1864.

——— . *Ninth Census of the United States.* Washington, D.C.: Government Printing Office, 1872.

U.S. Congress. House. *Biographical Directory of the American Congress, 1774–1927.* 69th Cong., 2d sess., 1927. H. Doc. 783.

——— . *Duty on Imported Salt.* 21st Cong.,. 2d sess., 1831. H. Rept. 70.

——— . *Reports on the Trade and Commerce of the British North American Colonies and upon the Trade of the Great Lakes and Rivers.* By Israel D. Andrews. 32d Cong., 2d sess., 1853. H. Exec. Doc. 136.

——— . *Salt Works—United States.* 21st Cong., 1st sess., 1830. H. Doc. 55.

U.S. Congress. Senate. *Documents Relating to the Manufacture, Quality, and Uses of Salt.* 25th Cong., 3d sess., 1839. S. Doc. 269.

——— . *Documents Relating to the Trade in, and Manufacture and Uses of, Salt.* 26th Cong., 1st sess., 1840. S. Doc. 196.

——— . *Memorial of the Manufacturers of Salt in the County of Kanawha, Virginia, against the Repeal of the Duty on Imported Salt.* 20th Cong., 1st sess., 1828. S. Doc. 47.

——— . *Memorial of the Manufacturers of Salt in the County of Kanawha, Virginia, against the Repeal of the Duty on Imported Salt.* 21st Cong., 1st sess., 1830. S. Doc. 134.

——— . *Report of the Committee on Manufactures.* 22d Cong., 1st sess., 1832. S. Doc. 105.

——— . *Report on the Repeal of the Salt Duty.* 19th Cong., 1st sess., 1826. S. Doc. 61.

——— . *Reports of the Majority and Minority of the Select Committee on the Origin and Character of Fishing Bounties and Allowances.* 26th Cong., 1st sess., 1840. S. Doc. 368.

U.S. Department of Interior. "Salt-Making Processes in the United States." By Thomas M. Chatard. In *Seventh Annual Report of the United States Geological Survey to the Secretary of the Interior, 1885–86,* 491–535. Washington, D.C.: Government Printing Office, 1888.

U.S. Department of Interior. Bureau of Mines. *Technology of Salt-Making in the United States.* By W.C. Phalen. Bulletin 146, Mineral Technology, no. 20. Washington, D.C.: Government Printing Office, 1917.

U.S. Department of Interior. U.S. Geological Survey. *Salt Resources of the United States.* By W.C. Phalen. Bulletin 669. Washington, D.C.: Government Printing Office, 1919.

Government Documents: State

Acts of the General Assembly of Virginia, 1812–1860.

Michigan Geological and Biological Survey. *Mineral Resources of Michigan with Statistical Tables of Production and Value of Mineral Products for 1918 and Prior Years.* Publication 29, Geological ser. 24. Fort Wayne, Ind., 1920.

New York State Museum. *Salt and Gypsum Industries of New York.* By Frederick J.H. Merrill. Albany: Univ. of the State of New York, 1893.

Virginia Geological Survey. *Report of the Geological Reconnaissance of the State of Virginia, Made under the Appointment of the Board of Public Works, 1835.* By William Barton Rogers. In *A Reprint of Annual Reports and Other Papers on the Geology of the Virginias,* by William Barton Rogers. New York: Appleton, and Co., 1884.

——— . *Report of the Progress of the Geological Survey of the State of Virginia for the Year 1839.* By William Barton Rogers. In *A Reprint of Annual Reports and Other Papers on the Geology of the Virginias,* by William Barton Rogers. New York: Appleton, and Co., 1884.

West Virginia Geological Survey. *Iron Ores, Salt and Sandstones.* By G.P. Grimsley. Vol. 4. Morgantown, W.Va.: Acme Publishing Co., 1909.

——— . *Kanawha County.* By Charles E. Krebs and D.D. Teets, Jr. Wheeling; W.Va.: Wheeling News Litho. Co., 1914.

——— . *Levels above Tide; True Meridians; Report on Coal.* By I.C. White. Vol. 2. Morgantown, W.Va.: Morgantown Post Co., 1903.

——— . *Petroleum and Natural Gas: Precise Levels.* By I.C. White. Vol. 1A. Morgantown, W.Va.: New Dominion Publishing Co., 1904.

——— . *Salt Brines of West Virginia.* By Paul H. Price, Charles E. Hare, J.B. McCue, and Homer A. Hoskins. Vol. 8. Morgantown, W. Va.: Morgantown Printing and Binding Co., 1937.

West Virginia University Agricultural Experiment Station. *Occurrence of Barium in the Ohio Valley Brines and Its Relation to Stock Poisoning.* By C.D. Howard. Bulletin 103. Morgantown, W.Va., June 1, 1906.

Secondary Sources

Ambler, Charles Henry. *Sectionalism in Virginia from 1776 to 1861.* Chicago: Univ. of Chicago Press, 1910.

Ambler, Charles Henry, and Festus Paul Summers. *West Virginia: The Mountain State.* 2d ed. Englewood Cliffs, N.J.: Prentice-Hall, 1958.

Anderson, Lorena Andrews. "Salt Industry of the Kanawha Valley." M.A. thesis, Marshall College, 1942.

Atkinson, George Wesley. *History of Kanawha County, from Its Organization in 1789 until the Present Time; Embracing Accounts of Early Settlements, and Thrilling Adventures with the Indians.* Charleston: West Virginia Journal, 1876.

Bateman, Fred, James D. Foust, and Thomas Weiss. "Large-Scale Manufacturing in the South and West, 1850–1860." *Business History Review* 45, no. 1 (Spring 1971): 1–17.

Bateman, Fred, and Thomas Weiss. *A Deplorable Scarcity: The Failure of Industrialization in the Slave Economy.* Chapel Hill: Univ. of North Carolina Press, 1981.

Bateman, Fred, and Thomas Weiss. "Market Structure before the Age of Big Business: Concentration and Profit in Early Southern Manufacturing." *Business History Review* 49, no. 3 (Autumn 1975): 312–36.

Benton, Elbert Jay. *The Wabash Trade Route in the Development of the Old Northwest.* Baltimore: Johns Hopkins Univ. Press, 1903.

Berry, Thomas Senior. "The Effect of Business Conditions on Early Judicial Decisions Concerning Restraint of Trade." *Journal of Economic History* 10, no. 1 (May 1950): 30–44.

——— . *Western Prices before 1861: A Study of the Cincinnati Market.* Cambridge, Mass.: Harvard Univ. Press, 1943.

Bidwell, Percy Wells, and John I. Falconer. *History of Agriculture in the Northern United States, 1620–1860.* Washington, D.C.: Carnegie Institution, 1925.

Bishop, John Leander. *A History of American Manufactures from 1608 to 1860.* 3 vols. Philadelphia: Edward Young and Co., 1866.

Blanton, Wyndham B. *Medicine in Virginia in the Nineteenth Century.* Richmond: Garrett and Massie, 1933.

Bodenhamer, David J., and James W. Ely, Jr., eds. *Ambivalent Legacy: A Legal History of the South.* Jackson: Univ. Press of Mississippi, 1984.

Bogart, Ernest L. "Early Canal Traffic and Railroad Competition in Ohio." *Journal of Political Economy* 21, no. 1 (Jan. 1913): 56–70.

Bruchey, Stuart. *Enterprise: The Dynamic Economy of a Free People.* Cambridge, Mass.: Harvard Univ. Press, 1990.

———. "Law and Economic Change in the Early American Republic." In *American Industrialization, Economic Expansion, and the Law,* ed. Joseph R. Frese and Jacob Judd, 85–111. Tarrytown, N.Y.: Sleepy Hollow Press and Rockefeller Archive Center, 1981.

Callahan, James Morton, *Semi-Centennial History of West Virginia.* N.p.: Semi-Centennial Commission of West Virginia, 1913.

Callender, G.S. "The Early Transportation and Banking Enterprises of the State in Relation to the Growth of Corporations." *Quarterly Journal of Economics* 17 (1903): 111–62.

Catterall, Ralph C.H. *The Second Bank of the United States.* Chicago: Univ. of Chicago Press, 1902.

Chandler, Alfred D., Jr. "The Railroads: Pioneers in Modern Corporate Management." *Business History Review* 39, no. 1 (Spring 1965): 16–40.

———. *Strategy and Structure: Chapters in the History of Industrial Enterprise.* Cambridge, Mass.: MIT Press, 1962.

———. *The Visible Hand: The Managerial Revolution in American Business.* Cambridge, Mass.: Harvard Univ. Press, 1977.

Clark, Christopher. *The Roots of Rural Capitalism: Western Massachusetts, 1780–1860.* Ithaca, N.Y.: Cornell Univ. Press, 1990.

Clark, John G. *The Grain Trade in the Old Northwest.* Urbana: Univ. of Illinois Press, 1966.

Clarkson, L.A. "Proto-Industrialization: The First Phase of Industrialization?" In *The Industrial Revolution: A Compendium,* ed. L.A. Clarkson, 149–209. Atlantic Highlands, N.J.: Humanities Press International, 1990.

Clemen, Rudolf Alexander. *The American Livestock and Meat Industry.* New York: Ronald Press Co., 1923.

———. "Waterways in Livestock and Meat Trade." *American Economic Review* 16, no. 4 (Dec. 1926): 640–52.

Cochran, Thomas Childs. *Frontiers of Change: Early Industrialism in America.* New York: Oxford Univ. Press, 1981.

Cohn, Raymond L. "Local Manufacturing in the Antebellum South and Midwest." *Business History Review* 54, no. 1 (Spring 1980): 80–91.

Collins, Lewis. *History of Kentucky.* Revised by Richard H. Collins. 2 vols. Louisville: John P. Morton and Co., 1924.

Cometti, Elizabeth, and Festus Paul Summers, eds. *The Thirty-fifth State: A Documentary History of West Virginia.* Morgantown: West Virginia University Library, 1966.

Committee of the Association of American Law Schools, comp. and ed. *Select Essays in Anglo-American Legal History.* 3 vols. Boston: Little, Brown 1907–9.

Craven, Avery Odelle. *Soil Exhaustion as a Factor in the Agricultural History of Virginia and Maryland, 1606–1860.* Urbana: Univ. of Illinois, 1926.

Crockett, Norman. *The Woolen Industry of the Midwest.* Lexington: Univ. Press of Kentucky, 1970.

Davis, Joseph S. *Essays in the Earlier History of American Corporations.* 2 vols. Cambridge, Mass.: Harvard Univ. Press, 1917.

Dawley, Alan. *Class and Community: The Industrial Revolution in Lynn.* Cambridge, Mass.: Harvard Univ. Press, 1976.

Degler, Carl N. "Slavery in Brazil and the United States: An Essay in Comparative History" *American Historical Review* 75, no. 4 (April 1970): 1004–28.

Dewey, Davis Rich. *Financial History of the United States.* 12th ed. New York: Longmans, Green and Co., 1934.

Dewing, Arthur Stone. *Corporate Promotions and Reorganizations.* 1913; New York: Harper and Row, 1969.

——— . *A History of the National Cordage Company.* Cambridge, Mass.: Harvard Univ. Press, 1913.

Dunaway, Wayland Fuller. *History of the James River and Kanawha Company.* New York: Columbia Univ., 1922.

Eavenson, Howard N. *The First Century and a Quarter of American Coal Industry.* Pittsburgh: Privately printed, 1942.

Eller, Ronald D. *Miners, Millhands, and Mountaineers: Industrialization of the Appalachian South, 1880–1930.* Knoxville: Univ. of Tennessee Press, 1982.

Esarey, Logan. *A History of Indiana.* 2 vols. Indianapolis: B.F. Bowen and Co., 1918.

Faler, Paul G. *Mechanics and Manufacturers in the Early Industrial Revolution: Lynn, Massachusetts, 1780–1860.* Albany: State Univ. of New York Press, 1981.

Fishlow, Albert. *American Railroads and the Transformation of the Ante-Bellum Economy.* Cambridge, Mass.: Harvard Univ. Press, 1965.

Friedman, Lawrence M. *A History of American Law.* New York: Simon and Schuster, 1973.

Gates, Paul W. *The Farmer's Age: Agriculture, 1815–1860.* Vol 3 of *The Economic History of the United States.* New York: Holt, Rinehart and Winston, 1960.

Goodall, Elizabeth J. "The Manufacture of Salt—Kanawha's First Commercial Enterprise." *West Virginia History* 26, no. 4 (July 1965): 234–50.

Goodnow, Frank J. "Trade Combinations at Common Law." *Political Science Quarterly* 12, no. 2 (June 1897): 212–45.

Goodrich, Carter. "The Virginia System of Mixed Enterprise." *Political Science Quarterly* 64, no. 3 (Sept. 1949): 355–87.

Grant, U.S. *Personal Memoirs of U.S. Grant.* 2 vols. New York: Charles L. Webster and Co., 1885.

Gras, N.S.B. *Business and Capitalism: An Introduction to Business History.* New York: F.S. Crofts and Co., 1939.

Gras, N.S.B. Introduction to *The Jacksons and the Lees: Two Generations of Massachusetts Merchants, 1765–1844.* By Kenneth Wiggins Porter. 1: xiii–xvi. Cambridge, Mass.: Harvard Univ. Press, 1937.

——— . "Stages in Economic History." *Journal of Economic and Business History* 2, no. 3 (May 1930): 395–418.

Gray, Lewis Cecil. *History of Agriculture in the Southern United States to 1860.* 2 vols. Washington, D.C.: Carnegie Institution, 1933.

Greer, Thomas H. "Economic and Social Effects of the Depression of 1819 in the Old Northwest." *Indiana Magazine of History* 44, no. 3 (Sept. 1948): 227–43.

Gutman, Herbert G. *The Black Family in Slavery and Freedom, 1750–1925.* New York: Pantheon Books, 1976.

——— . *Slavery and the Numbers Game: A Critique of Time on the Cross.* Urbana: Univ. of Illinois Press, 1975.

Habakkuk, H.J. *American and British Technology in the Nineteenth Century: The Search for Labour-Saving Inventions.* Cambridge: Cambridge Univ. Press, 1967.

Haeger, John Denis. "Eastern Financiers and Institutional Change: The Origins of the New York Life Insurance and Trust Company and the Ohio Life Insurance and Trust Company." *Journal of Economic History* 39, no. 1 (March 1979): 259–73.

———. *The Investment Frontier: New York Businessmen and the Economic Development of the Old Northwest.* Albany: State Univ. of New York Press, 1981.

Haites, Eric, James Mak, and Gary M. Walton. *Western River Transportation: The Era of Early Internal Development, 1810–1860.* Baltimore: Johns Hopkins Univ. Press, 1975.

Hale, J.P. "Historical and Descriptive Sketch of the Great Kanawha and New River Valleys from Point Pleasant to Hinton." *West Virginia Historical Magazine Quarterly* 1, no. 2 (April 1901): 5–22.

———. "Salt." In *Resources of West Virginia*, ed. M.F. Maury and William M. Fontaine, 274–305. Wheeling, W.Va.: Register Co., 1876.

Hale, J.P. *Trans-Allegheny Pioneers.* 2d ed. Charleston, W.Va.: Kanawha Valley Publishing Co., 1931.

Hammond, Bray. *Banks and Politics in America from the Revolution to the Civil War.* Princeton, N.J.: Princeton Univ. Press, 1957.

Handlin, Oscar, and Mary F. Handlin. "Origins of the American Business Corporation." *Journal of Economic History* 5, no. 1 (May 1945): 1–23.

Hedrick, Charles Embury. *Social and Economic Aspects of Slavery in the Transmontane prior to 1850.* Nashville: George Peabody College for Teachers, 1927.

Hill, Howard Copeland. "The Development of Chicago as a Center of the Meat Packing Industry." *Mississippi Valley Historical Review* 10, no. 3 (Dec. 1923): 253–73.

Hilliard, Sam Bowers. *Hog Meat and Hoecake: Food Supply in the Old South, 1840–1860.* Carbondale: Southern Illinois Univ. Press, 1972.

Hirsch, Arthur H. "The Construction of the Miami and Erie Canal." *Proceedings of the Mississippi Valley Historical Association* 10, pt. 2 (1919–20): 349–62.

Holdsworth, W.S. "Industrial Combinations and the Law in the Eighteenth Century." *Minnesota Law Review* 18, no. 4 (March 1934): 369–90.

Horwitz, Morton J. *The Transformation of American Law, 1780–1860.* Cambridge, Mass.: Harvard Univ. Press, 1977.

Hunter, Louis C. *Steamboats on the Western Rivers.* Cambridge, Mass.: Harvard Univ. Press, 1949.

———. *Studies in the Economic History of the Ohio Valley.* Northampton, Mass.: Smith College, 1934.

Hurst, James Willard. *The Growth of American Law: The Lawmakers.* Boston: Little, Brown, 1950.

———. *Law and Conditions of Freedom in the Nineteenth-Century United States.* Madison: Univ. of Wisconsin Press, 1956.

———. *Law and Economic Growth: The Legal History of the Lumber Industry in Wisconsin, 1836–1915.* Cambridge, Mass.: Harvard Univ. Press, 1964.

———. *Law and Social Process in United States History.* 1960; Buffalo, N.Y.: William S. Hein and Co., 1987.

———. *The Legitimacy of the Business Corporation in the Law of the United States, 1780–1970.* Charlottesville: Univ. Press of Virginia, 1970.

———. "Perspectives upon Research into Legal Order." *Wisconsin Law Review* (May 1961): 356–67.

Jakle, John Allais. "Salt and the Initial Settlement of the Ohio Valley." Ph.D. diss., Indiana University, 1967.

———. "Salt on the Ohio Valley Frontier, 1770–1820," *Annals of the Association of American Geographers* 59, no. 4 (Dec. 1969): 687–709.

Jones, Robert Leslie. *History of Agriculture in Ohio to 1880.* Kent, Ohio: Kent State Univ. Press, 1983.

Keller, Morton. "Business History and Legal History." *Business History Review* 53, no. 3 (Autumn 1979): 295–303.

Krenkel, John H. *Illinois Internal Improvements, 1818–1848.* Cedar Rapids, Iowa: Torch Press, 1958.

Kulikoff, Allan. "The Transition of Capitalism in Rural America." *William and Mary Quarterly* 3d ser., 46, no. 1 (Jan. 1989): 120–44.

Laidley, W.S. *History of Charleston and Kanawha County, West Virginia, and Representative Citizens.* Chicago: Richmond-Arnold Publishing Co., 1911.

———. "Col. Joseph Lovell." *West Virginia Historical Magazine Quarterly* 4, no. 4 (Oct. 1904): 295–302.

Langstroth, Charles S., and Wilson Stitz. *Railway Co-operation.* Philadelphia, 1899.

Larew, Marilynn Melton. "The Cincinnati Branch of the Second Bank of the United States and Its Effect on the Local Economy, 1817–1836." Ph.D. diss., University of Maryland, 1978.

Lewis, Ronald L. *Coal, Iron, and Slaves: Industrial Slavery in Maryland and Virginia, 1715–1865.* Westport, Conn.: Greenwood Press, 1979.

———. "From Peasant to Proletarian: The Migration of Southern Blacks to the Central Appalachian Coalfields." *Journal of Southern History* 55, no. 1 (Feb. 1989): 77–102.

Lippincott, Isaac. "The Early Salt Trade of the Ohio Valley." *Journal of Political Economy* 20, no. 10 (Dec. 1912): 1029–52.

Livermore, Shaw. *Early American Land Companies: Their Influence on Corporate Development.* 1939; New York: Octogon Books, 1968.

———. "Unlimited Liability in Early American Corporations." *Journal of Political Economy* 42, no. 5 (Oct. 1935): 674–87.

MacGill, Caroline E., et al. *History of Transportation in the United States before 1860.* Washington, D.C.: Carnegie Institution, 1917.

McGrane, Reginald Charles. *The Panic of 1837: Some Financial Problems of the Jacksonian Era.* New York: Russell and Russell, 1965.

Mak, James, and Gary M. Walton. "On the Persistence of Old Technologies: The Case of Flatboats." *Journal of Economic History* 33, no. 2 (June 1973): 444–51.

Martin, Louis A. "The Great Kanawha Valley in 1850." *West Virginia Historical Magazine Quarterly* 2, no. 3 (July 1902): 66–71.

Meigs, William. *The Life of Thomas Hart Benton.* Philadelphia: Lippincott, 1904.

Mendels, Franklin F. "Proto-Industrialization: The First Phase of the Industrialization Process." *Journal of Economic History* 32, no. 1 (March 1972): 241–61.

Miller, Randall M., and John David Smith, eds. *Dictionary of Afro-American Slavery.* Westport, Conn.: Greenwood Press, 1988.

Morison, Samuel Eliot. *The Maritime History of Massachusetts, 1783–1860.* Boston: Houghton Mifflin, 1921.

Multhauf, Robert P. *Neptune's Gift: A History of Common Salt.* Baltimore: Johns Hopkins Univ. Press, 1978.

Nettels, Curtis P. *The Emergence of a National Economy, 1775–1815.* Vol. 2 of *The Economic History of the United States.* New York: Holt, Rinehart and Winston, 1962.

Nevins, Allan. *John D. Rockefeller: The Heroic Age of American Enterprise.* 2 vols. New York: Scribner's, 1940.

——— . *Study in Power: John D. Rockefeller, Industrialist and Philanthropist.* 2 vols. New York: Scribner's, 1953.

Newton, James E., and Ronald L. Lewis, eds. *The Other Slaves: Mechanics, Artisans and Craftsmen.* Boston: G.K. Hall and Co., 1978.

Paskoff, Paul F. *Industrial Evolution: Organization, Structure, and Growth of the Pennsylvania Iron Industry, 1750–1860.* Baltimore: Johns Hopkins Univ. Press, 1983.

Pease, Louise McNeill. "The Great Kanawha in the Old South, 1671–1861: A Study in Contradictions." Ph.D. diss., West Virginia University, 1959.

Pessen, Edward. *Jacksonian America: Society, Personality, and Politics.* Rev. ed. Homewood, Ill.: Dorsey Press, 1978.

Pierce, Bessie L. *A History of Chicago.* 2 vols. New York: Knopf, 1937–40.

Porter, Glenn, and Harold C. Livesay. *Merchants and Manufacturers: Studies in the Changing Structure of Nineteenth-Century Marketing.* Baltimore: Johns Hopkins Press, 1971.

Preyer, Norris W. "Southern Support of the Tariff of 1816—A Reappraisal." *Journal of Southern History* 25, no. 3 (Aug. 1959): 306–22.

Prude, Jonathan. *The Coming of Industrial Order: Town and Factory Life in Rural Massachusetts, 1810–1860.* New York: Cambridge Univ. Press, 1983.

Pursell, Carroll W., Jr. *Early Stationary Steam Engines in America: A Study in the Migration of a Technology.* Washington: Smithsonian Institution Press, 1969.

Reynolds, Lloyd G. "Cutthroat Competition." *American Economic Review* 30, no. 4 (Dec. 1940): 736–47.

Rice, Otis K. "Coal Mining in the Kanawha Valley to 1861: A View of Industrialization in the Old South." *Journal of Southern History* 31, no. 4 (Nov. 1965): 393–416.

Ripley, William Z., ed. *Trusts, Pools and Combinations.* Rev. ed. New York: Harper and Brothers, 1929.

Roseboom, Eugene H. *The Civil War Era, 1950–1873.* Vol. 4 of *The History of the State of Ohio.* Edited by Carl Wittke. Columbus: Ohio State Archaeological and Historical Society, 1944.

Rosenberg, Charles E. *The Cholera Years: The United States in 1832, 1849, and 1866.* Chicago: Univ. of Chicago Press, 1962.

Rothbard, Murray N. *The Panic of 1819: Reactions and Policies.* New York: Columbia Univ. Press, 1962.

Ruffner, William Henry. "The Ruffners: Part III, David." *West Virginia Historical Magazine Quarterly* 1, no. 4 (Oct. 1901): 46–54.

Savitt, Todd L. *Medicine and Slavery: The Diseases and Health Care of Blacks in Antebellum Virginia.* Urbana: Univ. of Illinois Press, 1978.

Scheiber, Harry N. *Ohio Canal Era: A Case Study of Government and the Economy, 1820–1861.* Athens, Ohio: Ohio Univ. Press, 1969.

Scheiber, Harry N. "At the Borderland of Law and Economic History: The Contributions of Willard Hurst." *American Historical Review* 75, no. 3 (Feb. 1970): 744–56.

——— . "Federalism and the American Economic Order, 1789–1910." *Law and Society Review* 10 (Fall 1975): 58–67.

——— . "Government and the Economy: Studies of the 'Commonwealth' Policy in Nineteenth-Century America." *Journal of Interdisciplinary History* 3 (Summer 1972): 135–51.

——— . "The Ohio–Mississippi Flatboat Trade: Some Reconsiderations." In *The Frontier in American Development: Essays in Honor of Paul Wallace Gates*, ed. David M. Ellis, 277–98. Ithaca: Cornell Univ. Press, 1969.

——— . "Regulation, Property Rights, and Definition of 'The Market': Law and the American Economy." *Journal of Economic History* 41, no. 1 (March 1981): 103–9.

——— . "State Law and 'Industrial Policy' in American Development, 1790–1987." *California Law Review* 75, no. 1 (Jan. 1987): 415–44.

Schweikart, Larry. *Banking in the American South from the Age of Jackson to Reconstruction*. Baton Rouge: Louisiana State Univ. Press, 1987.

Scranton, Philip. *The Textile Manufacture at Philadelphia, 1800–1885*. New York: Cambridge Univ. Press, 1982.

Seager, Henry R., and Charles A. Gulick, Jr. *Trust and Corporation Problems*. New York: Harper and Brothers, 1929.

Seavoy, Ronald E. *The Origins of the American Business Corporation, 1784–1855: Broadening the Concept of Public Service during Industrialization*. Westport, Conn.: Greenwood Press, 1982.

Sellers, Charles. *James K. Polk*. 2 vols. Princeton, N.J.: Princeton Univ. Press, 1957–66.

——— . *The Market Revolution: Jacksonian America, 1815–1846*. New York: Oxford Univ. Press, 1991.

Sharp, James Roger. *The Jacksonians versus the Banks: Politics in the States after the Panic of 1837*. New York: Columbia Univ. Press, 1970.

Shaw, Ronald E. *Erie Water West: A History of the Erie Canal, 1792–1854*. Lexington: Univ. of Kentucky Press, 1966.

Shelton, Cynthia J. *The Mills of Manayunk: Industrialization and Social Conflict in the Philadelphia Region, 1787–1837*. Baltimore: Johns Hopkins Univ. Press, 1986.

Shultz, William J., and M.R. Crane. *Financial Development of the United States*. New York: Prentice-Hall, 1937.

Simpson, Alfred William Brian. "The Horwitz Thesis and the History of Contracts." *University of Chicago Law Review* 46, no. 3 (Spring 1979): 533–61.

Smith, John David, comp. *Black Slavery in the Americas: An Interdisciplinary Bibliography, 1865–1980*. 2 vols. Westport, Conn.: Greenwood Press, 1982.

Smith, Walter Buckingham, and Arthur Harrison Cole. *Fluctuations in American Business, 1790–1860*. Cambridge, Mass.: Harvard Univ. Press, 1935.

Snyder, Charles M. *Oswego: From Buckskin to Bustles*. Port Washington, N.Y.: Ira J. Friedman, 1968.

Somers, Harold M. "The Performance of the American Economy, 1789–1865." In *The Growth of the American Economy* ed. Harold Francis Williamson, 31–34. 2d ed. Englewood Cliffs, N.J.: Prentice-Hall, 1951.

Stampp, Kenneth M. *The Peculiar Institution: Slavery in the Ante-Bellum South*. New York: Knopf, 1956.

Stanwood, Edward. *American Tariff Controversies in the Nineteenth Century*. 2 vols. Boston: Houghton Mifflin, 1903.

Starobin, Robert S. "Disciplining Industrial Slaves in the Old South." *Journal of Negro History* 53, no. 2 (April 1968): 111–28.

——— . "The Economics of Industrial Slavery in the Old South." *Business History Review* 44, no. 2 (Summer 1970): 131–74.

——— . *Industrial Slavery in the Old South*. New York: Oxford Univ. Press, 1969.

Stealey, John Edmund, III. "George Clendinen and the Great Kanawha Valley Frontier: A Case Study of the Frontier Development of Virginia." *West Virginia History* 27, no. 4 (July 1966): 278–95.

Stevens, William H.S. "A Classification of Pools and Associations Based on American Experience." *American Economic Review* 3, no. 3 (Sept. 1913): 545–75.

——— , ed. *Industrial Combinations and Trusts*. New York: Macmillan, 1913.

Talley, William M. "Salt Lick Creek and Its Salt Works." *Register of the Kentucky Historical Society* 64, no. 2 (April 1966): 85–109.

Taussig, F.W. *The Tariff History of the United States*. 8th ed. New York: Putnam's, 1931.

Taylor, George Rogers, and Lucius F. Ellsworth, eds. *Approaches to American Economic History*. Charlottesville: Univ. Press of Virginia, 1971.

Teeven, Keven M. *A History of the Anglo-American Common Law of Contract*. Westport, Conn.: Greenwood Press, 1990.

Temin, Peter. *Causal Factors in American Economic Growth in the Nineteenth Century*. London: Macmillan, 1975.

——— . *The Jacksonian Economy*. New York: Norton, 1969.

Thoenen, Eugene David. *History of the Oil and Gas Industry in West Virginia*. Charleston, W.Va.: Education Foundation, 1964.

Tucker, Barbara M. "The Merchant, the Manufacturer, and the Factory Manager: The Case of Samuel Slater." *Business History Review* 55, no. 3 (Autumn 1981): 297–313.

——— . *Samuel Slater and the Origins of the American Textile Industry, 1790–1860*. Ithaca, N.Y.: Cornell Univ. Press, 1984.

Turner, Frederick Jackson. *The Frontier in American History*. New York: Henry Holt and Co., 1920.

Uselding, Paul. "Studies of Technology in Economic History." In *Research in Economic History; Supplement 1–1977: Recent Developments in the Study of Business and Economic History: Essays in Memory of Herman E. Kroos*, ed. Robert E. Gallman, 159–219. Greenwich, Conn.: JAI Press, 1977.

Wade, Richard C. *The Urban Frontier: The Rise of Western Cities, 1790–1830*. Cambridge, Mass.: Harvard Univ. Press, 1959.

Wallace, Anthony F.C. *Rockdale: The Growth of an American Village in the Early Industrial Revolution*. New York: Knopf, 1978.

——— . *St. Clair: A Nineteenth-Century Coal Town's Experience with a Disaster-Prone Industry*. New York: Knopf, 1987.

Walsh, Margaret. "The Dynamics of Industrial Growth in the Old Northwest, 1830–1870: An Interdisciplinary Approach." In *Business and Economic History Papers Presented at the Twenty-first Annual Meeting of the Business History Conference, 28 February-1 March 1975*, ed. Paul Uselding, 12–29, 2d ser., vol. 4. Urbana, Ill., 1975.

——— . "From Pork Merchant to Meat Packer: The Midwestern Meat Industry in the Mid Nineteenth Century." *Agricultural History* 56, no. 7 (Jan. 1982): 127–37.

——— . *The Manufacturing Frontier: Pioneer Industry in Antebellum Wisconsin, 1830–1860*. Madison: State Historical Society of Wisconsin, 1972.

——— . "Pork Packing as a Leading Edge of Midwestern Industry, 1835–1875." *Agricultural History* 51, no. 4 (Oct. 1977): 702–17.

——— . *The Rise of the Midwestern Meat Packing Industry*. Lexington: Univ. Press of Kentucky, 1982.

———— . "The Spatial Evolution of the Mid-Western Pork Industry, 1835–1875." *Journal of Historical Geography* 4, no. 1 (1978): 1–22.

Weisenburger, Francis Phelps. *The Passing of the Frontier, 1825–1850.* Vol. 3 of *The History of the State of Ohio.* Edited by Carl Wittke. Columbus: Ohio State Archaeological and Historical Society, 1941.

Yeager, Mary. *Competition and Regulation: The Development of Oligopoly in the Meat Packing Industry.* Greenwich, Conn.: JAI Press, 1981.

Index

Page numbers in italics indicate figures and tables.

Abram (a slave), 135, 149
Abram E. Sargent foundry, 126
Adams, Gilbert, 77
Adams, Samuel G., 19, 51, 134
Adcock, George C., 123
Adriatic Sea, salt imported from, 118
agricultural commodity markets, 4
Alderson, George, 10, 21
Alderson tract, 10-11, 12, 13, 21
Allen, Brayton, 93, 99, 131
Allen, William, 116
Alpin, William H., 142
Alton, Illinois, 43
alum salt, 64, 108, 111, 113
Amos (a slave), 150
Ananias (a slave), 142
Anderson, Alexander Outlaw, 117
Anderson, Robert, 90
Anderson, Robert N., 90
Anderson, Samuel Q., 90
Andrew Donnally (steamboat), 44
Andrew Donnally & Company, *138*
Andrew F. Donnally and Company, 164, 175
Ark (steamboat), 229 n 39
Armstrong, James S., 77, 83
Armstrong, Johnston, 77, 83, 84, 113
Armstrong, William, 77
Armstrongs, Grant and Company: refusal to pay tolls, 72; control of salt production by, 77-81, 83, 89; relationship with independent salt makers, 79-80; salt barrels used by, 123; profitability of, 183
Arnold, Enos S., *139*, 164
Arnold and Rand, 164
Artella Wood (steamboat), 171
Asiatic cholera, 146-48, 153

Baltimore and Ohio Railroad, 73
Bank of Cincinnati, 30
Bank of Kanawha, 67-68, 188

Bank of the United States, 35, 97
Bank of the Valley of Virginia, 67
Bank of Virginia, 33, 64-69, 90, 92, 94-95, 97
Barbary War, 103
barium, 55
barium chloride, 41
barrels: standards for construction of, 33, 60; inspection marks on, 60-61, 62, 167; standards for sizes of, 62, 64, 178-79; and cooperage industry, 122-24; slave labor in construction of, 142
Beardstown, Illinois, 43
Bell, Elisha, 122
Benton, Thomas Hart, 3, 107-18
Berry, Thomas Senior, 4, 151, 205 n 11
Best, Levi, 66
Beverley Randolph and Company, 23, 51
Biddle, Nicholas, 97
bittern, 55
Black Jack (a slave), 145-46
boss kettle tenders, 131, 136
Bosworth, Nathaniel, 51
Bream, James, 24, 25, 67, 84, 93, 94, 105, 113, 127
bricklaying, 125
brick making industry, 4
Brigham, William A., 34, 164
Brooks, Ann, 145
Brooks, Elisha, 9-10
Brooks, Frederick F., 79, 80, 89, 92, 94, 98, *138*, 164, 174, 177
Brooks, James S.O., *138*, 140, 164, 175
Brooks, Martin P., 145
Brooks, Nathaniel S., 130, 131, 164
Brooks, William C., *138*, 145, 164
Brown, Charles, 14-15, 20, 26, 27
Brown, Samuel B., 142
Buffalo Commercial Advertiser, 46
building construction industry, 4
Bureau, John Peter Roman, 21

254 Index

Bureau, Madelain Françoise Charlotte, 21
Burke, Sally, 140
Burning Spring Creek, 21
Burning Spring tract, 20, 21

Cabell, John J., 26, 27, 33-34, 84, 112, 131, 145-47, 155
Cabell, N.B., 171
calcium chloride, 41
Calhoun, John C., 112, 115
Campbell's Creek, 9, 10, 21, 127
canals: construction of, 39, 44-47; tolls for shipments on, 46, 69-73, 74-75, 86, 177
Capehart, James, 67
Capehart, John, 229 n 39
carpentry, 124, 125
Chandler, Alfred Dupont, Jr., 5, 130
Chappell, Henry, 139, 164
Cheek, Macker, 29
Chicago, 189
Chillicothe, Ohio, 42, 44
cholera, 146-48, 153
Cincinnati: pork-packing industry in, 1, 42, 175, 189; banking in, 30, 69; salt sales in, 36, 85, 97, 99, 110, 151, 152, 158, 162, 163, 165, 170, 171-74, 178, 180-81, 182, 184, 187, 189-90, 193; merchant capital from, 39; steamboat traffic at, 44; salt inspection in, 64; moral condition of, 119
Cincinnati Chronicle, 128
Cincinnati Price-Current, 182, 189
Cist, Charles, 187
Civil War, 2, 134, 186, 190
Clarkson, John N., 138, 153, 164
class system, 5
Clay, Henry, 107, 113, 114, 115-16, 118
Clendinen, George, 9
Clendinen, Jemima, 9
Clifton, William B., 67
coal-bank managers, 131-32, 136
Coalburg (Brooks) coal, 127
coal mining: industrial, 2, 5, 6; in salt industry, 4, 45, 51-53, 56, 126-29; anthracite combination in, 22, 197; labor costs in, 129; occupational hazards of, 142-43; rising interest in, 185, 186, 197
Coalport Salt Company, 179, 180
Coal Ridge Salt Company, 180
Coal River, 71
coarse salt, 64, 94
Cobb, Martin and Company, 176
Cochran, Thomas Childs, 1
Coleman, Nelson B., 185
Coleman and Company, 123
Coleman & Ingles, 139

combination. See salt monopoly (combination)
commission merchants, 39, 82-88, 122, 162-63, 171, 173-74, 175, 181. See also merchant capitalists
Committee on Behalf of the Manufacturers, 109
Commonwealth of Virginia, impact on salt industry, 1-2, 57-75, 86
company housing, 5, 131
company stores, 4, 5, 84-85, 93, 120, 150, 167, 171
Conemaugh River salines, 44, 177
contract law, 195
conveyances industry, 4
cooperage industry, 122-24, 142
cooperative agreements, 101, 102, 158, 163
copartnerships, 22, 26-28, 194-95, 196. See also Kanawha Salt Company
coppersmithing, 125
cordage pool, 22, 197
corporations, origins of, 194-95, 196. See also incorporation
cotton trade, international, 4, 43, 97, 186
Cowey, James, 130-31, 134, 143
Cox, E.V., 138
Cox, William R., 89, 92, 95, 98, 99
Craik, James, 66, 86, 216 n 34
Crallé, Richard K., 112
Crockett, John B., 35
cutthroat competition, concept of, 191-92
C.W. Atkinson salt works, 136

Daniel Webster (steamboat), 146
Darneal, Jacob S., 139
Davis, John, 117
Davis, Zalinda L., 147
Davis Creek, 21
Davy Crockett (steamboat), 120
Dawley, Alan, 2
Dewing, Arthur Stone, 196
Dickerson, Mahlon, 114
Dickinson, Col. John, 9, 10, 12, 13
Dickinson, William, 84, 134, 148-49, 161, 185-86
Dickinson and Shrewsbury: independence maintained by, 26, 80, 93, 158, 168, 169, 182, 183, 185-86, 195; in joint ventures, 83, 84, 94; slave labor in, 134, 138, 140-41, 148-49
Dickinson, Armstrongs and Company, 83
Dickinson, Ruffner and Company, 84
Dickinson salt spring, 9-11, 50. See also Kanawha Salines
disease. See Asiatic cholera
distilling industry, 4

Donnally, Andrew, Jr.: as salt maker, 10, 13, 14, 19, 20, 22, 23, 24, 26, 27, 29, 31, 34, 36, 37-39, 54, 77, 80, 84, 89, 92, 93, 101, 123, 127, *138*; steamboats owned by, 43-44; and banking, 67, 95; and transportation systems, 70, 71, 72; and salt tariff, 105
Donnally, Andrew, Sr., 19
Donnally, Andrew F., 164, 175
Donnally, Lewis F., 164
Donnally, Van B., 131
Donnally, William, 164
Donnally and Noyes, 121, 122
Donnally and Steele and Company, 19, 20, 21-22, 23, 121, 126
Donnally, Bream and Company, 84, 85
Donnally, Noyes and Patrick, 94, 96, 99
Doyle and Kline, 125
Draper's Meadows settlement, 9
Dunlap's Creek, 69
Dupuy, William, 10

Early, Samuel H., *138*, 142, 161, 164
East Saginaw Salt Manufacturing Company, 190
Elija (a slave), 140
Eliza (steamboat), 44
Elk River, 17-18, 37, 69, 71, 72
English, Job, 90, 161, 164
Enos S. Arnold salt works, *139*
entrepreneurship, 5, 130
Erie Canal, 45, 177
E.V. Cox & William Hedrick salt works, *138*
excess capacity, 191-92, 196
extractive industries, Appalachian, 5, 185-86, 197

factories. *See* salt factories
fair trade, 3. *See also* free trade
Fairy Queen (steamboat), 44
Fann (a slave), 140
Farmers' and Mechanics' Bank, 30
Farmers' Bank of Virginia, 64, 67
fishing industry, 104, 106, 108, 115, 117
Fitzhugh, Mr., 145
Fitzhugh, Henry, 89, 92
flatboats and flatboat pilots, 44, 71, 121-22, 124-25, 171-72, 232-33 n 10
Fletcher, Joseph, 20
flour industry, 4
foreign salt. *See* salt, imported
forest industries, 5, 6. *See also* lumber industry
Frank (a coal miner/slave), 143-44
Frank (a woodcutter/slave), 135
Franklin Noyes salt works, *139*

Frederick Brooks salt works, *138*
free trade, 3, 87, 109, 111, 112, 117
French settlers, 8
Friedman, Lawrence M., 194
Friend, Joseph, 98, *138*, 161
Friend, Thomas, 135, 136, 150
frontier, role of salt in, 8, 202 n 1
Fry, James H., *139*, 164
Fry, Joseph, 73
Fuqua, Moses M., 84, 89, 92, 145
furnaces: numbers of, 4, 10, 12, 14, 15, 17, 18, 20, 21, 26, 57, 78, 79, 106; maintainence of, 22, 49, 99-101, 109, 125; technology of, 48, 51-53, 54-55, 56, 99, 125-26; trust conveyances of, 82; managers of, 130-32

Gallatin, Albert, 103
Gallatin County, Illinois, salines, 45
Gatewood (a slave), 145
gentleman's agreements, 196
George H. Warth salt works, *139*
George's Creek, 21, 127
G.H. Warth and Company, 164
Gilbert, James, 145
Giles, William G., 72
glassmaking industry, 4
Gleason and Downward, 136
Goose Creek Salt Works, Kentucky, 44
grande gabelle (French salt tax), 111
Grant, Jesse Root, 214-15 n 7
Grant, Peter, 77, 79, 80
Grant, Ulysses S., 214-15 n 7
Great Britain, salt tax in, 111
Great Buffalo Lick, 8, 9
Great Kanawha River: land ownership along, 1, 9-10, 12-13, 14-15, 36, 37, 38-39, 87; location of salines along, 1, 8, 11-12; flooding of, 2, 36, 188; mineral and forest industries along, 4, 5, 6, 20, 45, 51-53, 56, 123-24, 126-29, 185-86, 197; fertility of soil near, 9; navigation of, 69-73
Green (a slave), 148
Greenbrier River, 69
Greenlee, John, 124
gristmills, 4
Guiteau, Calvin, 54, 94
gypsum, 41

Hale, John P., *138*, 164
Hamilton, Alexander, 103
Hamilton, Ohio, 42
Hannah, Samuel, 99, 142
Harman, Middleton, 125
Harris, James E., 21
Harrison, William Henry, 104-5, 107

Harry (a slave), 143
Harry Tompkins (steamboat), 96
Hatch, Nathaniel, 90, 92, 135
Hawksbill Creek, 9
Hayne, Robert Y., 113
Hays, John, 145
Hedrick, William, 138
Henderson, A.M., 44
Hening, Robert, 19
Henry (a slave), 142
Henry Chappel salt works, 139
Henry H. Wood salt works, 138
Heth, Harry, 19, 23, 51, 134, 148
Hewitt, Clarice Grant (Mrs. James), 79
Hewitt, James, 67, 77, 80, 83, 84, 85, 89, 92, 93, 94
Hewitt, Roe and Company, 171, 176
Hewitt, Ruffner and Company: establishment of, 68, 74, 89-99, 102; relationship with independent salt makers, 93-94, 96; currency circulated by, 95; slave labor used by, 145; problems in, 164; profitability of, 183
Hewitt & Willcox, 90, 92, 93
Hildreth, Dr. S.P., 126
Hocking Valley, Ohio, salines, 46
holding corporations, 196
Horwitz, Morton J., 195
Howard's Creek, 69
Howe, Henry, 96
Hudson, Robert F., 126
Hugh L. White (steamboat), 96
Hurst, James Willard, 193, 194-95
Hurt, Ira, 139, 164
Hurt, Richard A., 139, 164
H.W. Reynolds and Company, 125

Ice's Creek, West Virginia, 179
Illinois: salt production in, 15, 45, 86; canals in, 45; railroads in, 189
Illinois and Michigan Canal, 45
incorporation, 85-88, 158, 194-95, 196
Indiana: meat-packing in, 42; canals in, 45; railroads in, 47, 189
Indians. See native Americans
industrial hazards, 86, 131, 142-44
industrial sabotage, 29
Ingles, Crockett, 90, 92, 131, 147-48, 164
Ingles, Mary, 9
Ira Hurt & Son, 139, 164
iron manufacturing industry, 4, 109, 125-26
Isaac (a slave), 145
Isaac & Franklin, 93
Isam (a slave), 142

Jack (a slave), 147-48
Jackson, O.F., 171

Jacob S. Darneal salt works, 139
James Cowey and Company, 143-44
James H. Fry salt works, 139
James River, 70
James River and Kanawha Company, 74-75, 84, 95
James River Company, 69-72, 73-74
James S.O. Brooks salt works, 138
Jarred, Cle, 14
Jarret, Eli, 21
Jefferson, Thomas, 103, 115
Jefferson, Madison, and Indianapolis Railroad, 47
Jenatte, John B., 29
Jim (a hired slave), 148
Jim (a leased slave), 142-43
Jim (an uncooperative slave), 149
John (a hired slave), 148
John (a steam engine operator/slave), 144
John D. Lewis salt works, 138
John H. Piatt and Company, 30
John N. Clarkson salt works, 138
John P. Hale salt works, 138
John R. Smith and Company, 147
Johnson, Col. Robert, 14
joint stock companies, 68, 77, 89, 158, 163, 193, 194, 196
Jones, William, 30
Joseph Friend salt works, 138
Joseph Ruffner salt works, 139
J.Q. Dickinson & Company Salt Factory, 52, 100

Kanawha Banner, 109, 147
Kanawha County, population of, 133-34, 136-40, 153, 154
Kanawha County Court, 63, 64, 69, 76
Kanawha County Courthouse, 32, 36, 66, 71
Kanawha Salines (Terra Salis or Malden): location of, 1, 8; ownership of, 1, 9-10, 12-13, 14-15, 18-40 passim, 87, 92; well construction at, 9-10, 11-12, 49, 125; furnaces at, 10, 12, 13, 14, 15, 17, 18, 20, 21, 22, 25, 26; exploration at, 11-12, 13-15; first salt production at, 13; production capacity at, 15, 16, 17, 18, 27, 31, 54, 79, 84, 85, 95, 99, 136, 158, 184, 190; location of bank at, 67-68; moral condition of, 119-21; decline of, 184-90
Kanawha Salines Savings Institution, 68
Kanawha Salt Association, 158-63, 170
Kanawha Salt Company (various enterprises and proposals): establishment of, 22, 26-27, 193; purpose of, 22, 26, 27; production capacity of, 27; directors of, 27-28; relationship with independent

salt makers, 28-29; failure of, 29-30; incorporation of, 86
Kanawha Savings Institution, 65
Kanawha Valley Star, 184
Kentucky: salt production in, 8, 15, 44; industrial sabotage in, 29; salt sales in, 35; objections to Kanawha Valley salt combinations in, 80-81
King's Salt Works, 58-59, 117
Kiskiminetas River salines, 44, 177

labor regulations, 135, 141
labor supply: availability of, 5, 86, 120, 129, 156; cost of, 56, 150-56, *155;* description of, 119-22; and furnace managers, 130-32, 136; foreign, 186; and excess capacity, 192. *See also* salt factories, slave labor in
Lacy, John, 140
Lafayette, Indiana, 42
Laidley, James M., 66
Laidley, W.S., 121
land: speculation in, 6; value of, 31, 69, 184-85
lease-hire system, 5, 150-57
Leftwich, Joel, 78
Leftwich, Littleberry, 78
legal and economic history, borderland of, 3
legal history, 2-3, 195
Lelia (steamboat), 229 n 39
Leonard Morris and Sons, 20
Lett, L.C., 142
Lewis (a drowned slave), 145
Lewis (a suffocated slave), 143
Lewis, Col. Andrew, 9
Lewis, Betty Washington, 24
Lewis, Col. Fielding, 24
Lewis, Howell, 24
Lewis, John, 89, 92
Lewis, John D., 67, 77, 84, 89, 90, 92, 102, 136, *138,* 161, 164
Lewis, R., 14
Lewis, William A., 171
Lewis family, 20
Lewis Ruffner salt works, *138*
Lewis & Shrewsbury, 90, 92, 93, 164
lime sulfate, 55
Little Miami Railroad, 47, 179
Livermore, Shaw, 194
Liverpool, salt imported from, 17, 18, 43, 103, 106, 118, 175, 176, 181
Livesay, Harold C., 192-93
local government, domination by salt makers, 6. *See also* Commonwealth of Virginia
Lord Dunmore's War, 9

Louisiana Purchase, 103
Louisville: pork-packing industry in, 1, 42, 175; salt sales in, 43, 110, 165, 171, 172, 173, 175, 176, 180, 193; salt inspection in, 64
Lovell, Betty Washington Lewis, 24
Lovell, Joseph: as legal counsel, 24-26, 193-94; in Kanawha Salt Company, 26, 27; land ownership by, 38, 127; and transportation systems, 70, 71, 72, 73; and salt tariff, 105, 106, 107, 113; as salt maker, 175
Lovell, Richard C.M., 101, 134, *139,* 155, 162, 163, 164, 167-68, 183
lumber industry, 4, 6, 20, 51, 123-24, 126, 197
Lynchburg (steamboat), 96
Lynn, Massachusetts, 2

McCommas, Lucinda, 140
McConihay, John, 147
McDowell, James, 128-29
McDowell, Woodford G., 129
McFarland, James C., 66, 73, 83, 84, 89, 90, 92, 95, 113
machinery construction industry, 4
McMullin, William A., 75, *139,* 164
Macon, Nathaniel, 107
Madison, Indiana, 42, 96, 162
Mad River and Lake Erie Railroad, 47, 179
magnesium chloride, 41
Malden, West Virginia, 1
Marietta, Ohio, 43
marketing techniques, changes in, 192-93
Marshall, John, 69
Mason County, Virginia, salines, 179, 186, 187
May, Jacob, 131
Maysville, Kentucky, 80-81, 163, 175
Maysville Eagle, 81
meat-packing industry, 41-43, 105, 108, 111, 175, 189
Mediterranean Sea, salt imported from, 176
Medium (steamboat), 229 n 39
Meigs County, Ohio, salines, 179, 186, 187
Mendels, Franklin F., 6
merchant capitalists, 39, 82-88, 191. *See also* commission merchants
Miami (Ohio) Canal, 45
Miami Exporting Company, 30, 31
Michigan, salt production in, 22, 190, 197
Michigan Salt Association, 22, 197
Mid (a slave), 143
Miller, Samuel A., 164, 170

mineral industries, 5. *See also* coal mining
Mitchell, James, 171
Moore, Samuel, 121
Morris, Charles, 26, 27
Morris, John, 21
Morris, Leonard, 20, 26, 27, 78
Morris, William ("Billy"), 49
Murphy, Edward C., 143
Murray, John (4th earl of Dunmore), 9
Muskingum, Ohio, salines, 43, 44, 45, 46, 86, 176, 177
Myers, Conrad, 128

Napoleonic Wars, 31
Nathaniel V. Wilson salt works, *138*
National Salt Company, 196
native Americans, use of salt licks by, 8-9
natural gas, 129-30, 185, 197
New River, 69
New York State: salt production in, 15, 16, 17, 44, 45-46, 86, 105, 175, 176, 177, 178, 179, 190; canals in, 45, 46
Norton, James, 91, 161, 162
Norton, Moses, 229 n 39
Norton and Kline, 136
Noyes, Bradford, 26, 27, 54, 83, 84, 98, 127, 185
Noyes, Bradford, Jr., 90
Noyes, Franklin, *139*, 164
Noyes, Isaac: as salt maker, 15, 26, 27, 34, 54, 83, 84, 93, 127; steamboats owned by, 43-44; and salt tariff, 105, 113
Noyes, Rand & Smith, 90, 92

occupational hazards, 86, 131, 142-44
Ohio: salt production in, 13, 15, 43, 44, 46, 54, 86, 175, 179-80, 186, 187; canals in, 45, 46, 86, 105, 146, 177, 179; New York State salt consumed in, 46, 178, 187; railroads in, 47, 188-89; salt prices in, 105, 178; escape of slaves to, 144-46, 149, 150, 229 n 39
Ohio Board of Public Works, 46
Ohio Canal, 46, 86, 146, 179
Ohio Life Insurance and Trust Company, 187-88
oil (petroleum), 185, 197
Old Lick, 14
Onondaga, New York, salines, 15, 16, 17, 44, 45-46, 86, 105, 177, 178, 179, 190
ownership: of saline wells and springs, 1, 9-10, 12-13, 14-15, 18-40 passim, 87, 92; decentralized, 5, 18, 40, 88; legal forms for, 22, 193. *See also* copartnerships; incorporation; joint stock companies; lease-hire system; sales agency plans; salt monopoly (combination)

Panic of 1819, 18, 30-31
Panic of 1837, 65, 66, 97, 118, 164, 187
Panic of 1857, 187
Parkersburg, Virginia, 43
Parks, Andrew, 38, 71, 72, 74, 113
partnerships. *See* copartnerships
Patrick, George H., 54, 66
Patrick, Dr. Spicer, *138*, 183
Patterson, Samuel, 150
Penn, Moses, 131
Pennsylvania, salt production in, 43, 44, 86, 175, 176-77
Philips, William B., 77
plantation slavery system: in salt industry, 1, 5, 56, 79, 86, 123, 125, 129, 131, 132, 133-57, 186; and managerial slaves, 136, 149; and escape of slaves, 144-46, 149, 150, 229 n 39; and control of slaves, 148-49; and humane treatment of slaves, 149-50; and rental prices for slaves, 150-53; traditional, 156; and excess capacity, 192
Pocatalico River, 37
police district, 120
Polk, James Knox, 117, 118
Pollard, Ann, 143
Pomeroy, Ohio, salines, 54, 174, 179, 180, 187
Pomeroy Salt Company, 179, 180
pools, 22, 193, 196, 197
pork-packing industry, 1, 41-43, 105, 108, 111, 175, 189
Porter, Glenn, 192-93
Potter, John, 148
pottery industry, 4
Preston (a slave), 142
Prewitt, Stokes, 124
private property rights, 116
proto-industrialization, 6, 191
Publius (pseudonym), 109-10
Putney, Richard E., 89, 92, 93, 113, 129

Quarrier, Gustavius B., 164

Rachel (a slave), 140
Radcliff, Stephen, 26, 27
railroads: study of, 4; legal combinations in, 22; impact on salt distribution, 47, 73, 118; and coal transport, 128; freight rates on, 179; and new trade patterns, 188; expansion of, 188-89, 197
Rand, William I., 90, 164
Randolph, Beverley, 19, 51-53, 58, 134
rational organization, 5
R.C.M. Lovell & Company, *139*
Return (steamboat), 171
Reuben (a slave), 135

Reynolds, Charles G., 89, 93, 143
Reynolds, John, 20, 21, 26, 27
Reynolds, Lloyd G., 191-92
Reynolds, Silas, 14, 20, 93
Richard (a slave), 142
Ritter, Jackson, 224-25 n 42
roads, improvements in, 76-77
robber barons, 7
Robert F. Hudson foundry, 126
Robinson, Stuart, 144
Rogers, John, 67, 85, 161
Rogers, John, Jr., 89
Rogers, Joseph H., 171, 172-74, 178-79,
  180-82
Rogers, Leonora C., 164
Rogers, William Barton, 126
Rooks, Stephen, 122
Roy, Larkin C., 123
Roy, Rueben, 85
Royall, Anne Newport, 119, 120, 210 n 5
Ruffner, Abraham (son of Joseph), 10, 13
Ruffner, Daniel (son of Joseph), 10, 14, 26,
  27, 70, 90, 92, 113, 128
Ruffner, David (son of Joseph): as salt
  maker, 10, 11-13, 14, 15, 17, 20, 21, 26,
  27, 39, 49, 51, 53, 127; and banking, 66,
  69; and transportation systems, 71, 72
Ruffner, Dr. Henry (son of David), 11, 13,
  14, 23, 39, 53, 119
Ruffner, Isaac, 90, 92, 93
Ruffner, John, 127
Ruffner, Joseph, Jr. (son), 10, 11-13, 14, 15,
  49, 53, 139
Ruffner, Joseph, Sr., 9, 10
Ruffner, Lewis: as salt maker, 53, 56, 84,
  85, 89, 90, 91, 92, 93, 98, 102, 130, 131,
  161, 164, 181; and banking, 66, 67, 95;
  and salt tariff, 105, 106, 113; and slave
  labor, 138, 143, 145; as Louisville sales
  agent, 171; and salt speculation, 176;
  inspection of Onondaga furnaces
  by, 178
Ruffner, Tobias (son of Joseph), 10, 14, 21,
  26, 27
Ruffner, Donnally and Company: salt distribution by, 122, 170-83, 186-87, 188,
  193; establishment of, 163-69; dissolution
  of, 184
Ruffner, Hale and Company, 184
rural capitalism, 6-7
Rush Creek, 21
Russel, Thomas, 121

Sainte Genevieve, Missouri, 8
St. Louis, 43
St. Ubes, salt imported from, 118
Salem (steamboat), 171

sales agency plans, 33, 83-84, 89, 110, 114,
  158, 184, 193, 196
salt: demand for, 1, 8, 16, 41-42, 57, 108-9;
  price of, 3, 4, 12, 13, 15-16, 17, 21, 24,
  25, 29-30, 31-34, 39-40, 56, 57, 58, 59, 61,
  76, 80, 81, 83, 85, 93, 94, 96, 97, 99, 102,
  105-6, 109-10, 113-14, 158, 162-63, 170,
  175, 179, 180, 181, 184, 238 n 13;
  imported, 3-4, 8, 17, 36, 41, 42, 43, 45,
  70, 81, 86, 103-18 passim, 175-76, 181,
  186, 190; availability of, 5, 8, 17; discovery of, 6; shortages of, 8; rate of production of, 13, 14, 15; lick weight of, 174. See
  also salt factories; salt industry; salt tariff; salt tax; salt trade
Salt Creek Works, Kentucky, 44
salt duty. See salt tariff
salt factories: slave labor in, 1, 5, 56, 79,
  86, 123, 125, 129, 131, 132, 133-57, 186;
  impermanence of, 2, 48-49; inspection
  by state, 2, 57, 59-64, 77, 82; compo-
  nents of, 55-56; and pollution, 119
salt industry: markets for, 1, 18, 31, 35,
  36, 40; manufacturing costs in, 13, 24,
  25, 38-39, 48, 76, 86, 183; depressions in,
  18, 30-31, 38, 39, 58, 106, 153, 158; price
  controls in, 23, 24, 26-27, 29-30, 31-34,
  35-36, 68, 77, 79, 80-81, 84, 87, 90, 93,
  94, 96, 105, 158, 159, 160, 162-63, 170,
  175, 182, 187, 193, 197; sabotage in, 29;
  technological innovations in, 40, 48-56,
  99; inventories in, 57; licensing in, 57,
  58; banking for, 64-69, 94-95; recessions
  in, 85, 99, 101, 187-88; reliance on flatboat pilots, 121-22. See also salt factories;
  salt monopoly (combination); salt trade
Salt Lick (pseudonym), 81-82
salt monopoly (combination): and Benton's attack on salt tariff, 3, 107-18; purpose of, 3, 5, 23, 193; establishment of,
  18-19, 22, 31, 35, 65, 87; legal form for,
  22, 193; fear of, 88, 109, 111; temporary
  nature of, 195-96
saltpeter, 41
salt producers' associations, 22, 65, 116,
  158-63, 170
salt tariff, 87, 103-18, 186
salt tax, 2, 57-59
salt trade: domestic competition in, 4, 15,
  16, 17, 43, 44-47, 86, 106, 109, 118, 163,
  174-75, 176-77; limitations on, 15; suspended in 1819, 30; and speculation,
  174, 176, 193; cutthroat competition in,
  191-92. See also free trade; salt, imported
Samuel H. Early salt works, 138
Samuel Q. Anderson and Company,
  90, 92

Sanford, Walker J.L., 131
Sargent, Abram E., 126
Sargent, Lemuel H., 180, 190
Saunders, Henry B., 125
sawmills. *See* lumber industry
Scheiber, Harry N., 3
Scioto Salt Works, Ohio, 13, 15, 44
Second Bank of the United States, 30, 31, 108, 116
Sharpe, Marcella, 140
Shawneetown, Illinois, salines, 45. *See also* United States Saline, Illinois
shoemaking industry, 2
Shrewsbury, Charles L., 89
Shrewsbury, Joel, Jr., 66, 67, 89
Shrewsbury, Joel, Sr., 19, 26, 27, 29-30, 31, 35, 53, 67, 70, 71, 72, 80, 84, 95, 105, 134, 135, 140, 141, 145, 146, 148, 161, 185-86
Shrewsbury, John, 20, 21, 26, 27, 35
Shrewsbury, John D., 20, 21, 26, 27, 35
Shrewsbury, Samuel, Jr., 14, 20, 21, 26, 27, 90, 92
Shrewsbury, William D., 84, 89, 90, 92, *138*, 164
Shrewsbury and Fitzhugh, 136
Simon (a slave), 136
Simony Creek, 20
Sinclair, Sir John, 112
Slaughter, Reuben, 20
Slaughter's Creek, 71, 72
slavery, industrial. *See* plantation slavery system
Smith, Adam, 3, 7, 191
Smith, Benjamin H., 90
Smith, Daniel, 73
Smith, John B., 171, 178, 180, 182
Smith, John R., 147
Smithers, Benjamin S., 130
Solomon (a slave), 229 n 39
South Carolina, and salt tariff, 114
Spencer (a slave), 135, 149
Spicer Patrick salt works, *138*
Spinks, Jabez, 125
Squire (a slave), 150
Standard Oil Trust, 22
Starobin, Robert S., 141
states' rights, 112
Staunton and Potomac Railroad, 73
steamboats: impact on salt distribution, 18, 36, 39, 43-44, 70, 103, 104, 106, 124; owned by salt makers, 43-44, 96, 124, 171; and slavery, 146, 229 n 39
Steele, Adam, 19, 20, 22, 23-24, 36, 37, 38
Steele, Ellen Joel Lewis (wife of Robert M.), 24, 37
Steele, Col. John, 19, 20, 21, 37

Steele, Martha Breckinridge Makemie (mother), 19
Steele, Richard, Jr., 19, 20, 22, 23-24, 36, 37, 38
Steele, Richard, Sr. (father), 19
Steele, Robert Makemie, 19, 21, 22, 23-24, 33-35, 36, 37, 76
Steele, William, 19-24, 26, 27, 33-37, 76, 127
Steele, Donnally and Steeles: establishment of, 22, 23-24; ownership of, 23-24; production capacity of, 24; expansion of, 26; profitability of, 26; price controls by, 27, 29-30; suspension of trade in 1820 by, 30, 31; indebtedness of William Steele to, 36, 37-38; suit for damages against flatboat pilot by, 121
Stella (steamboat), 171
Stephens, George, 178
Stephens, William J., 179
Stockton, Aaron, 26, 27, 34-35, 78, 224-25 n. 42
Stone, Martha, 148
stonemasonry, 125
Stout, James H., 177
Stratton, Joseph D., 84
Summers, George W., 71, 72, 73, 87-88, 142-43
Summers, Lewis, 16, 65, 71, 73, 74, 84-88, 95, 99, 101-2, 105, 145, 209 n 10

tallow, in salt, 28
tanning industry, 4
task system, 136
taxation. *See* salt tax
Tazewell, Littleton Walker, 105
Tennessee: salt sales in, 35, 78, 193; money in Bank of Virginia, 95
Tennessee River, 78
Terra Salis, 1
Terre Haute, Indiana, 42
Terry, William, 148
textile industry, 2, 4, 191
Thirteen Mile Chute, 122
Thomas, John, 128
Thompson, Francis, 146
Thompson, Philip A., 73
Thompson, Robert A., 66
Thoroughfare Gap, 8, 9
Three Furnace property, 21
Tide Shylock (steamboat), 96
timber industry. *See* lumber industry
tobacco industry, 133
Tom (a boss kettle tender), 136
Tom (a cooper/slave), 142
Tom (a slave laborer), 135, 149
Tompkins, Henry, 91

Tompkins, Jane M. Grant, 79
Tompkins, Rachel Marie Grant, 79
Tompkins, William: as salt maker, 34, 56, 78, 89, 90, 91, 92, 98, 129-30; and banking, 67, 97
Trackwell, Thompson, 121
trading companies, 84-85
transportation systems: state role in, 3, 69-75; impact on salt distribution, 4, 15, 18, 43-47, 69, 77, 118, 186; and tolls, 46, 69-73, 74-75, 86. *See also* canals; flatboats and flatboat pilots; railroads; steamboats
Trimble, Walter, 33-34, 77-78
Truro Furnace, 129
trust, legal: formation of, 22, 196; conveyed by William Steele, 36-37; for furnaces, 82
Tuckahoe (steamboat), 145
Turk's Island, salt imported from, 43, 103, 106, 118, 176, 181
Turnbull, Edward, 144
Turner, Frederick Jackson, 202 n 1
Turner, Jane, 140
Tyler, John, 105, 118

U.S. Senate Committee on Agriculture, 104
U.S. Senate Committee on Finance, 113, 115
U.S. Senate Committee on Manufactures, 113-14
United States Saline, Illinois, 15. *See also* Shawneetown, Illinois, salines

Vanceburg, Kentucky, salines, 44
Venable, Charles, 19, 79
"View of the Salt-Works on the Kanawha" (Howe), *96*
Virginia. *See* Commonwealth of Virginia
Virginia Board of Public Works, 72, 73
voluntary associations, 194. *See also* Kanawha Salt Association; Michigan Salt Association; salt producers' associations

Wabash and Erie Canal, 45
Wabash Salines, 15
Waid, John, 142
Walker, Robert J., 118
Wallace, Anthony F.C., 2
War of 1812, 2, 6, 17, 18, 44, 48, 59, 104, 105, 133
Warth, George H., 90, *139*, 144, 161, 164

Warth, John A., 20, 21, 90, 164
Warth & English, 90, 92, 130, 136, 148, 164
Washington (a slave), 149
Washington, George, 24
Washington family, 20
Watson and Jones, 126
W.C. Brooks & Company, *138*
weights and scales: standards for, 60, 61, 64, 82; and lick weight, 174
Welch, Levi: as salt maker, 38, 46, 84, 90, 91, 92, 94, 102; and banking, 66, 67, 92, 95; and salt tariff, 113; death of, 147
Welch laborers, 186
Welch, Wood and Company, 84
well construction, 9-10, 11-12, 49-51, 125
well tenders, 132, 136
West Columbia Mining and Manufacturing Company, 156, 179, 180
Western Virginian, 64
Wheeling, West Virginia, 43, 44, 177
White, Cunningham and Company (commission merchants), 173
Whitteker, Levi, 15
Whitteker, William, 14, 15, 20, 49
Will (a slave), 149
Willcox, Luke, 67, 89-90, 140, 142, 143, 147
William A. McMullin salt works, *139*
William and Jones, 136
Williams, John, 123
Williams, William, 129
William Shrewsbury and Company, 89, 92, *138*
William Steele and Company, 23, 24, 26, 27, 33, 36, 37, 38, 121
Wilson, Dr. Goodrich, 67
Wilson, James, 127
Wilson, John, 123
Wilson, Nathaniel V., 129, *138*, 161, 164
Witcher's Creek, 20
Wood, Henry H., 84, 90, 92, 93, *138*, 149, 161, 164, 175
Woodbridge and Pierce (commission merchants), 21
Woodbury, Levi, 104
Woods, Wiley P., 144
Woods and Seay (commission merchants), 35
Woodyard, James, 121
work regulations, 135, 141
Wright, Silas, 115

Young, Arthur, 112